D1420560

GRIDS

GRIDS

2nd Edition

Creative Solutions for Graphic Designers

RotoVision

A RotoVision Book

Published and distributed by RotoVision SA
Route Suisse 9
CH-1295 Mies
Switzerland

RotoVision SA
Sales and Editorial Office
Sheridan House, 114 Western Road
Hove BN3 1DD, UK

Tel: +44 (0)1273 72 72 68
Fax: +44 (0)1273 72 72 69
www.rotovision.com

10 9 8 7 6 5 4 3 2 1

ISBN: 978-2-88893-155-3

Design: Studio Ink
Photography for Introduction: Andrew Penketh
Grid tutorials: Tony Seddon

Printed in China by 1010 Printing International Ltd.

The CD and tutorials

The grids featured in this book are included on the accompanying CD, and have been recreated in both InDesign and QuarkXPress. To locate the grid you wish to utilize in either of these applications, simply look for the file name that matches the page number on which the grid appears in the book.

Also included on the CD are five Illustrator grids and six exclusive tutorials that introduce readers to the working methods behind successful grid design.

Measurements

All measurements have been given in millimeters or points. If you prefer working in inches, most applications provide this option in the measurements palette.

Contents

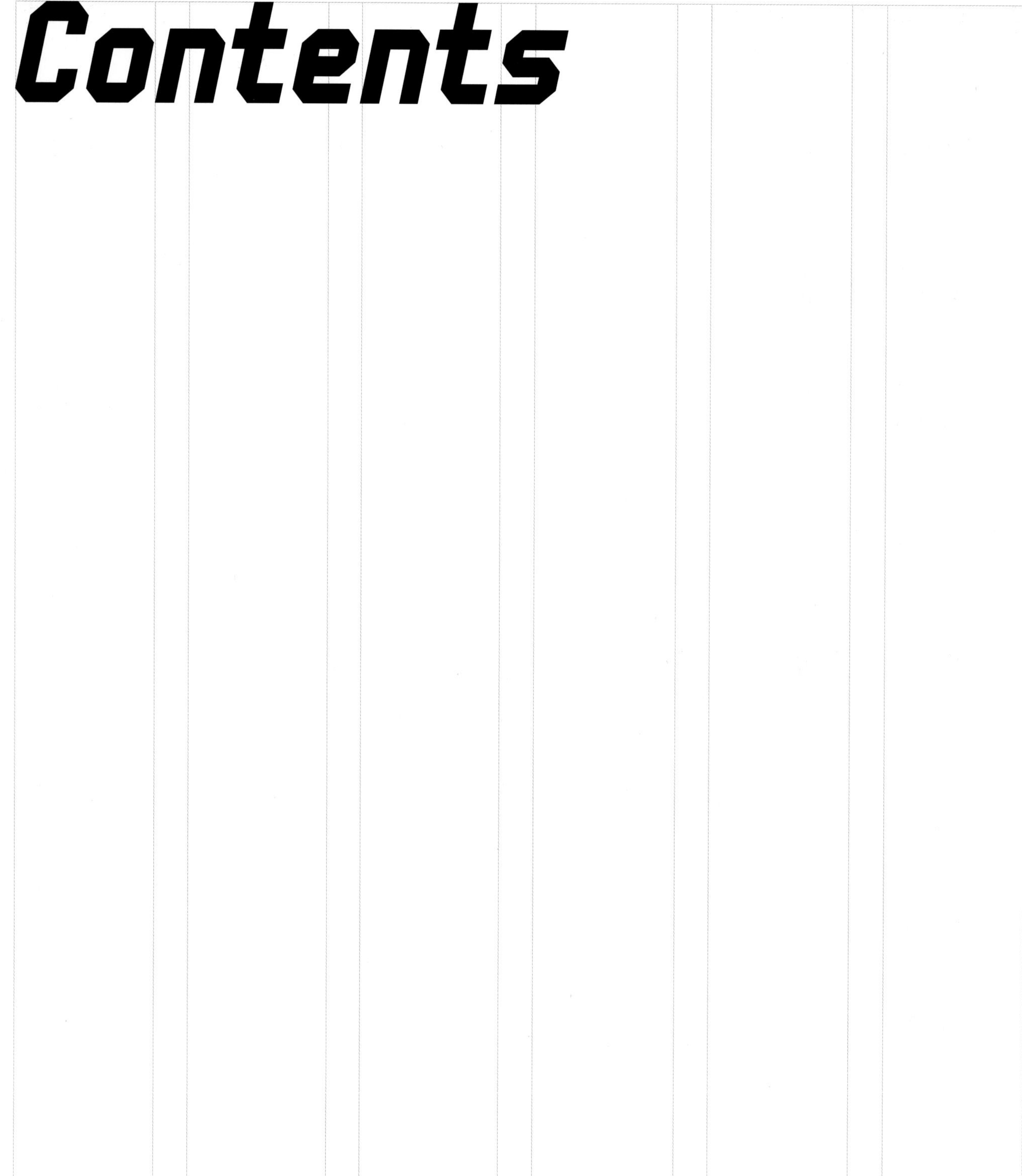

Introduction 008

Catalogs, leaflets & brochures 020

Exhibitions 040

Illustrated books 060

Identities 104

Magazines, newspapers & newsletters 126

Packaging 172

Posters & fliers 188

Index 222

Introduction

This whole business of grids is so difficult for graphic designers. Most of us love them. But we're scared of revealing any nerdy or, worse still, despotic tendencies so we jump nervously from foot to foot, simultaneously belittling and venerating the grid. We've got to appear to be casual about it—but not so much so that our peers think we're grid lightweights.

The problem is partly one of association. A grid is generally a series of straight vertical and horizontal lines so, if you're interested in grids are you "straight" in other ways too? This book sets out to demonstrate that, ultimately, it's not the notion of the grid that is important—it's the hand that constructs, the brain that computes, and the perspicacious eye that exploits these invisible structures.

A graphic-design grid is a bit like magic (now you see it, now you don't) sets of intersecting lines that help the designer decide where to put things, but that generally no one else sees. The benefits of using a grid are multifarious, ranging from the psychological to the functional, and, of course, the aesthetic. The grid embodies all the contradictions that designers struggle with. This is the designer's very own enigma code that can elevate design discourse to that of a science, and eradicate the creative block by "virtually" filling the blank page.

What is a grid?

A grid subdivides a page vertically and horizontally into margins, columns, inter-column spaces, lines of type, and spaces between blocks of type and images. These subdivisions form the basis of a modular and systematic approach to the layout, particularly for multipage documents, making the design process quicker, and ensuring visual consistency between related pages.

At its most basic, the sizes of a grid's component parts are determined by ease of reading and handling. From the sizes of type to the overall page or sheet size, decision-making is derived from physiology and the psychology of perception as much as by aesthetics. Type sizes are generally determined by hierarchy—captions smaller than body text and so on—column widths by optimum word counts of eight to ten words to the line, and overall layout by the need to group related items. This all sounds rather formulaic, and easy. But designers

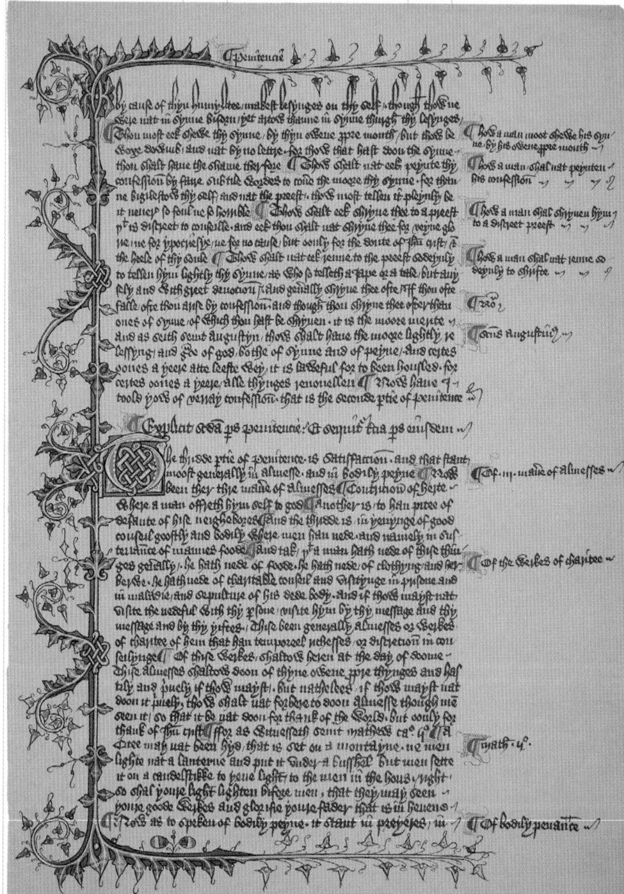

Left

This facsimile page is from a fourteenth-century English manuscript. The overall layout is asymmetric, and therefore surprisingly modern. The main column is positioned to the left of the page, with a large right-hand margin used for notes. All text is calligraphic and ranged left.

whose grids produce dynamic or very subtle results take these rules as a starting point only, developing flexible structures in which their sensibility can flourish.

The first five hundred years

Philosophers and linguists have argued that nothing exists in our consciousness unless it is named and we have a language with which to discuss it. Neither "graphic design" nor "grids" were talked about until the mid-twentieth century. Once named, complex grid structures comprising multiple columns, fields, baseline grids, and so on poured forth as never before, but it's not true to say that designers or their predecessors—commercial artists, printers, and scribes—hadn't been thinking about content, proportion, space, and form before this.

Even prior to typesetting and printing there were texts available to read. These were religious texts laid out by scribes in calligraphy. The pages were surprisingly modern, often using more than one column, with lettering that was ranged left, and color and variations in letter size used for emphasis. Just as the first cars resembled a horse-drawn carriage, the first printed pages took their cue from the manuscript page. But over time one major difference was introduced—justified setting. In this, spaces between words in continuous text are adjusted in each line so that columns align on both left and right sides. Although manuscript pages were symmetrical when viewed as spreads, the ranged-left lettering made them essentially asymmetric. With justified setting came 450 years of symmetry, and it wasn't until the twentieth century that this convention was truly challenged.

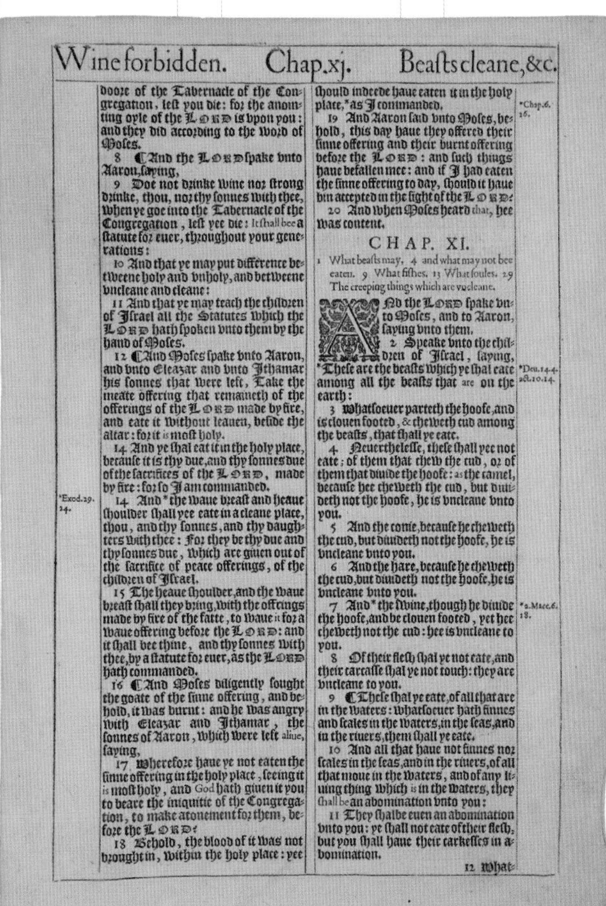

Wine forbidden. Chap.xj. Beasts cleane,&c.

doore of the Tabernacle of the Congregation, lest you die: for the anoin-
ting oyle of the LORD is vpon you:
and they did according to the word of
Moses.
8 ¶And the LORD spake vnto
Aaron, saying,
9 Doe not drinke wine nor strong
drinke, thou, nor thy sonnes with thee,
when ye goe into the Tabernacle of the
Congregation, lest yee die: It shall bee a
statute for euer, throughout your generations:
10 And that ye may put difference betweene holy and vnholy, and betweene
vncleane and cleane:
11 And that ye may teach the children
of Israel all the Statutes which the
LORD hath spoken vnto them by the
hand of Moses.
12 ¶And Moses spake vnto Aaron,
and vnto Eleazar and vnto Ithamar
his sonnes that were left, Take the
meate offering that remaineth of the
offerings of the LORD made by fire,
and eate it without leauen, beside the
altar: for it is most holy.
14 And ye shal eat it in the holy place,
because it is thy due, and thy sonnes due
of the sacrifices of the LORD, made
by fire: for so I am commanded.
*Exod.29. 24. 14 And *the waue breast and heaue
shoulder shall yee eate in a cleane place,
thou, and thy sonnes, and thy daugh-
ters with thee: For they be thy due and
thy sonnes due, which are giuen out of
the sacrifice of peace offerings, of the
children of Israel.
15 The heaue shoulder, and the waue
breast shall they bring, with the offrings
made by fire of the fatte, to waue it for a
waue offering before the LORD: and
it shall bee thine, and thy sonnes with
thee, by a statute for euer, as the LORD
hath commanded.
16 ¶And Moses diligently sought
the goate of the sinne offering, and behold, it was burnt: and he was angry
with Eleazar and Ithamar, the
sonnes of Aaron, which were left aliue,
saying,
17 Wherefore haue ye not eaten the
sinne offering in the holy place, seeing it
is most holy, and God hath giuen it you
to beare the iniquitie of the Congregation, to make atonement for them, before the LORD?
18 Behold, the blood of it was not
brought in, within the holy place: yee
should indeede haue eaten it in the holy
place, *as I commanded. *Chap.6. 26.
19 And Aaron said vnto Moses, behold, this day haue they offered their
sinne offering and their burnt offering
before the LORD: and such things
haue befallen mee: and if I had eaten
the sinne offering to day, should it haue
bin accepted in the sight of the LORD?
20 And when Moses heard that, hee
was content.

CHAP. XI.

1 What beasts may, 4 and what may not bee
eaten. 9 What fishes. 13 What foules. 29
The creeping things which are vncleane.

AND the LORD spake vn-
to Moses, and to Aaron,
saying vnto them,
2 Speake vnto the chil-
dren of Israel, saying,
*These are the beasts which ye shal eate *Deu.14.4. act.10.14.
among all the beasts that are on the
earth:
3 Whatsoeuer parteth the hoofe, and
is clouen footed, & cheweth cud among
the beasts, that shall ye eate.
4 Neuerthelesse, these shall yee not
eate; of them that chew the cud, or of
them that diuide the hoofe: as the camel,
because hee cheweth the cud, but diuideth not the hoofe, he is vncleane vnto
you.
5 And the conie, because he cheweth
the cud, but diuideth not the hoofe, he is
vncleane vnto you.
6 And the hare, because he cheweth
the cud, but diuideth not the hoofe, he is
vncleane vnto you.
7 And *the swine, though he diuide *2.Macc.6. 18.
the hoofe, and be clouen footed, yet hee
cheweth not the cud: hee is vncleane to
you.
8 Of their flesh shal ye not eate, and
their carcasse shal ye not touch: they are
vncleane to you.
9 ¶These shal ye eate, of all that are
in the waters: whatsoeuer hath finnes
and scales in the waters, in the seas, and
in the riuers, them shall ye eate.
10 And all that haue not finnes nor
scales in the seas, and in the riuers, of all
that moue in the waters, and of any li-
uing thing which is in the waters, they
shall be an abomination vnto you:
11 They shalbe euen an abomination
vnto you: ye shall not eate of their flesh,
but you shall haue their carkesses in a-
bomination.
12 What-

Left

Although derived from calligraphic forms, this lettering is actually type. Taken from a late-sixteenth-century English Bible, this page shows how printers quickly adopted symmetry. The text is justified and the two columns placed symmetrically on the page, with hanging notes also positioned according to a central axis.

Proportion and geometry

From the beginnings of printing (from the mid-fifteenth century) until the Industrial Revolution (late eighteenth century), the book was the primary output of printing. Apart from verse, type was generally set in one justified column per page, placed symmetrically on the spread with larger outer margins than inner, and a larger margin at the foot than at the head. But just as each decision made in minimal art is hugely significant, so too were the relative relationships of these few elements on the page. The proportions of these pages and margins were determined by geometry, concerned with the relation of points, lines, surfaces, and solids to one another rather than their measurement.

There are many geometrical constructions that can produce a beautiful page, but the golden section is usually cited as the most successful. As it is a geometrically derived form, it can be drawn with a setsquare and a compass—no measuring required. For those who do like to know measurements, the relationship of short to long side of a golden rectangle is 1:1.618. Many contemporary designers find this apparently irregular ratio unsettlingly chaotic, but others feel that the number sequence at its core has almost magical properties. By adding the lengths of the long and short edges it is possible to arrive at the next measurement in the sequence to give a bigger rectangle of the same proportions. This also works in reverse in order to make a smaller rectangle.

Adding two numbers to find the next in a series is also the basis of the number progression of the Fibonacci sequence, named after the thirteenth-century Italian mathematician who first identified it in many natural forms, from the arrangements of petals to the spirals of seashells. A combination of the golden section and Fibonacci sequence (1, 1, 2, 3, 5, 8, 13, etc) was often used to determine the overall proportion of the page and margins of the classical book.

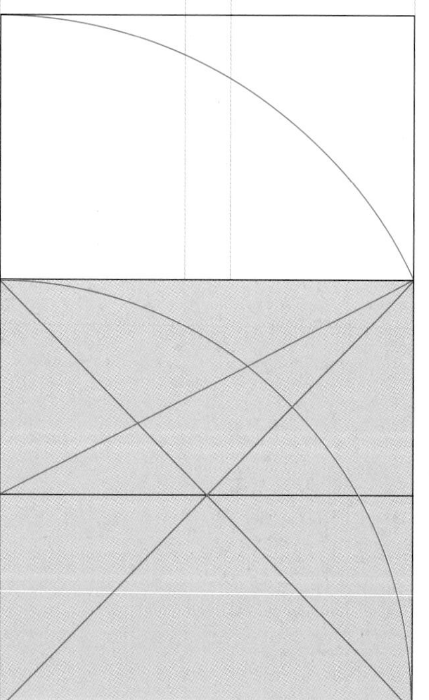

Left

This diagram shows how to draw a golden-section rectangle using only a set square and a compass. The resulting proportions are considered to be some of the most aesthetically pleasing. Start by using a set square to draw a right angle. Place a compass in one corner and draw an arc to arrive at a square, then draw a line horizontally through its center. Use the compass to join the two points shown to complete the rectangle.

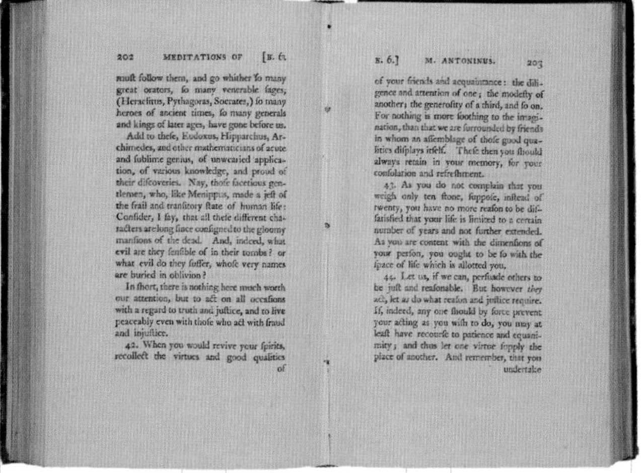

202 MEDITATIONS OF [B. 6.

muſt follow them, and go whither ſo many great orators, ſo many venerable ſages, (Heraclitus, Pythagoras, Socrates,) ſo many heroes of ancient times, ſo many generals and kings of later ages, have gone before us.

Add to theſe, Eudoxus, Hipparchus, Archimedes, and other mathematicians of acute and ſublime genius, of unwearied application, of various knowledge, and proud of their diſcoveries. Nay, thoſe facetious gentlemen, who, like Menippus, made a jeſt of the frail and tranſitory ſtate of human life: Conſider, I ſay, that all theſe different characters are long ſince conſigned to the gloomy manſions of the dead. And, indeed, what evil are they ſenſible of in their tombs? or what evil do they ſuffer, whoſe very names are buried in oblivion?

In ſhort, there is nothing here much worth our attention, but to act on all occaſions with a regard to truth and juſtice, and to live peaceably even with thoſe who act with fraud and injuſtice.

42. When you would revive your ſpirits, recollect the virtues and good qualities of

B. 6.] M. ANTONINUS. 203

of your friends and acquaintance: the diligence and attention of one; the modeſty of another; the generoſity of a third, and ſo on. For nothing is more ſoothing to the imagination, than that we are ſurrounded by friends in whom an aſſemblage of thoſe good qualities diſplays itſelf. Theſe then you ſhould always retain in your memory, for your conſolation and refreſhment.

43. As you do not complain that you weigh only ten ſtone, ſuppoſe, inſtead of twenty, you have no more reaſon to be diſſatiſfied that your life is limited to a certain number of years and not further extended. As you are content with the dimenſions of your perſon, you ought to be ſo with the ſpace of life which is allotted you.

44. Let us, if we can, perſuade others to be juſt and reaſonable. But however *they* act, let *us* do what reaſon and juſtice require. If, indeed, any one ſhould by force prevent your acting as you wiſh to do, you may at leaſt have recourſe to patience and equanimity; and thus let one virtue ſupply the place of another. And remember, that you undertake

Above

This spread from The Meditations of Marcus Aurelius Antoninus, *published in 1792, uses the golden section to determine the text area, and the Fibonacci sequence to arrive at relative margin sizes (inner margin 3 units; top and outer margins 5 units; bottom margin 8 units). The gutter is treated as the central axis, and there is one column of text. The outer and bottom margins are larger than the inner and top. These optical adjustments ensure that the text doesn't appear to be falling off the bottom of the page.*

The next hundred years

The Industrial Revolution marked the beginning of a capital-based economy, with mass production at its heart. Graphic design was born, although still not named as such. Its job was to communicate diverse messages to an increasingly literate people. The rise in print output was phenomenal—posters, leaflets, and advertising of all kinds, newspapers, timetables, and all manner of information-based design. Suddenly designs competed for attention. Images, initially in the form of engravings and then as photographs, had to be incorporated along with an ever-expanding array of display typefaces. Highly skilled and educated printers stayed firmly in the land of the book, while jobbing printers and compositors struggled to lay out this diverse material for which the classical book was not a useful precedent.

Toward the end of the nineteenth century, artists and thinkers identified this as a problem that had to be solved. Although the work produced by William Morris and the Arts and Crafts movement may appear very different from that of modernism, Arts and Crafts was its forerunner in one important respect. Morris believed that form and function were inextricably entwined. Running almost concurrently with these ideas were the revolutionary cubist experiments of Picasso and Braque,

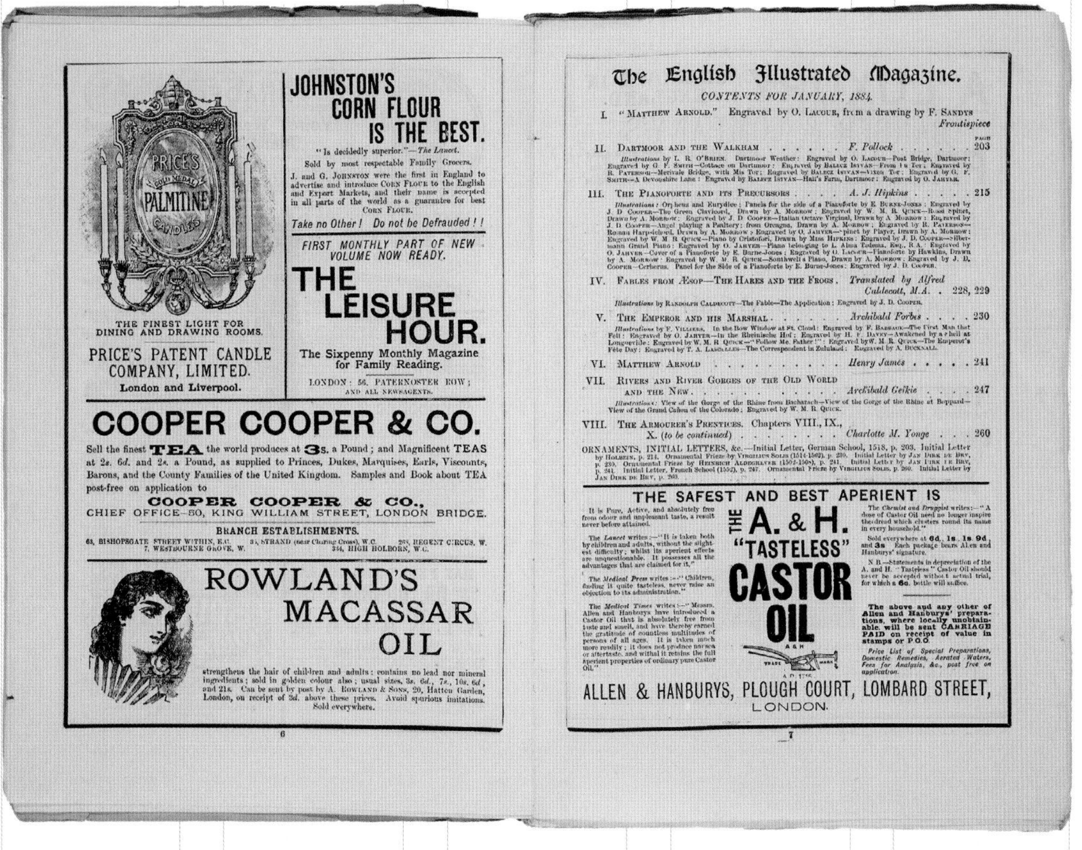
PRICE'S GOLD MEDAL PALMITINE CANDLES

THE FINEST LIGHT FOR DINING AND DRAWING ROOMS.

PRICE'S PATENT CANDLE COMPANY, LIMITED.
London and Liverpool.

JOHNSTON'S CORN FLOUR IS THE BEST.

"Is decidedly superior."—*The Lancet.*

Sold by most respectable Family Grocers.

J. and G. Johnston were the first in England to advertise and introduce Corn Flour to the English and Export Markets, and their name is accepted in all parts of the world as a guarantee for best Corn Flour.

Take no Other! Do not be Defrauded!!

FIRST MONTHLY PART OF NEW VOLUME NOW READY.

THE LEISURE HOUR.

The Sixpenny Monthly Magazine for Family Reading.

LONDON: 56, PATERNOSTER ROW; AND ALL NEWSAGENTS.

COOPER COOPER & CO.

Sell the finest TEA the world produces at 3s. a Pound; and Magnificent TEAS at 2*s.* 6*d.* and 2*s.* a Pound, as supplied to Princes, Dukes, Marquises, Earls, Viscounts, Barons, and the County Families of the United Kingdom. Samples and Book about TEA post-free on application to

COOPER COOPER & CO.,
CHIEF OFFICE—50, KING WILLIAM STREET, LONDON BRIDGE.

BRANCH ESTABLISHMENTS.
63, BISHOPSGATE STREET WITHIN, E.C. 3, STRAND (near Charing Cross), W.C. 268, REGENT CIRCUS, W.
7, WESTBOURNE GROVE, W. 334, HIGH HOLBORN, W.C.

ROWLAND'S MACASSAR OIL

strengthens the hair of children and adults: contains no lead nor mineral ingredients; sold in golden colour also; usual sizes, 3*s.* 6*d.*, 7*s.*, 10*s.* 6*d.*, and 21*s.* Can be sent by post by A. Rowland & Sons, 20, Hatton Garden, London, on receipt of 3*d.* above these prices. Avoid spurious imitations. Sold everywhere.

6

The English Illustrated Magazine.

CONTENTS FOR JANUARY, 1884.

I. "Matthew Arnold." Engraved by O. Lacour, from a drawing by F. Sandys ... *Frontispiece*

II. Dartmoor and the Walkham ... *F. Pollock* ... 203

Illustrations by L. R. O'Brien. Dartmoor Weather: Engraved by O. Lacour—Post Bridge, Dartmoor: Engraved by G. F. Smith—Cottage on Dartmoor: Engraved by Balecz Istvan—From Ira Tor: Engraved by R. Paterson—Merivale Bridge, with Mis Tor: Engraved by Balecz Istvan—Vixen Tor: Engraved by G. F. Smith—A Devonshire Lane: Engraved by Balecz Istvan—Hall's Farm, Dartmoor: Engraved by O. Jahyer.

III. The Pianoforte and its Precursors ... *A. J. Hipkins* ... 215

Illustrations: Orpheus and Eurydice; Panels for the side of a Pianoforte by E. Burne-Jones: Engraved by J. D. Cooper—The Green Clavicord, Drawn by A. Morrow: Engraved by W. M. R. Quick—Rossi Spinet, Drawn by A. Morrow: Engraved by J. D. Cooper—Italian Octave Virginal, Drawn by A. Morrow: Engraved by J. D. Cooper—Angel playing a Psaltery: from Orcagna, Drawn by A. Morrow: Engraved by R. Paterson—Roman Harpsichord, Drawn by A. Morrow: Engraved by O. Jahyer—Spinet by Player, Drawn by A. Morrow: Engraved by W. M. R. Quick—Piano by Cristofori, Drawn by Miss Hipkins: Engraved by J. D. Cooper—Silbermann Grand Piano: Engraved by O. Jahyer—Piano belonging to L. Alma Tadema, Esq., R.A.: Engraved by O. Jahyer—Cover of a Pianoforte by E. Burne-Jones; Engraved by O. Lacour—Pianoforte by Hawkins, Drawn by A. Morrow: Engraved by W. M. R. Quick—Southwell's Piano, Drawn by A. Morrow: Engraved by J. D. Cooper—Cerberus. Panel for the Side of a Pianoforte by E. Burne-Jones; Engraved by J. D. Cooper.

IV. Fables from Æsop—The Hares and the Frogs. *Translated by Alfred Caldecott, M.A.* ... 228, 229

Illustrations by Randolph Caldecott—The Fable—The Application: Engraved by J. D. Cooper.

V. The Emperor and his Marshal ... *Archibald Forbes* ... 230

Illustrations by F. Villiers. In the Bow Window at St. Cloud: Engraved by F. Babbage—The First Man that Fell: Engraved by O. Jahyer—In the Rheinische Hof: Engraved by H. F. Davey—Awakened by a Shell at Longueville: Engraved by W. M. R. Quick—"Follow Me, Father!": Engraved by W. M. R. Quick—The Emperor's Fête Day: Engraved by T. A. Lascelles—The Correspondent in Zululand: Engraved by A. Bucknall.

VI. Matthew Arnold ... *Henry James* ... 241

VII. Rivers and River Gorges of the Old World and the New ... *Archibald Geikie* ... 247

Illustrations: View of the Gorge of the Rhine from Bacharach—View of the Gorge of the Rhine at Boppard—View of the Grand Cañon of the Colorado; Engraved by W. M. R. Quick.

VIII. The Armourer's Prentices. Chapters VIII., IX., X. (*to be continued*) ... *Charlotte M. Yonge* ... 260

ORNAMENTS, INITIAL LETTERS, &c.—Initial Letter, German School, 1518, p. 203. Initial Letter by Holbein, p. 214. Ornamental Frieze by Virgilius Solis (1514-1562), p. 230. Initial Letter by Jan Dirk de Bry, p. 230. Ornamental Frieze by Heinrich Aldegrever (1502-1558), p. 241. Initial Letter by Jan Dirk de Bry, p. 241. Initial Letter, French School (1552), p. 247. Ornamental Frieze by Virgilius Solis, p. 260. Initial Letter by Jan Dirk de Bry, p. 260.

THE SAFEST AND BEST APERIENT IS

THE A. & H. "TASTELESS" CASTOR OIL

It is Pure, Active, and absolutely free from odour and unpleasant taste, a result never before attained.

The *Lancet* writes:—"It is taken both by children and adults, without the slightest difficulty; whilst its aperient effects are unquestionable. It possesses all the advantages that are claimed for it."

The *Medical Press* writes:—"Children, finding it quite tasteless, never raise an objection to its administration."

The *Medical Times* writes:—"Messrs. Allen and Hanburys have introduced a Castor Oil that is absolutely free from taste and smell, and have thereby earned the gratitude of countless multitudes of persons of all ages. It is taken much more readily; it does not produce nausea or aftertaste, and withal it retains the full aperient properties of ordinary pure Castor Oil."

The *Chemist and Druggist* writes:—"A dose of Castor Oil need no longer inspire the dread which clusters round its name in every household."

Sold everywhere at 6d., 1s., 1s. 9d., and 3s. Each package bears Allen and Hanburys' signature.

N.B.—Statements in depreciation of the A. and H. "Tasteless" Castor Oil should never be accepted without actual trial, for which a 6d. bottle will suffice.

The above and any other of Allen and Hanburys' preparations, where locally unobtainable, will be sent CARRIAGE PAID on receipt of value in stamps or P.O.O.

Price List of Special Preparations, Domestic Remedies, Aerated Waters, Fees for Analysis, &c., post free on application.

ALLEN & HANBURYS, PLOUGH COURT, LOMBARD STREET, LONDON.

7

Left
Design as we know it was born partly in response to the Industrial Revolution. As this spread from the English Illustrated Magazine *of 1884 shows, designs were suddenly competing for attention. The resulting visual confusion may have a certain charm, but these random layouts were confusing and often inaccessible. Contemporary designers considered this a problem to solve and started to explore different theoretical approaches to their work.*

who were exploring how to represent 3-D forms on 2-D planes, producing increasingly abstract results. Artists, and then designers, were influenced by this work, and re-evaluated composition as a result.

The early twentieth-century art movements—futurism, dadaism, surrealism, constructivism, suprematism, and expressionism—also had an influence on the development of the grid. Artists were united in trying to represent a new, industrialised age exemplified by speed of travel and faster communication. They recognized the power of the word and broke with all previous print tradition by using type at conflicting angles or on curves; introducing extreme variation in type sizes; using drawn, abstracted letterforms; and generally ignoring the vertical and horizontal nature of type. For the first time, space was used as a dynamic component in typographic layout. The ethos that underpins this work was the antithesis of the rational and logical approach implicit in the grid. But in drawing such a resolute line under the past, it opened the door to de Stijl, the Bauhaus, and typographers like Herbert Bayer and Jan Tschichold, who called for some order to be imposed on what seemed like fractured chaos.

LACERBA 53

MOVIMENTO DI 2 STANTUFFI

VENTO — **negatore** pigrizia inerzia congelare tutto con stelle letterarie sradicate dalla carne (NOTTE LIBRARIA) seppellire tutto con odore di ascelle materassi di profumi mammelle cotte piacere + 7000 ragionamenti scettici

SANGUE — **affermatore** ottimismo forza respingere il vento pessimismo caldo o freddo andare senza scopo per FARE VIVERE CORRERE ESSERE

Karazuc zuczuc Karazuc zuczuc Nadl nadl AAAaaaaaaaaa

SOLE OLIATORE UNIVERSALE

MENU D'UN PRANZO DI 6 COPERTI AL LUME DI UNA LUCCIOLA

tlac tlac cic-cioc

1. Antipasto di kakawicknostalgin
2. Angoscette al sugo
3. rimorschif in bianco
4. presentimentlung allo spiedo
5. grappoli emorroidali
6. orina d'asceta frappée

aih aiiiiii aiiiiii fuuuuut — sedersi comodamente in quattro sulla punta d'uno spillo snellezza signorile grigioperla del vento che porta a spasso l'incendio-levrette-vestita-di-rosso

FEROCISSIMO SOLE

SENTIMENTALE

accecato di lagrime — sui giovani esploratori traditi da mogli amanti solennità d'un cornuto sulla linea dell'equatore — accecante di lagrime rosse

(andante grazioso con pizzicato)

letterina tiepida sudante sul petto dilataaaaARSI d'una parola scritta gomito nudo affusolarsi di nuvola — mano — tenne nel caldo 3 giorni di marcia dune dune dune
COSTA il **POSTALE**
8 GIORNI **GENOVA** Parma eccomi baci **zingzing zingzing** tradizionale di un letto di provincia
Karazuc - zuczuc Karazuc - zuczuc seistatuneroe **zingzingcuic Naldl Naldl AAAAAAaaaaa zingzingcuic** floscezza di campane bagnate mature cadenti **cadeeenti**

Tempo di Cake-Walk

daal ramo altissimo antichiiiiissimo odore-di-bucato-acacie-muffa-legnotarlato-cavolicotti-**zing-zang**-di-casseruole buio ammoniacale d'una tenda di beduini dune dune dune

MARINETTI

CARRÀ.

Costruzione spaziale. Simultaneità di ritmi.

Deformazione dinamica.

Una tela bianca non ha spazio.

Lo spazio s'inizia con l'arabesco plastico, man mano che i valori di superficie e di profondità vanno prendendo i caratteri speciali all'emozione che guida il pittore.

Un insieme di colore-tono scaturisce e si sviluppa da un dato colore che ne è in qualche modo il centro generatore.

Il valore spaziale di una data forma, concreta e subordina a sè i diversi valori plastici di un quadro in una unità d'espressione.

Il pittore futurista non si limita a considerare il problema plastico dal punto di vista elementare dell'impresionismo.

Egli sa che non varcherebbe i confini limitatissimi dell'impressionismo se si accontentasse di rendere la deformazione formale d'un oggetto nel solo suo *succedersi-ritmico* di onde colorate.

Il pittore futurista supera il principio pittorico dell'impressionismo cogliendo *in ogni forma e zona di colore* la forza emotiva propria ad ogni forma e ad ogni zona di colore e raggiunge così il carattere ben definito di *espressione spaziale*.

Questa espressione spaziale potrebbe essere definita *prospettiva astratta di forma-colore*.

I ritmi organati sull'asse della *spazialità* ci danno gli accordi e disaccordi orchestrali di colore-forma-forza. La spazialità ci dà la quantità

Above

This page is from an issue of the Futurist magazine Lacerba, *published in 1914. By breaking with previous approaches to layout and design, early twentieth-century art movements had an influence on the development of the grid. The work was often intentionally chaotic, but as the old rules were broken, a new, more rational system was given the space to develop.*

de Stijl, the Bauhaus, and Jan Tschichold

In 1917 Dutch architect, designer, and painter Theo van Doesburg founded de Stijl. The importance of this movement to the grid is that it explored form as determined by function, and placed this in a political context. Arguing that simplicity of form was accessible and democratic, its members advocated minimalism, using only rectilinear forms, and eradicating surface decoration other than as a byproduct of a limited color palette: the primaries plus black and white. The typographers affiliated to de Stijl wanted to apply these ideas in the real world, not just for their artistic cause. Designers like Piet Zwart and Paul Schuitema used these principles to produce commercial advertising and publicity materials.

The Bauhaus opened its doors in Weimar, Germany, in 1919, with the architect Walter Gropius as its Director. His belief that architecture, graphic art, industrial design, painting, sculpture, and so on were all interrelated had a profound impact on the development of typography and graphic design long after the school was forced to close by the Nazis in the 1930s. Within an astonishingly short period of time, graphic artists were marrying analytical skills with abstract form to arrive at mass-produced designs determined as much by political idealism as by a desire for self-expression. In 1925, Herbert Bayer was appointed to run the new printing and advertising workshop. He paid attention to typographic detail, experimenting with a limited typographic palette in order to achieve greater visual clarity and easily navigable pages.

During the late 1920s and the 1930s, typographer Jan Tschichold set out his typographic principles in two seminal books: *The New Typography* (1928), and *Asymmetric Typography* (1935). Tschichold's work was more refined than much of that which had preceded it. He wrote of typographic consistency as a necessary precursor to understanding, described designers as akin to engineers, and argued compellingly for asymmetry as a central tenet of modernism. It was the logical way to lay out text that is read from left to right, and produced "natural" rather than "formalist" solutions to the new design challenges than classicism, with its enforced central axis. In his work Tschichold explored subtle horizontal and vertical alignments, and used a limited range of fonts, type sizes, and type weights.

Josef Albers: Wall picture, etched in black-and white double-layer glass. 1928.

Subjectless painting is usually called abstract, but to be precise what it deals with is not abstract, but real – a line, a circle, an area signify themselves, while in representative painting they stand for something else. Therefore it is not wrong to apply the word 'abstract' to representative painting. The expression 'absolute painting' is also objectionable. Theo von Doesburg and the AC group were right when they first used the term 'concrete painting' in 1930. This term however, is not suitable in the English language.

A painting with a subject consists of two things and most people think only of one, namely the subject. They are pleased if a picture re-

80

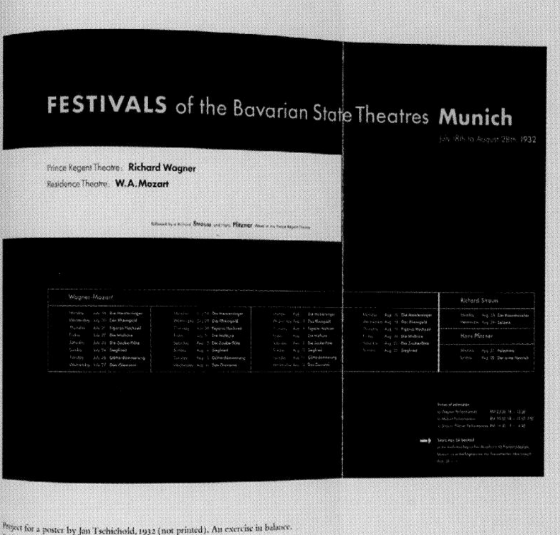

Project for a poster by Jan Tschichold, 1932 (not printed). An exercise in balance. Such a design might still be used to advertise electronic music.

Left

This spread and throw-out is from Jan Tschichold's seminal work Asymmetric Typography, *originally published in 1935. In it Tschichold argued that typographic consistency is a necessary precursor to understanding, and described designers as akin to engineers. His work was nevertheless aesthetically refined and dynamic. Here he explains the parallels between abstract art and typographic layout.*

The grid and Swiss typography

Early modernists had explored layout, space, and scale. They had talked of the democratizing benefits of mass production, and had used the language of science as much as art. They had argued for consistency and minimalism as a mark of design confidence and greater accessibility. During WWII, and in the decades that followed, these ideas coalesced into a coherent design manifesto with a new design device at its core—the grid.

The grid and Swiss typography are synonymous. Switzerland was neutral during the war. Not only did it attract many intellectual refugees, including designers like Jan Tschichold, but also most peacetime activities continued as normal, and supplies of such things as ink and paper weren't rationed. Added to this, publications had to be set in its three official languages—French, German, and Italian—which called for a modular approach, using multiple column structures.

Several Swiss artist/designers, most notably Max Bill and Richard Paul Lohse, explored systematic forms in their paintings concurrently with graphic design, while the graphic designers Emil Ruder and Josef Müller-Brockmann both wrote educative texts explaining what grids were and how to use them. They approached the subject with great rigor, arguing passionately that "integral design" required structures that would unite all the elements in both 2-D and 3-D design: type, pictures, diagrams, and space itself. Despite their enthusiasm for order and precision, they both understood the value of artistic intuition.

"No system of ratios, however ingenious, can relieve the typographer of deciding how one value should be related to another... He must spare no effort to tutor his feeling for proportion... He must know intuitively when the tension between several things is so great that harmony is endangered. But he must also know how to avoid relationships lacking in tension since these lead to monotony." **Emil Ruder**, *Typography*

The grid and the design philosophy of which it is a part have been criticized for placing the narcissistic designer at the heart of the solution, and generating formulaic solutions that are mechanistic, unyielding, and rigid. But for Ruder, Müller-Brockmann, and many other designers since, the grid was the natural response to a design problem. It was also a metaphor for the human condition, and was found in all areas of human endeavor.

"Just as in nature, systems of order govern the growth and structure of animate and inanimate matter, so human activity itself has, since the earliest times, been distinguished by the quest for order... The desire to bring order to the bewildering confusion of appearances reflects a deep human need." **Josef Müller-Brockmann**, *Grid Systems in Graphic Design*

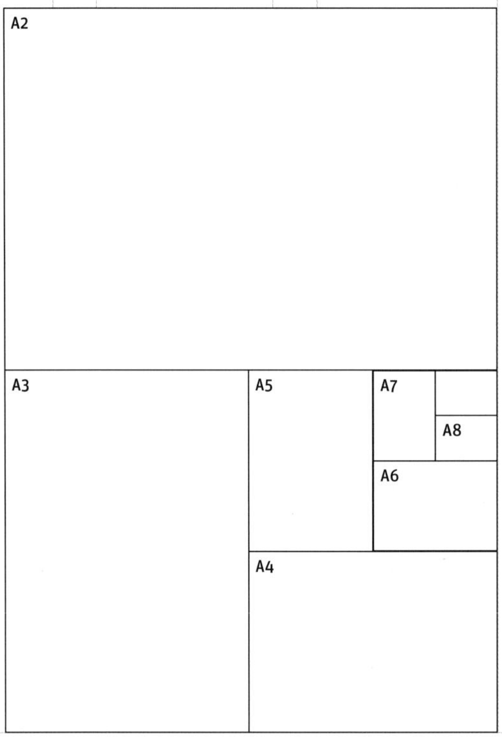

A2

A3

A5

A7

A8

A6

A4

Right

The ingenuity of the "A" paper sizing system appeals to designers who are interested in modular approaches to design. For the true modernist, working with standard paper sizing is more economic and celebrates mass production. But, for designers who want to usurp the system, there are countless ways to subdivide the sheet sizes to arrive at more unusual formats.

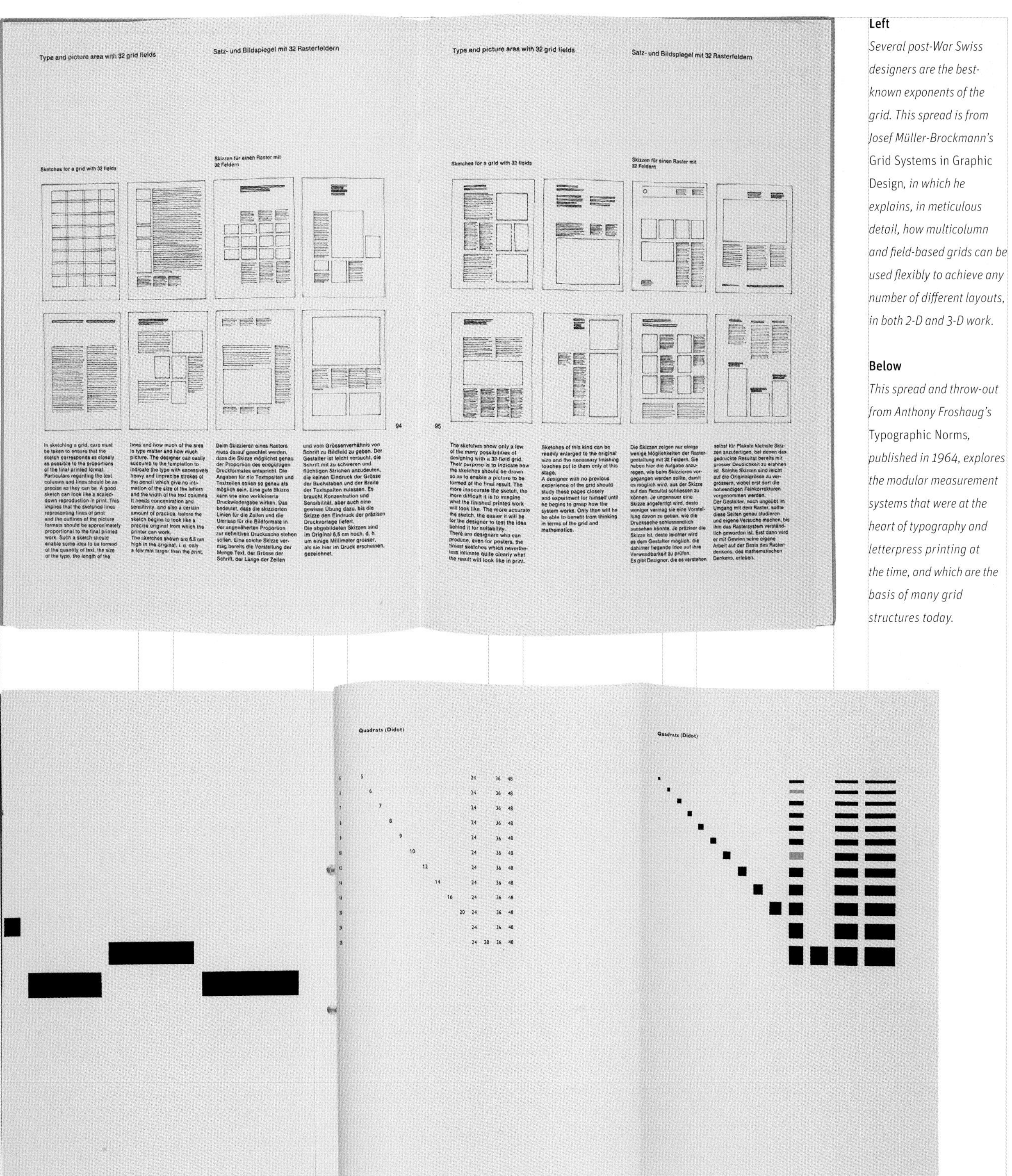

Type and picture area with 32 grid fields

Satz- und Bildspiegel mit 32 Rasterfeldern

Sketches for a grid with 32 fields

Skizzen für einen Raster mit 32 Feldern

In sketching a grid, care must be taken to ensure that the sketch corresponds as closely as possible to the proportions of the final printed format. Particulars regarding the text columns and lines should be as precise as they can be. A good sketch can look like a scaled-down reproduction in print. This implies that the sketched lines representing lines of print and the outlines of the picture formats should be approximately proportional to the final printed work. Such a sketch should enable some idea to be formed of the quantity of text, the size of the type, the length of the lines and how much of the area is type matter and how much picture. The designer can easily succumb to the temptation to indicate the type with excessively heavy and imprecise strokes of the pencil which give no intimation of the size of the letters and the width of the text columns. It needs concentration and sensitivity, and also a certain amount of practice, before the sketch begins to look like a precise original from which the printer can work.
The sketches shown are 6.5 cm high in the original, i. e. only a few mm larger than the print.

Beim Skizzieren eines Rasters muss darauf geachtet werden, dass die Skizze möglichst genau der Proportion des endgültigen Druckformates entspricht. Die Angaben für die Textspalten und Textzeilen sollen so genau als möglich sein. Eine gute Skizze kann wie eine verkleinerte Druckwiedergabe wirken. Das bedeutet, dass die skizzierten Linien für die Zeilen und die Umrisse für die Bildformate in der angenäherten Proportion zur definitiven Drucksache stehen sollen. Eine solche Skizze vermag bereits die Vorstellung der Menge Text, der Grösse der Schrift, der Länge der Zeilen und vom Grössenverhältnis von Schrift zu Bildfeld zu geben. Der Gestalter ist leicht versucht, die Schrift mit zu schweren und flüchtigen Strichen anzudeuten, die keinen Eindruck der Grösse der Buchstaben und der Breite der Textspalten zulassen. Es braucht Konzentration und Sensibilität, aber auch eine gewisse Übung dazu, bis die Skizze den Eindruck der präzisen Druckvorlage liefert.
Die abgebildeten Skizzen sind im Original 6,5 cm hoch, d. h. um einige Millimeter grösser, als sie hier im Druck erscheinen, gezeichnet.

94

95

The sketches show only a few of the many possibilities of designing with a 32-field grid. Their purpose is to indicate how the sketches should be drawn so as to enable a picture to be formed of the final result. The more inaccurate the sketch, the more difficult it is to imagine what the finished printed work will look like. The more accurate the sketch, the easier it will be for the designer to test the idea behind it for suitability.
There are designers who can produce, even for posters, the tiniest sketches which nevertheless intimate quite clearly what the result will look like in print. Sketches of this kind can be readily enlarged to the original size and the necessary finishing touches put to them only at this stage.
A designer with no previous experience of the grid should study these pages closely and experiment for himself until he begins to grasp how the system works. Only then will he be able to benefit from thinking in terms of the grid and mathematics.

Die Skizzen zeigen nur einige wenige Möglichkeiten der Rastergestaltung mit 32 Feldern. Sie haben hier die Aufgabe anzuregen, wie beim Skizzieren vorgegangen werden sollte, damit es möglich wird, aus der Skizze auf das Resultat schliessen zu können. Je ungenauer eine Skizze angefertigt wird, desto weniger vermag sie eine Vorstellung davon zu geben, wie die Drucksache schlussendlich aussehen könnte. Je präziser die Skizze ist, desto leichter wird es dem Gestalter möglich, die dahinter liegende Idee auf ihre Verwendbarkeit zu prüfen.
Es gibt Designer, die es verstehen selbst für Plakate kleinste Skizzen anzufertigen, bei denen das gedruckte Resultat bereits mit grosser Deutlichkeit zu erahnen ist. Solche Skizzen sind leicht auf die Originalgrösse zu vergrössern, wobei erst dort die notwendigen Feinkorrekturen vorgenommen werden.
Der Gestalter, noch ungeübt im Umgang mit dem Raster, sollte diese Seiten genau studieren und eigene Versuche machen, bis ihm das Rastersystem verständlich geworden ist. Erst dann wird er mit Gewinn seine eigene Arbeit auf der Basis des Rasterdenkens, des mathematischen Denkens, erleben.

Left
Several post-War Swiss designers are the best-known exponents of the grid. This spread is from Josef Müller-Brockmann's Grid Systems in Graphic Design, *in which he explains, in meticulous detail, how multicolumn and field-based grids can be used flexibly to achieve any number of different layouts, in both 2-D and 3-D work.*

Below
This spread and throw-out from Anthony Froshaug's Typographic Norms, *published in 1964, explores the modular measurement systems that were at the heart of typography and letterpress printing at the time, and which are the basis of many grid structures today.*

Grids and mathematics

The difference between grids as we know them and the page layouts of the past rests in increased flexibility and mathematical dexterity. This starts with considering format and ends with baseline grids, for which lines are often subdivided into units as small as 2pt. The computer has made greater precision easy, and contemporary grids subdivide the page into small component parts that can be combined in numerous ways that still ensure cohesion in the design. Small columns are joined to make wider columns, numbers of baseline units are joined to make fields, and so on.

Karl Gerstner's grid for the journal *Capital*, designed in 1962, is still often cited as near-perfect in terms of its mathematical ingenuity. The smallest unit in Gerstner's grid, or matrix as he called it, is 10pt—the baseline to baseline measurement of the text. The main area for text and images is a square, with an area above for titles and running heads. The cleverness lies in the subdivision of the square into 58 equal units in both directions. If all intercolumn spaces are two units, then a two-, three-, four-, five-, or six-column structure is possible without any leftover units.

Above
The Swiss designer Karl Gerstner's 1962 grid for the periodical Capital *is near perfect. His unit, both horizontally and vertically, was 10pt—the baseline to baseline measurement of the text type. The type area was a square of 58 units. Allowing for intercolumn spaces, this gave Gerstner grids of two, three, four, five, and six columns and fields.*

The grid made visible

Grids are generally made visible only through use, but some designers have exposed the workings of the graphic design machine to demonstrate that the grid is something not only of utility, but also of beauty. Once visible, the precision of the grid acts as evidence of design credibility, and its purity of form has a mystical draw.

The Dutch designer Wim Crouwel pioneered the application of systematic design in the Netherlands during the 1950s and 1960s. His identity for the Vormgevers exhibition at the Stedelijk Museum in Amsterdam in 1968 used an exposed grid in the layout of posters and catalogs, which was also the basis of the lettering. In 1990, issue 7 of 8vo's influential journal *Octavo* ran grids with coordinates, like maps, under

Right
Dutch designer Wim Crouwel is known for his exploration and experimentation with grids. In this poster for the Vormgevers exhibition in 1968, he made the grid visible. This device then formed the basis not only for the layout, but also for the lettering.

each spread. *Octavo* called their method of working "visual engineering."

"To get things built, you have to be able to describe them... The act of specifying requires one to define the structure of a design very precisely... It places one's design under intense scrutiny in terms of structure and logical process. Very different to the 'drag and drop' computer screen environment, where close enough is often good enough." **Mark Holt and Hamish Muir**, *8vo: On the Outside*

Designer Astrid Stavro has taken this one stage further. Inspired by a diverse set of grids, from the Gutenberg Bible to the *Guardian* newspaper, Stavro's GRID-IT notepads celebrate the usually invisible graphic-design grid in its purist form—unused and unsullied. Perhaps we can take this as a sign that designers no longer worry about being a little nerdy or despotic.

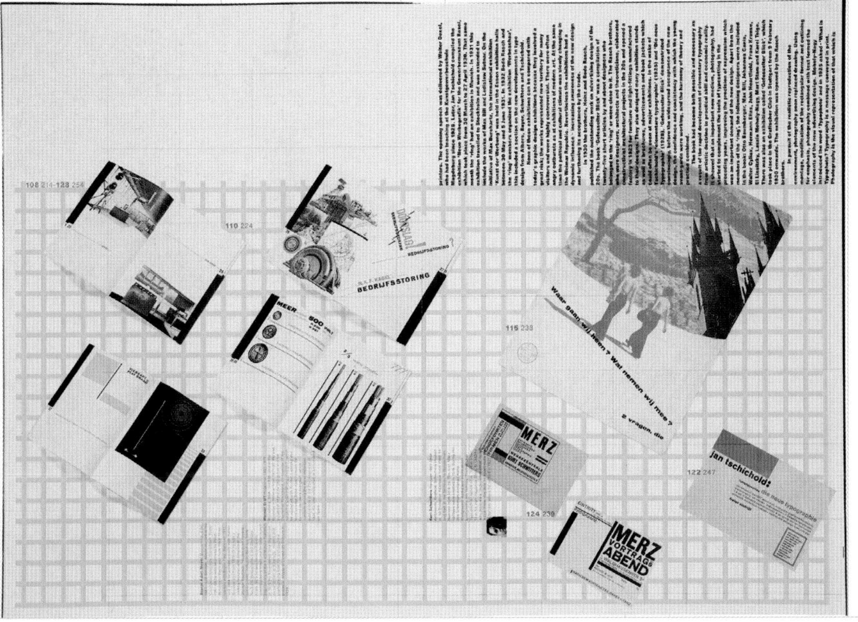

Left
Having started the journal Octavo, *designers 8vo edited and designed it from the mid 1980s to the early 1990s. The design often explored systematic and modular approaches, but in issue 7 the designers chose to reveal their methods by giving the grid coordinates, like a map, and printing it as a background to each page.*

Above
Italian designer Astrid Stavro worked on the Grid-it! Notepads project while studying at London's Royal College of Art. The intention is to celebrate the notion of the grid in its pure form. Each pad shows a different grid. These range from Tschichold and Müller-Brockmann *classics to* the Gutenberg Bible and Guardian *newspaper. [Photographer: Mauricio Salinas]*

Catalogs, leaflets & brochures

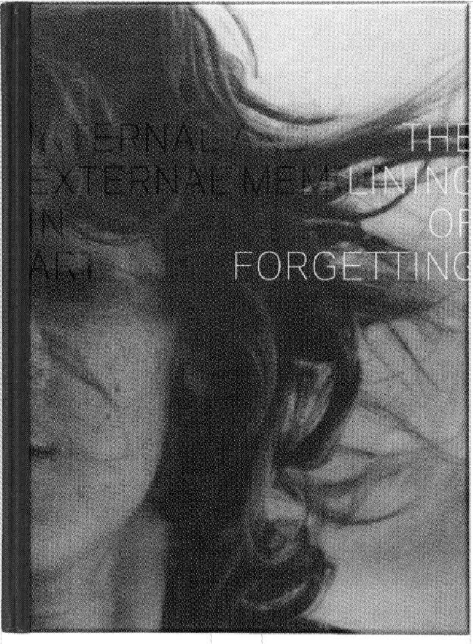

THE LINING OF FORGETTING

Pablo Helguera
Louise Bourgeois
Deborah Aschheim
Edgar Arceneaux
Dinh Q. Lê
John Coplans
Janice Caswell
Emma Kay
Scott Lyall
David Rokeby
Mungo Thomson
Cody Trepte
Kerry Tribe
Rachel Whiteread

THE LINING OF FORGETTING
Internal & External Memory in Art

Curated by
Xandra Eden

With essays by
John Roberts
and
Sarah Cook

Weatherspoon Art Museum
The University of North Carolina at Greensboro

DIRECTOR'S FOREWORD

Nancy Doll

WE MAKE NOTES SO WE WON'T FORGET. We ask others to help us remember. We rely on all kinds of systems to retain data we need and want. We live in an ironic time: The more information our technological world readily makes available to us, the more we need those same technologies to store and retrieve it, to even prompt us at times to remember that it's there.

Together, memory and the loss of memory comprise one of the seminal issues of our world today. The list of related topics seems to expand daily: the aging of the baby boomers; new discoveries about the way the brain works; new technology-aided neurosurgical procedures; the rise of dementia and Alzheimer's disease; the exponential increase of available information; the growing use of memory surrogates. As challenging as these issues may be, other aspects of memory persist relatively unchanged: our fondness for certain memories and the converse—how we wish we could forget some things; memory as a subject and metaphor in art and literature; the way we form mental pictures.

From the photo album and Facebook to Marcel Proust and *Memento*, it seems fair to say that, as humans, we are obsessed with memory. We record, document, represent, and depict—all so that we don't forget. This catalogue will serve as the instrument by which the exhibition *The Lining of Forgetting: Internal and External Memory in Art* essentially will be remembered. *The Lining of Forgetting* is an ambitious and forward-reaching project that traverses the sphere of memory and its loss. The Weatherspoon's curator of exhibitions, Xandra Eden, is to be congratulated for intelligently and beautifully realizing a project of such breadth and complexity. She joins me in wholeheartedly thanking the artists for their willing participation: Edgar Arceneaux, Deborah Aschheim, Louise Bourgeois, Janice Caswell, John Coplans, Pablo Helguera, Emma Kay, Dinh Q. Lê, Scott Lyall, David Rokeby, Mungo Thomson, Cody Trepte, Kerry Tribe, and Rachel Whiteread. Their galleries have been most helpful in the project's organization. We especially wish to thank Susanne Vielmetter and Gosia Wojas, Susanne Vielmetter Los Angeles Projects; Wendy Williams, Louise Bourgeois Studio; Amanda Means, The John Coplans

We often imagine our brain as a large filing system or computer database (if a slightly malfunctioning one), but the human mind is nothing so aseptic. In 1983, French filmmaker Chris Marker pronounced, as his alter ego Sandor Krasna, in *Sans Soleil*:

> *I will have spent my life trying to understand the function of remembering, which is not the opposite of forgetting, but rather its lining. We do not remember. We rewrite memory much as history is rewritten.*

This concept of memory as a process that is, first, mostly about forgetting, and, second, forever in editing mode, is central to the exhibition *The Lining of Forgetting: Internal and External Memory in Art*. The

artists—Edgar Arceneaux, Deborah Aschheim, Louise Bourgeois, Janice Caswell, John Coplans, Pablo Helguera, Emma Kay, Dinh Q. Lê, Scott Lyall, David Rokeby, Mungo Thomson, Cody Trepte, Kerry Tribe, and Rachel Whiteread—address not only these issues but more through such diverse media as sculpture, video, book works, photography, installation, and computer-generated works. Organized around three thematic headings—Media Is the Memory, *Une Mémoire Involuntaire*, and The Work of Memory—the exhibition encourages an examination of the mutable nature of memory and the complex interconnections between both the internal and external variety. The categories are by no means watertight; many of the works move across thematics. Long-term, declarative memory, rather than short-term memory or procedural memory, predominates in these works, with most pertaining to episodic memory (the recollection of a particular occasion or event) or semantic memory (memory of knowledge, often accrued over time), although there are several works that deal with implicit memory (memory that comes into play without conscious awareness). Most important, the artists highlight memory as a creative endeavor that involves as much fact as fiction.

Memory is built and destroyed, reformed and

blocked, obsessed over and forgotten in much the same way that Marker's eye describes the world for us on the screen. His consideration of the role that technology plays within the realm of memory, both in *Sans Soleil* and his earlier film *La Jetée* (1962), provides a compelling platform from which to rethink how our notion of memory, its applications and potential, may be evolving. Marker's work exhibits a nonlinear structure that juxtaposes seemingly unrelated images and moments in time, and encourages subsequent reinterpretation with each viewing. Internal memory is no system

KERRY TRIBE
Episode
2006, stills from "Report on Memory" sequence; DW-TV Archives Capture, Berlin.

THE WORK OF MEMORY

> *The only hope for survival lay in time.*
> – Marker, *La Jetée*

> *The new bible will be an eternal magnetic tape of a time that will have to reread itself constantly, just to know it existed.*
> – Marker, *Sans Soleil*

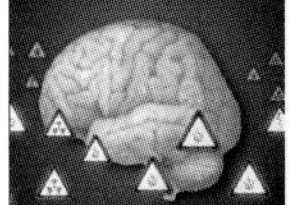

28

Personal memory is a vast, mysterious territory, and our efforts at consistency in recollection are often thwarted. The slow buildup of knowledge and history involves a great amount of loss; although this dissolution is sometimes intentional, other times it is because of the particular aspects we choose to focus upon and the manner in which we attempt to string ideas together. That one could forget, or refuse to acknowledge, an accepted truth, seems sinful in the face of so much access to external memory. But forgetting involves labor equal to that of remembering, and personal memory plays an active role in sorting through the plethora of external memory available to us. We see an examination of the process in the work of Janice Caswell, Emma Kay, and David Rokeby, while the project of conceptualizing the legacy of knowledge in concrete form takes center stage in the work of Scott Lyall and Edgar Arceneaux. In all cases, the accumulation of information is shown to be highly valued in our culture; the question is, how do we fit the pieces together?

Arceneaux and Lyall explore the ways that knowledge can both shape and limit our perception of the world through methods of visualizing its storage and use. An encounter with Lyall's

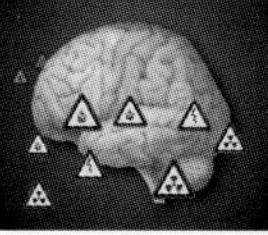

work is similar to the experience of Internet browsing. The random and nonlinear processes at work in *the little contemporaries* (2007) suggest narrative, but viewers must make their own associations to the field of information provided and create an individual pathway through it. Arceneaux uses more simplistic imagery to invite us to balance upon a similar threshold of incomprehensibility. In *Blocking Out the Sun*, alternating images of idealistic sunsets are blocked and unblocked by the artist's thumb, suggesting that by indulging in the known or familiar we may limit our potential to achieve greater knowledge.

Relying solely on her own memory—without recourse to books, films, or other research aids—Kay wrote out as

KERRY TRIBE
Episode
2006, stills from "Report on Memory" sequence; DW-TV Archives Capture, Berlin.

hold onto the memory of Clementine, hiding her away in unrelated and obscure parts of his past. But no memory is so buried as to evade the dispassionate erasure services of Lacuna.

All of us, whether young or old, have been frustrated by inadequacies of memory, or have wished we had the ability to forget selectively. In *The Seven Sins of Memory*, Daniel L. Schacter proposes that while we may feel guilt or embarrassment over our memory's fallibility, these mishaps are simply part of the necessary adaptive process of the brain.[7] But responsibility to personal memory, in relation to ourselves and others, is similar to the responsibility we feel to help build an accurate collective memory. We are deeply concerned with the methods by which we store memory today, as well as with the subsequent writing and rewriting of history over time. As has been shown, however, memory will always be a selective reshaping of the past, not only because it requires another medium to be articulated but because it is forever dependent upon our perception of the present and the future.

NOTES

1. Victoria Nelson, *The Secret Life of Puppets* (Cambridge: Harvard University Press, 2001), 190.
2. Russell J. A. Kilbourn, "Architecture and Cinema: The Representation of Memory in W. G. Sebald's *Austerlitz*," in *W. G. Sebald: A Critical Companion*, J. J. Long and Anne Whitehead, eds. (Seattle: University of Washington Press, 2004), 140.
3. Edward L. Wilding and Helen Sharp, "Episodic Memory Encoding and Retrieval: Recent Insights from Event-Related Potentials," in *The Cognitive Electrophysiology of the Mind and Brain*, Alberto Zani and Alice Proverbio, eds. (New York: Elsevier, 2003), 169–96.
4. Estimate is from a study at Johns Hopkins University: Ron Brookmeyer, Elizabeth Johnson, Kathryn Ziegler-Graham, and H. Michael Arrighi, "Forecasting the Global Burden of Alzheimer's Disease" (January 2007). For more information on Alzheimer's, please visit www.actionalz.org.
5. Marcel Proust, in an interview with Élie-Joseph Bois for *Le Temps* (vol. 88), 289. As cited by Mary Warnock, in *Memory* (London: Faber and Faber Ltd., 1987), 92.
6. *60 Minutes*, June 14, 2007.
7. See Daniel L. Schacter, *The Seven Sins of Memory: How the Mind Forgets and Remembers* (Boston: Houghton Mifflin Company, 2001).

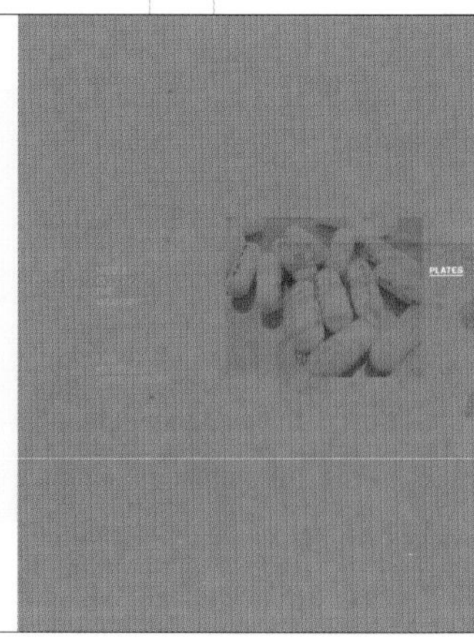

THE LINING OF FORGETTING

Xandra Eden

We often imagine our brain as a large filing system or computer database (if a slightly malfunctioning one), but the human mind is nothing so aseptic. In 1983, French filmmaker Chris Marker pronounced, as his alter ego Sandor Krasna, in *Sans Soleil*:

> *I will have spent my life trying to understand the function of remembering, which is not the opposite of forgetting, but rather its lining. We do not remember. We rewrite memory much as history is rewritten.*

This concept of memory as a process that is, first, mostly about forgetting, and, second, forever in editing mode, is central to the exhibition *The Lining of Forgetting: Internal and External Memory in Art*. The

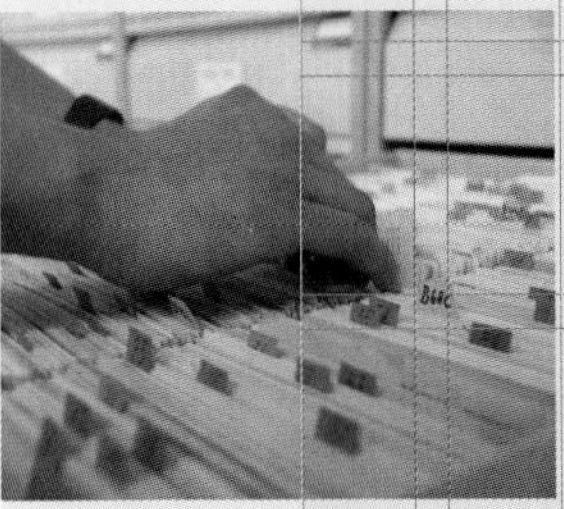

artists—Edgar Arceneaux, Deborah Aschheim, Louise Bourgeois, Janice Caswell, John Coplans, Pablo Helguera, Emma Kay, Dinh Q. Lê, Scott Lyall, David Rokeby, Mungo Thomson, Cody Trepte, Kerry Tribe, and Rachel Whiteread—address not only these issues but more through such diverse media as sculpture, video, book works, photography, installation, and computer-generated works. Organized around three thematic headings—Media Is the Memory, *Une Mémoire Involuntaire*, and The Work of Memory—the exhibition encourages an examination of the mutable nature of memory and the complex interconnections between both the internal and external variety. The categories are by no means watertight; many of the works move across thematics. Long-term, declarative memory, rather than short-term memory or procedural memory, predominates in these works, with most pertaining to episodic memory (the recollection of a particular occasion or event) or semantic memory (memory of knowledge, often accrued over time), although there are several works that deal with implicit memory (memory that comes into play without conscious awareness). Most important, the artists highlight memory as a creative endeavor that involves as much fact as fiction.

Memory is built and destroyed, reformed and

blocked, obsessed over and forgotten in much the same way that Marker's eye describes the world for us on the screen. His consideration of the role that technology plays within the realm of memory, both in *Sans Soleil* and his earlier film *La Jetée* (1962), provides a compelling platform from which to rethink how our notion of memory, its applications and potential, may be evolving. Marker's work exhibits a nonlinear structure that juxtaposes seemingly unrelated images and moments in time, and encourages subsequent reinterpretation with each viewing. Internal memory is no system

KERRY TRIBE
Episode
2006, stills from "Report on Memory" sequence: DW-TV Archives Capture, Berlin.

GRID SPECIFICATIONS

Page size (trimmed)	165 x 215.9mm
Top margin	25.4mm
Bottom margin	38mm
Outside margin	38mm
Inside margin	19mm
Number of columns	6
Gutter width	4.25mm
Extras	N/A

THE LINING OF FORGETTING EXHIBITION CATALOG

Design: Volume Inc.

The primary themes of this exhibition were those of memory and forgetting, exploring the ways we remember and highlighting how we mostly forget, rewrite, or fabricate memory, rather than accurately recalling our past. Volume Inc. envisioned the catalog metaphorically as a journey through a person's memory, using its typography, imagery and grid structure in ways that evoke how memories fade in and out of our conscious minds.

MEDIA IS THE MEMORY

Untitled (From Vietnam to Hollywood)

Lê offers a sobering perspective on our susceptibility to transform the imagery and narratives that are produced and disseminated by popular culture into dominant sources of recollection. His large-scale woven photographs literally intertwine archival images documenting the Vietnam War with stills from such popular Hollywood films as *Apocalypse Now*. He creates large printouts of these different photographic images, cuts them into strips, and then, using the tradition of grass-mat weaving that he learned from his aunt in Vietnam, weaves them together.

Lê's family escaped the Khmer Rouge and immigrated to Los Angeles in 1979. The works from his series *From Vietnam to Hollywood* elucidate how personal memory can fuse with the fictional memories created by mass media. The stark contrast between the black-and-white documentary photographs and Hollywood's lush, full-color representation of the American perspective is emblematic of the power of popular media to mold collective memory, and reveals contemporary Western culture's tendency to allow the reality of traumatic events to be subsumed by highly mediated narratives.

June 10

Aschheim has produced a significant body of work that integrates the clinical studies of laboratory research on the brain with the more mutable personal and emotional content of memory. A large part of her practice has involved working with neurobiologists; after making fMRI scans of her own brain, she was inspired to serve as both scientist and subject by mapping the dense memory matrix of her first, fifth, and sixth year birthday parties.

Every time one remembers something, it is newly encoded by the brain, and this process permanently alters that memory in accordance with the recalled context. To recover her long-forgotten memories, Aschheim used 8mm films shot by her father as retrieval cues. The final work, *June 10*, consists of three large-scale suspended sculptures, each with its own central pod, showing a video of a birthday in progress, surrounded by a field of outlying nodes that resemble brain neurons and their interconnecting synapses. The proximity of each node to the main video pod and the LED light emitting from them indicates the strength of the memory Aschheim experienced as she watched the videos as an adult. A more descriptive account of the people, colors, shapes, and ideas that each node represents to Aschheim is featured in accompanying drawings.

|ðē|past|
|iz|ā|
|ˈfôrən|
|ˈkəntrē|

|ðē|
|ˈfyoōchər|
|iz||nät|
|(h)wät|it|
|yoōzd|
|toō||bē|

Photo Album

Trepte's work explores the way that computers have come to serve as the external memory for even the most personal correspondence and family photographs. He demonstrates that, today, little of this information is actually printed out in physical form—it lies dormant on various computer hard drives or CDs, materials at risk of deteriorating or becoming quickly outdated by subsequent technology. For *Photo Album*, Trepte produced seventy-five bound books between 2006 and 2007. A text plate on the exterior of each book describes a family photograph, but, upon opening the book, we see the image only in terms of data. For, unlike film-based photography, most of our computer-generated memories exist in the impersonal and abstract 0s and 1s of computer code. They are indecipherable without the aid of external media, such as that offered by computers and software applications. Trepte encourages us to consider whether someday we will lament our diminishing habit of printing out and preserving evidence of our past.

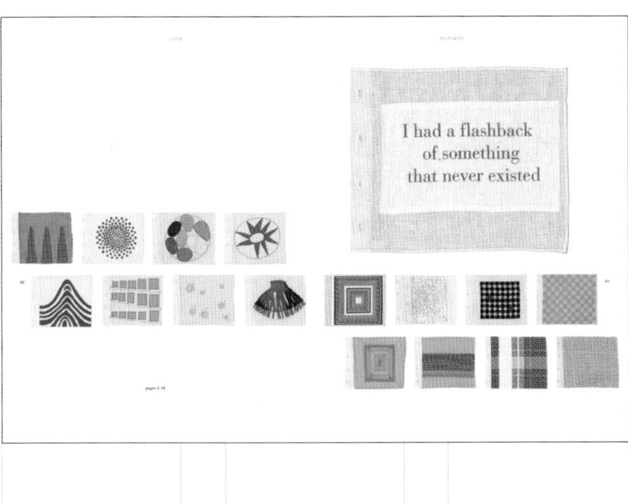
I had a flashback
of something
that never existed

collective memory into historical memory that has characterized much of the new critical work on memory during this period. The recourse to testimony as part of a reflection on history and representation and art's engagement with the world-historical event—the Holocaust, apartheid, the collapse of Soviet Communism—has been widespread. Similarly, a Benjaminian-inspired mnemotechnics has had some influence theoretically in cultural practice and theory on the critique of the posthistoricity of postmodernism and the fantasies of neoliberal "progress." As Tom Cohen has argued, in one of the more sophisticated versions of this position, mnemotechnics, as a critical summons to, and denaturalization of, the ruling representations and symbols of the present and the past, "holds open the possibility of actively deforming and negating the signifying

order out of which [history's] own present had been generated."[19] In this, it codifies the textual work of anamnesis—inscription and reinscription—as a politics of the event, trace and testimony. Out of a mnemotechnic cultural politics, "alternate models of reference, causality, the historical, and the 'event' become possible."[20] Chris Marker's important photofilm works and "fiction" documentaries are similarly mnemotechnical in this sense. Memory images are juxtaposed and choreographed, not just as a bulwark

CHRIS MARKER
La Jetée
1962, film stills. © Jonas Films and Argos Films.

against the erosion and fading of (revolutionary) memory but also as an interrogation of the process of memory as representation, as the labor of reinscription.[21]

But if a politicized mnemotechnics has shifted postconceptual practice into a new and fruitful engagement with the document and archive in art—into new sequential and relational wholes, so to speak[22]—memory-work has also seen an accompanying fetishization of memory as the default position of a dominant postpolitical culture. The invocation of personal memory as an attachment to the lost object of desire has become a commonplace conceit in a lot of work that mourns the possibility of praxis, in a world seemingly devoid of praxis. The use of memory as a surrogate of closure, "endism" and "postism," or as an identification, simply, with the commemorative, has become commonplace. Significantly, in integrating living memory and historical memory into a politicized mnemotechnics, we also require a critique of memory-work itself. Not only

CHRIS MARKER
La Jetée
1962, film stills. © New Yorker Films.

NETWORKED MEMORY: "ALWAYS LIVE AND YET ALWAYS AN ARCHIVE"

Sarah Cook

NETWORKED MEMORY: "ALWAYS LIVE AND YET ALWAYS AN ARCHIVE"

In 1996, Australian artist Denis Beaubois performed *In the event of amnesia the city will recall...*in Sydney. He stood in front of a surveillance camera and held up a series of hand-printed signs. On one occasion, the signs said, "I have amnesia," "You are watching me," "[You have been watching me] all day, everywhere I go," "Maybe you can help," and "Who am I? What's my name?" Beaubois's action suggests what it is to put one's trust in the network of CCTV cameras capturing the life of the city. It presupposes that the networked and distributed video image is a more reliable record of events than anything an individual alone could write, make, or do.[1]

As society becomes increasingly subject to and reliant upon the objective workings of databases and networks—from CCTV networks assuring our "security" in the city to the GPS network ensuring we don't get too lost in the country—the place of individual experience and memory is called into question. It is only through consideration and reflection that information (the facts of who, what, where,

DENIS BEAUBOIS
In the event of amnesia the city will recall...
1996, documentation of performance

> *Contemporary media artists appear to be doing nothing else than adapting this Bergsonist vocation to the concrete demands of the information age: by placing the embodied viewer-participant into a circuit with information, the installations and environments they create function as laboratories for the conversion of information into corporeally apprehensible images.*[10]

This is exactly what David Rokeby's project *The Giver of Names* (1990) does in asking viewers to choose colorful plastic toys from a pile on the floor and place them on a pedestal, so that the seeing-eye computer can look at them, analyze their shapes and colors, and "name" them, using artificial-intelligence software that draws on a database populated with language and grammatical constructs.[11] Rokeby's art is to assign intent to the machine, relying on the connection between its perception and that of the viewer—the informational circuit—to complete the process of naming and remembering. But the work's "machine memory," as with its artificial intelligence, differs from our human memory:

> *Both are making a kind of selection or censorship of information...Our memory, because of our perception, is a process of selecting maybe 1% or 10%...to be able to survive and to communicate between us. So most of the information...is just thrown away. Psychology describes the function of our memory [as] mainly throwing away information. One can analyze with philosophy or phenomenology your intentions, your needs, and so on. Artificial memory has no capacity of that kind of phenomenological attitude which makes our memory useful for us and the way we use it for survival. [Artificial memory] is more mechanical...So even if we have a huge capacity for artificial memory...it is very difficult to make any kind of regulation or protocol to decide what we will keep and what we will forget.*[12]

All of David Rokeby's work, including his *Machine for Taking Time (Boul. Saint-Laurent)* (2006–7), illuminates, indeed reveals, the process by which some bits of information are perceived and

DAVID ROKEBY
Machine for Taking Time (Oakville)
2001–4. Commissioned by Oakville Galleries, Oakville, Ontario.

ISLINGTON

Islington has long been known as one of London's most fashionable and stylish boroughs. It draws its vibrant character from around the world and there is a real sense of community in this thriving and prosperous area. Home to some of the most diverse shopping in London, it offers unrivalled choice.

Crafted by CARROT

L'ÉCOLE

L'École, a former Victorian schoolhouse and architectural landmark, located on the northern fringes of Islington, has been crafted into 52 spacious apartments by Carrot. L'École consists of two buildings, a sympathetic conversion of the Victorian schoolhouse and a contemporary new building. The two buildings sit side by side, designed in unison and working together to create a distinctive development where 21st-century technology is mixed with classic Victorian elegance. The development embodies Carrot's philosophy of creating individually crafted spaces with a modern style, whilst retaining a warm, sensuous feel.

ISLINGTON Islington has long been known as one of London's most fashionable and stylish boroughs. It draws its vibrant character from around the world and there is a real sense of community in this thriving and prosperous area. Home to some of the most diverse shopping in London, it offers unrivalled choice.

Crafted by CARROT

GRID SPECIFICATIONS

Page size (trimmed)	330 x 310mm
Top margin	25mm
Bottom margin	18mm
Outside margin	25mm
Inside margin	15mm
Number of columns	8
Gutter width	5mm
Extras	Baseline grid, 21.5pt starting at 35.7mm

L'ÉCOLE PROPERTY BROCHURE

Design: Brad Yendle at Design Typography

L'École, a former school in north London, was redeveloped by Carrot into a variety of apartments. The building took shape in several phases, so designers Brad Yendle and Zoë Bather were briefed to develop a flexible system that could be updated and added to easily over time. This requirement informed all aspects of the design. The publication is loose-leaf and loop bound. The binding is not only practical, but also unusually utilitarian in feel—both Design Typography and its client were keen to ensure that the publication reflected the detailing of the development and wasn't dismissed as a predictably glossy promotion. The grid is based on eight small columns that can be used in different combinations to accommodate text, images, maps, plans, and diagrams.

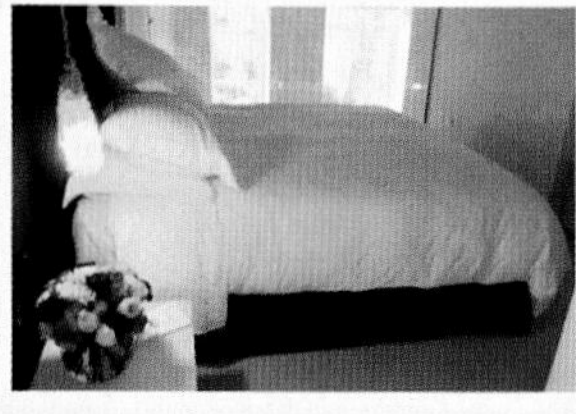

Contemporary architecture and spacious layouts dominate the feel of the new build apartments at L'École. Building in a U-shape around the communal courtyard garden has given the development a real sense of community.

The Winter Gardens add a unique focal feature to the front elevation, providing a fabulous enclosed glass space all year round, offering seclusion and serenity in this bustling London borough.

At the top of the buildings sit the stunning penthouses, whose abundant use of glass ensures they are always flooded with light. The penthouse lifestyle offered at L'École is one of true indulgence – whilst relaxing on the terrace, one can enjoy panoramic views across Islington.

Crafted by CARROT.

KITCHENS
- Individual Swedish-designed black high-gloss 'Kvanum' kitchens combined with white 'Corian' worktops
- Fully integrated 'Siemens' appliances: dishwasher, fridge freezer, ceramic hob, oven & extractor hood

BATHROOMS
- Underfloor electric heating
- 'Porcelanosa' porcelain floor & wall tiles in 'Cube Nature'

BEDROOMS
- Bespoke floor to ceiling wardrobes in master bedrooms
- Satellite TV point
- Telephone socket
- Wall lights
- Carpets

GENERAL
- Oak wide-board floors
- Fully wired for home entertainment system installation

SPECIFICATION

Throughout L'École, detail and finish are second to none and this is synonymous with the Carrot brand and concept. Each L'École apartment is individually crafted by Carrot with precise attention to detail using high-quality materials to the highest level of specification.

Crafted by CARROT.

Q – WHERE IS L'ÉCOLE SITUATED?

A – JUST 2 STOPS AWAY FROM PARIS ON THE EUROSTAR

ALL THAT YOU WILL EVER NEED…

Whether it is a theatre, university, museum, green space, antique shop or good transport links that you need, living at L'École will ensure that it is right on your doorstep.

1 King's Cross St Pancras, Eurostar
2 Arsenal, Highbury Fields, Metropolitan University
3 Upper Street, N1 Shopping Centre, Business Design Centre, Almeida Theatre, Antiques Arcade
4 Sadler's Wells Theatre, Exmouth Market, Clerkenwell
5 The City, St Paul's
6 Camden Passage Market
7 Hampstead Heath
8 Tate Modern, London Eye
9 Regent's Park
10 2012 Olympic Site

CARROT® Carrot Limited is a niche property developer specialising in bespoke residential and mixed use schemes in city centres – creating inspiring urban homes which focus on space and design quality.

Carrot was formed in 2001 by Tim Carr. Tim has been in the Central London property business since 1975, by way of estate agencies and consultancy, with a particular dexterity in acting for developers and house builders in acquisitions, site disposal and marketing.

Prior to setting up Carrot, Tim co-founded CYZ. For the past 12 years his management of CYZ has ensured that it has built a reputation as a 'class act' in urban regeneration and warehouse conversions, notably in Clerkenwell, London.

Tim founded Urban Construction Management Ltd (UCM) in 2001, the construction company for all Carrot projects. This relationship ensures a tighter control of the cost and management of the construction process, allowing Carrot to exercise 'hands-on' control of its schemes. Since formation, UCM have consistently delivered projects on budget and to planned timescales.

Central London is Carrot's core market. However, Bristol in the South West, where Carrot is already developing, has been identified as having similar regeneration potential and market characteristics, allowing the Company's expertise to be fruitfully applied in a new city.

For more information about L'École and other developments, please contact Charlotte Steedman.

Carrot Ltd
48 Britton Street
London EC1M 5UL
T +44 (0)20 7251 3999
F +44 (0)20 7251 8008
E charlottesteedman@carrotltd.com
www.lecolecarrot.com

lost souls
S/S 07

lost souls
S/S 07

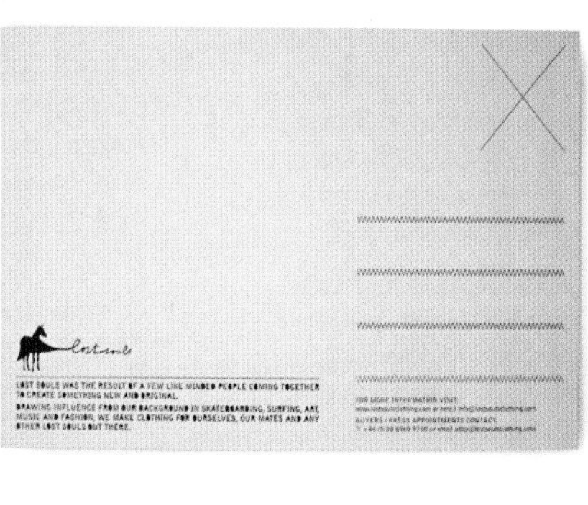
LOST SOULS WAS THE RESULT OF A FEW LIKE MINDED PEOPLE COMING TOGETHER TO CREATE SOMETHING NEW AND ORIGINAL.
DRAWING INFLUENCE FROM OUR BACKGROUND IN SKATEBOARDING, SURFING, ART, MUSIC AND FASHION, WE MAKE CLOTHING FOR OURSELVES, OUR MATES AND ANY OTHER LOST SOULS OUT THERE.
FOR MORE INFORMATION VISIT:
BUYERS / PRESS APPOINTMENTS CONTACT:

S/S 07

LOST SOULS WAS THE
RESULT OF A FEW LIKE
MINDED PEOPLE COMING
TOGETHER TO CREATE
SOMETHING NEW
AND ORIGINAL.
DRAWING INFLUENCE
FROM OUR BACKGROUND
IN SKATEBOARDING,
SURFING, ART, MUSIC
AND FASHION, WE MAKE
CLOTHING FOR OURSELVES,
OUR MATES AND ANY
OTHER LOST SOULS
OUT THERE.

LOST SOULS LOOKBOOK

Design: Julian Harriman-Dickinson at Harriman Steel

The humble postcard was the inspiration behind this promotional "lookbook" for Lost Souls clothing company, designed by Julian Harriman-Dickinson. Consisting of four postcards inserted into the folds of a double-sided A3 (297 × 420mm [11¾ × 16½in]) poster, the overall design utilizes the grid generated by the folding process. Graphic-design grids are generally invisible to the end user and, although determined by format, are additions to it. Here the grid is completely visible and inseparable from the format. This reinterpretation of the grid is, by its nature, three-dimensional, and creates unexpected relationships between text and image as the structure unfolds and the content is revealed.

GRID SPECIFICATIONS

Page size (trimmed)	167 x 193mm
Top margin	7mm
Bottom margin	7mm
Outside margin	9mm
Inside margin	12mm
Number of columns	5
Gutter width	4mm
Extras	6 horizontal fields

mosaic

apabilities
process, but as
her, it takes some
you present
e way possible.
friendly
cation
abilities

eco-friendly

mPower

c.j. appleton
Favorite Ice Cream
Favorite Quote
Best Birthday Gift Ever
Reality TV Show On Which He'd Appear
Most Prominent Cocktail Table Magazine
His Karaoke Song
Meal He'd Eat For A Week

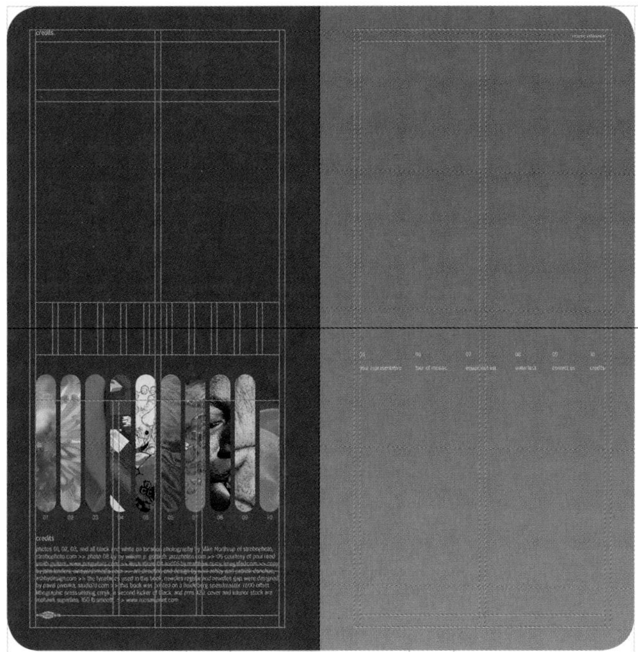

GRID SPECIFICATIONS

Page size (trimmed)	171.5 x 343mm
Top margin	12.7mm
Bottom margin	12.7mm
Outside margin	12.7mm
Inside margin	19mm
Number of columns	2
Gutter width	4.25mm
Extras	

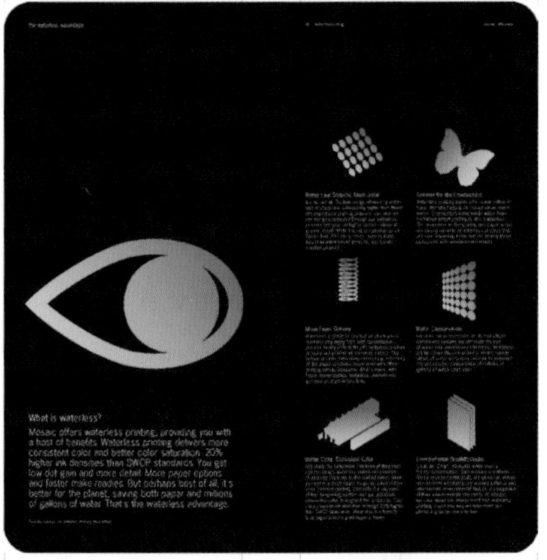

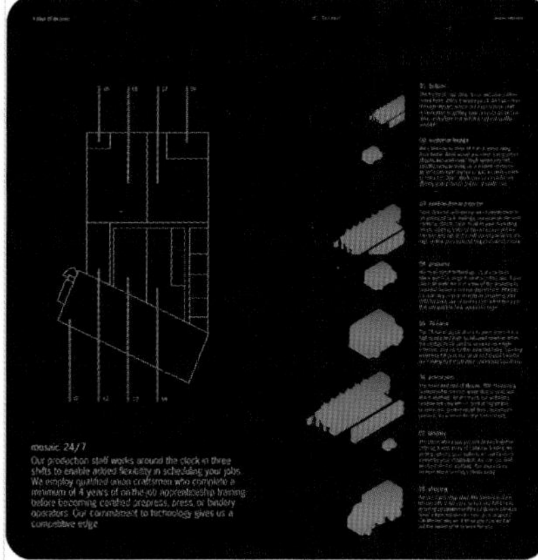

MOSAIC BROCHURE

Design: Neal Ashby and Patrick Donohue at Ashby Design

This spiral bound, 40 page brochure was created to highlight the range of services offered by Mosaic Print. The binding allowed for the possibility of personalizing each brochure with a specific print representative's biography and contact information. Each brochure featured the first 24 pages cut in half, creating a grid consisting of quadrants which allowed for multiple combinations of content.

The designers drew inspiration from the client's name to produce a patchwork of imagery made up of photographs, illustrations and copy. Pages were cut in half to allow the viewer to flip the top and bottom halves independently, creating a variety of different combinations of spreads. The resulting effect is that of a dynamic 'mosaic' of services, capabilities, and information.

UN
FILTER
ED
IN THE PAST I HAVE
AND
I
DON'T
FLOSS.
I'M
A
REPUBLICAN.
FILTER
800
336
0809

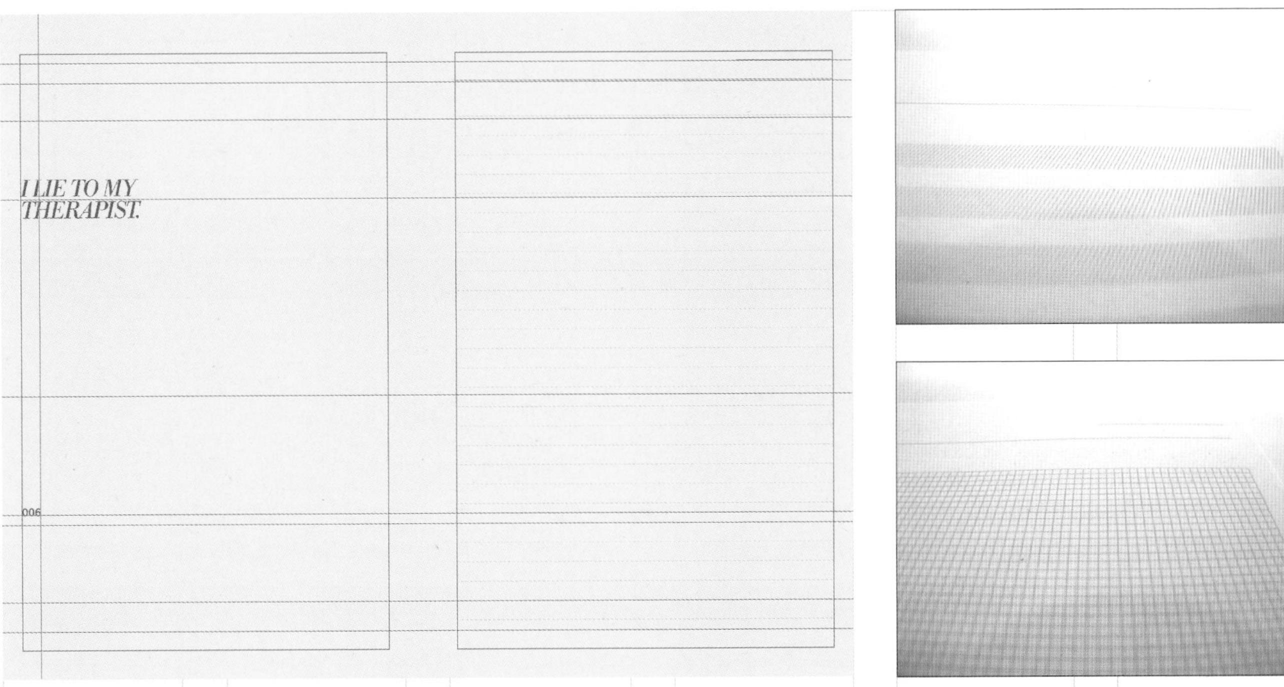
I LIE TO MY
THERAPIST.
006

GRID SPECIFICATIONS

Page size (trimmed)	139.7 x 215.9mm
Top margin	12.7mm
Bottom margin	12.7mm
Outside margin	6.35mm
Inside margin	12.7mm (left page) and 9.5mm (right page)
Number of columns	1
Gutter width	N/A
Extras	N/A

FILTER "UNFILTERED" JOURNAL

Design: Turnstyle

Filter is a staffing agency and production studio focused on the creative industry. As part of their celebrations during the holiday season, they threw a party for clients and partners that carried the theme of leaving the past behind. As a gift for attendees, Turnstyle created a hard-bound journal that included real confessions by employees and members of the Filter talent pool. Quotes such as "I eat other peoples' lunches" and "I wish I had robot legs" pepper the book in between gridded and lined journal pages. The designers at Turnstyle drew their inspiration from designer rants, confessions, moleskin journals, graphs, and grids.

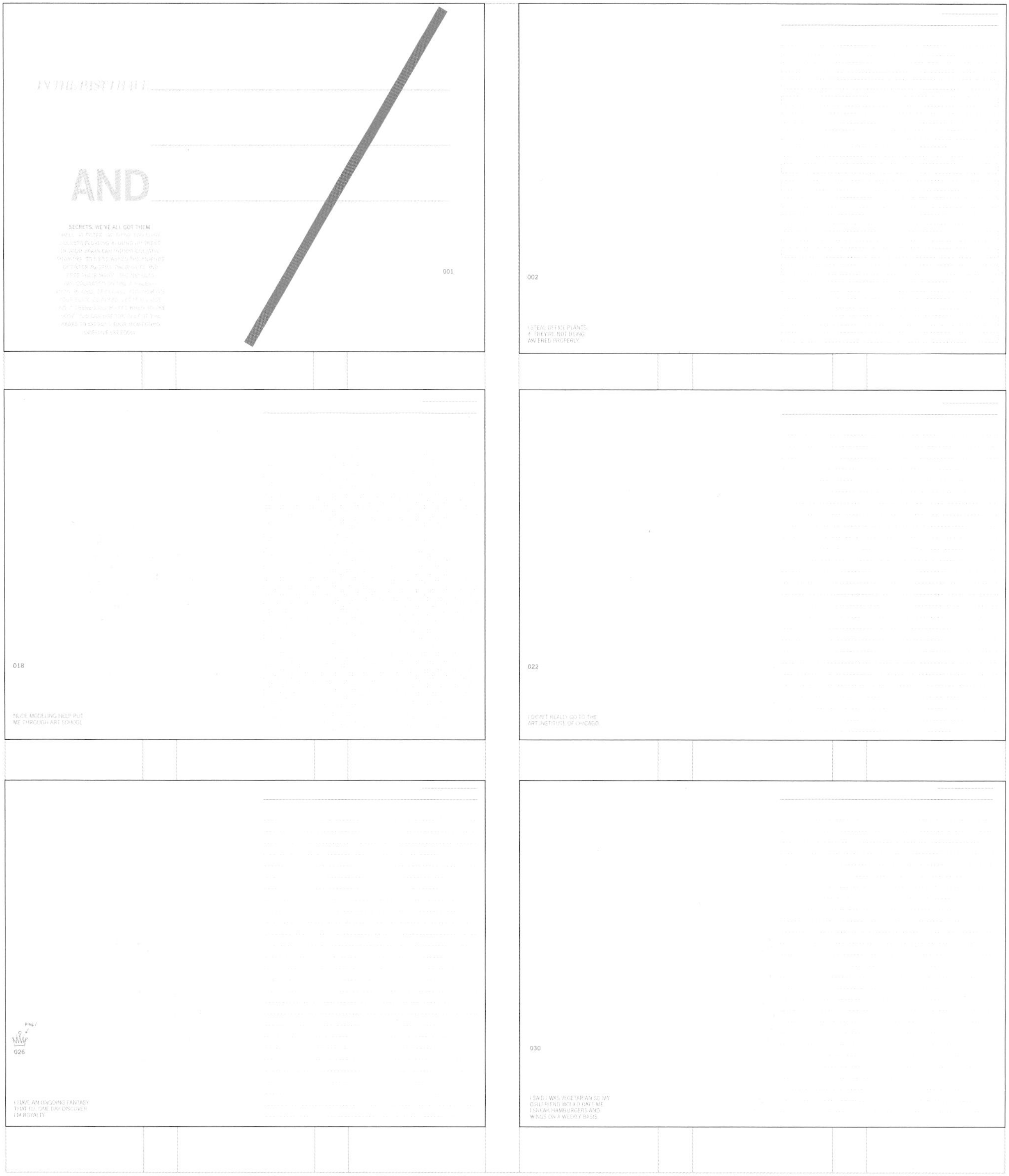

IN THE PAST I HAVE

AND

SECRETS. WE'VE ALL GOT THEM.

001

002

I STEAL OFFICE PLANTS
IF THEY'RE NOT BEING
WATERED PROPERLY.

018

NUDE MODELING HELP PUT
ME THROUGH ART SCHOOL

022

I DIDN'T REALLY GO TO THE
ART INSTITUTE OF CHICAGO.

026

I HAVE AN ONGOING FANTASY
THAT I'LL ONE DAY DISCOVER
I'M ROYALTY.

030

I SAID I WAS VEGETARIAN SO MY
GIRLFRIEND WOULD DATE ME.
I SNEAK HAMBURGERS AND
WINGS ON A WEEKLY BASIS.

034

I HAVE HAD A CRUSH
ON RICHARD DREYFUSS
SINCE JAWS

I WISH I HAD ROBOT LEGS.

112

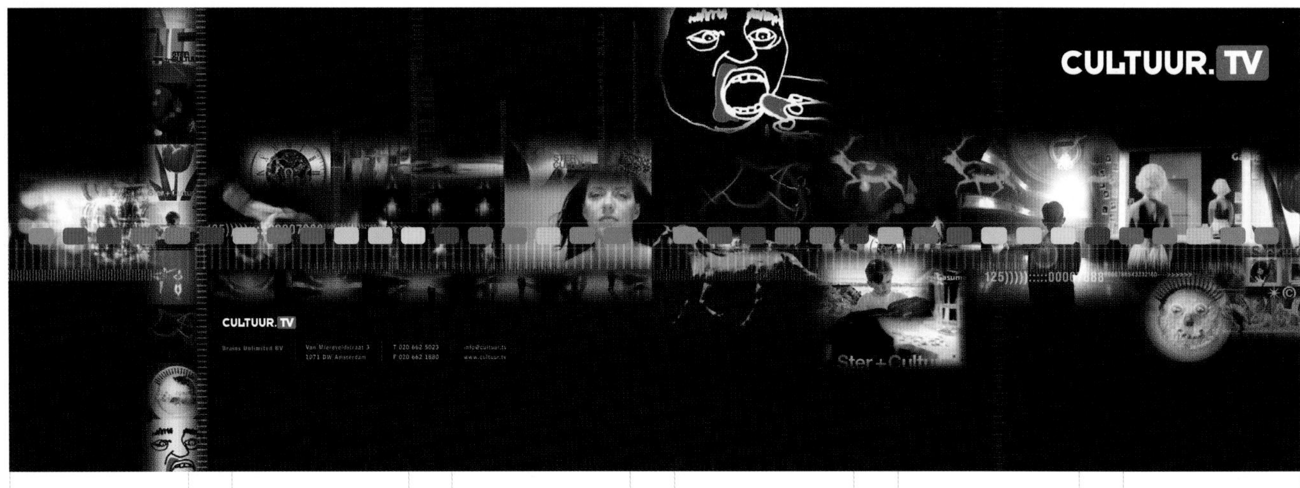

CULTUUR.TV

Cultuur.tv

5|6

Wat is Cultuur.tv precies?
Cultuur.tv is hét reclameblok op televisie voor de culturele sector. Cultuur.tv wordt 13 keer per week op de Nederlandse publieke zenders uitgezonden en bereikt daarmee een miljoenenpubliek. De uitzendtarieven in Cultuur.tv bedragen 10 à 20% van het normale commerciële uitzendtarief. Om gebruik te kunnen maken van deze mogelijkheid moet de commercial voldoen aan een aantal voorwaarden. Deze voorwaarden vindt u op www.cultuur.tv.

Ieder Cultuur.tv blok wordt voorafgegaan door een introductiefilmpje van acht seconden gesponsord door Gasunie. Na de introductiefilm worden maximaal vijf Cultuurspots uitgezonden, van elkaar gescheiden door een break van twee seconden. Het gehele blok wordt afgesloten door een bumper van drie seconden. De bumper toont onder meer het webadres www.cultuur.tv.

Nu ook Cultuurspots van 12 seconden
De lengte van een cultuurspot is zeven seconden. Met de introductie van de nieuwe naam Cultuur.tv bieden we voortaan ook de mogelijkheid een spot van 12 seconden uit te zenden. In deze langere spot kunt u meer beelden communiceren, hetgeen bij sommige culturele boodschappen zeer goed kan werken. Denkt u bijvoorbeeld aan het weergeven van een fragment uit een dans of toneelvoorstelling. Bovendien heeft deze langere Cultuurspot natuurlijk een extra attentiewaarde binnen het blok van Cultuur.tv.

Waarom adverteren in Cultuur.tv?
Cultuur.tv is dé manier om op televisie te adverteren tegen een sterk gereduceerd tarief, in een culturele context en op zeer gunstige uitzendmomenten, waardoor u snel een groot en nieuw publiek bereikt. Door in Cultuur.tv te adverteren, kunt u de volgende doelen bereiken:
- het werven van algemene bekendheid voor uw culturele boodschap;
- publiekswerving voor een specifiek evenement;
- verbetering van uw imago.

Vanaf www.cultuur.tv kunnen bezoekers doorlinken naar de website van uw organisatie. Geïnteresseerden kunnen zo met één muisklik informatie over het evenement of uw instelling krijgen. Hieraan zijn geen extra kosten verbonden

Uitzendtijden Cultuur.tv
Cultuur.tv wordt 13 keer per week uitgezonden op de publieke zenders Nederland 1 en Nederland:
- Drie keer per week (woensdag, zaterdag en zondag) op Nederland 3, tussen 18.00 en 19.00 uur, rondom de populaire Z@ppelinprogramma's en het goed bekeken Jeugdjournaal.
- Drie keer per week (donderdag, vrijdag en zaterdag) op Nederland 1 rondom het 20:00 uur Journaal.
- Dagelijks vóór het 22:00 uur Journaal op Nederland 3.

Kijkersprofielen Nederland 1 en Nederland 3
Tijdens de uitzendmomenten van Cultuur.tv rond het Jeugdjournaal bestaan de kijkers overwegend uit ouders met kinderen. Dit maakt deze culturele reclameblokken dus geschikt om culturele evenementen met een zeer brede doelgroep (8-80 jaar) in één klap landelijke bekendheid te geven.
Door Cultuur.tv in te zetten rondom het 20.00 uur Journaal op Nederland 1 bereikt u een breed miljoenenpubliek. Rondom het 22.00 uur Journaal op Nederland 3 is het publiek kleiner, maar specifieker. Op dit tijdstip kijken overwegend cultuur-geïnteresseerden en hoger opgeleiden. Met 10 uitzendingen in Cultuur.tv, verspreid over Nederland 1 en Nederland 2, genereert u circa 3 miljoen kijkerscontacten.

Boeken in Cultuur.tv
Om zeker te zijn van zendtijd bestaat de mogelijkheid om geheel vrijblijvend, tot drie weken voor uitzendtijd, een optie te plaatsen. Zo'n optie verplicht tot niets, maar verzekert u wel van de gewenste plaats in een blok van Cultuur.tv.

Uitzendtarieven
Voor de eerste 12 uitzendingen betaalt u een vast tarief per uitzending, afhankelijk van de lengte van de spot. Als u meer dan 12 keer uitzendt, wordt vanaf de 13de uitzending een lager tarief per uitzending gerekend. De kracht van een campagne in Cultuur.tv ligt in de herhaling, daarom adviseren we een minimum van 8 uitzendingen. Er is geen maximum verbonden aan het aantal uitzendingen.

7 seconde spot
€ 385,- per uitzending (€ 370,- vanaf de 13e uitzending)

12 seconde spot
€ 660,- per uitzending (€ 635,- vanaf de 13e uitzending)

N.B.: Prijzen zijn exclusief BTW en geldig tot 1 januari 2005

introductie films CULTUUR.TV

Gasuniefilms
In 2001 werden de Gasuniefilms gelanceerd; het resultaat van een samenwerkingsverband tussen Ster+Cultuur (Brains Unlimited) en de Gasunie. Deze films introduceren de culturele reclameblokken Ster+Cultuur.
De input voor deze korte kunstzinnige films wordt geleverd door jonge kunstenaars en filmmakers. Per jaar worden er twintig Gasuniefilms van acht seconden geproduceerd op basis van de scripts die deze jonge creatieven insturen voor de Gasuniescriptwedstrijd. Deze wedstrijd vindt twee keer per jaar plaats. Het resultaat is een unieke serie films, die vervolgens een half jaar op televisie worden uitgezonden.

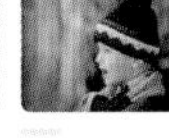

Gasuniefilms

9|10

Het succes van de Gasuniefilms
Meteen al het eerste jaar zijn de Gasuniefilms een enorm succes gebleken. Ieder jaar doen er meer jonge creatieven mee aan de scriptwedstrijd. Vier films werden genomineerd voor de Sponsor Ring 2001, een Nederlandse prijs voor succesvolle, vernieuwende en inspirerende vormen van sponsoring. In hetzelfde jaar werd de Gasuniefilm 'Douche' genomineerd tijdens het filmfestival in Lausanne.
Oorspronkelijk was het idee om in de scripts de koppeling van warmte en energie aan de ene kant, en cultuur aan de andere kant tot uiting te laten komen. Nadat er een groot aantal Gasuniefilms naar dit idee waren geproduceerd, bleek er behoefte aan meer afwisseling en nieuwe invalshoeken. Vanaf 2002 is er aan de scriptwedstrijd elke keer een ander thema verbonden. Thema's als 'Groei', 'Verwondering', Cool&Staal', 'Vet&'Plastic', 'Edward Muybridge' en 'Sergej Diaghilev' inspireren jonge kunstenaars en creatieven tot steeds betere en inhoudelijk interessante inzendingen. Inmiddels zijn er in totaal bijna 70 Gasuniefilms geproduceerd. Al deze films zijn nu te zien op www.cultuur.tv en absoluut de moeite waard van een sitebezoekje waard. Ook op bijgevoegde cd-rom staan tal van deze filmpjes.

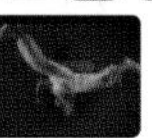

Meedoen aan scriptwedstrijd?
Als u mee wil doen aan de volgende Gasuniescriptwedstrijd stuur dan een e-mail naar info@cultuur.tv. U krijgt dan de eerstvolgende briefing met alle details, zoals thema en deadline. Doe mee, want dit is de kans dat uw idee wordt verfilmd en uitgezonden op televisie. En niet geheel onbelangrijk: de winnaars ontvangen ter aanmoediging € 1135,-.

Ga voor meer informatie over de Gasuniefilms en Gasuniescriptwedstrijd naar www.cultuur.tv.

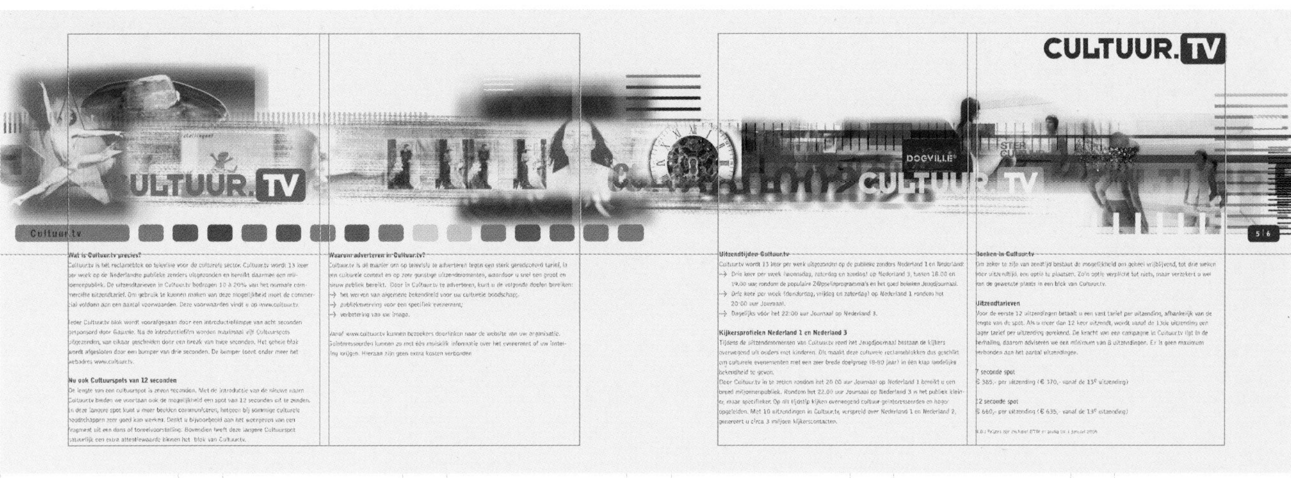

CULTUUR TV

Design: Maestro Design & Advertising

Culturr TV features a combination of commercials and promotions for cultural events on Dutch television. Tasked with creating a promotional brochure for the channel, the design team at Maestro took inspiration from the wide variety of events being publicized, using small cultural clips and images within the layouts, as well as favoring a large and varied color palette. The grid was developed as a series of rectangles based on screen format, allowing scope to show multiple screen images and also affording the freedom to bleed larger images across the pages.

GRID SPECIFICATIONS	
Page size (trimmed)	285 x 200mm
Top margin	10mm
Bottom margin	14mm
Outside margin	30mm
Inside margin	30mm
Number of columns	2
Gutter width	4mm
Extras	N/A

Exhibitions

ON-SITE
ARQUITECTURA CONTEMPORÁNEA
EN LA COMUNIDAD DE MADRID
PROMOMADRID

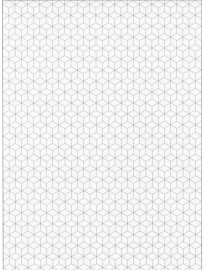

GRID SPECIFICATIONS

Page size (trimmed)	Resizable, as required
Top margin	½ base unit
Bottom margin	½ base unit
Outside margin	½ base unit
Inside margin	½ base unit
Number of columns	Flexible
Gutter width	2.5mm
Extras	Grid developed from base unit—hexagon

ON-SITE EXHIBITION GUIDELINES

Design: BaseDESIGN

The exhibition On-Site: New Architecture in Spain documented recent Spanish architectural innovation. A Museum of Modern Art initiative, the exhibition opened in New York before moving to Madrid. BaseDESIGN's graphic solution uses the architectonic form of a cube (suggested by the perspective of the hexagon) as a basis for the identity. The three visible sides of the cube symbolize the exhibition, tours, and talks, which are also color-coded as red, blue, and green, respectively. Although not a conventional typographic grid, this is a highly flexible modular system that provides the framework for a range of color and pattern combinations to communicate the diversity in form, scale, and geography of the exhibits.

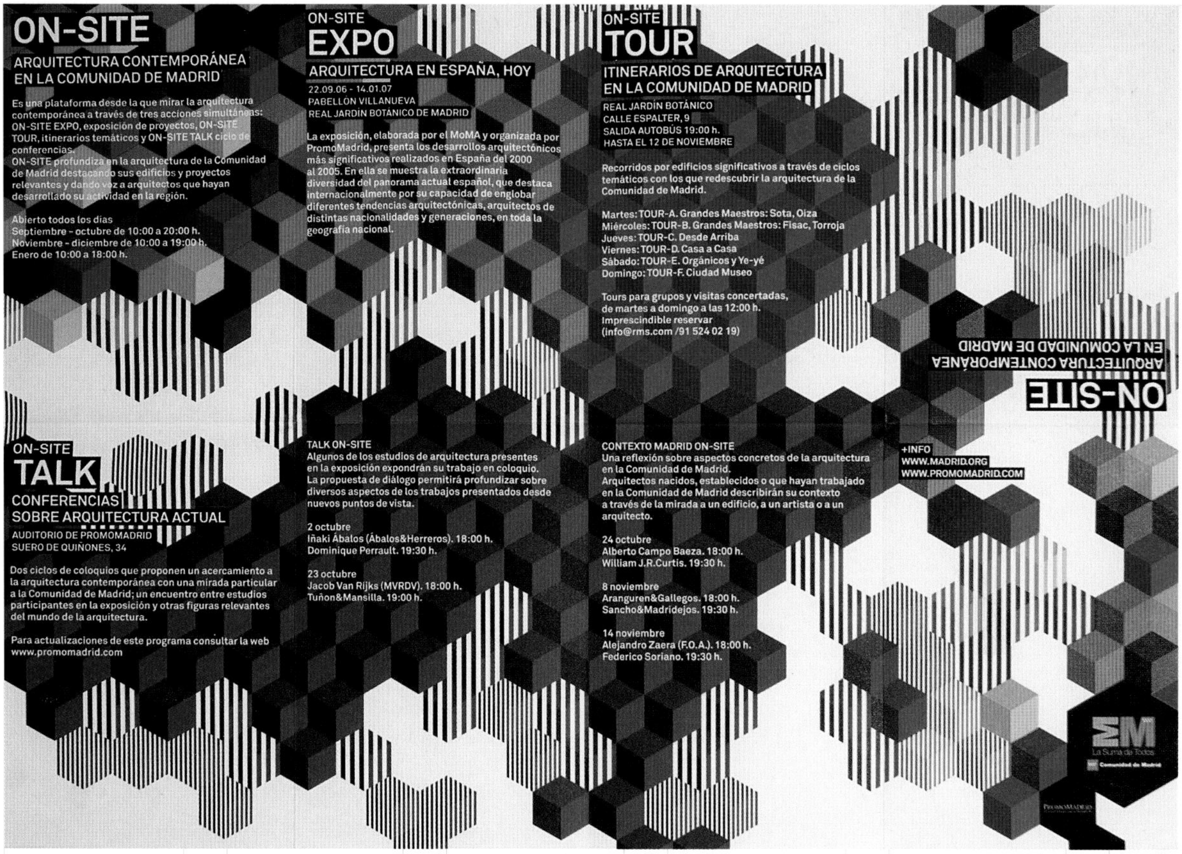

ON-SITE

ARQUITECTURA CONTEMPORÁNEA
EN LA COMUNIDAD DE MADRID

Es una plataforma desde la que mirar la arquitectura contemporánea a través de tres acciones simultáneas: ON-SITE EXPO, exposición de proyectos, ON-SITE TOUR, itinerarios temáticos y ON-SITE TALK ciclo de conferencias.
ON-SITE profundiza en la arquitectura de la Comunidad de Madrid destacando sus edificios y proyectos relevantes y dando voz a arquitectos que hayan desarrollado su actividad en la región.

Abierto todos los días
Septiembre - octubre de 10:00 a 20:00 h.
Noviembre - diciembre de 10:00 a 19:00 h.
Enero de 10:00 a 18:00 h.

ON-SITE EXPO

ARQUITECTURA EN ESPAÑA, HOY
22.09.06 - 14.01.07
PABELLÓN VILLANUEVA
REAL JARDÍN BOTÁNICO DE MADRID

La exposición, elaborada por el MoMA y organizada por PromoMadrid, presenta los desarrollos arquitectónicos más significativos realizados en España del 2000 al 2005. En ella se muestra la extraordinaria diversidad del panorama actual español, que destaca internacionalmente por su capacidad de englobar diferentes tendencias arquitectónicas, arquitectos de distintas nacionalidades y generaciones, en toda la geografía nacional.

ON-SITE TOUR

ITINERARIOS DE ARQUITECTURA
EN LA COMUNIDAD DE MADRID
REAL JARDÍN BOTÁNICO
CALLE ESPALTER, 9
SALIDA AUTOBÚS 19:00 h.
HASTA EL 12 DE NOVIEMBRE

Recorridos por edificios significativos a través de ciclos temáticos con los que redescubrir la arquitectura de la Comunidad de Madrid.

Martes: TOUR-A. Grandes Maestros: Sota, Oiza
Miércoles: TOUR-B. Grandes Maestros: Fisac, Torroja
Jueves: TOUR-C. Desde Arriba
Viernes: TOUR-D. Casa a Casa
Sábado: TOUR-E. Orgánicos y Ye-yé
Domingo: TOUR-F. Ciudad Museo

Tours para grupos y visitas concertadas, de martes a domingo a las 12:00 h.
Imprescindible reservar
(info@rms.com /91 524 02 19)

ON-SITE
ARQUITECTURA CONTEMPORÁNEA
EN LA COMUNIDAD DE MADRID

ON-SITE TALK

CONFERENCIAS
SOBRE ARQUITECTURA ACTUAL
AUDITORIO DE PROMOMADRID
SUERO DE QUIÑONES, 34

Dos ciclos de coloquios que proponen un acercamiento a la arquitectura contemporánea con una mirada particular a la Comunidad de Madrid; un encuentro entre estudios participantes en la exposición y otras figuras relevantes del mundo de la arquitectura.

Para actualizaciones de este programa consultar la web www.promomadrid.com

TALK ON-SITE
Algunos de los estudios de arquitectura presentes en la exposición expondrán su trabajo en coloquio. La propuesta de diálogo permitirá profundizar sobre diversos aspectos de los trabajos presentados desde nuevos puntos de vista.

2 octubre
Iñaki Ábalos (Ábalos&Herreros). 18:00 h.
Dominique Perrault. 19:30 h.

23 octubre
Jacob Van Rijks (MVRDV). 18:00 h.
Tuñon&Mansilla. 19:00 h.

CONTEXTO MADRID ON-SITE
Una reflexión sobre aspectos concretos de la arquitectura en la Comunidad de Madrid.
Arquitectos nacidos, establecidos o que hayan trabajado en la Comunidad de Madrid describirán su contexto a través de la mirada a un edificio, a un artista o a un arquitecto.

24 octubre
Alberto Campo Baeza. 18:00 h.
William J.R.Curtis. 19:30 h.

8 noviembre
Aranguren&Gallegos. 18:00 h.
Sancho&Madridejos. 19:30 h.

14 noviembre
Alejandro Zaera (F.O.A.). 18:00 h.
Federico Soriano. 19:30 h.

+INFO
WWW.MADRID.ORG
WWW.PROMOMADRID.COM

La Suma de Todos
Comunidad de Madrid

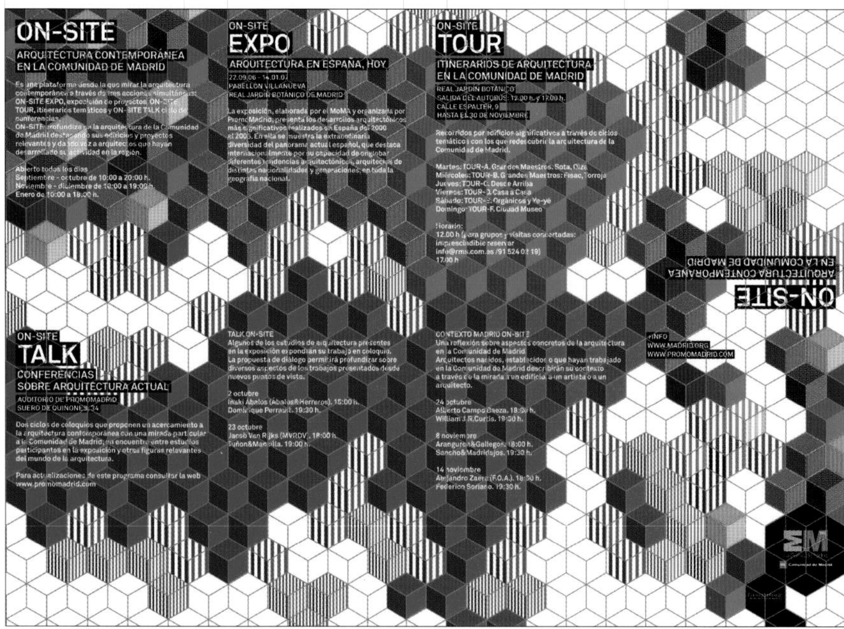

ON-SITE
TOUR
TOUR-A
GRANDES MAESTROS:
SOTA, OIZA

ON-SITE
TOUR
TOUR-A
GRANDES MAESTROS:
SOTA, OIZA

TORRES BLANCAS
Francisco Javier Sáenz de Oiza
1961-1968
Avenida de América, 37
Juan Huarte, promotor y gran mecenas de la arquitectura madrileña de los sesenta, quiso construir un nuevo modelo de residencias en altura. Siguiendo las ideas de Le Corbusier, Oiza propuso un proyecto ideal de torre que tuviera todas las ventajas de las viviendas unifamiliares. Decidió apilar un conjunto de villas en vertical formando una estructura arbórea, donde las raíces son el acceso semienterrado conectado con la ciudad y prolongado bajo tierra en aparcamientos e instalaciones; las viviendas forman el tronco y la parte alta, las ramas, agrupan todos los elementos sociales de la torre: restaurante, tiendas, piscina, gimnasio, etc., inclusión que permite segregar los usos domésticos en favor de la privacidad, así como optimizar recursos, mejorar la calidad de vida y fomentar el intercambio social.
Originalmente concebida como una pareja de torres, de las que solamente se llevó a cabo una, fue construida con pantallas semicirculares de hormigón armado.
Alrededor del núcleo central de comunicaciones se disponen cuatro viviendas por planta, algunas en dúplex, todas con amplios balcones semicirculares que amplifican el límite entre el interior y el exterior, dotando al conjunto de una gran expresividad plástica desarrollada en la Basílica de Arânzazu y culminada en Torres Blancas, convertidas voluntariamente en uno de los iconos de la arquitectura madrileña.
No te pierdas…
todo el edificio, cada una de sus esquinas merece la pena: la piscina, el restaurante, los apartamentos, el portal, los núcleos de comunicación…
→ Metro Línea 7 Cartagena

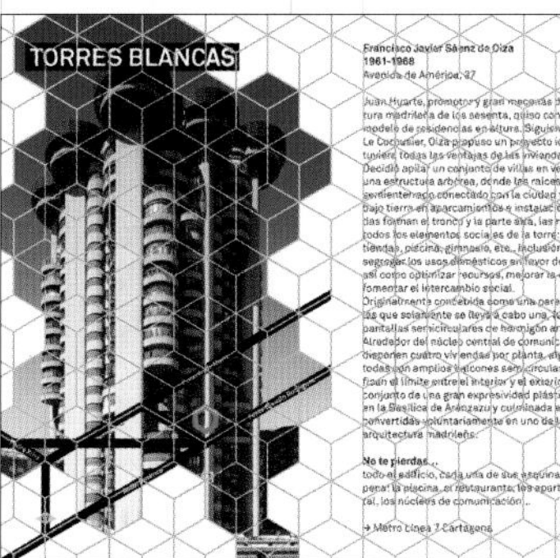
TORRES BLANCAS
Francisco Javier Sáenz de Oiza
1961-1968
Avenida de América, 37
Juan Huarte, promotor y gran mecenas de la arquitectura madrileña de los sesenta, quiso construir un nuevo modelo de residencias en altura. Siguiendo las ideas de Le Corbusier, Oiza propuso un proyecto ideal de torre que tuviera todas las ventajas de las viviendas unifamiliares. Decidió apilar un conjunto de villas en vertical formando una estructura arbórea, donde las raíces son el acceso semienterrado conectado con la ciudad y prolongado bajo tierra en aparcamientos e instalaciones; las viviendas forman el tronco y la parte alta, las ramas, agrupan todos los elementos sociales de la torre: restaurante, tiendas, piscina, gimnasio, etc., inclusión que permite segregar los usos domésticos en favor de la privacidad, así como optimizar recursos, mejorar la calidad de vida y fomentar el intercambio social.
Originalmente concebida como una pareja de torres, de las que solamente se llevó a cabo una, fue construida con pantallas semicirculares de hormigón armado.
Alrededor del núcleo central de comunicaciones se disponen cuatro viviendas por planta, algunas en dúplex, todas con amplios balcones semicirculares que amplifican el límite entre el interior y el exterior, dotando al conjunto de una gran expresividad plástica desarrollada en la Basílica de Arânzazu y culminada en Torres Blancas, convertidas voluntariamente en uno de los iconos de la arquitectura madrileña.
No te pierdas…
todo el edificio, cada una de sus esquinas merece la pena: la piscina, el restaurante, los apartamentos, el portal, los núcleos de comunicación…
→ Metro Línea 7 Cartagena

ON-SITE
ARQUITECTURA CONTEMPORANEA
EN LA COMUNIDAD DE MADRID
ON-SITE
EXPO
ARQUITECTURA EN ESPAÑA, HOY
22.09.06 - 14.01.07
PABELLÓN VILLANUEVA
REAL JARDÍN BOTÁNICO DE MADRID
ON-SITE
TOUR
ITINERARIOS DE ARQUITECTURA
EN LA COMUNIDAD DE MADRID
ON-SITE
TALK
CONFERENCIAS
SOBRE ARQUITECTURA ACTUAL
+INFO: WWW.PROMOMADRID.COM
PROMOMADRID

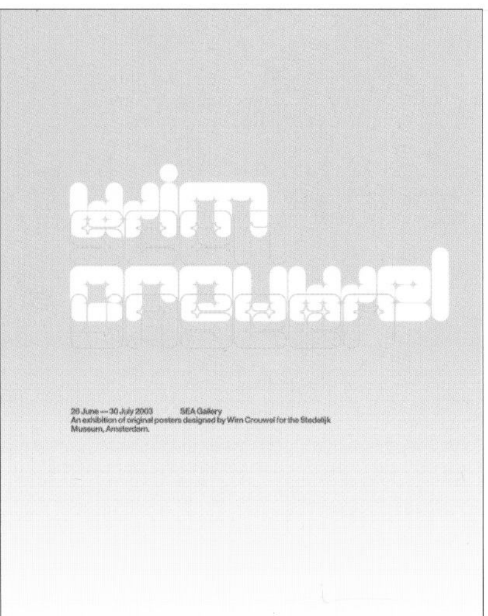

wim
crouwel
26 June — 30 July 2003
SEA Gallery
An exhibition of original posters designed by Wim Crouwel for the Stedelijk Museum, Amsterdam.

WIM CROUWEL EXHIBITION CATALOG

Design: SEA

SEA self-published this catalog to accompany an exhibition of Wim Crouwel posters held at its gallery in London. Renowned for his fascination with grid structures and a systematic approach to design, Crouwel's posters juxtapose highly structured letterforms, often hand-drawn, with carefully composed typographic layouts. SEA's catalog uses a nine-column grid divided horizontally into 11 fields. This structure gives great flexibility while ensuring unity throughout the publication. Columns are joined in different combinations to allow for varying text measures. Both images and text hang at different heights determined by the fields. By leaving columns and fields empty, SEA has used space creatively to add emphasis and to help the reader navigate the page.

Mason Wells
North Design

06—07

I was disappointed that I had to comment on the Léger poster, not because I dislike it, but because I wanted to pay homage to Vormgevers (a personal favourite, and I hazard a guess, the one everyone else wanted to pass comment on). But examining an early piece such as this allows one to re-assess things in terms of the evolution of Crouwel's work.

It goes without saying that Crouwel's posters meet all the right criteria in terms of what constitutes a good poster — they are legible, they work at varying proximities, they are compositionally perfect and they are built on content. You almost take it for granted that all the right bits are in the right places.

What really makes his work so outstanding, is the custom letterforms and typefaces (which feature in seven of the eight posters on display). In the case of the Léger poster, the title is created as an interlocking linear structure, presumably in reference to the cubist forms of the artist. This would be easy on a Mac, but three decades before, it brought along a new set of problems.

Crouwel placed no boundaries on himself and his constant re-invention of typeforms (whether manipulated or drawn from scratch) kept his work free from the dogmas associated with the work of many of his contemporaries, ensuring that each new artwork was fresh. Looking at this poster, it's easy to see how it pre-empts his later work such as Vormgevers, Visuele communicatie and New Alphabet.

What is hard to comment on are the bits that contextualise it. Tangible elements such as colour, print process and scale—even mistakes such as misaligned registration and over-specified colour trap—become impossible to pass comment on when all one has as reference are miniscule reproductions (in this case an absolutely knackered Mode en Module and a few Dutch design books). It's like criticising a piece of architecture without visiting the building—you have to go there and experience it to truly understand it.

Fernand Léger

Silkscreen, 88x60cm
Stedelijk Van
Abbemuseum
Eindhoven
1957

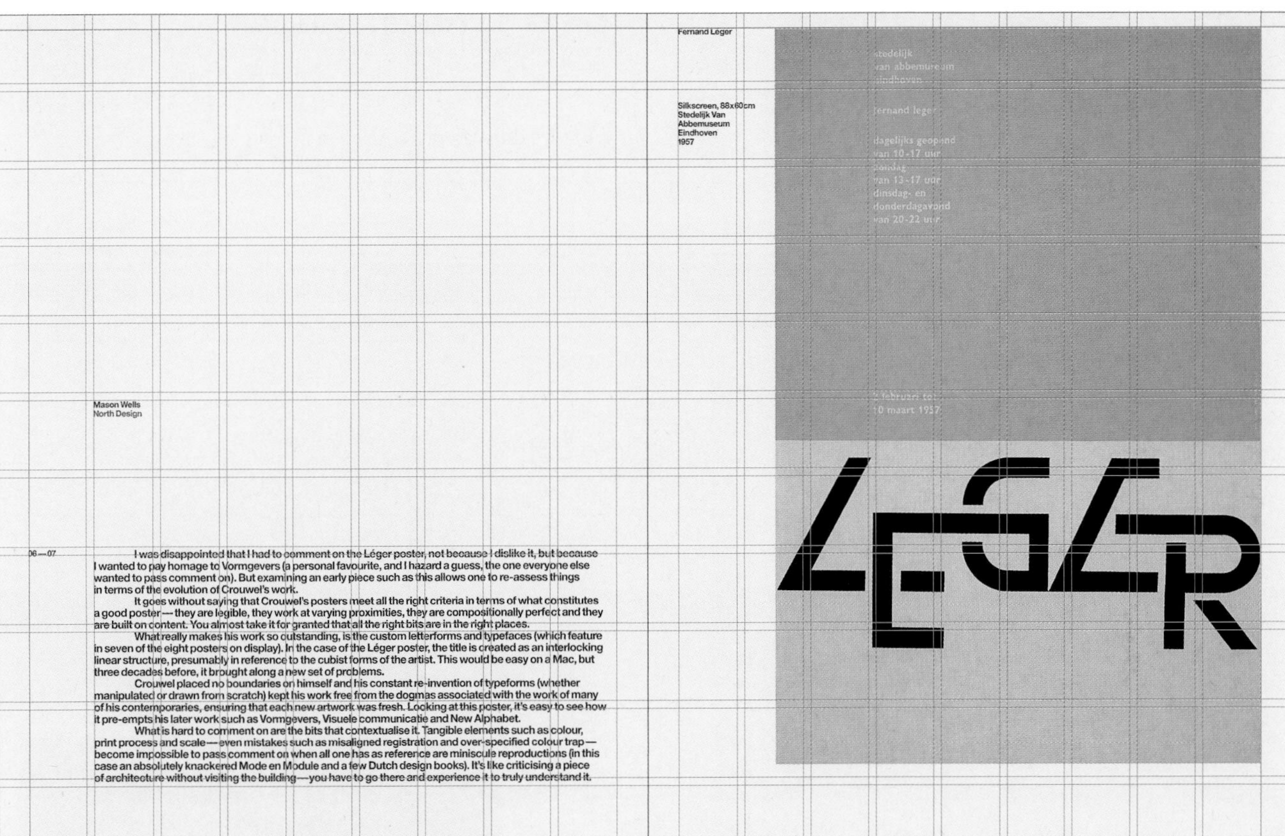

Mason Wells
North Design

06—07

I was disappointed that I had to comment on the Léger poster, not because I dislike it, but because I wanted to pay homage to Vormgevers (a personal favourite, and I hazard a guess, the one everyone else wanted to pass comment on). But examining an early piece such as this allows one to re-assess things in terms of the evolution of Crouwel's work.

It goes without saying that Crouwel's posters meet all the right criteria in terms of what constitutes a good poster — they are legible, they work at varying proximities, they are compositionally perfect and they are built on content. You almost take it for granted that all the right bits are in the right places.

What really makes his work so outstanding, is the custom letterforms and typefaces (which feature in seven of the eight posters on display). In the case of the Léger poster, the title is created as an interlocking linear structure, presumably in reference to the cubist forms of the artist. This would be easy on a Mac, but three decades before, it brought along a new set of problems.

Crouwel placed no boundaries on himself and his constant re-invention of typeforms (whether manipulated or drawn from scratch) kept his work free from the dogmas associated with the work of many of his contemporaries, ensuring that each new artwork was fresh. Looking at this poster, it's easy to see how it pre-empts his later work such as Vormgevers, Visuele communicatie and New Alphabet.

What is hard to comment on are the bits that contextualise it. Tangible elements such as colour, print process and scale — even mistakes such as misaligned registration and over-specified colour trap — become impossible to pass comment on when all one has as reference are miniscule reproductions (in this case an absolutely knackered Mode en Module and a few Dutch design books). It's like criticising a piece of architecture without visiting the building — you have to go there and experience it to truly understand it.

Fernand Leger

Silkscreen, 88x60cm
Stedelijk Van
Abbemuseum
Eindhoven
1957

GRID SPECIFICATIONS

Page size (trimmed)	210 x 265mm
Top margin	5mm
Bottom margin	5mm
Outside margin	10mm
Inside margin	10mm
Number of columns	9
Gutter width	2.5mm
Extras	11 horizontal fields

02—03

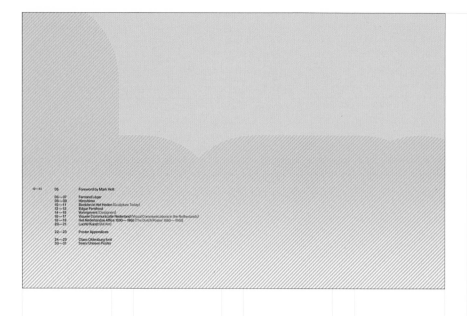

05 Foreword by Mark Holt

06—07 Fernand Léger
08—09 Hiroshima
10—11 Beelden in Het Heden (Sculpture Today)
12—13 Edgar Fernhout
14—15 Vormgevers (Designers)
16—17 Visuele Communicatie Nederland (Visual Communications in the Netherlands)
18—19 Het Nederlandse Affice 1890—1968 (The Dutch Poster 1890—1968)
20—21 Lucht/Kunst (Air/Art)

22—23 Poster Appendices

24—29 Claes Oldenburg font
30—31 Seen/Unseen Poster

Vormgevers
(Designers)

Offset, 95x64cm
Stedelijk Museum,
Amsterdam
1968

stedelijk museum amsterdam
5 april t/m 23 juni 1968

vorm
gevers

Mark Holt
Mark Holt Design

14—15

For this poster, Crouwel revealed the grid he had used on all his previous posters (and the later posters he would produce) for the Stedelijk Museum. Place a number of Stedelijk posters alongside Vormgevers and it is remarkable to see the grid used time and time again to anchor each poster's design elements.

Each grid square and corresponding interval is equal to five units, which predetermines the height of the two sizes of font used on Vormgevers. The diameter of the rounded corners of the larger font, is equal to the width of a single unit. The font's form grows out of the grid itself, letter and grid are one. Resolved it certainly is. And if anyone needed proof that black and white need not be a poverty then surely this poster is it.

My favourite detail? The numeral five which starts the second text line, set to the x-height of the font and placed directly under the 's' of Stedelijk. In this context, quite possibly the most bizarre five I think I've ever seen.

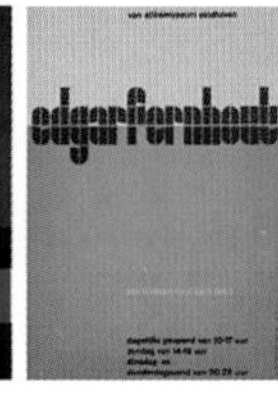

22—23

Fernand Léger
1957

One of Crouwel's best known posters, and a personal favourite of his. Drawn without the aid of graph paper, the poster's strong diagonal black lines reveal Crouwel's initial point of reference — it was a continuation from his New Acquisitions poster of 1956.

The Léger poster is simply constructed, with a letter 'r' which is formed from part of a pure circle, rather than being optically corrected.

Crouwel was very impressed by Léger's paintings and he has described this piece as being a typographic, if somewhat poetic, interpretation of the artist's work.

Hiroshima
1957

Designed in the same year as the Léger poster, this poster marked an exhibition of Japanese drawings based on Hiroshima. The background colour was similar to that of Japanese lacquer and the word Hiroshima is based on a small Grotesk — the way the letters were constructed determined their very tight spacing.

Crouwel wanted the word Hiroshima to appear heavy and threatening, and likens the ascenders to singed chimneys rising up from the black form.

Beelden in Het Heden
1959

A poster which was designed for an exhibition of sculpture. Crouwel designed the poster in portrait format to look like a landscape with three vertical sculptures, but it was always hung horizontally by mistake.

The bands of colour represent earth, sky and the horizon and the letterforms form the three sculptures. The letters are tightly spaced and the serifs extended to give the effect of a solid sculpture — they were individually drawn, pushed together and then painstakingly drawn again.

Edgar Fernhout
1963

In this poster for an exhibition of paintings by Edgar Fernhout, Crouwel was influenced by the artist's abstract landscapes, which were painted using small brushstrokes. The letterforms which were influenced to some extent by Tschichold, were divided into four equal parts, two above and two below the 'horizon' that Crouwel created through the middle of the text, also in reference to the artist's work.

Crouwel only designed these letters at the time of making the poster — he did not make them into a complete alphabet until four years later.

Vormgevers
1968

One of Crouwel's most talked about pieces, this poster featured a visible grid that was used for the layouts of all of the catalogues Crouwel designed for the Stedelijk.

The original graph sheets were printed in light grey — for this poster, Crouwel made the lines more visible and composed the letterforms inside them. The letterforms were a precursor to Crouwel's Fodor typeface, which was designed three years later.

Visuele Communicatie Nederland
1968

Designed for the Dutch Art Directors Club, this poster combines simplified pointed letterforms, all three points wide, which sit on a background inspired by the first bar codes.

The letterforms were reduced to very simple forms and are similar to those in Crouwel's soft alphabet, designed for his Claes Oldenburg poster of 1970.

Although it is a poster about visual communication, Crouwel admits that it is the most illegible poster that he has made.

Het Nederlandse Affice 1890—1968
1968

This poster was created for an exhibition about posters and features a folded down corner in the top left hand side, which reveals the Stedelijk marque and is a reference to the transient nature of the artform.

The letterforms are constructed around a square, and give rise to a strong sense of perspective, creating striking diagonals. The letters that form the word 'Affiche' go off the page on both sides, suggesting a fleeting glimpse of a poster as you walk past it.

Lucht/Kunst
1971

This poster is for an exhibition that was devoted to art made with air — pieces that were inflatable. Crouwel rounded off the letterforms (which are constructed from a narrow Grotesk) and pushed them together to give them a feeling of being blown full of air.

Both the outline and the spaces between the letters become very significant and the speech bubble is another (somewhat more literal) take on the subject matter.

claes
oldenburg
sm

HORROR VACUI
Urban implosions in the Netherlands
Text: Hans Ibelings
Photos: Roel Backaert

HORROR VACUI
Urban implosions in the Netherlands
Text: Hans Ibelings
Photos: Roel Backaert
implosões urbanas na Holanda

HORROR VACUI
Implosões urbanas na Holanda
Texto: Hans Ibelings
Fotografia: Roel Backaert

GRID SPECIFICATIONS

Page size (trimmed)	Panels: 1100 x 1100mm/ Booklet: 170 x 235mm
Top margin	Panels: 52.5mm/Booklet: 7.8mm
Bottom margin	Panels: 200mm/Booklet: 7.8mm
Outside margin	Panels: 52.5mm/Booklet: 7.8mm
Inside margin	Panels: 52.5mm/Booklet: 0mm (interior)
Number of columns	Panels: 5/Booklet: 5 (sideways)
Gutter width	Panels: 30mm/Booklet: 5mm
Extras	N/A

HORROR VACUI EXHIBITION PANELS

Design: Arjan Groot and Julia Müller

These panels and booklet were designed for the traveling exhibition Horror Vacui: Urban Implosions in the Netherlands, initially shown at the Lisbon Architecture Triennial. The exhibition looked at how gaps are filled within the urban fabric of Dutch cities—the term "horror vacui" translates as "fear of empty spaces." The designers took this theme as the starting point for their design. They filled any empty spaces on their pages with a graphic pattern influenced by textile weavings and Scottish tartans. Reminiscent of op art, this pattern creates a kind of visual vertigo appropriate to the overall subject matter. These repetitive graphic marks are, in themselves, an elaborate grid, and form the basis of the more conventional typographic grid used for the text and image layouts.

HORROR VACUI

Urban implosions in the Netherlands

Cities in the Netherlands, from Groningen in the north to Maastricht in the south, are undergoing a remarkable transformation. While Dutch cities, with the exception of Almere, are scarcely growing at all in terms of population, a great deal of building is going on. Open areas, 'overshot' zones, and disused port and industrial areas are, or soon will be, turned into new fragments of city, with urban densities and urban-looking buildings; consolidation is under way in city centres and around the railway stations; in nearly every city residential and office towers are under construction or in the pipeline; dual land use is an undeniable trend, manifested in road-straddling construction and tunneling beneath or building on top of existing buildings. The gaps in the urban fabric that were an accepted part of Dutch cities until the mid 1980s, are fast disappearing.

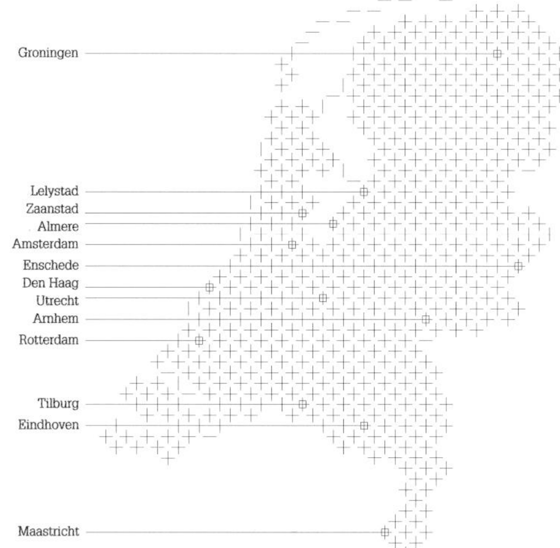

This exhibition is produced by the Netherlands Architecture Institute in collaboration with A10 new European architecture, with financial support from the Netherlands Architecture Fund.

Curators: Hans Ibelings + Kirsten Hannema. Exhibition design: Marta Malé-Alemany + José Pedro Sousa (ReD). Graphic design: Arjan Groot + Julia Müller. Photography: Roel Backaert. Production: Suzanne Kole + Marinke van der Horst. Supervisor: Martien de Vletter. International coordinator: Agnes Wijers

Special thanks to: AAS Architecten, ARCADIS Bouw en Vastgoed BV, Architectenbureau Art Zaaijer, Architectenbureau Marlies Rohmer, Architectuurstudio Herman Hertzberger, Atelier Rijksbouwmeester, Benthem Crouwel Architekten BV, Bouwfonds MAB Development, Bureau B+B stedebouw en landschapsarchitectuur, City of Eindhoven, City of Tilburg, Claus en Kaan Architecten, De Architekten Cie, De Zwarte Hond, Department of Physical Planing and Economic Affairs Groningen, Department of Physical Planning Amsterdam, Dick van Gameren architecten B.V., Dienst Stedelijke Ontwikkeling – City of The Hague, dS+V Rotterdam, (EEA) Erick van Egeraat associated architects, FARO Architecten bv, FPW Rotterdam, hvdn Architecten, JHK Architecten, Jo Coenen & Co Architecten, KCAP Architects&Planners, Köther | Salman | Koedijk | Architecten bv, Meyer en Van Schooten Architecten BV, MVRDV, NL Architects, OD 205 architectuur bv, Office for Metropolitan Architecture, OMS Beheer bv (City of Lelystad and William Properties bv), ONL [Oosterhuis_Lénárd], Ontwikkelingsbedrijf Rotterdam, Pierre Gautier architecture, PPKS Architects Ltd., Project Organisation Stationsgebied – City of Utrecht, Projectbureau Amsterdam Zuidas – City of Amsterdam, Projectbureau Zuidelijke IJ-oevers – City of Amsterdam, Rijnboutt Van der Vossen Rijnboutt bv, S333 architects, Soeters Van Eldonk Architecten, Stadsdeel Geuzenveld-Slotermeer – City of Amsterdam, Tania Concko Architectes, THALEN\BASELINE, UN Studio, Van Sambeek & Van Veen Architecten, Vera Yanovshtchinsky architecten, vof ontwikkelingscombinatie IMA (ING, MOESbouw, AM), West 8 urban design & landscape architecture b.v., Wiel Arets Architects, Ymere Ontwikkeling, Zwarts & Jansma Architects

Groningen Ciboga

Rotterdam Wijnhaven

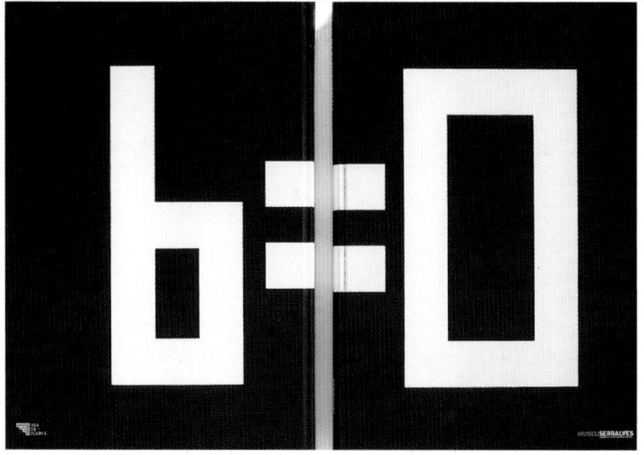

considerada então como «demasiado *engagé*». Tendo por objectivo único transformar-se num agrupamento «completamente atrasado mental», logo ficou decidido que os Ena Pá deveriam assumir como seu objectivo fazer a «pior música possível», utilizando apenas um ou dois acordes, a qual seria ainda servida por letras «absolutamente idiotas». Procurariam a todo o custo transformar-se num grupo de rock português que, «tal como os Sex Pistols ou os Ramones», exibisse a sua «mediocridade de modo transbordante e esplendoroso». A ideia fez o seu caminho, que deve já aqui ficar enunciado. Na futura formação musical, espécie de braço musical da homeostética, esteve, além de Vieira, Francisco Ferro. O primeiro concerto, ou melhor, a primeira «representação de concerto rock», aconteceria ainda em Dezembro de 1982 – no meio de uma festa operária e num prédio em construção, a ela tendo apenas assistido Portugal, Proença, uma rapariga anónima e seu cão – e o disco inicial viria a ser publicado cinco anos depois: trata-se de um single em vinil com duas músicas apenas, «Pão, Amor e Totobola» e «Telephone call». A partir de 1984, muitas das canções dos Ena Pá 2000 passaram a ser escritas por Fernando Brito, ao lado de Manuel Vieira. Em Anelhe, os passeios pelo campo e as imensas refeições, naquele Verão de 1982, foram intercalados também com a realização de várias pinturas. Pedro Portugal, que desde aí se atribuiu no movimento o papel do sujeito que cola as partes e as faz operar – «os budistas chamam a estas pessoas pontes», assinala a propósito –, começou a registar fotograficamente todas estas viagens, bem como as performances efectuadas pelos seis artistas e companheiros na ESBAL, daí resultando um acervo composto por milhares de negativos de «fotos oficiais» ou «autorizadas». E é facto indesmentível que a memória homeostética adquire, através das fotografias de Pedro Portugal, uma extensão desconhecida de outros agrupamentos estéticos. Os três passaram ainda pelo festival de Vilar de Mouros, onde viriam a conhecer as irmãs Medeiros, Maria e Inês, que pouco depois começariam a aparecer no Grupo de Teatro da Escola de Belas-Artes, animado por Xana e que viria também a ser integrado por Vieira e Proença. Estes dois partiriam, ainda em meados de Agosto, para o Algarve e em Lagos – onde se encontrava Xana de férias – tocaram bandolim e guitarra nas ruas durante dias seguidos, tendo com isso conseguido arrecadar algumas moedas. Rumaram em seguida à Fuzeta, localidade em que lhes surgiria a personagem Capitão Nemo, cujas cartas, relatando viagens imaginárias, foram escritas num espírito de absoluta desconversa. No mês seguinte, Vieira e Portugal foram até Paris tirar mais fotografias e ver o que «estava a acontecer».

–54–

–55–

considerada então como «demasiado *engagé*». Tendo por objectivo único transformar-se num agrupamento «completamente atrasado mental», logo ficou decidido que os Ena Pá deveriam assumir como seu objectivo fazer a «pior música possível», utilizando apenas um ou dois acordes, a qual seria ainda servida por letras «absolutamente idiotas». Procurariam a todo o custo transformar-se num grupo de rock português que, «tal como os Sex Pistols ou os Ramones», exibisse a sua «mediocridade de modo transbordante e esplendoroso». A ideia fez o seu caminho, que deve já aqui ficar enunciado. Na futura formação musical, espécie de braço musical da homeostética, esteve, além de Vieira, Francisco Ferro. O primeiro concerto, ou melhor, a primeira «representação de concerto rock», aconteceria ainda em Dezembro de 1982 – no meio de uma festa operária e num prédio em construção, a ela tendo apenas assistido Portugal, Proença, uma rapariga anónima e seu cão – e o disco inicial viria a ser publicado cinco anos depois: trata-se de um single em vinil com duas músicas apenas, «Pão, Amor e Totobola» e «Telephone call». A partir de 1984, muitas das canções dos Ena Pá 2000 passaram a ser escritas por Fernando Brito, ao lado de Manuel Vieira. Em Anelhe, os passeios pelo campo e as imensas refeições, naquele Verão de 1982, foram intercalados também com a realização de várias pinturas. Pedro Portugal, que desde aí se atribuiu no movimento o papel do sujeito que cola as partes e as faz operar – «os budistas chamam a estas pessoas pontes», assinala a propósito –, começou a registar fotograficamente todas estas viagens, bem como as performances efectuadas pelos seis artistas e companheiros na ESBAL, daí resultando um acervo composto por milhares de negativos de «fotos oficiais» ou «autorizadas». E é facto indesmentível que a memória homeostética adquire, através das fotografias de Pedro Portugal, uma extensão

desconhecida de outros agrupamentos estéticos. Os três passaram ainda pelo festival de Vilar de Mouros, onde viriam a conhecer as irmãs Medeiros, Maria e Inês, que pouco depois começariam a aparecer no Grupo de Teatro da Escola de Belas-Artes, animado por Xana e que viria também a ser integrado por Vieira e Proença. Estes dois partiriam, ainda em meados de Agosto, para o Algarve e em Lagos – onde se encontrava Xana de férias – tocaram bandolim e guitarra nas ruas durante dias seguidos, tendo com isso conseguido arrecadar algumas moedas. Rumaram em seguida à Fuzeta, localidade em que lhes surgiria a personagem Capitão Nemo, cujas cartas, relatando viagens imaginárias, foram escritas num espírito de absoluta desconversa. No mês seguinte, Vieira e Portugal foram até Paris tirar mais fotografias e ver o que «estava a acontecer».

-54- -55-

GRID SPECIFICATIONS

Page size (trimmed)	252 x 356mm
Top margin	15mm
Bottom margin	15mm
Outside margin	25mm
Inside margin	15mm
Number of columns	12
Gutter width	4mm
Extras	Baseline grid, 14pt

6 = 0 EXHIBITION CATALOG

Design: Lizá Ramalho, Artur Rebelo, and Nuno Bastos at R2 design

This catalog accompanied an exhibition by 1980s Portuguese art collective Homeosteticos, held at the Serralves Museum of Contemporary Art, Porto. The title, 6=0, reflected how under-appreciated this group of six artists felt. Designers Lizá Ramalho, Artur Rebelo, and Nuno Bastos emphasized this notion by reversing the equation of the title and placing a zero on the front cover and a six on the back.

Poemas Homeostéticos

1 O ORGÃO HUMANO
2 AZERTES DE UMA GALINHA
3 SAGA DE PEDRO PUTANHEIRO NA CIDADE DO PORTO
4 DOIS POEMAS: AU TOUR DE LA CRITIQUE
5 A IDADE DA CHUPETA
6 VANGUARDA, ONDE ESTÁS?
7 AS ORELHAS DE BUGS BUNNY
8 FRAGMENTO DO «NEOLÍTICO POSTLÍTICO»
9 EX-LÍRICO
10 ROSA EXTRAVAGANTE (LADO B)
11 SONHO (PIRAMIDAL) DE RENATO ORNATO
12 PRÁTICO
13 OS REIS QUE COMIAM SARDINHAS À SOBREMESA
14 A COBRA COM CABEÇA DE ARANHA
15 QUADRAS
16 PLUM PUDDING POEM
17 ANA COMENA
18 SONHO DISCRETO
19 AMEI
20 SOPA DE LEGUMES
21 LET ME KISS YOU TIZIANO
22 PARANÁLISE
23 EU AMO O NÉON
24 DOIS POEMAS A DESPROPÓSITO [1] [2]
25 FIZ DA ARTE UM CAMINHO
26 FRÁGIL, 17/10/85
27 TRIOLOGIA DE UMA DÚZIA (O QUE FICOU!)
28 ATELIER
29 GÉNESIS
30 TESEIDA
31 A FAINA
32 ESTÁDIO
33 ESTRANHO PÁSSARO

Edição

-143-

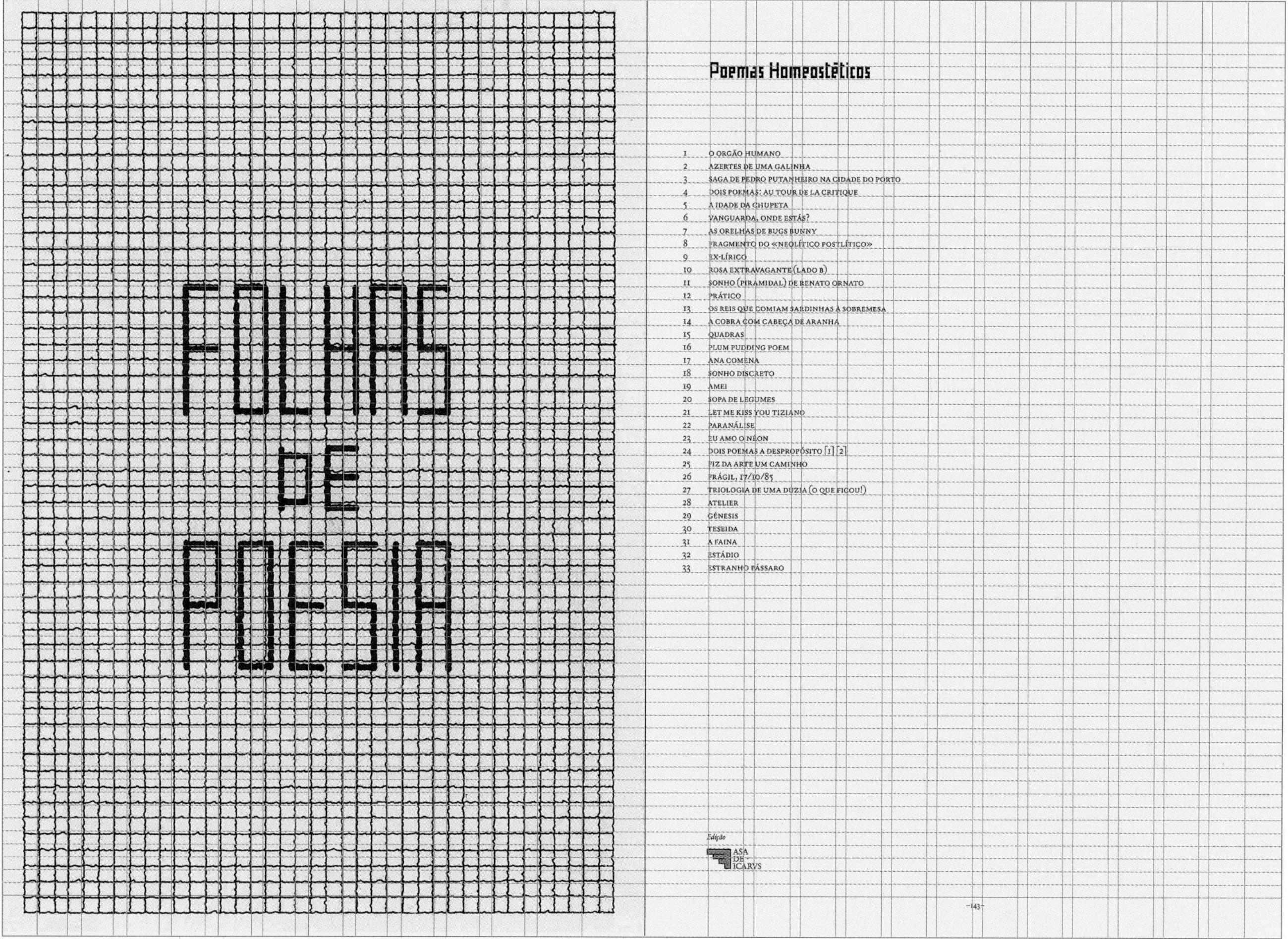

Poemas Homeostéticos

1 O ORGÃO HUMANO
2 AZERTES DE UMA GALINHA
3 SAGA DE PEDRO PUTANHEIRO NA CIDADE DO PORTO
4 DOIS POEMAS: AU TOUR DE LA CRITIQUE
5 A IDADE DA CHUPETA
6 VANGUARDA, ONDE ESTÁS?
7 AS ORELHAS DE BUGS BUNNY
8 FRAGMENTO DO «NEOLÍTICO POSTLÍTICO»
9 EX-LÍRICO
10 ROSA EXTRAVAGANTE (LADO B)
11 SONHO (PIRAMIDAL) DE RENATO ORNATO
12 PRÁTICO
13 OS REIS QUE COMIAM SARDINHAS À SOBREMESA
14 A COBRA COM CABEÇA DE ARANHA
15 QUADRAS
16 PLUM PUDDING POEM
17 ANA COMENA
18 SONHO DISCRETO
19 AMEI
20 SOPA DE LEGUMES
21 LET ME KISS YOU TIZIANO
22 PARANÁLISE
23 EU AMO O NÉON
24 DOIS POEMAS A DESPROPÓSITO [1] [2]
25 FIZ DA ARTE UM CAMINHO
26 FRÁGIL, 17/10/85
27 TRIOLOGIA DE UMA DUZIA (O QUE FICOU!)
28 ATELIER
29 GÉNESIS
30 TESEIDA
31 A FAINA
32 ESTÁDIO
33 ESTRANHO PÁSSARO

Edição
ASA DE ICARVS

-143-

The selection of work for the publication was made in collaboration with contributing artist Pedro Portugal by putting work up on the studio walls and editing intuitively. The composition of the pages attempts to capture this; the scattering of images within the multi-column grid reflects the organic nature of the selection process, and resembles the composition in progress on the studio wall. The grid is designed to allow flexibility, but still gives the publication a strong overall structure.

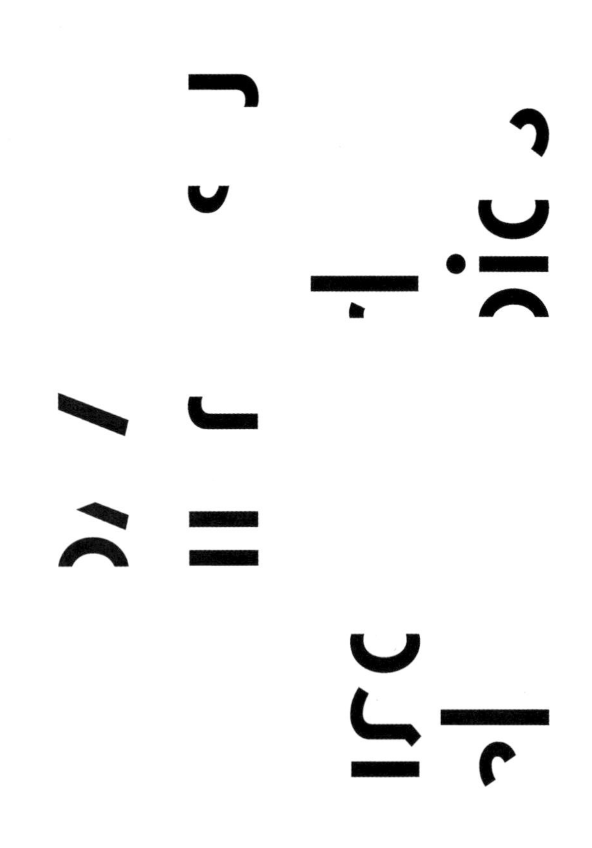

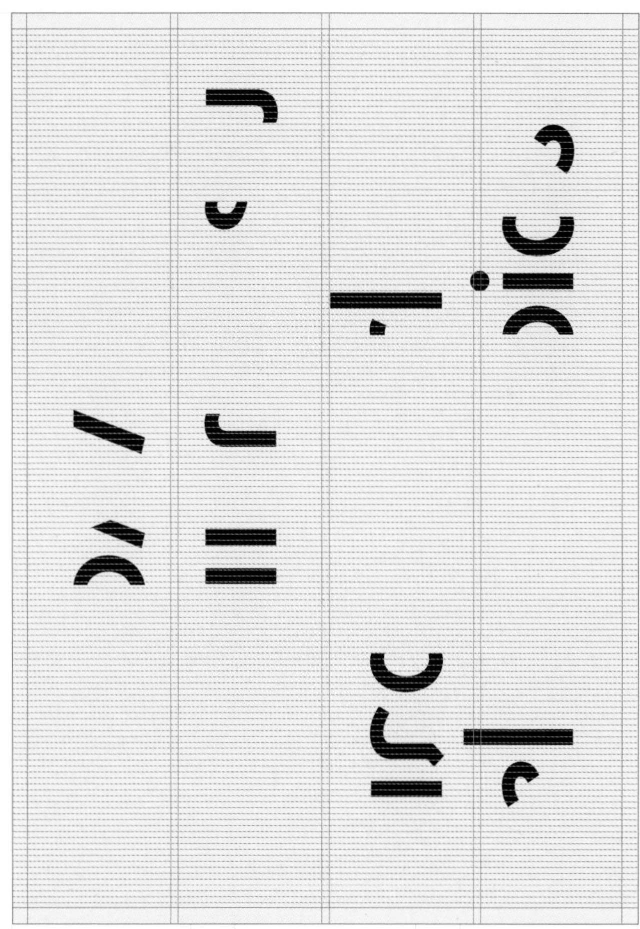

URBAN VOIDS EXHIBITION CATALOG

Design: Lizá Ramalho, Artur Rebelo, and Liliana Pinto at R2 design

This promotional material for the Lisbon Architecture Triennial was designed to reflect the overarching theme of the event—urban voids. Designers Lizá Ramalho, Artur Rebelo, and Liliana Pinto wanted to use graphic forms to communicate ideas of abandonment, and also to draw attention to city spaces that are often overlooked. By choosing a stencil font, and showing it in its fragmented form, the designers produced what at first appears to be a dislocated composition. But, by printing on different densities of translucent paper (as used in architectural projects), the name of the event becomes clear once the publication is folded to size. The overall grid structure is simple, but the hanging heights of the text further reinforce the sense of isolation and temporary dislocation.

GRID SPECIFICATIONS

Page size (trimmed)	420 x 594mm
Top margin	10mm
Bottom margin	10mm
Outside margin	10mm
Inside margin	10mm
Number of columns	4
Gutter width	5mm
Extras	Baseline grid, 11pt

vazios urbanos
urban voids
Trienal de Arquitectura de Lisboa 2007
Lisbon Architecture Triennale 2007
31/05 — 31/07
Principais exposições / Main exhibitions
www.trienaldelisboa.com

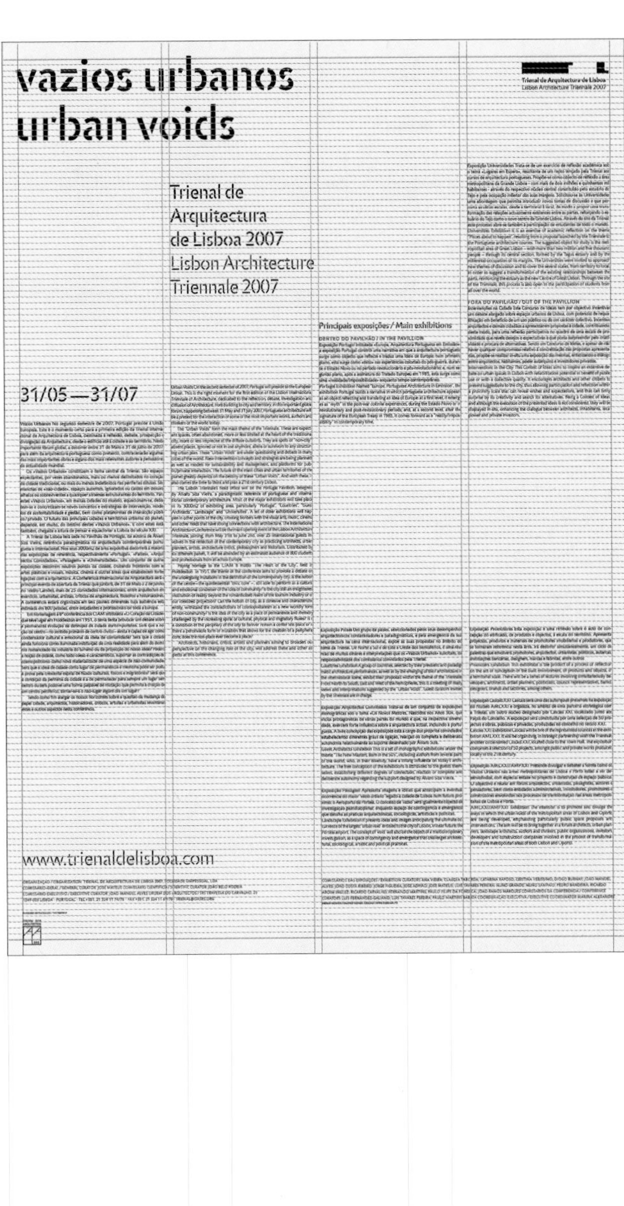
vazios urbanos
urban voids
Trienal de Arquitectura de Lisboa 2007
Lisbon Architecture Triennale 2007
31/05 — 31/07
Principais exposições / Main exhibitions
www.trienaldelisboa.com

Illustrated books

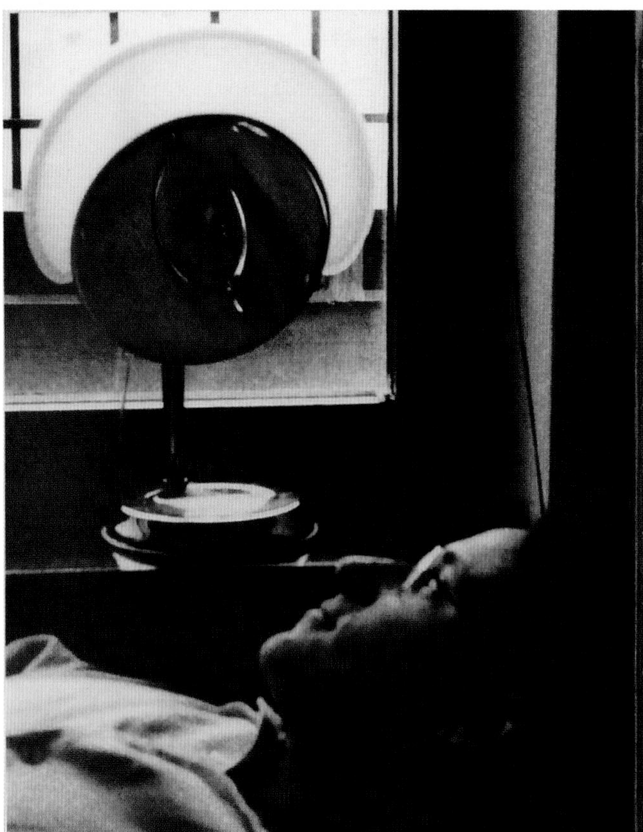

The Art of the Jester

Chip Kidd. Photograph by Duane Michals, 2001.

Pull a book at random from your bookcase and look at its cover. 7
That is all you need to do to travel back to that specific moment in your life when you first read it. As compact as a time capsule, a book jacket holds forever the memory of the brief cultural period when it was in print. But a short shelf life is the price a book jacket must pay for leaving a vivid impression in the mind. My 1987 hardcover edition of Tom Wolfe's *The Bonfire of The Vanities*, so promising when it came out during the heady days of the Reagan administration, looks and feels today like a dear old friend wearing a toupee.[1] However, the fact that most book jackets look dated within a couple of years of their publication does not take anything away from their graphic appeal. One of the things we love about books is the way they age along with us.

Yet today, newness is considered a critical design element of a book jacket. Indeed, when I survey bookstores, the future obsolescence of the latest best-sellers' covers is the furthest thing from my mind. Even though I am aware that the current jackets will one day have the same emotional patina as award-winning jackets designed or art directed a decade ago by Louise Fili, Carin Goldberg, Sara Eisenman, Paula Scher, Frank Metz, Krystyna Skalski, Fred Marcellino or Neil Stuart, I cannot help but be seduced by the allure of instant modernity that the new books seem to capture. One of the things that tells me that a book is brand new is the presence of photography on its cover. Over the last couple of years, I have been conditioned to equate the use of conceptual photography on American book jackets with cutting-edge, contemporary literature. In contrast, if a book has an illustrated jacket, I regret to admit that I assume that its content is somewhat behind the curve. Graphic profiling, like racial profiling, is an inescapable reality in the world in which we live today.

The now popular photographic approach was originally pioneered in the late 1980s by a group of young designers working for the Knopf Publishing Group. Famous for its emblematic Borzoi logo, the Knopf

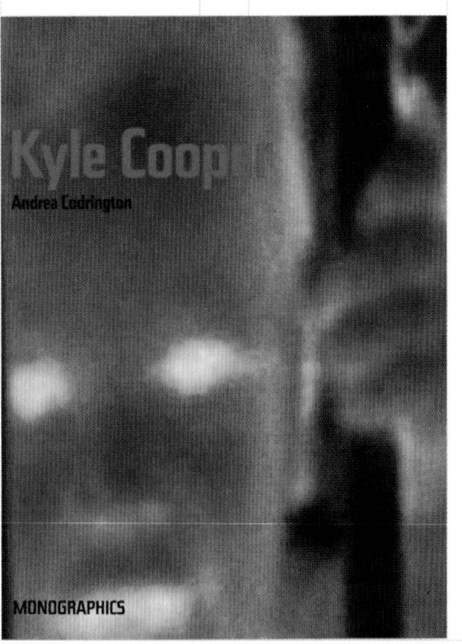

Donnie Brasco

Director – Mike Newell, 1997
Titles – Kyle Cooper (dir.)
for Imaginary Forces

One of the first main titles to be done under the Imaginary Forces name, *Donnie Brasco* is a micro-narrative so moody and evocative that it had one *New Yorker* critic praising it above the film itself. Using a combination of predominantly black-and-white and colour stills shot in surveillance style – complete with Kodak markings and grease pencil scribblings – Cooper choreographs an unsettling sequence about friendship, betrayal and the implosion of relationships caught in the middle. Accompanied by a delicate piece of music by Beethoven, the grainy still images become animated thanks to a carefully choreographed edit that favours slow fades punctuated by rapid cut action sequences and the occasional piece of live footage. The titles begin and end with a view of Johnny Depp's dark-ringed eyes looking from outside – an imposter cop in the midst of New York wise guys.

56

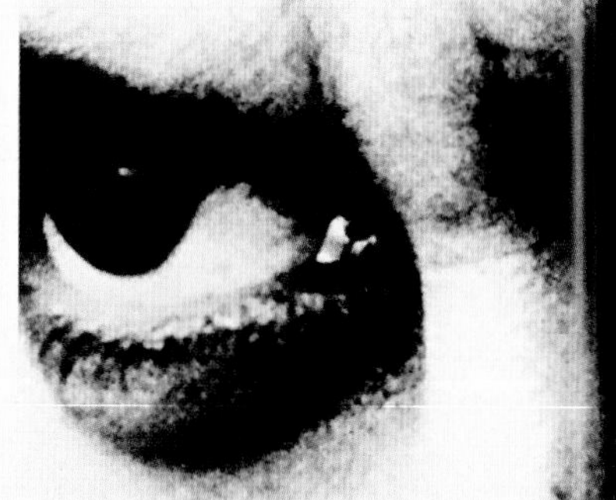

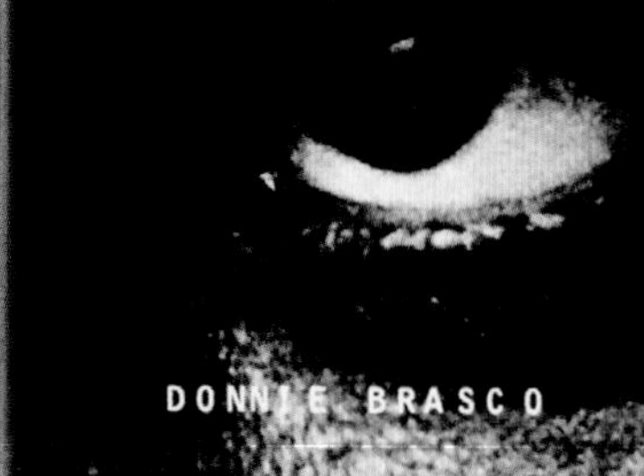

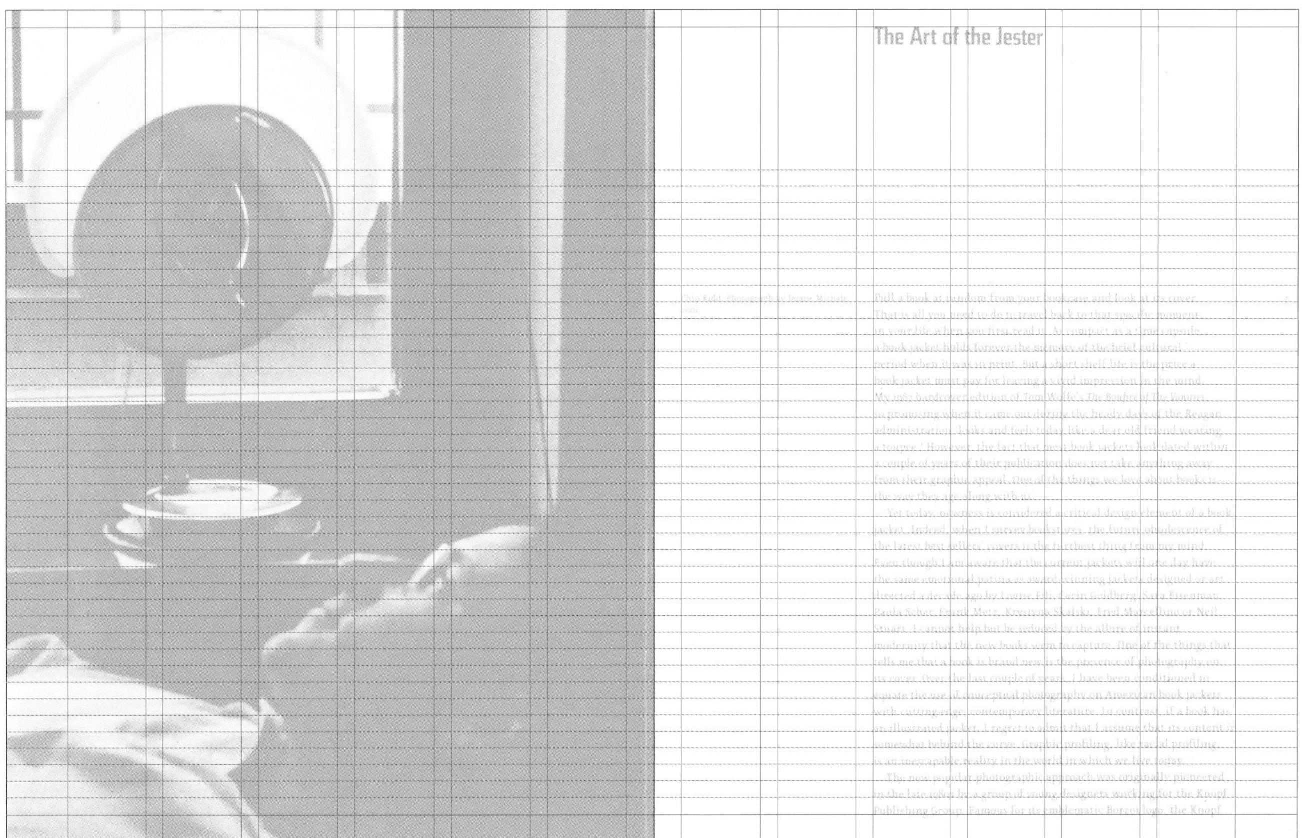

GRID SPECIFICATIONS

Page size (trimmed)	189 x 238mm
Top margin	5mm
Bottom margin	10mm
Outside margin	8mm
Inside margin	18mm
Number of columns	6
Gutter width	5mm
Extras	Baseline grid, 13.25pt starting at 45.5mm

MONOGRAPHICS SERIES

Design: Brad Yendle at Design Typography

Each book in Laurence King's Monographics series concentrates on the work of one creative practitioner. The series style has to be recognizable, but flexible, and has to act as a fairly neutral backdrop to the work featured. These considerations informed designer Brad Yendle's decision to create what he describes as a considered, but quite austere design. Herbert Spencer's *Typographica* magazine and the *Graphis* annuals from the 1960s were his inspiration. Yendle's grid is a multicolumn structure that can accommodate continuous text, captions, and index easily. Its large top margin introduces welcome breathing space to pages that include visual examples and formats from a range of disciplines—movie stills and titles, book covers and spreads, prints and comic books.

Véronique Vienne

Chip Kidd

Laurence King Publishing

Through the Glass Darkly

Kyle Cooper. Photograph by Michael Power.

Kyle Cooper is a postmodern paradox. He is an iconoclast who loves what he transgresses, whether the tenets of modernist typography, the idea of apple-pie America or even the belief in an all-loving, all-powerful God. He is by nature betwixt and between, not quite fitting into the commercial world of Hollywood and not entirely at home in the realm of high-design discourse. He is a true-believing Christian whose oeuvre has often lingered on the sinister themes of murder and madness. The work that he has created over the past decade – first at R/Greenberg and then at Imaginary Forces, the studio he cofounded in 1996 with Peter Frankfurt and Chip Houghton – distinctively plays off this tension to great effect. 7

In an age predicated on irony – the knowing collusion between auteur and audience via winking references made at breakneck speed – Cooper's work comes into bold relief, for it is marked by something that seems all but lost in our cleverness-as-king culture: earnestness. This may sound an odd description for a designer who first came to
36 fame with the opening titles for David Fincher's 1995 film *Seven*, a sequence characterized by degraded, hand-scrawled type and nerve-jangling imagery. But Cooper has realized something important: desecration is all the more effective when the ideals being torn down are ones that are dearly held by the desecrater.

Kyle Cooper's short-form artistry is particularly appreciated in a culture known for its collective attention deficit disorder because it delivers intense experiences in quick bursts. The fact that such jags of entertainment have snuck into the unassuming cultural spaces of legally mandated credit sequences is a testament to both the creative urge and, perhaps, consumer culture's discomfort in the presence of blank, unmediated space. Cooper himself displays a tendency toward fitful absorption – darting associatively in conversation from one topic to the next, multi-tasking to such an extent that many of the interviews that fill his dictionary-sized book of press clippings were given on his cell phone while driving the freeways of Los Angeles

The homey quality of Kidd's art direction in these spreads from *Peanuts* is reminiscent of a family photo album. Changes of scale give the pages their texture. The comic strips are photographed from the original pulp pages, showing wear and tear and discolouration. Because Schulz didn't have anything that could be called an archive in his studio, assembling this book was like a scavenger hunt for Kidd and Spear.

104

105

48

The Cold Six Thousand
James Ellroy
Main photograph – Mell Kilpatrick
2001 New York ALFRED A. KNOPF
[Hardback]

The blurred colour photograph of a neon Las Vegas landscape sets the location for a tale of violence and corruption amid the desert casinos. The bloodied crime scene offers a macabre invitation to enter a world peopled with amoral characters who both repel and fascinate.

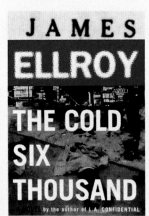

White Jazz
James Ellroy
Photograph – Robert Morrow
1992 New York ALFRED A. KNOPF
[Hardback]

"Chip Kidd frames the front cover in pristine white – a color at once stark, innocent and inviting. Centered in that white expanse: an LAPD patrol car door shot full of holes. The potential book buyer/reader has been presented with a statement and a challenge – forceful, simple, elegant: Read This Book!"
– *James Ellroy*

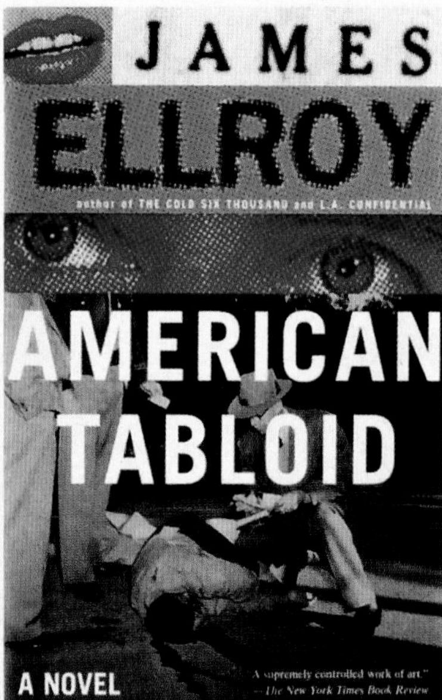

American Tabloid
James Ellroy
Main photograph – Mell Kilpatrick
2001 New York ALFRED A. KNOPF
[Paperback]

The saturated and grainy colour images of eyes and lips highlight our voyeuristic attraction to scenes of bloodshed and mayhem. The vintage shot of a crime scene makes reference to the American underworld in the years before and after the Bay of Pigs.

49

Daniel Raeburn

Chris Ware

Laurence King Publishing

any of his own many moods. In one strip he made Jimmy into an old grouch; in the next, an irrepressible gee-whiz kid. At the time, Ware was new to Chicago and had no money, no friends, no girlfriend, nowhere to go and no way to get there even if he did. (Working late one night at the School of the Art Institute, Ware broke both his legs by jumping out of the window after the keepers of the building locked him inside – a perfect metaphor for Ware's experience of art school.) Basically, Ware was a lonely schlub on crutches, just like Jimmy. All of Ware's characters began like Jimmy, as a joke that the legendarily self-critical cartoonist played on himself. The frump from "Tales of To-Morrow" parodied Ware's own sedentary pursuit of happiness in

an online consumer utopia; the roly-poly hoarders Rusty Brown and Chalky White lampooned his frenzies of toy collecting. Ware diagnosed this idiosyncrasy as his "Benny Hill" syndrome, because it appears as though one guy – a doughy, bald version of Chris Ware – is playing all of the major roles.

Because Ware cracked these jokes at his own expense, the characters had a reflexivity that soon imbued his stereotypical visions with a humanity he did not at first grant them. When Jimmy Corrigan hobbled out of Chicago to find his fictional father, marking the beginning of his novel and his life as a more fleshed-out character, he ceased to be a cipher and became instead an Everyman. Rusty Brown is no longer the odious flea market hound but, in the book bearing his name, the same bullied schoolboy that Ware once was. Both Jimmy and Rusty became more specific, more like Ware and oddly more universal. "I don't understand how that happened," Ware says. "I think it's just my immaturity as a writer and an artist, but I'm not able to start out with a specific character. Any time that I start out taking a character really, deeply seriously, it's a miserable failure. Strangely, most of the mean-spirited gags that I've done have ended up being the characters that I truly care about." Ware may begin by caricaturing himself, but in time he turns his caricature into his character.

Art is supposed to imitate life, but in Ware's case the relationship also worked eerily in reverse. When Ware was a toddler his father abandoned him and his mother. Twenty or so years later Ware began to work in earnest on Jimmy Corrigan, which begins with Jimmy receiving a letter from the father who abandoned him. The letter requests that they meet. As Ware was midway through drawing out this fictional meeting, his father telephoned him and suggested a meeting. At first Ware thought it was a joke, but it was in fact his real father, and they did face each other, and their conversation was as pained as the imaginary one Ware had already written. The two finished their dinner and agreed awkwardly to meet again some day. Ware went back to work on his book and ended it, years later, with the death of Jimmy's father. Within one month Ware learned that his own father had just died. Ware appended to his novel a corrigendum in which he noted that the four or five hours it takes to read his book is the same amount of time that he had ever spent with his father. The book itself, he concluded, encloses the same quantity of physical matter as the urn holding his father's ashes. By equating his life's

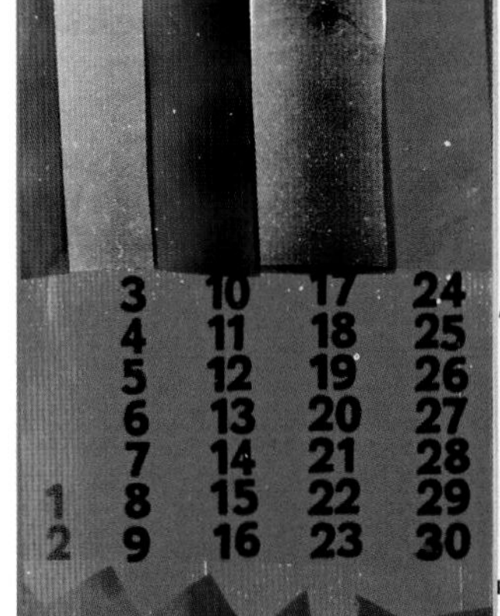

H.N. Werkman

Alston W. Purvis

Laurence King Publishing

but almost everything had to be liquidated. He retained only two employees, one being Bos, and moved the remnants of his business to a seventh-floor loft in a warehouse along a canal. According to his brother, Werkman "then began to live according to his own philosophy, sincerely and frankly, and to again seek his solace in an art form that he had cultivated and developed on his own, and one in which he would find compensation for all of the misery in his life".

Ironically, Werkman's adversities became a form of salvation, giving him a fresh sense of independence. He later wrote that although the 1920s constituted his most destitute period it was then that he "realized that the better purposes in life are to be found somewhere else". Werkman had always used printing to serve his clients but now realized that he had never treated it as his heart demanded. At the age of 41, he experienced an epiphany, and the means that had once only afforded him a living now became an artistic tool. The Belgian artist Michel Seuphor, pseudonym of F. Berckelaers, the publisher of *Het Overzicht* (The Review), soon became one of Werkman's most active correspondents and his main link with the European avant-garde. Werkman wrote to Seuphor in 1930: "It seems that my objective in life has become to redress myself for all that I have overlooked until now and could have done." The two discussed their financial straits, Seuphor explaining how he and his collaborator Jozef Peeters had endured great hardship and Werkman responding with optimism: "We have also been experiencing some uneasy times lately, but aware of the irrelevance of all these things, we attempt to lose ourselves in our work and in the joy of life."

For Werkman, 1923 was a turning point when the past was closed and the future lay open. On 12 September of that year, a simple flyer was delivered to Werkman's colleagues in De Ploeg. Opening with "GRONINGEN BERLIN PARIS MOSCOW 1923 – Beginning of the Violet Season", it announced a new publication and declared the dawn of an artistic epoch: "It must be attested and affirmed ... Art is everywhere." Beginning with the second issue this publication would be titled *The Next Call*, the slogan of Werkman's entreaty for a new artistic beginning.

"To view *The Next Call* as a 'cri de coeur' is no exaggeration", Ad Petersen wrote in his book on De Ploeg. Werkman later reflected on the significance of this period for him: "Like a wet poodle I shook off everything that for me was annoying and stood then for a while virtually alone. To tell the truth I did not understand it myself at times. Still I continued: everything that you now lose is gain ..."

Werkman's German hand press made by Christian Dingler in 1850.

New art movements were then flourishing in Berlin, Paris and Moscow, major cultural centres of the time, and although Groningen was comparatively insignificant, Werkman hoped that something similar could take root there as well. However, in 1923 Groningen was a provincial city and attempting a publication there such as *The Next Call* was a bold endeavour. Werkman wrote to Seuphor in 1924, lamenting the parochialism of his environment: "Much to my regret I have to admit that Groningen sits in a corner which almost no sound penetrates." Or as the poet Hendrik de Vries (also a Groninger) wrote, "Only one who derives his energy from his own loneliness can thrive here", a fitting description of Werkman.

One objective of *The Next Call* was to generate innovation and force certain De Ploeg members to shake off their complacent demeanours and question the legacies of their academic training. Its abrupt appearance was provocative in itself, but afterwards most of De Ploeg dismissed it as a curiosity produced by an eccentric colleague. What *The Next Call did* do was provide Werkman with an outlet for his experimental typography and his few attempts at poetry. It was also a convenient way to keep abreast of the international avant-garde. Most of all, however, it kept Werkman spiritually alive in what was for him a claustrophobic and provincial environment.

From 1923 until 1926, *The Next Call* was published in nine random issues in editions of around 40 copies and was sent without charge. The first four issues were distributed mainly to De Ploeg members, friends and business acquaintances, but with the fifth number it was sent to the editors of other avant-garde publications, both in the Netherlands and abroad. The first issue articulated in large, uneven, uppercase sans serif letters Werkman's present frustrations with his immediate milieu and his future outlook:

EEN RIL DOORKLIEFT (a chill permeates)
HET LIJF DAT VREEST (the body that fears)
DE VRIJHEID VAN DE GEEST (the freedom of the soul)

Werkman produced *The Next Call* on a German hand press made in 1850 by Christian Dingler. By treating type as an artistic element in its own right, independent of its logical communicative function,

Notes

Selected Bibliography

IDEAS
this is an idea
Or to be more precise, its a *symbol* that *represents* an idea.
Almost *everything* can represent *something*. In fact, it's very hard to find anything, whether natural or man-made, that represents *nothing* - that has or has had no symbolic value whatsoever to someone, somewhere, at some point in time.
If you can find one of these rare things, they represent one thing and one thing only - *themselves*.

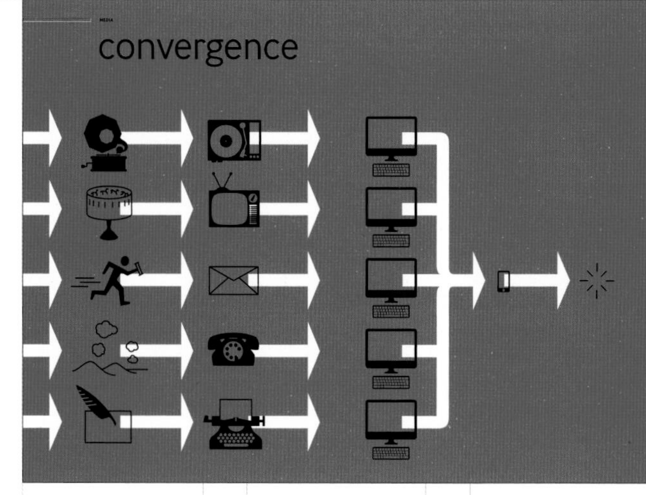
MEDIA
convergence

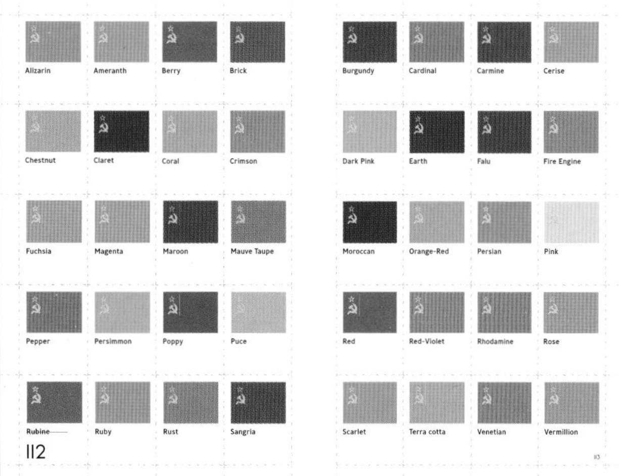
Alizarin
Ameranth
Berry
Brick
Burgundy
Cardinal
Carmine
Cerise
Chestnut
Claret
Coral
Crimson
Dark Pink
Earth
Falu
Fire Engine
Fuchsia
Magenta
Maroon
Mauve Taupe
Moroccan
Orange-Red
Persian
Pink
Pepper
Persimmon
Poppy
Puce
Red
Red-Violet
Rhodamine
Rose
Rubine
Ruby
Rust
Sangria
Scarlet
Terra cotta
Venetian
Vermillion
112

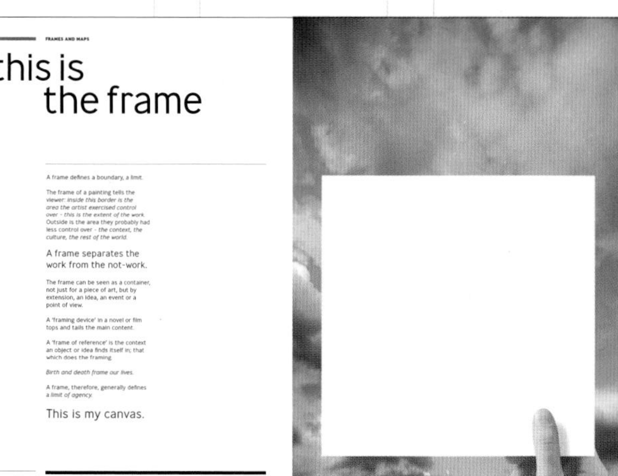
FRAMES AND MAPS
this is the frame
A frame defines a boundary, a limit.
The frame of a painting tells the viewer: *inside this border is the area the artist exercised control over - this is the extent of the work.* Outside is the area they probably had less control over - *the context, the culture, the rest of the world.*
A frame separates the work from the not-work.
The frame can be seen as a container, not just for a piece of art, but by extension, an idea, an event or a point of view.
A 'framing device' in a novel or film tops and tails the main content.
A 'frame of reference' is the context an object or idea finds itself in; that which does the framing.
Birth and death frame our lives.
A frame, therefore, generally defines a *limit of agency.*
This is my canvas.
134
120 NEGATIVE SPACE
120
248 ART? YEAH!

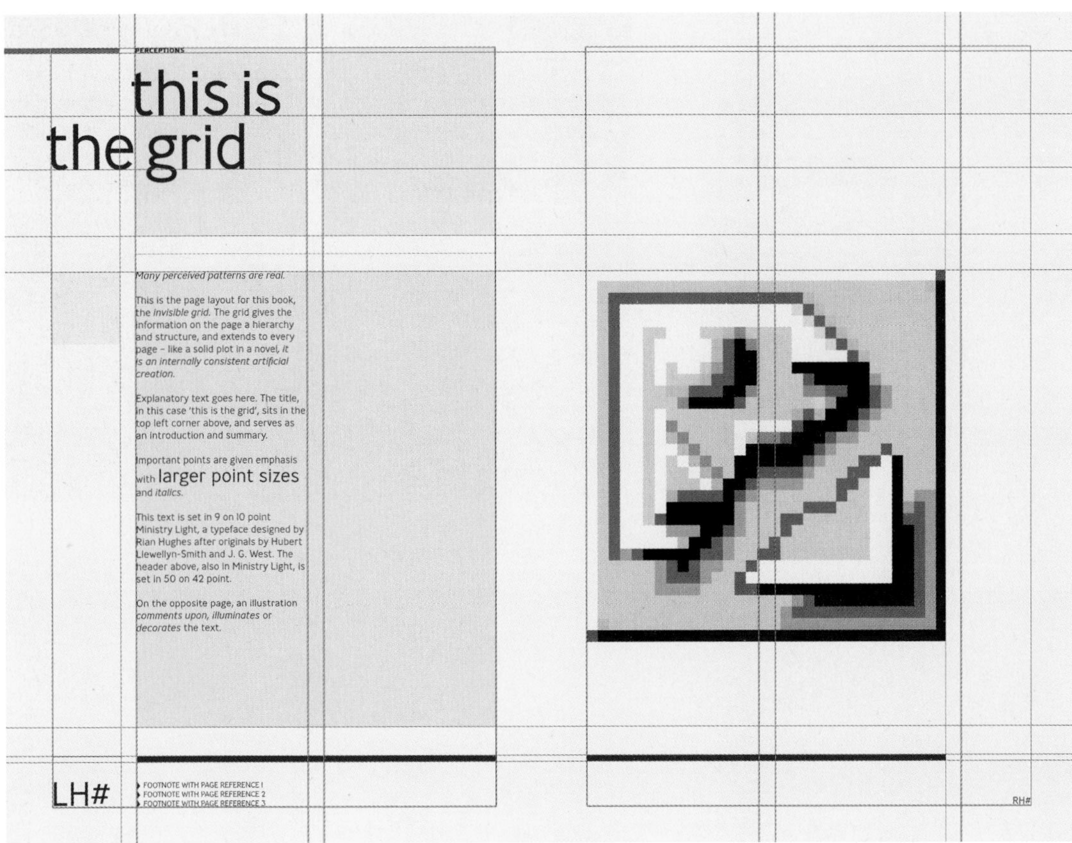

GRID SPECIFICATIONS

Page size (trimmed)	152.4 x 228.6mm
Top margin	9mm
Bottom margin	10mm
Outside margin	12mm
Inside margin	12mm
Number of columns	3
Gutter width	5mm
Extras	N/A

CULT-URE

Design: Rian Hughes at Device

The average person living in today's message-driven environment is continually bombarded with visual ciphers and symbols that must be understood and decoded. With the Internet now providing an ever more powerful means of transporting these messages throughout society, never before has our cultural landscape been in such a constant state of rapidly changing flux. Written and designed by Rian Hughes, *Cult-Ure* is an extended essay in graphic design form, exploring color, symbols, themes, and ideas. Throughout the book the underlying framework and organization of information is analyzed in relation to the overall concept. Hughes also includes highlighted visible grids in order to reveal the hidden structure beneath the organization of material within the book.

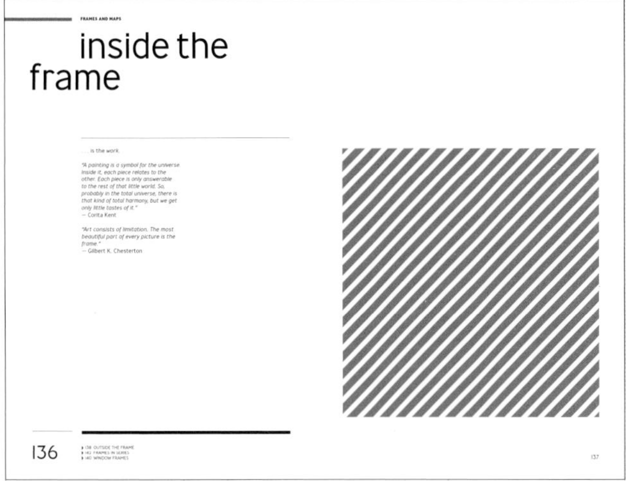
FRAMES AND MAPS
inside the
frame
... is the work
"A painting is a symbol for the universe inside it, each piece relates to the other. Each piece is only answerable to the rest of that little world. So, probably in the total universe, there is that kind of total harmony, but we get only little tastes of it."
— Corita Kent
"Art consists of limitation. The most beautiful part of every picture is the frame."
— Gilbert K. Chesterton
136
138 OUTSIDE THE FRAME
140 WINDOW FRAMES
137

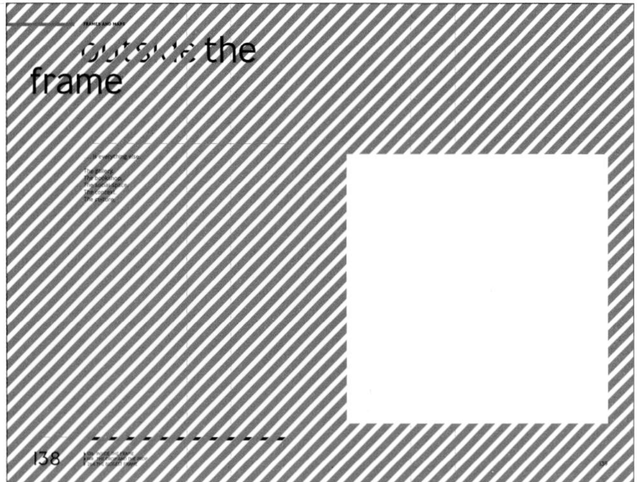
the
frame
138

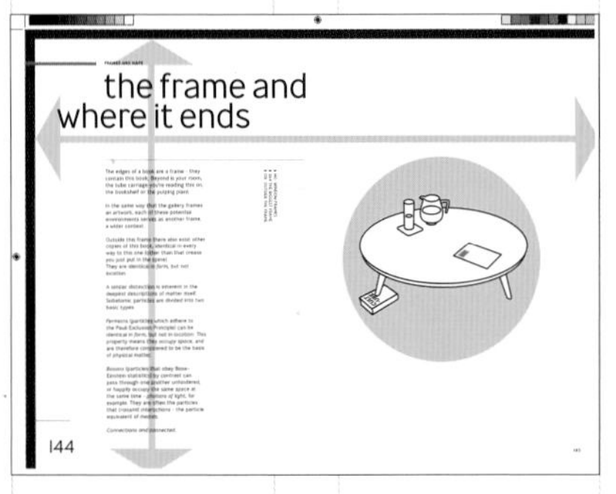
the frame and
where it ends
144

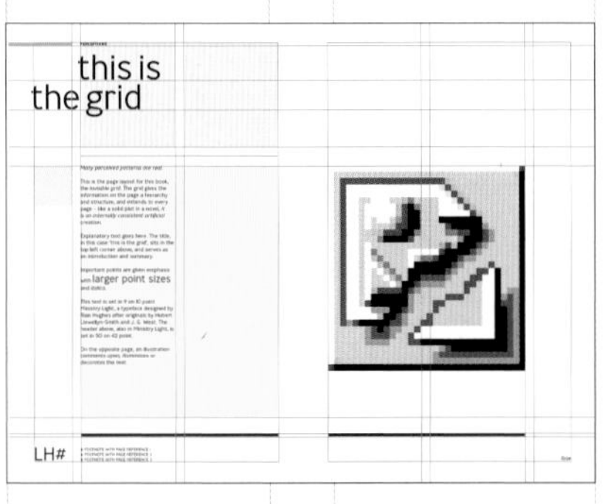
this is
the grid
larger point sizes
LH#

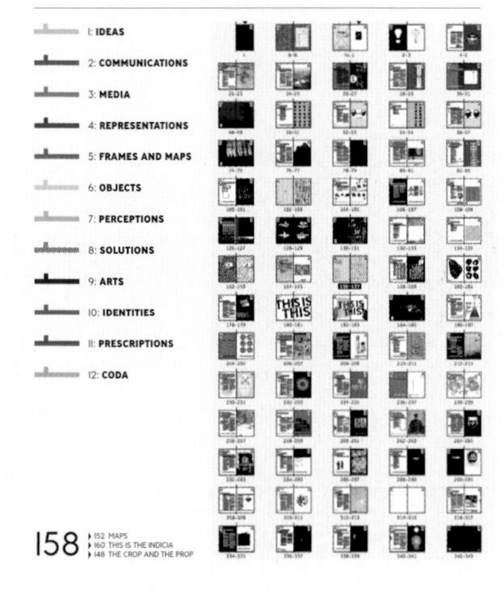
FRAMES AND MAPS
this is the
map of
this book
1: IDEAS
2: COMMUNICATIONS
3: MEDIA
4: REPRESENTATIONS
5: FRAMES AND MAPS
6: OBJECTS
7: PERCEPTIONS
8: SOLUTIONS
9: ARTS
10: IDENTITIES
11: PRESCRIPTIONS
12: CODA
158
152 MAPS
160 THIS IS THE INDICIA
148 THE CROP AND THE PROP

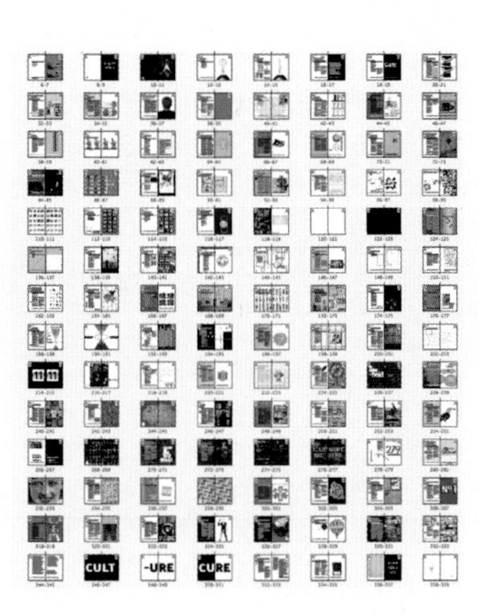
CULT
-URE
CURE

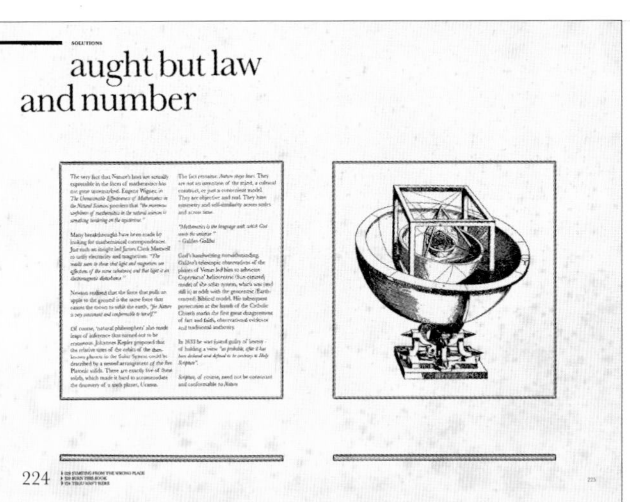
SOLUTIONS

aught but law and number

The very fact that Nature's laws are actually expressible in the form of mathematics has not gone unremarked. Eugene Wigner, in *The Unreasonable Effectiveness of Mathematics in the Natural Sciences* ponders that *"the enormous usefulness of mathematics in the natural sciences is something bordering on the mysterious."*

Many breakthroughs have been made by looking for mathematical correspondences. Just such an insight led James Clerk Maxwell to unify electricity and magnetism: *"The results seem to show that light and magnetism are affections of the same substance, and that light is an electromagnetic disturbance."*

Newton realised that the force that pulls an apple to the ground is the same force that causes the moon to orbit the earth, *"for Nature is very consonant and conformable to herself."*

Of course, 'natural philosophers' also made leaps of inference that turned out to be erroneous. Johannes Kepler proposed that the relative sizes of the orbits of the then-known planets in the Solar System could be described by a nested arrangement of the five Platonic solids. There are exactly five of these solids, which made it hard to accommodate the discovery of a sixth planet, Uranus.

The fact remains: *Nature obeys laws.* They are not an invention of the mind, a cultural construct, or just a convenient model. They are objective and real. They have symmetry and self-similarity across scales and across time.

"Mathematics is the language with which God wrote the universe."
– Galileo Galilei

God's handwriting notwithstanding, Galileo's telescopic observations of the phases of Venus led him to advocate Copernicus' heliocentric (Sun-centred) model of the solar system, which was (and still is) at odds with the geocentric (Earth-centred) Biblical model. His subsequent persecution at the hands of the Catholic Church marks the first great disagreement of fact and faith, observational evidence and traditional authority.

In 1633 he was found guilty of heresy – of holding a view *"as probable, after it has been declared and defined to be contrary to Holy Scripture"*.

Scripture, of course, need not be consonant and conformable to Nature.

224

225

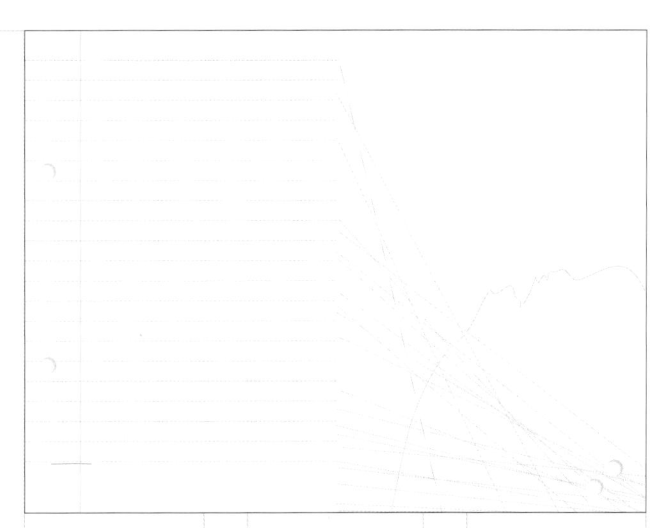

PRESCRIPTIONS

a democracy of ideas

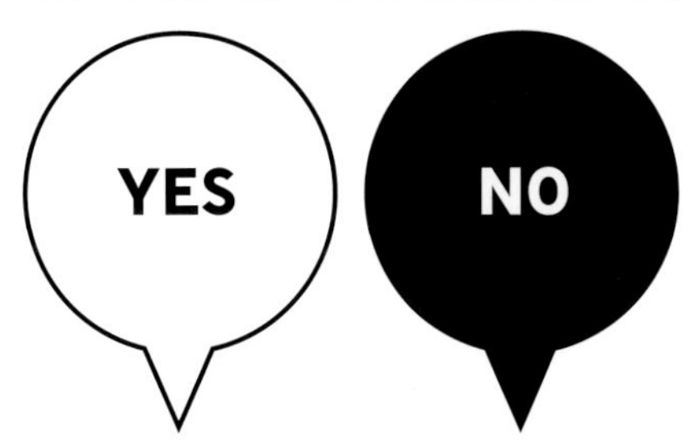

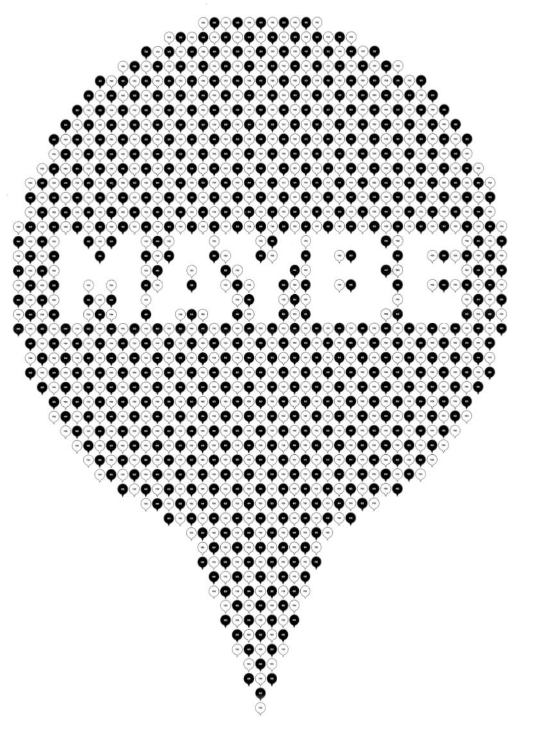

330

▸ 324 ORDER, ORDER
▸ 332 THE THIN FORMICA VENEER OF CIVILISATION
▸ 258 SELL ME A DREAM, SHOW ME A WAY TO BE

331

6

A New Style: American Design at Mid-Century 1950–1959

'Modern businessmen have come to recognize that design can and should be used to express the character and identity of business organizations. Design is a function of management, both within an industry and the world outside it. Industry is the institution that reaches further into our civilization than government and therefore has a greater opportunity and responsibility to influence the quality of life.'

Herbert Bayer quoted in *A Tribute to Herbert Bayer*, 1979

THE AMERICAN SCENE

The American economy continued to boom in the 1950s. Despite the 'police action' in Korea, Americans generally knew peace, prosperity and conformity in this decade. The nation had a certain naïvety, a simple and optimistic approach to life which preceded the turbulent changes to come in the 1960s. It was the calm before the storm. Improved mass-market technology made television sets affordable for many more people and brought advertising for a vast range of products straight into people's homes. Strikingly different product forms became available. The critic Thomas Hine referred to the 1950s as a time when 'everything from a T-bird to a toaster took on a shape that seemed to lean forward, ready to surge ahead'. It was as if the streamlined Art Deco style of the 1930s had been updated for a new audience. Detroit produced cars with exaggerated tail fins and gleaming chrome.

But despite the bright and shining optimism, the early 1950s were also the era of the McCarthy Communist witch hunts, the beginning of a deep dissent in the land – a conflict between liberalism and xenophobic conservatism. Jack Kerouac's book *On The Road* (1957) and Allen Ginsberg's poetry gave voice to the underground counterculture of the Beat Generation. Music lost its squeaky-clean image and became dissonant and more subversive. Art became more expressive and abstract. The definition of art was even challenged by Claes Oldenberg's soft sculptures and Allan Kaprow's 'Happenings'. The art of New York finally eclipsed that of Paris – the Americans had arrived on the scene with a vengeance. The 1950s was the decade that saw the emergence of the painter Jackson Pollock. His work grew out of a dynamic, improvisational Zeitgeist that characterized both the progressive jazz of the time and the writings of the Beat Generation. Socially, the beginnings of the civil rights movement happened in 1950 as Rosa Parks sparked the bus boycott in Montgomery, Alabama. Signs of deep change were on the horizon as Americans basked in the postwar optimism while they cruised around the new suburbs in their gas-guzzling cars with huge fins on each rear fender.

Opposite top *Portfolio* magazine was a major professional achievement for Alexey Brodovitch. In this experimental arts publication he was able to combine optimum editorial and design quality. This two-page spread from 1951 presented an article on the painter Jackson Pollock. Scale contrast in the photography plus the understated typography combines to create a layout of great elegance.

Opposite bottom Advertising designer Robert Gage worked for Doyle Dane Bernbach, Inc. He produced this ad for the New York rye bread company, Levy's. A whole series of similar ads followed, appearing even as late as 1967. These ads represented the simple, direct, humorous and sometimes controversial approach to print advertising that was common in the 1950s.

136

ADVERTISING IN THE 1950S

By the late 1940s and early 1950s, an increasing consciousness about graphic design and designers was evident because Modernism became more visible on the creative scene. Design became a more dominant force in the corporations and in the advertising business. An important debate occurred between typographic purists and those who believed in excitement and experimentation. The most effective examples of design in the 1950s were able to mediate these differences, excite their readers and be legible. In advertisements, copy was shorter, headlines more brief, and text functioned to support the illustration. Photography, both colour and black-and-white, was the dominant medium of advertising illustration. Creativity was the big word in this decade, especially in advertising. Towards the end of the 1950s, at a New York Art Directors Club conference, keynote speakers stated that designers were now moving away from being just layout men to assuming creative responsibility for the whole job. Many designers opened their own businesses; companies specializing just in graphic design. In corporations, the title 'graphic design' finally meant something. Those who practised this

A New Style: American Design at Mid-Century 1950–1959 137

Contents
1
The Basis for the New: The Cradle of Modernism
1850–1899
7
2
A New World Forming: The Impact of Modernism
1900–1919
15
3
American Design in Transition: Traditional to Modernism
1920–1929
33
4
Into the Design Scene: Modernism Arrives in America
1930–1939
47
5
At War and After: The Creative Forties in America
1940–1949
83
6
A New Style: American Design at Mid-Century
1950–1959
135
7
Design Since Mid-Century: Diversity and Contradiction
1960–1999
157
BAZAAR

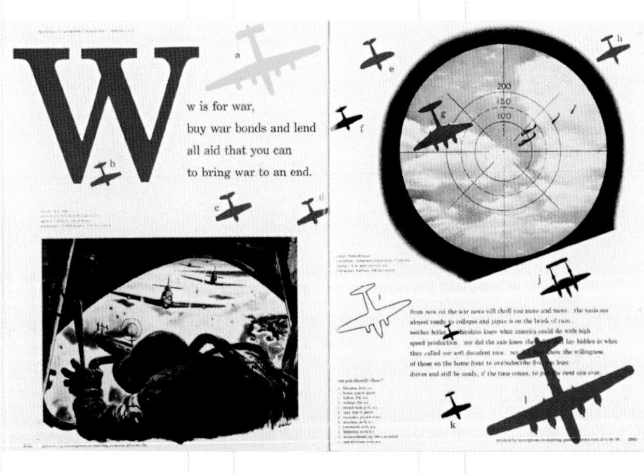

w is for war,
buy war bonds and lend
all aid that you can
to bring war to an end.

6

A New Style: American Design at Mid-Century 1950–1959

'Modern businessmen have come to recognize that design can and should be used to express the character and identity of business organizations. Design is a function of management, both within an industry and the world outside it. Industry is the institution that reaches further into our civilization than government and therefore has a greater opportunity and responsibility to influence the quality of life.'

Herbert Bayer quoted in *A Tribute to Herbert Bayer*, 1979

THE AMERICAN SCENE

The American economy continued to boom in the 1950s. Despite the 'police action' in Korea, Americans generally knew peace, prosperity and conformity in this decade. The nation had a certain naivety, a simple and optimistic approach to life which preceded the turbulent changes to come in the 1960s. It was the calm before the storm. Improved mass-market technology made television sets affordable for many more people and brought advertising for a vast range of products straight into people's homes. Strikingly different product forms became available. The critic Thomas Hine referred to the 1950s as a time when 'everything from a T-bird to a toaster took on a shape that seemed to lean forward, ready to surge ahead'. It was as if the streamlined Art Deco style of the 1930s had been updated for a new audience. Detroit produced cars with exaggerated tail fins and gleaming chrome.

But despite the bright and shining optimism, the early 1950s were also the era of the McCarthy Communist witch hunts, the beginning of a deep dissent in the land – a conflict between liberalism and xenophobic conservatism. Jack Kerouac's book *On The Road* (1957) and Allen Ginsberg's poetry gave voice to the underground counterculture of the Beat Generation. Music lost its squeaky-clean image and became dissonant and more subversive. Art became more expressive and abstract. The definition of art was even challenged by Claes Oldenberg's soft sculptures and Allan Kaprow's 'Happenings'. The art of New York finally eclipsed that of Paris – the Americans had arrived on the scene with a vengeance. The 1950s was the decade that saw the emergence of the painter Jackson Pollock. His work grew out of a dynamic, improvisational Zeitgeist that characterized both the progressive jazz of the time and the writings of the Beat Generation. Socially, the beginnings of the civil rights movement happened in 1950 as Rosa Parks sparked the bus boycott in Montgomery, Alabama. Signs of deep change were on the horizon as Americans basked in the postwar optimism while they cruised around the new suburbs in their gas-guzzling cars with huge fins on each rear fender.

Opposite top *Portfolio* magazine was a major professional achievement for Alexey Brodovitch. In this experimental arts publication he was able to combine optimum editorial and design quality. This two-page spread from 1951 presented an article on the painter Jackson Pollock. Scale contrast in the photography plus the understated typography combines to create a layout of great elegance.

Opposite bottom Advertising designer Robert Gage worked for Doyle Dane Bernbach, Inc. He produced this ad for the New York rye bread company, Levy's. A whole series of similar ads followed, appearing even as late as 1967. These ads represented the simple, direct, humorous and sometimes controversial approach to print advertising that was common in the 1950s.

136

JACKSON POLLOCK

ADVERTISING IN THE 1950s

By the late 1940s and early 1950s, an increasing consciousness about graphic design and designers was evident because Modernism became more visible on the creative scene. Design became a more dominant force in the corporations and in the advertising business. An important debate occurred between typographic purists and those who believed in excitement and experimentation. The most effective examples of design in the 1950s were able to mediate these differences, excite their readers and be legible. In advertisements, copy was shorter, headlines more brief, and text functioned to support the illustration. Photography, both colour and black-and-white, was the dominant medium of advertising illustration. Creativity was the big word in this decade, especially in advertising. Towards the end of the 1950s, at a New York Art Directors Club conference, keynote speakers stated that designers were now moving away from being just layout men to assuming creative responsibility for the whole job. Many designers opened their own businesses: companies specializing just in graphic design. In corporations, the title 'graphic design' finally meant something. Those who practised this

You don't have
to be Jewish
to love Levy's
real Jewish Rye

A New Style: American Design at Mid-Century 1950–1959 137

AMERICAN MODERNISM: GRAPHIC DESIGN 1920 TO 1960

Design: Brad Yendle at Design Typography

The design for this book needed to be anonymous and discrete. Many of the designers included now have iconic status—Lester Beall, Alexey Brodovitch, Lou Dorfsman, Paul Rand, Ladislav Sutnar, and Massimo Vignelli—and their work is often extremely bold and strong. The book explores the extraordinary influence that European émigrés had on American design. Appropriately, designer Brad Yendle used two complementary fonts, one designed by a German—Futura—and the other by an American—New Caledonia. Referring to Jost Hochuli's work as a book designer, Yendle developed a six-column grid. By combining these small columns in different configurations, the text, captions, and images are easily accommodated.

GRID SPECIFICATIONS	
Page size (trimmed)	280 x 215mm
Top margin	23mm
Bottom margin	27.5mm
Outside margin	15mm
Inside margin	16mm
Number of columns	6
Gutter width	4mm
Extras	Baseline grid, 15.5pt starting at 23mm

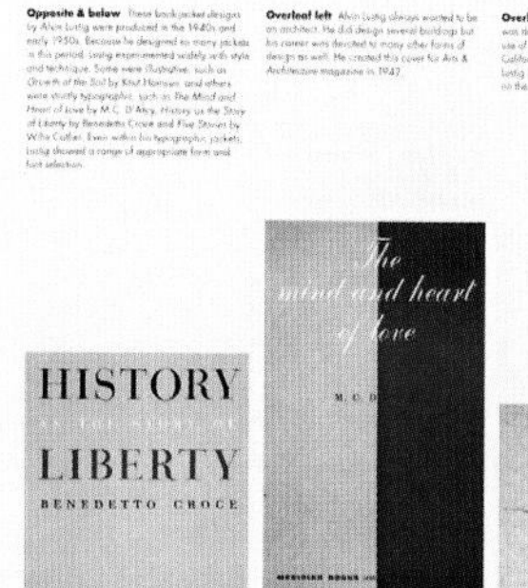

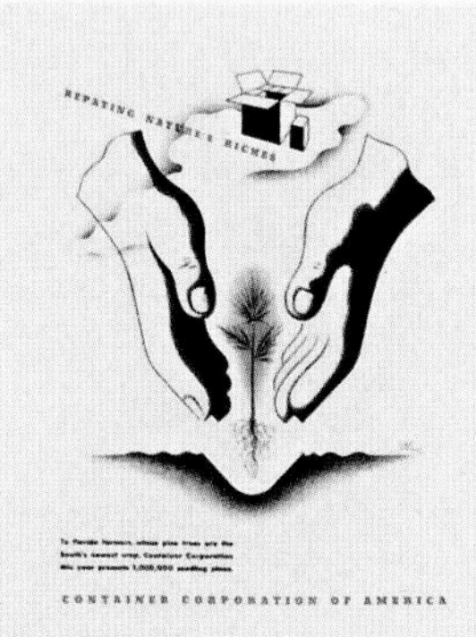

Above left The French poster artist Jean Carlu lived in New York during World War II. He designed many advertisements and posters on behalf of the war effort. This ad for the Container Corporation of America was created in 1942. Entitled 'Repaying America's Riches', it represented the CCA's public service support in presenting one million pine tree seedlings to Florida farmers in terms of understandable imagery.

Above right This ad, designed by Paul Rand, ran in consumer magazines in the United States in 1946. It was the first ad in a long series in which each of the 48 United States was featured. The headline read, 'U.S. 48 States light the road to world peace and commerce'. The ad reflected the post-World War II optimism for peace and prosperity. Rand's visualization was characteristic in the simplified synthesis of illustration with graphic symbolic form.

talent – tenacity, diplomacy and salesmanship. It is no good to create a beautiful layout if disintegration sets in at any one of the important points of production.'[7] In the postwar period, with the economy moving again, more and more Modernist designers were active in producing imaginative advertisements and receiving recognition for bringing fresh, design-oriented solutions to the world of marketing.

GRAPHIC DESIGN ACROSS AMERICA

Two prominent designers, Paul Rand and Bradbury Thompson, emerged during the war and made major contributions to the new direction in American graphic design. They shared an interest in bringing the formal ideas of the European avant-garde into their work at the same time as being firmly grounded in the realities of the American business scene.

Rand, a native New Yorker, worked through the 1940s at the Weintraub Advertising Agency, designing outstanding campaigns for Orbachs, Stafford Fabrics, Disney Hats and others. His covers for *Direction* magazine afforded the opportunity to explore new approaches in form and content interpretation. The covers show Rand's unique understanding of perceptual values, his

Above left Montana was the birth state of E. McKnight Kauffer. He had spent most of his career in England but participated in the Container Corporation of America's 48 States campaign with this ad for his home state in 1944. The CCA ad campaign featured a prominent artist or illustrator from each of the 48 states.

Above right Fernand Léger was a famous French artist who waited out World War II in New York. While he was in the U.S., art directors such as Charles Coiner asked Léger to produce work for Container Corporation of America's ad campaigns. This ad, from 1941, emphasized the fact that the CCA organization was a full-service packaging business. Léger also designed covers for *Fortune* magazine.

Overleaf Between 1947 and 1949, Paul Rand designed a series of ads for Disney Hats. In the campaign, each ad was different but was composed of similar elements, namely a hat, the outline of a figure, the company seal and the copy. This series showed Rand's ingenuity at presenting a visually uninteresting product line with creativity and visual interest.

104

At War and After: The Creative Forties in America 1940 – 1949

105

I FUTURISTI PER FIUME ITALIANA

FUTURISTI CONTRO OGNI REAZIONE

FIUMANIZZIAMO L'ITALIA

Alle ore 21 del Giorno 4 novembre adunatevi tutti in Piazza Colonna

Novembre 1920

F. T. Marinetti Mario Carli Mino Somenzi

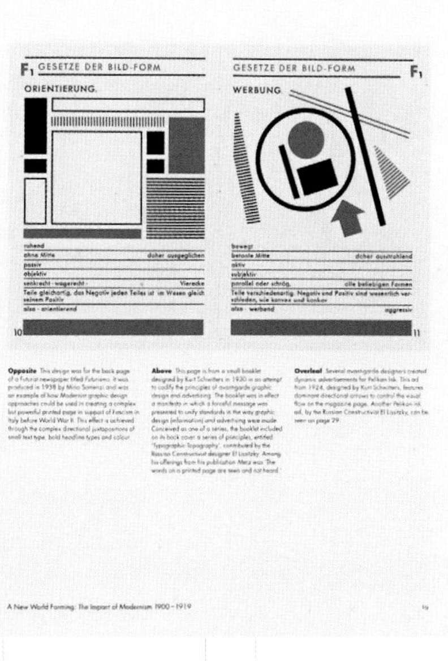
F1 GESETZE DER BILD-FORM

ORIENTIERUNG.

ruhend	
ohne Mitte	daher ausgeglichen
passiv	
objektiv	
senkrecht · wagerecht ·	Vierecke
Teile gleichartig, das Negativ jeden Teiles ist im Wesen gleich seinem Positiv	
also · orientierend	

10

GESETZE DER BILD-FORM F1

WERBUNG.

bewegt	
betonte Mitte	daher ausstrahlend
aktiv	
subjektiv	
parallel oder schräg,	alle beliebigen Formen
Teile verschiedenartig. Negativ und Positiv sind wesentlich verschieden, wie konvex und konkav	
also · werbend	aggressiv

11

Opposite This design was for the back page of a Futurist newspaper titled *Futurismo*. It was produced in 1938 by Mino Somenzi and was an example of how Modernist graphic design approaches could be used in creating a complex but powerful printed page in support of Fascism in Italy before World War II. This effect is achieved through the complex directional juxtapositions of small text type, bold headline types and colour.

Above This page is from a small booklet designed by Kurt Schwitters in 1930 in an attempt to codify the principles of avantgarde graphic design and advertising. The booklet was in effect a manifesto in which a forceful message was presented to unify standards in the way graphic design (information) and advertising were made. Conceived as one of a series, the booklet included on its back cover a series of principles, entitled 'Typographic Topography', contributed by the Russian Constructivist designer El Lissitzky. Among his offerings from his publication *Merz* was 'The words on a printed page are seen and not heard.'

Overleaf Several avantgarde designers created dynamic advertisements for Pelikan Ink. This ad from 1924, designed by Kurt Schwitters, features dominant directional arrows to control the visual flow on the magazine page. Another Pelikan ink ad, by the Russian Constructivist El Lissitzky, can be seen on page 29.

A New World Forming: The Impact of Modernism 1900–1919

BATES BROS
BUILDING

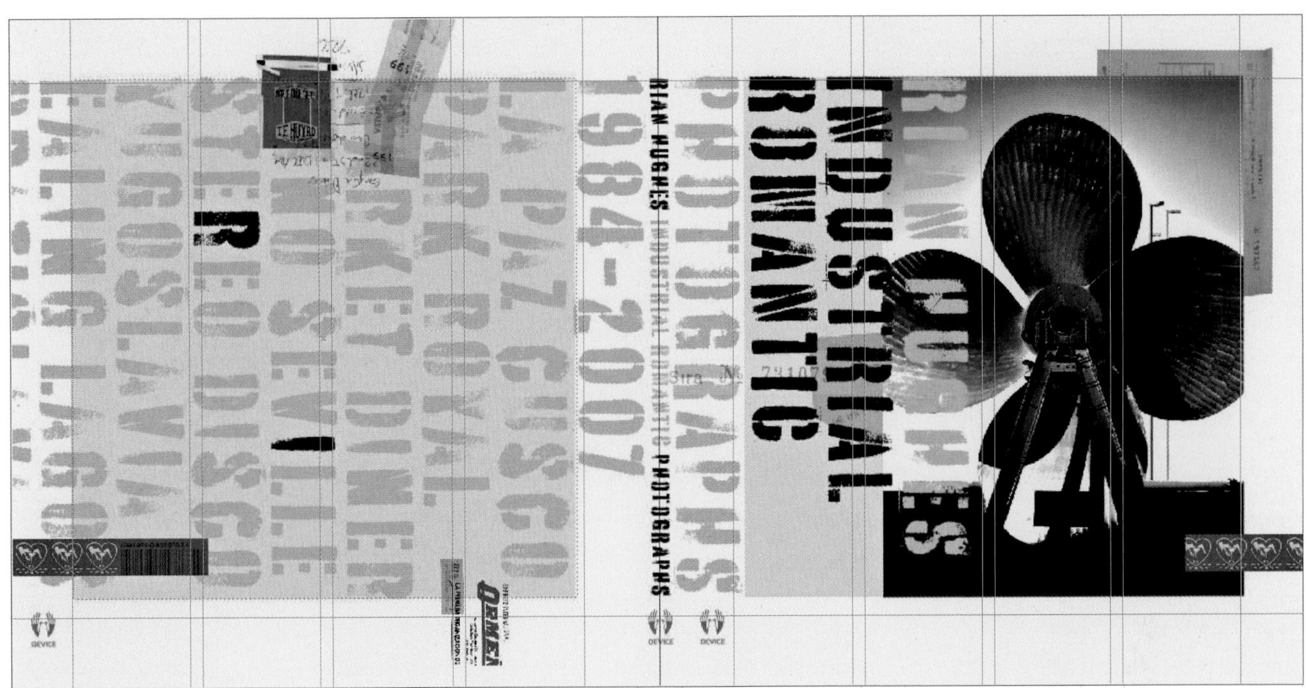

GRID SPECIFICATIONS

Page size (trimmed)	260 x 260mm
Top margin	25mm
Bottom margin	27mm
Outside margin	25mm
Inside margin	30mm
Number of columns	4
Gutter width	5mm
Extras	N/A

INDUSTRIAL ROMANTIC

Design: Rian Hughes at Device

Rian Hughes is best known as an illustrator, and a graphic and font designer, but this book focuses on his photographs. It was a challenge to develop a system that would accommodate images with such a variation in size and proportion. Hughes decided to use a square format for the book, which he found sensitive to both portrait and landscape images. His four-column grid had to be used flexibly. Hughes consistently aligned three sides of his photographs with the grid, but allowed one edge to break it, determined by the best crop and scale for that particular shot. He selected the images for each spread based on their relative size as well as their subject matter. The layout is then disrupted by the more randomly placed related ephemera.

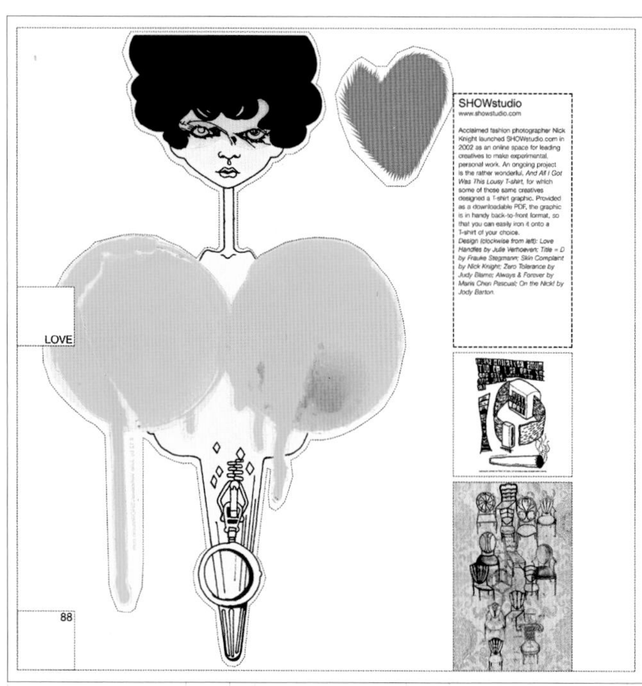

SHOWstudio
www.showstudio.com
Acclaimed fashion photographer Nick Knight launched SHOWstudio.com in 2002 as an online space for leading creatives to make experimental, personal work. An ongoing project is the rather wonderful, *And All I Got Was This Lousy T-shirt*, for which some of those same creatives designed a T-shirt graphic. Provided as a downloadable PDF, the graphic is in handy back-to-front format, so that you can easily iron it onto a T-shirt of your choice.
Design (clockwise from left): Love Handles by Julie Verhoeven; Title = D by Frauke Stegmann; Skin Complaint by Nick Knight; Zero Tolerance by Judy Blame; Always & Forever by Maria Chen Pascual; On the Nick! by Jody Barton.
LOVE
88

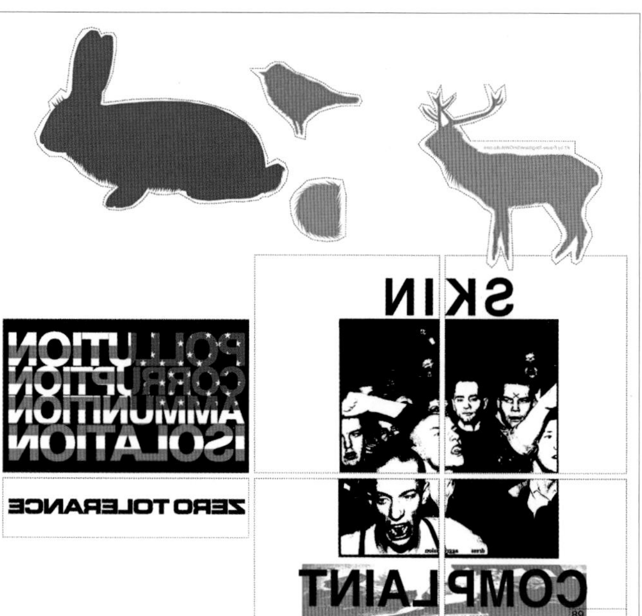

SKIN
POLLUTION
CORRUPTION
AMMUNITION
ISOLATION
ZERO TOLERANCE
COMPLAINT
89

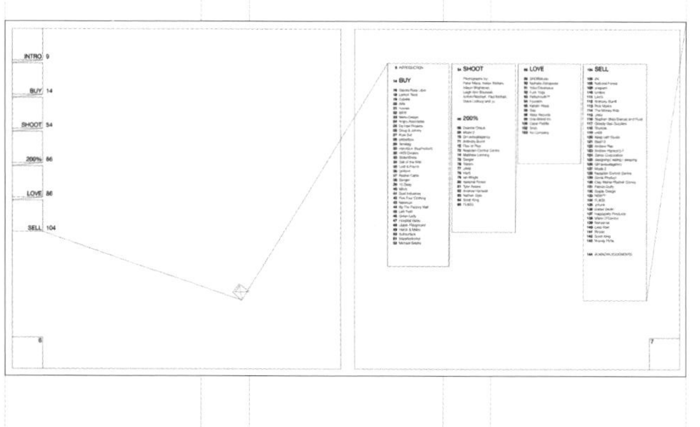

INTRO 9
BUY 14
SHOOT 54
200% 66
LOVE 86
SELL 104

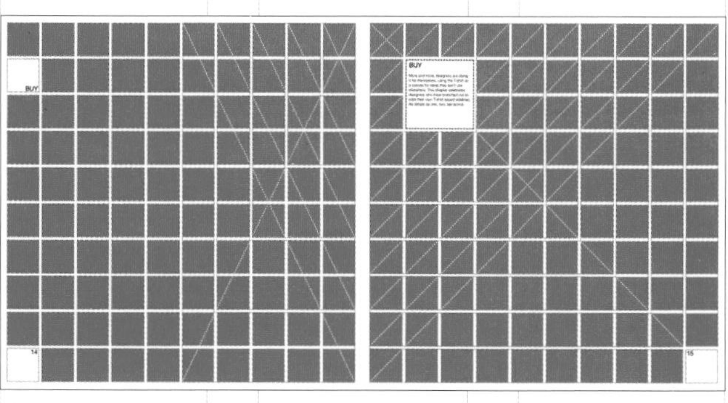

BUY
14
15

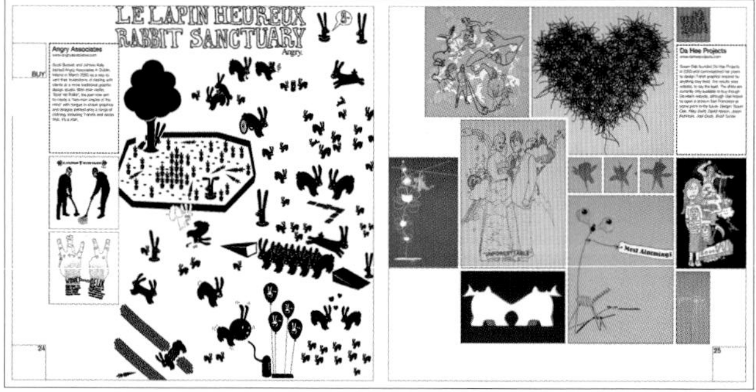

LE LAPIN HEUREUX
RABBIT SANCTUARY
Angry Associates
BUY
Da Hee Projects
24
25

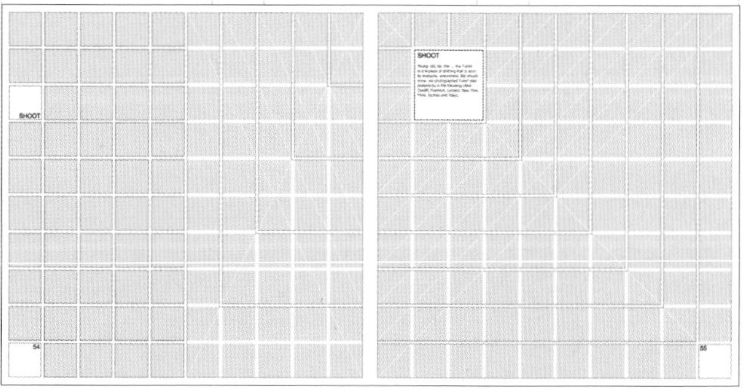

SHOOT
54
55

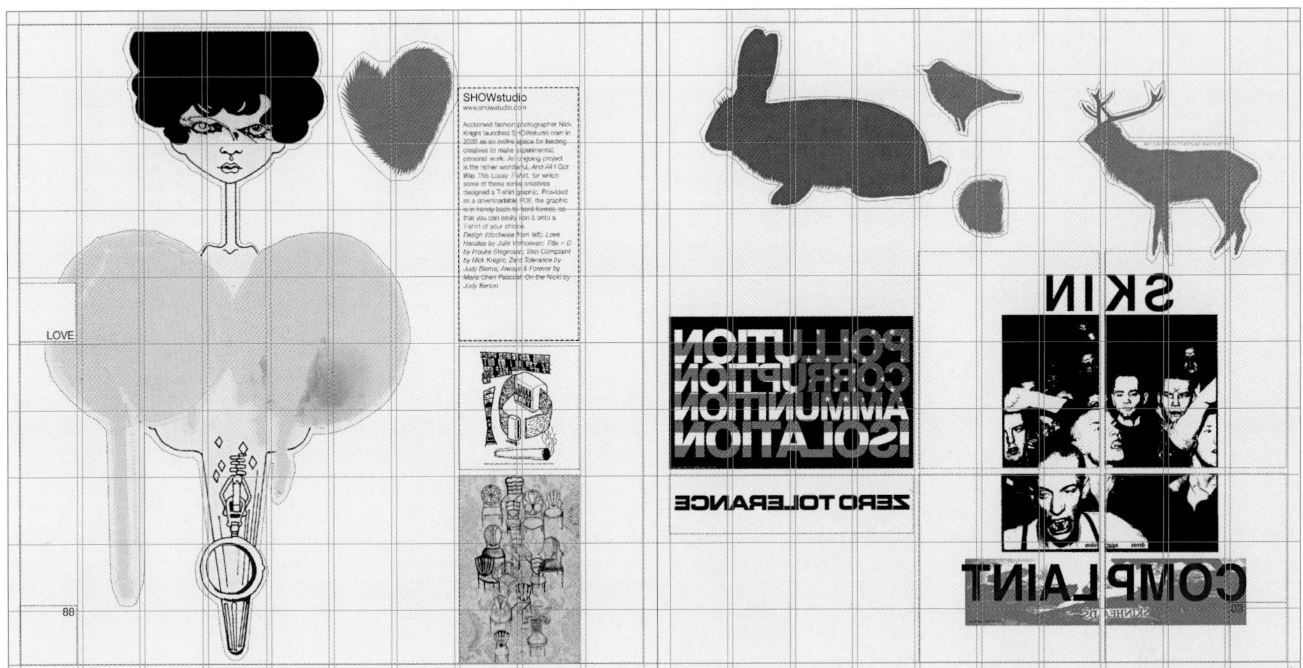

GRID SPECIFICATIONS

Page size (trimmed)	250 x 250mm
Top margin	5mm
Bottom margin	5mm
Outside margin	5mm
Inside margin	5mm
Number of columns	10
Gutter width	2mm
Extras	10 horizontal fields

200% COTTON: NEW T-SHIRT GRAPHICS and 300% COTTON: MORE T-SHIRT GRAPHICS

Design: Agathe Jacquillat and Tomi Vollauschek at Fl@33

These image-based books contain over 1,000 illustrations each. The grid had to be flexible, provide consistency, and make the design process relatively systematic. Designers Agathe Jacquillat and Tomi Vollauschek developed a multicolumn grid with 10 horizontal fields. In *200%* dotted rules form threadlike outlines to frame and connect images and text, foregrounding the grid in a playful way, and making a subtle association with fashion and needlework. The brief for *300%* was to refresh the layout while maintaining the visual identity of the previous title in the series. Jacquillat and Vollauschek chose to exploit the versatility of the grid by introducing diagonals to the layout. The result is a lively reinterpretation of the previously used system.

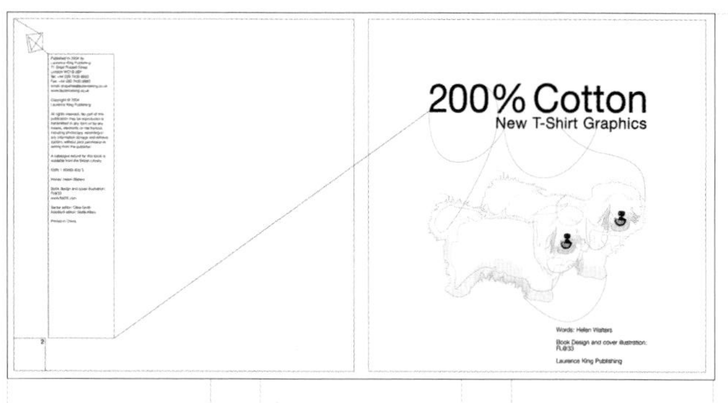
200% Cotton
New T-Shirt Graphics
Words: Hellen Walters
Book Design and cover illustration: FL@33
Laurence King Publishing

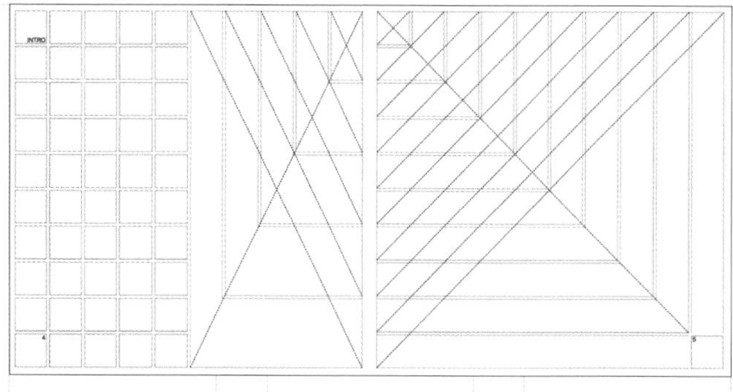

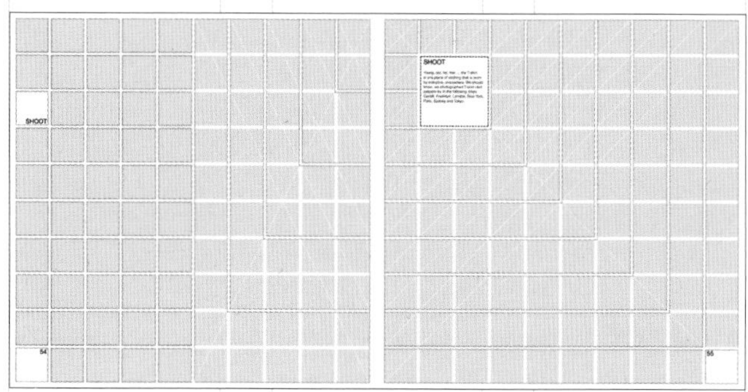

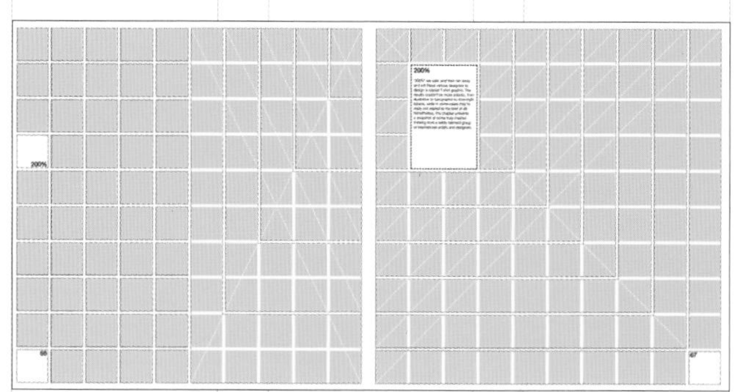

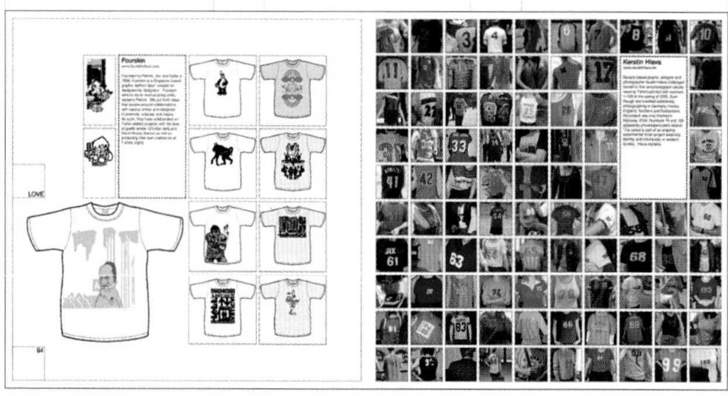

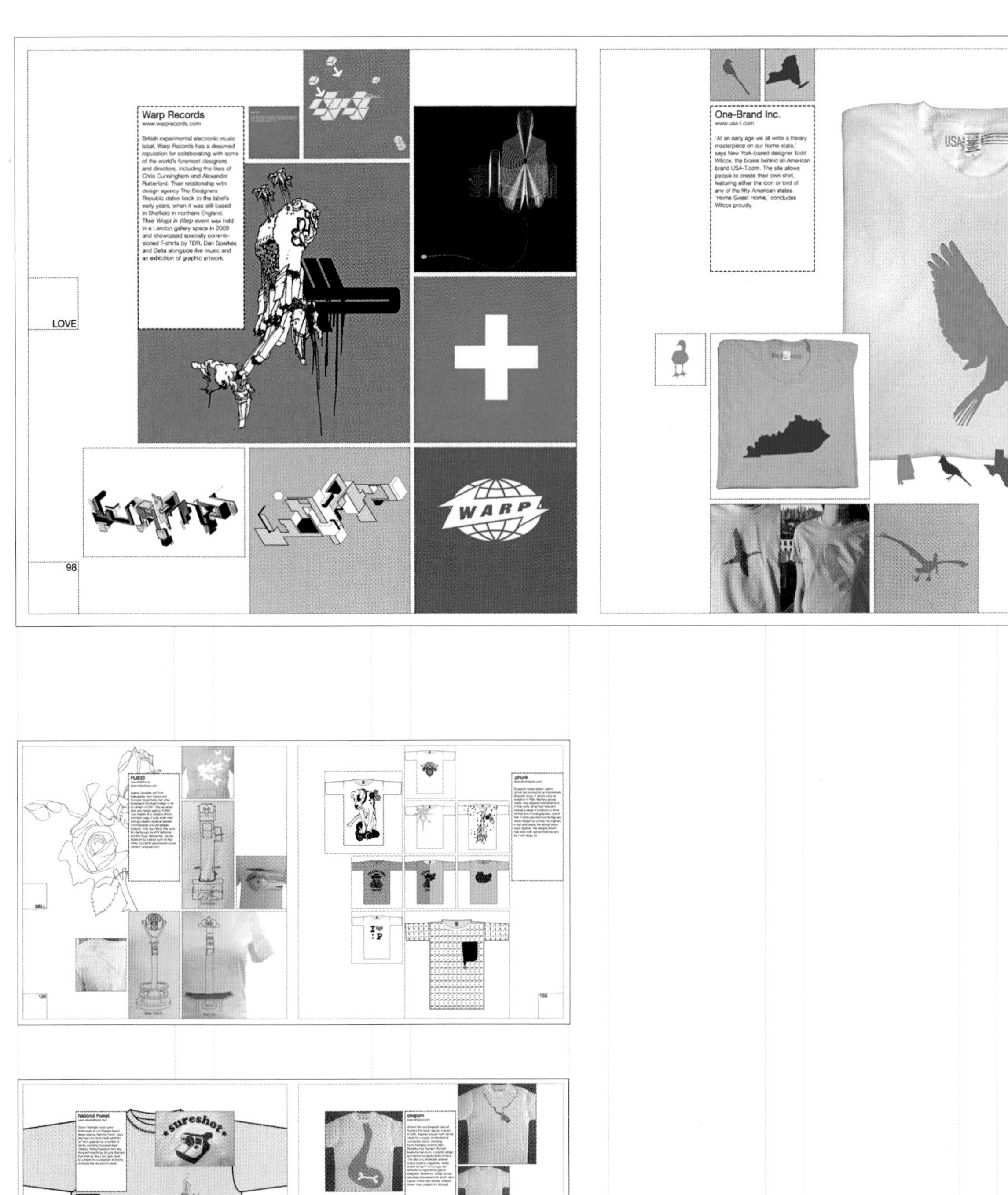

LOVE

Warp Records

www.warprecords.com

British experimental electronic music label, Warp Records has a deserved reputation for collaborating with some of the world's foremost designers and directors, including the likes of Chris Cunningham and Alexander Rutterford. Their relationship with design agency The Designers Republic dates back to the label's early years, when it was still based in Sheffield in northern England. Their *Wrapt in Warp* event was held in a London gallery space in 2003 and showcased specially commissioned T-shirts by TDR, Dan Sparkes and Delta alongside live music and an exhibition of graphic artwork.

98

One-Brand Inc.

www.usa-t.com

'At an early age we all write a literary masterpiece on our home state,' says New York-based designer Todd Wilcox, the brains behind all-American brand USA-T.com. The site allows people to create their own shirt, featuring either the icon or bird of any of the fifty American states. 'Home Sweet Home,' concludes Wilcox proudly.

99

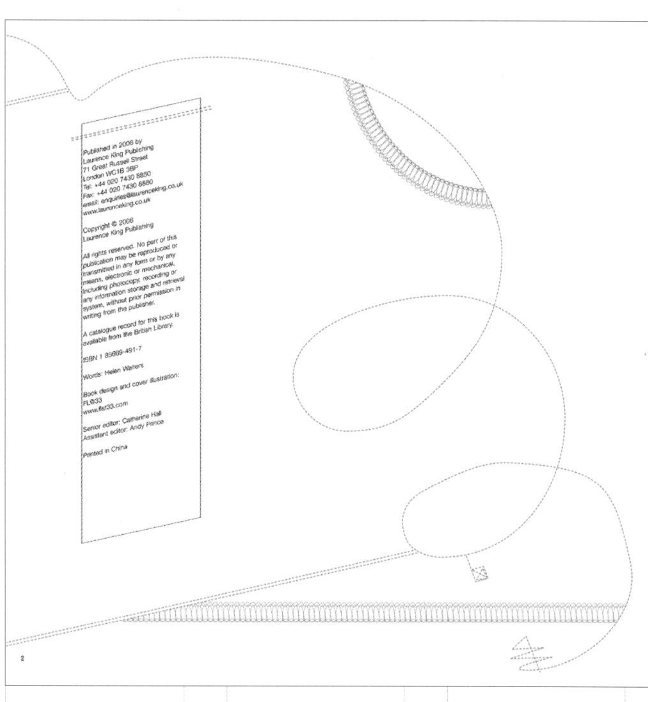
Published in 2006 by
Laurence King Publishing
71 Great Russell Street
London WC1B 3BP
Tel: +44 020 7430 8850
Fax: +44 020 7430 8880
email: enquiries@laurenceking.co.uk
www.laurenceking.co.uk
Copyright © 2006
Laurence King Publishing
All rights reserved. No part of this publication may be reproduced or transmitted in any form or by any means, electronic or mechanical, including photocopy, recording or any information storage and retrieval system, without prior permission in writing from the publisher.
A catalogue record for this book is available from the British Library.
ISBN 1 85669-491-7
Words: Helen Walters
Book design and cover illustration: FL@33
www.flat33.com
Senior editor: Catherine Hall
Assistant editor: Andy Prince
Printed in China
2
300% Cotton
More T-Shirt Graphics
Words: Helen Walters
Book design and cover illustration: FL@33
Laurence King Publishing
3

Intro

The Imaginary Foundation
Future Relic
Happiness is a new idea
Make
Make

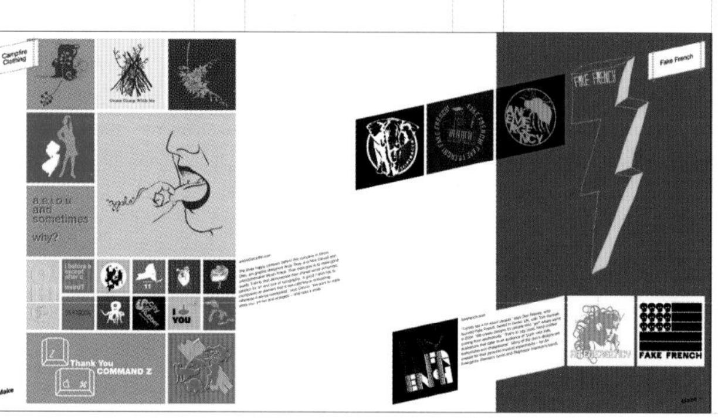
Campfire Clothing
Fake French
and sometimes why?
Thank You COMMAND Z
FAKE FRENCH
Make
Make

Love
Love
Love

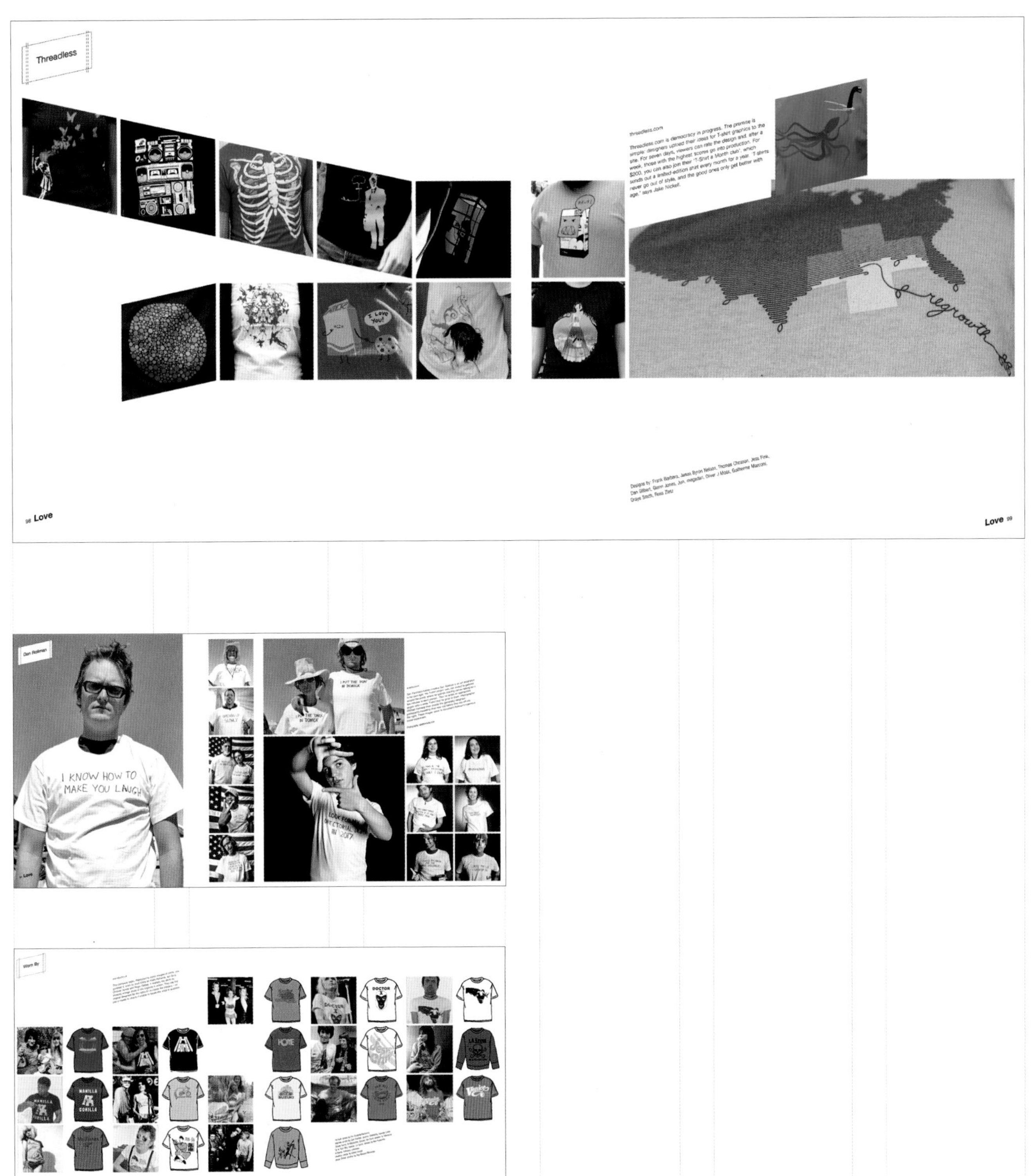
Threadless
threadless.com
Threadless.com is democracy in progress. The premise is simple: designers upload their ideas for T-shirt graphics to the site. For seven days, viewers can rate the design and, after a week, those with the highest scores go into production. For $200, you can also join their 'T-Shirt a Month club', which sends out a limited-edition shirt every month for a year. 'T-shirts never go out of style, and the good ones only get better with age,' says Jake Nickell.
Designs by: Frank Barbara, Jason Byron Nelson, Thomas Chciason, Jess Fink, Dan Gilbert, Glenn Jones, Jun, megadan, Oliver J Moss, Guilherme Marconi, Graye Smith, Ross Zietz
98 Love
Love 99
I KNOW HOW TO MAKE YOU LAUGH
I PUT THE 'FUN' IN DONKUK
LOOK FOR MY DIRECTORIAL DEBUT IN 2017
Worn By
DOCTOR
HOME
LA STENE
MANILLA GORILLA

INTRODUCTION

'Take any form you please and repeat it at regular intervals and, as surely as recurrent sounds give rhythm or cadence, whether you want it or not, you have pattern.'

Lewis F. Day

This book is a collection of a number of contemporary surface patterns created between 2000 and 2005 by designers and artists from many different cultures and backgrounds.

The patterns have been achieved by a number of techniques, which include drawing, painting, collage, embroidery, appliqué, hand dyeing and screen printing. Many of the designs have been digitally manipulated. As this was a project facilitated almost entirely by e-mail and digitalized images, this is not surprising. What has been surprising is the range and variety of initiating ideas, as outlined by the artists themselves. These run from 'Mary Poppins Dissected' to 'The Cornish Seascape' to 'Chaos Theory'! I have included the artists' own comments on their inspiration and content wherever possible.

The patterns themselves have been chosen subjectively by me for their perceived qualities of beauty and balance, their use of colour and overall aesthetic appeal. They have been grouped into families following a contemporary understanding of the traditional surface design categories, and I have also arranged the patterns so that they fall in a definite and, I trust, pleasing colour order within each category.

006

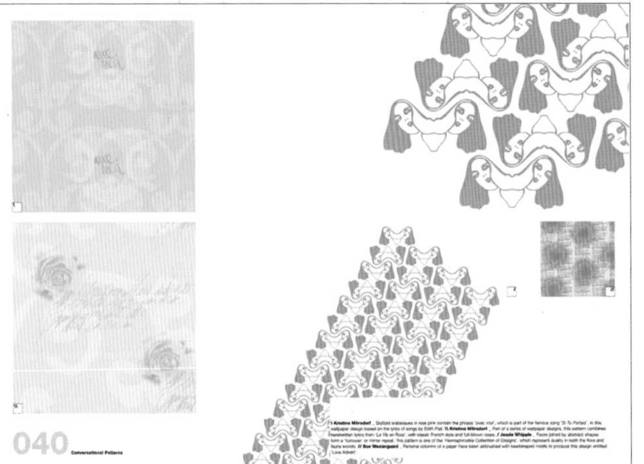

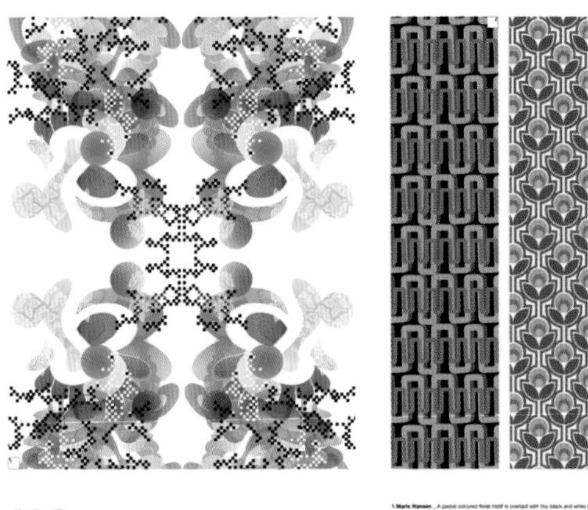

INTRODUCTION

'Take any form you please and repeat it at regular intervals and, as surely as recurrent sounds give rhythm or cadence, whether you want it or not, you have pattern.'

Lewis F. Day

This book is a collection of a number of contemporary surface patterns created between 2000 and 2005 by designers and artists from many different cultures and backgrounds.

The patterns have been achieved by a number of techniques, which include drawing, painting, collage, embroidery, appliqué, hand dyeing and screen printing. Many of the designs have been digitally manipulated. As this was a project facilitated almost entirely by e-mail and digitalized images, this is not surprising. What has been surprising is the range and variety of initiating ideas, as outlined by the artists themselves. These run from 'Mary Poppins Dissected' to 'The Cornish Seascape' to 'Chaos Theory'! I have included the artists' own comments on their inspiration and content wherever possible.

The patterns themselves have been chosen subjectively by me for their perceived qualities of beauty and balance, their use of colour and overall aesthetic appeal. They have been grouped into families following a contemporary understanding of the traditional surface design categories, and I have also arranged the patterns so that they fall in a definite and, I trust, pleasing colour order within each category.

006

PATTERNS: NEW SURFACE DESIGN

Design: Agathe Jacquillat and Tomi Vollauschek at Fl@33

Coming up with a system that would accommodate examples of elaborate and visually rich pattern making sensitively was a challenge for designers Agathe Jacquillat and Tomi Vollauschek. They had little editorial control over the selection or grouping of the images, which was determined by the author. But, their highly flexible grid allowed them to vary the scale and area used for each example to ensure that the visual relationships between patterns were sympathetic, and potential clashes between designs could be avoided. The page is divided into 12 vertical columns and 17 horizontal fields, with a folio, running foot, and caption zone at the bottom of the page.

GRID SPECIFICATIONS	
Page size (trimmed)	170 x 240mm
Top margin	8mm
Bottom margin	16mm
Outside margin	8mm
Inside margin	8mm
Number of columns	12
Gutter width	5mm
Extras	17 horizontal fields

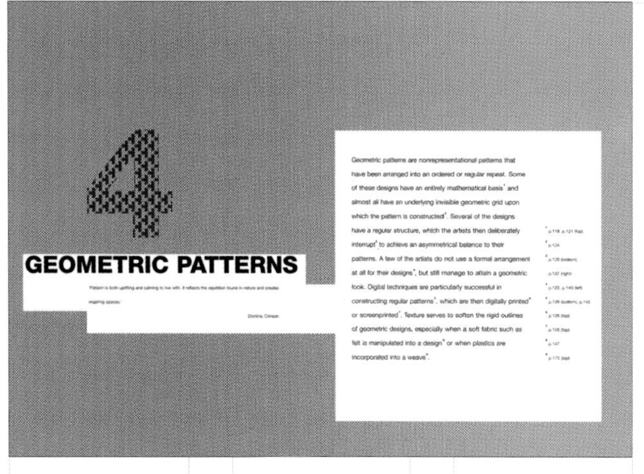
4
GEOMETRIC PATTERNS
Geometric patterns are nonrepresentational patterns that have been arranged into an ordered or regular repeat. Some of these designs have an entirely mathematical basis and almost all have an underlying invisible geometric grid upon which the pattern is constructed. Several of the designs have a regular structure, which the artists then deliberately interrupt to achieve an asymmetrical balance to their patterns. A few of the artists do not use a formal arrangement at all for their designs, but still manage to attain a geometric look. Digital techniques are particularly successful in constructing regular patterns, which are then digitally printed or screenprinted. Texture serves to soften the rigid outlines of geometric designs, especially when a soft fabric such as felt is manipulated into a design or when plastics are incorporated into a weave.

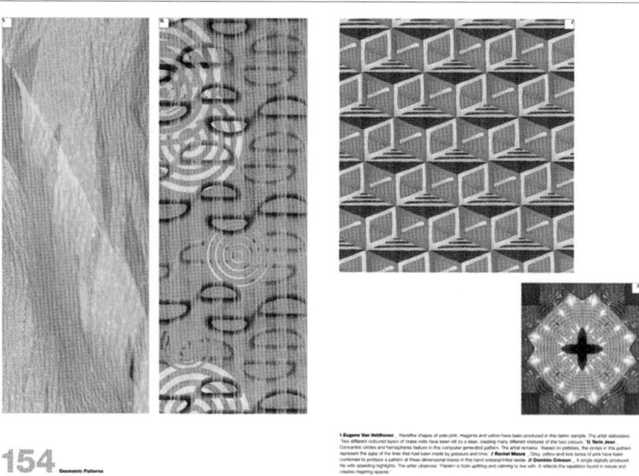
154
Geometric Patterns

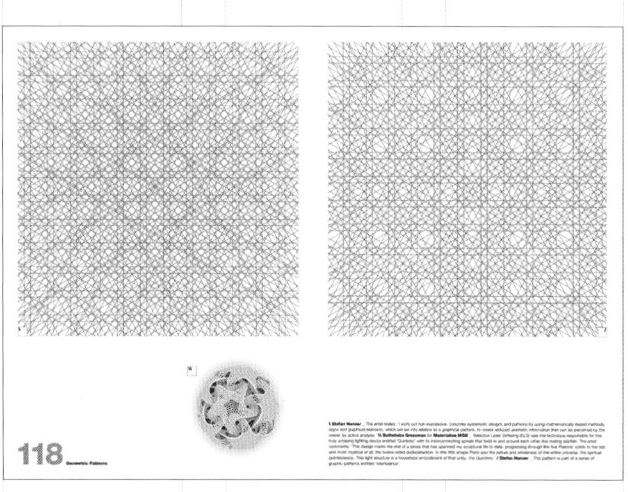
118
Geometric Patterns

168
Geometric Patterns

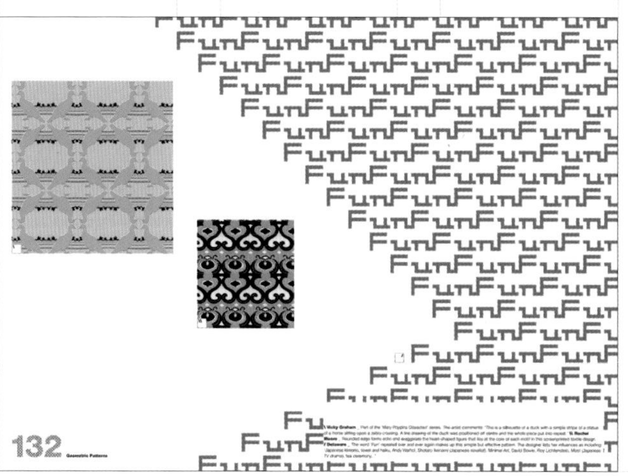
FunFunFunFunFunFunFun
132
Geometric Patterns

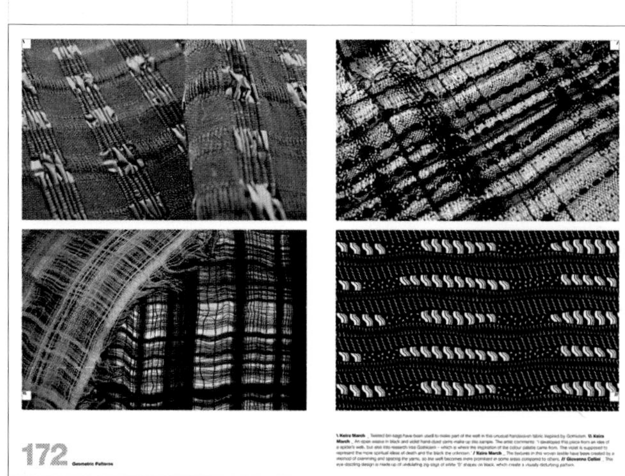
172
Geometric Patterns

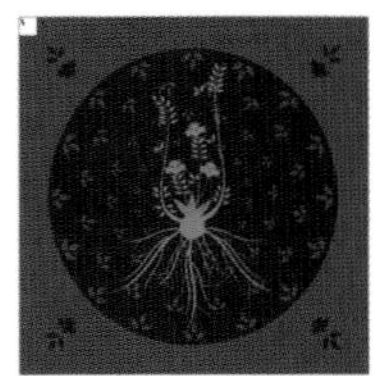

210 Organic Patterns

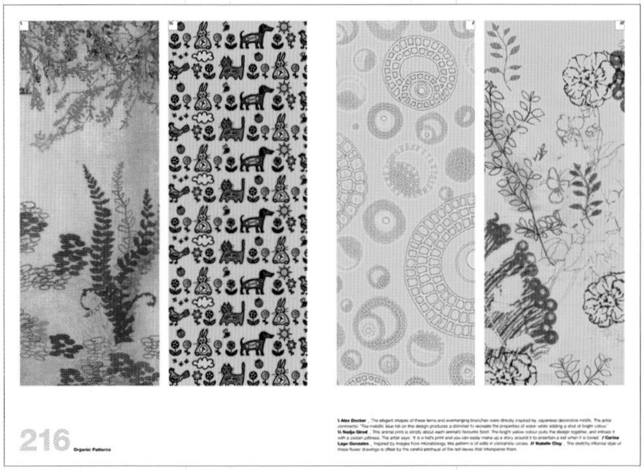

216 Organic Patterns

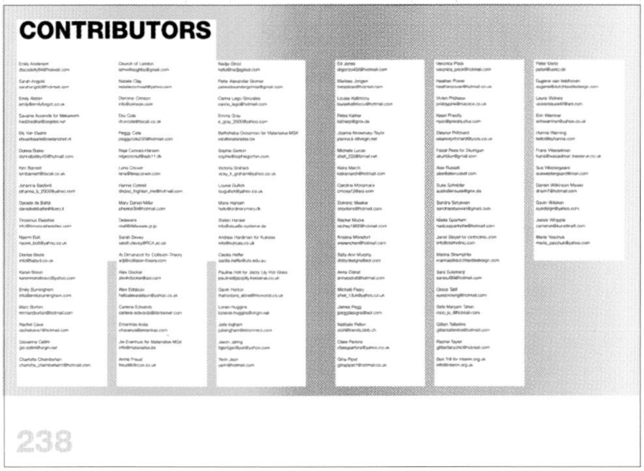

CONTRIBUTORS

238

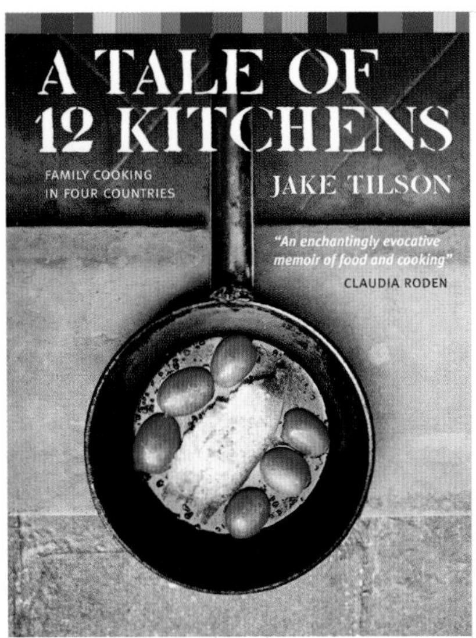

A TALE OF
12 KITCHENS
FAMILY COOKING
IN FOUR COUNTRIES
JAKE TILSON
"An enchantingly evocative memoir of food and cooking"
CLAUDIA RODEN

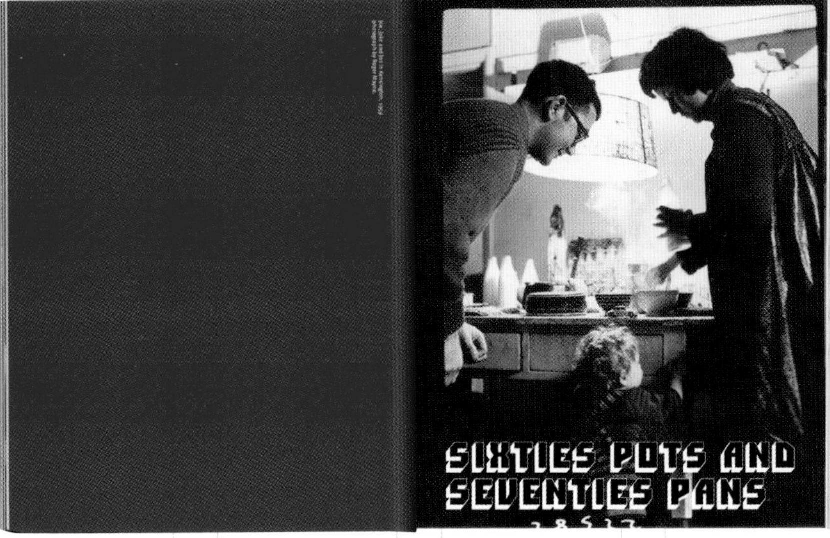

DON'T GO TO ANY TROUBLE BACKSTREET COUSCOUS

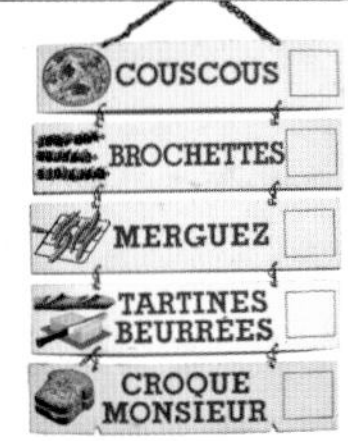

A dish that encourages interpretation and invention. I assemble mine with the assimilated memories of smoke-filled Tunisian restaurants in Paris and three memorable meals in a frenzied visit to Morocco in my youth. In Paris they tend towards the separation of the meat from the stew. This becomes an inspiring triad of tastes and texture – soft, dry couscous grains, crisp roast meat accompanied by the wet vegetable stew. Couscous is the name for both the semolina grain and the dish itself. Serve with roasted meat, chicken, lamb, fish or sausages.
Serves 8

5 carrots, sliced in rounds
5 courgettes, sliced in rounds
3 onions, roughly chopped
3 large cabbage leaves, shredded
3 cups chickpeas, precooked or canned
600ml (1 pint) of chicken stock
3 cloves of garlic, chopped
3 tablespoons of tomato purée and/or 1 400g (14oz), can of tomatoes, finely mashed

spices
1 stick of cinnamon
1 teaspoon ground cumin
1 teaspoon ground coriander
1 teaspoon ground ginger
1 teaspoon freshly ground cumin seeds
10 threads of saffron
15 sprigs of fresh coriander, tied in a bunch
15 sprigs of fresh parsley, tied in a bunch

Vegetable stew – quick method
To achieve a backstreet Parisian-Tunisian style vegetable stew, adopt a nonchalant approach. Put all the ingredients in a large pan, cover with water and simmer for 30 minutes. Done. Serve with couscous grains and roasted or grilled meats.

Variations
You could add harder root vegetables first and softer ones towards the end of cooking for a more consistent bite. Some cooks first fry the spices, onions and garlic until transparent, before adding the remaining ingredients. The key items are carrots, courgettes and chickpeas. Improvise with chicory, shredded cabbage, diced squash or even a stray potato.

Couscous grains
I use a medium wholegrain couscous from our local Iranian store. Barley couscous is also good, with a nutty flavour. I use a quick method for preparing the couscous grains taught to me by a Parisian friend. A medium-grain couscous is easier to cook than fine.
Serves 8

2 cups of medium-grain couscous
salt
saffron (optional)
1 tablespoon butter
30 sultanas for decoration

Put the couscous grains into a bowl with a few strands of saffron and a little salt. Gently pour boiling water onto the couscous until the water just breaks the surface of the grains, do not mix it. Leave to soak for 20 minutes. Melt a knob of butter in a large pan. The bowl of soaked couscous grains will appear to be a solid mass. With a fork gently plough away the top layer of grains off into the hot buttered pan. Slowly loosen off all of the grains into the pan. Heat through, stirring with a flat-ended wooden spoon for a few minutes. You can cover the pan and reheat later.

Heap the cooked couscous in a pyramid on a warmed round plate and dot a ring of sultanas around the edge.

Accompaniment
Any roasted meat or fish forms the final point of the couscous triad. Country chicken (p 82), *agnello scotaditto* without the sage (p 65). Merguez sausages, grilled fish or fried sardines. A leg of lamb rubbed with cumin, coriander and teaspoon of harissa, then roasted on a bed of outer cabbage leaves sprinkled with caraway seeds.
A *couscous royale* in Paris is a mixed platter of chicken, lamb and merguez.

To serve
Transfer the stew to a deep serving bowl with a ladle. Each plate requires a heap of couscous grains, meat and a ladle of vegetable stew. Throughout the meal the couscous grains seem never to diminish on your plate if replenished with enough liquid stew.

GRID SPECIFICATIONS

Page size (trimmed)	250 x 196mm
Top margin	11mm
Bottom margin	11mm
Outside margin	15mm
Inside margin	15mm
Number of columns	6
Gutter width	3mm
Extras	N/A

A TALE OF 12 KITCHENS

Design: Jake Tilson at Jake Tilson Studio

As author, designer, photographer, and cook, every aspect of this book is the creation of passionate cook, and artist, Jake Tilson. It provides a distinctive multisensory perspective on seeing and tasting food, from the way it is grown, packaged, and bought, to how it is cooked and remembered. The underlying structure of the book had to support an evocative memoir and a functional cookery book. The grid divides the page into four equal columns and two narrower columns, plus horizontal fields. Although Tilson's recipe layouts are conventional, eclectic combinations of photos, fonts, and ephemera surround them. His goal was to share how much fun food can be, and to produce a guide for his daughter on the significance of cooking and eating in the life of their family.

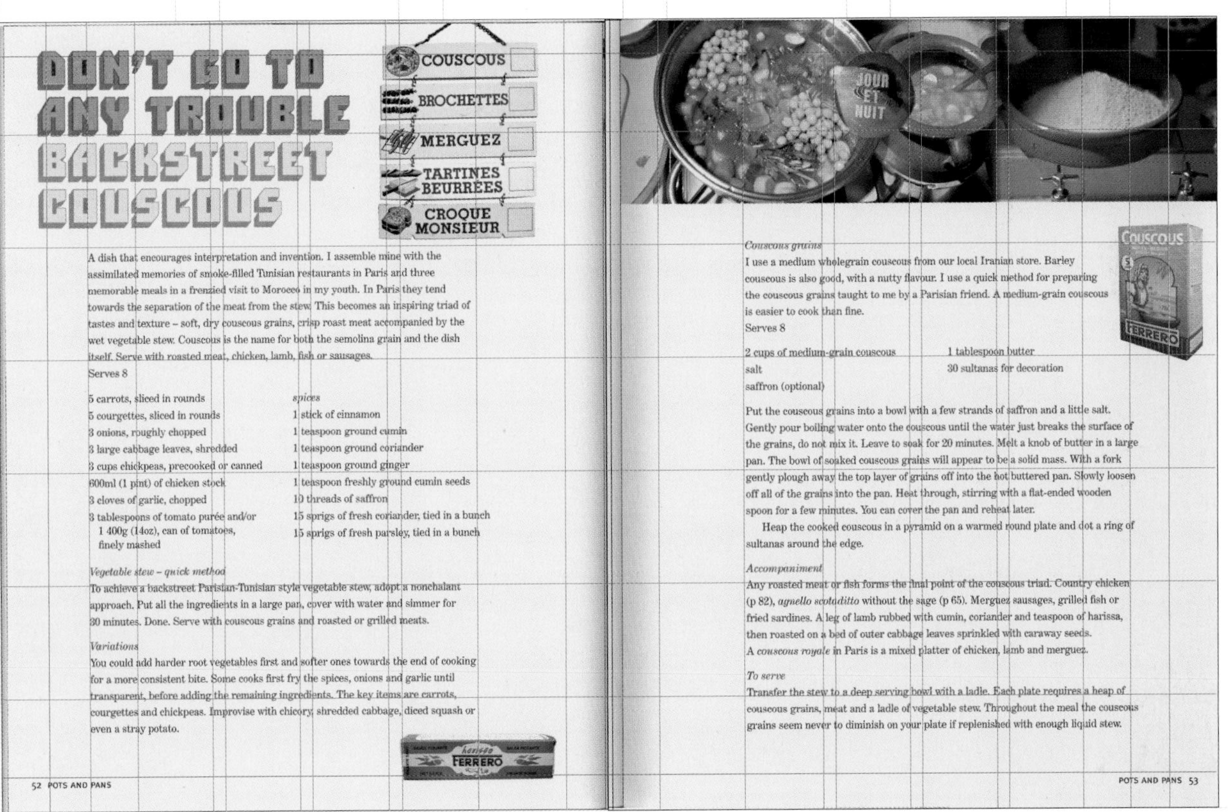

DON'T GO TO ANY TROUBLE BACKSTREET COUSCOUS

A dish that encourages interpretation and invention. I assemble mine with the assimilated memories of smoke-filled Tunisian restaurants in Paris and three memorable meals in a frenzied visit to Morocco in my youth. In Paris they tend towards the separation of the meat from the stew. This becomes an inspiring triad of tastes and texture – soft, dry couscous grains, crisp roast meat accompanied by the wet vegetable stew. Couscous is the name for both the semolina grain and the dish itself. Serve with roasted meat, chicken, lamb, fish or sausages.

Serves 8

5 carrots, sliced in rounds
5 courgettes, sliced in rounds
3 onions, roughly chopped
3 large cabbage leaves, shredded
3 cups chickpeas, precooked or canned
600ml (1 pint) of chicken stock
3 cloves of garlic, chopped
3 tablespoons of tomato purée and/or 1 400g (14oz), can of tomatoes, finely mashed

spices
1 stick of cinnamon
1 teaspoon ground cumin
1 teaspoon ground coriander
1 teaspoon ground ginger
1 teaspoon freshly ground cumin seeds
10 threads of saffron
15 sprigs of fresh coriander, tied in a bunch
15 sprigs of fresh parsley, tied in a bunch

Vegetable stew – quick method
To achieve a backstreet Parisian-Tunisian style vegetable stew, adopt a nonchalant approach. Put all the ingredients in a large pan, cover with water and simmer for 30 minutes. Done. Serve with couscous grains and roasted or grilled meats.

Variations
You could add harder root vegetables first and softer ones towards the end of cooking for a more consistent bite. Some cooks first fry the spices, onions and garlic until transparent, before adding the remaining ingredients. The key items are carrots, courgettes and chickpeas. Improvise with chicory, shredded cabbage, diced squash or even a stray potato.

52 POTS AND PANS

Couscous grains
I use a medium wholegrain couscous from our local Iranian store. Barley couscous is also good, with a nutty flavour. I use a quick method for preparing the couscous grains taught to me by a Parisian friend. A medium-grain couscous is easier to cook than fine.
Serves 8

2 cups of medium-grain couscous
salt
saffron (optional)
1 tablespoon butter
30 sultanas for decoration

Put the couscous grains into a bowl with a few strands of saffron and a little salt. Gently pour boiling water onto the couscous until the water just breaks the surface of the grains, do not mix it. Leave to soak for 20 minutes. Melt a knob of butter in a large pan. The bowl of soaked couscous grains will appear to be a solid mass. With a fork gently plough away the top layer of grains off into the hot buttered pan. Slowly loosen off all of the grains into the pan. Heat through, stirring with a flat-ended wooden spoon for a few minutes. You can cover the pan and reheat later.

Heap the cooked couscous in a pyramid on a warmed round plate and dot a ring of sultanas around the edge.

Accompaniment
Any roasted meat or fish forms the final point of the couscous triad. Country chicken (p 82), *agnello scottadito* without the sage (p 65). Merguez sausages, grilled fish or fried sardines. A leg of lamb rubbed with cumin, coriander and teaspoon of harissa, then roasted on a bed of outer cabbage leaves sprinkled with caraway seeds.
A *couscous royale* in Paris is a mixed platter of chicken, lamb and merguez.

To serve
Transfer the stew to a deep serving bowl with a ladle. Each plate requires a heap of couscous grains, meat and a ladle of vegetable stew. Throughout the meal the couscous grains seem never to diminish on your plate if replenished with enough liquid stew.

POTS AND PANS 53

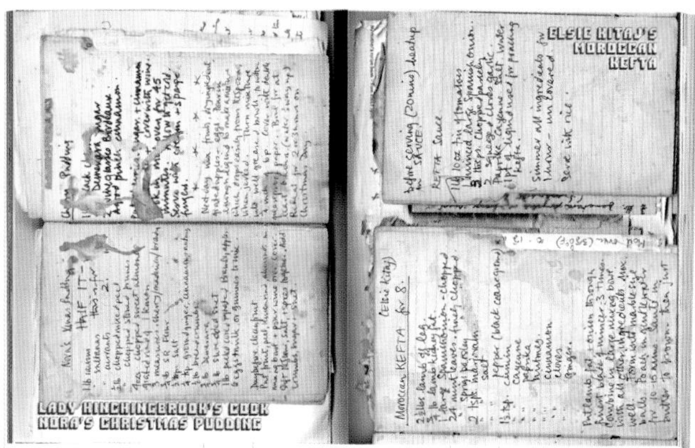

COOKING AMID THE HEAT AND DUST ON OUR OUTDOOR WOOD-BURNING STOVE SURROUNDED BY SINGING BIRDS AND INSECTS REMINDS ME OF UDAIPUR IN RAJASTHAN. AS THE SUN GOES DOWN WE ARE EMBALMED BY THE SOUND OF CICADAS. THE FLAMES GIVE THE ROTIS THEIR FINAL COLOUR NEXT TO A WOK OF SIMMERING COCKERELS IN COCONUT.

90 TUSCANY

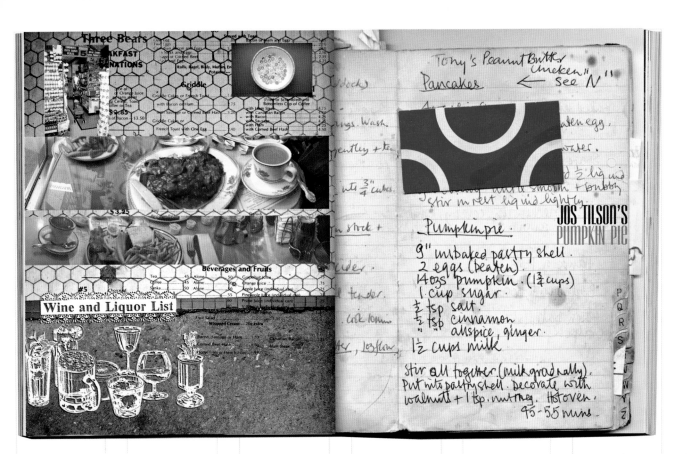

Three Bears

Wine and Liquor List

Tony's Peanut Butter "Chicken" see "N"

Pancakes

JOS TILSON'S PUMPKIN PIE

Pumpkin pie.

9" unbaked pastry shell.
2 eggs (beaten).
14 ozs pumpkin. (1¾ cups)
1 cup sugar.
½ tsp salt.
½ tsp cinnamon
" " allspice, ginger.
1½ cups milk

Stir all together (milk gradually). Put into pastry shell. Decorate with walnuts + 1 tsp. nutmeg. Hot oven. 45-55 mins.

2 DESIGN THIS DAY

FOREWORD 3

FOREWORD

ROSS LOVEGROVE

Sitting here in my London studio, in the tranquility of the early morning before my assistants arrive, I look around me at a space filled with organic shapes, nature's forms, and modern technology all living in a certain harmony together. This precious silence allows my mind to wander, contemplating the future and the role that design will play in its success or failure.

In a recent interview between Ettore Sottsass and Hans-Ulrich Obrist, Sottsass reminded us of the question he and his collaborators posed at the outset of Memphis...should we be creating in the service of humanity or the service of industry? I have read in previous interviews that he also states there is a difference between Design and Industrial Design, with the former emerging the moment first humans scratched a mark on a bone as a free artistic act, and the latter merely requiring the service of someone qualified to deliver a working solution to the Industry.

These ideas have stayed with me over recent months as I have tried to relate the concept of progression and relevance in the design field: understanding that there is something incredible in the transformation of materials and technology by mankind into the supporting tools of our culture and existence. This places all endeavours, however advanced or primitive, in the same evolutionary pot. To understand the future, one has to first have a sense of the past.

What unites these polarities is our sense of self, our place in the universe, and our potential. But what defines our civilization are the incredible moments of innovation inspired partly by previous achievements and the seamless passage of knowledge, and even more so by our instinctive sense of possibility. This instinct is extremely rare and is something deeply primordial, similar to an anticipatory sixth sense that allows one to look into the future with logic and purpose.

Technology is nothing without instinct and instinct is nothing without technology. We see this even more as we enter a new age whereby the last century already feels as if it is an eternity away.

The new millennium was approached with great expectation and uncertainty as designers lost their direction in search of "safe" options, looking back to a retro world that was taking us nowhere.

I try to imagine what the world felt like 80 years ago when futurism was a fabulous incubator of dreams, with everything out there waiting to be invented, and an aesthetic identity assigned to common artifacts and modes of transportation. The incredible visions created by a soft pencil on paper and then beaten to shape out of new alloys, first out of polymers, an organic seductive material which transposed a new kind of energy into material objects.

"Streamlining," as it was termed, was a style with attitude. It gave form to technology and created an interface that was anatomic and liquid.

The Meat Slicer No. 195, called the "Streamliner" by Egmont H. Arens and Theodore C. Brookhart, remains a masterpiece that would not look out of place today. The Water Kettle Model No. 4133, called the "Magnalite" by John Gordon Rideout, the Electric Drill Model No. 315, "The Craftsman," designed by John R. Morgan in 1940 for Sears, Roebuck and Co in Chicago, and the Polaroid Lamp Model No. 114 designed by Walter Dorwin Teague in 1939, were all very reflexive responses to ergonomic and functional needs. They were also pure examples of the industrial aesthetics of the time, architectonic but not so obviously influenced by the architectural vernacular of the day which gives them great strength of character as a smoothed out evolution of Art Nouveau. These designs helped define the age whereby the concept of dynamic, fluid form became a language that permeated society and embraced a style that transcended its origins.

The big ideas of the day related to a new consumer economy, new modes of transport, flight, speed, and the infinite possibility of machine invention. The shift from need to want, the concept of desire and experience—and all the imagery that surrounded the thrust forward to the modern age—created some of the most celebrated industrial designers of all time, such as Raymond Loewy and Walter Dorwin Teague, whose flare and instinct for form made them glamorous superheroes of a wealth-generating era.

The "Fast Commuter" railway car designed by Loewy in 1936, the 1938 Teague Car of the Future, or "A New Transoceanic Treat" by Bohn Aluminium and Brass Company in 1946 are visions that inspired me as a child to draw, create, and imagine a new genre of transport that would help define our creative potential.

As my mind's eye lingers on such visions, I lean back for a moment to look around me and see the white fluid forms of my Go Chair in front of the large sculptural-form studies in aluminium I create to satisfy my own dreams of form, material, and lightness in trinity.

In front of me is my Ty Nant water bottle, next to meringue and a bear skull, both related through proteins and polysaccharides—the future, perhaps, of biodegradable products. Against the window glass is a futuristic study model of a supersonic aircraft given to my son by Luigi Colani and beyond that a stereo lithographical model of a house called "Frozen Elasticity," completely organic and impossible to make in real terms.

This is indeed a new world, and a world of today that I inhabit.

I wish to live and work within the potential of my time to deliver solutions that embrace and reflect the hopes and fears of our collective world.

Issues that impact our future, such as sustainability; resource drawdowns; the quest for new, clean energy; the quality of our air and water; the need to be resourceful rather than greedy; the need to share, the need to be humanistic and real.

This is the world that consumes me and the young people who assist my ambition...we share common goals and objectives, hoping that the work we do here speculates and capitalizes on the advanced processes of today. Here we keep a balance that embraces context and understanding; we want to contribute to the dream of putting form to the abstract forces of materials and science in a way that is human-centric and responsible.

This massive soup that I have fallen into today, as I spill out this text from my mind's eye, opens me up to unite the incredible visions of the past with the insights and knowledge of the present.

What man envisions ultimately becomes reality; it's just a matter of time.

How can one deny the possibility of existence to a vision in one's mind, however extreme or unfeasible, when surely if it has been imagined by a human mind, then by definition, it can relate to mankind itself? All share the ability to speculate. But only some have the innate sense of seeing the future in glorious Technicolor, and fewer still have the will and passion to bring it to life. I believe Walter Dorwin Teague showed that will during his life.

If those who, across oceans and continents, share the same visions via collective empathy then the opportunity to make exponential progress in our industrial society with logic and beauty is there for our loss or beautiful gain.

DESIGN THIS DAY: 8 DECADES OF INFLUENTIAL DESIGN

Design: Steve Watson, Ben Graham, Jason Gómez, and Bryan Mamaril at Turnstyle

This limited-edition book was produced to commemorate industrial design company Teague's 80th anniversary. Designers Steve Watson, Ben Graham, Jason Gómez, and Bryan Mamaril wanted the graphic design to reflect the attention to detail characteristic of Teague's design solutions. The typography and navigational devices are clean and systematic, but allow for subtle changes between sections. Reminiscent of some of the complex grids developed by the Swiss

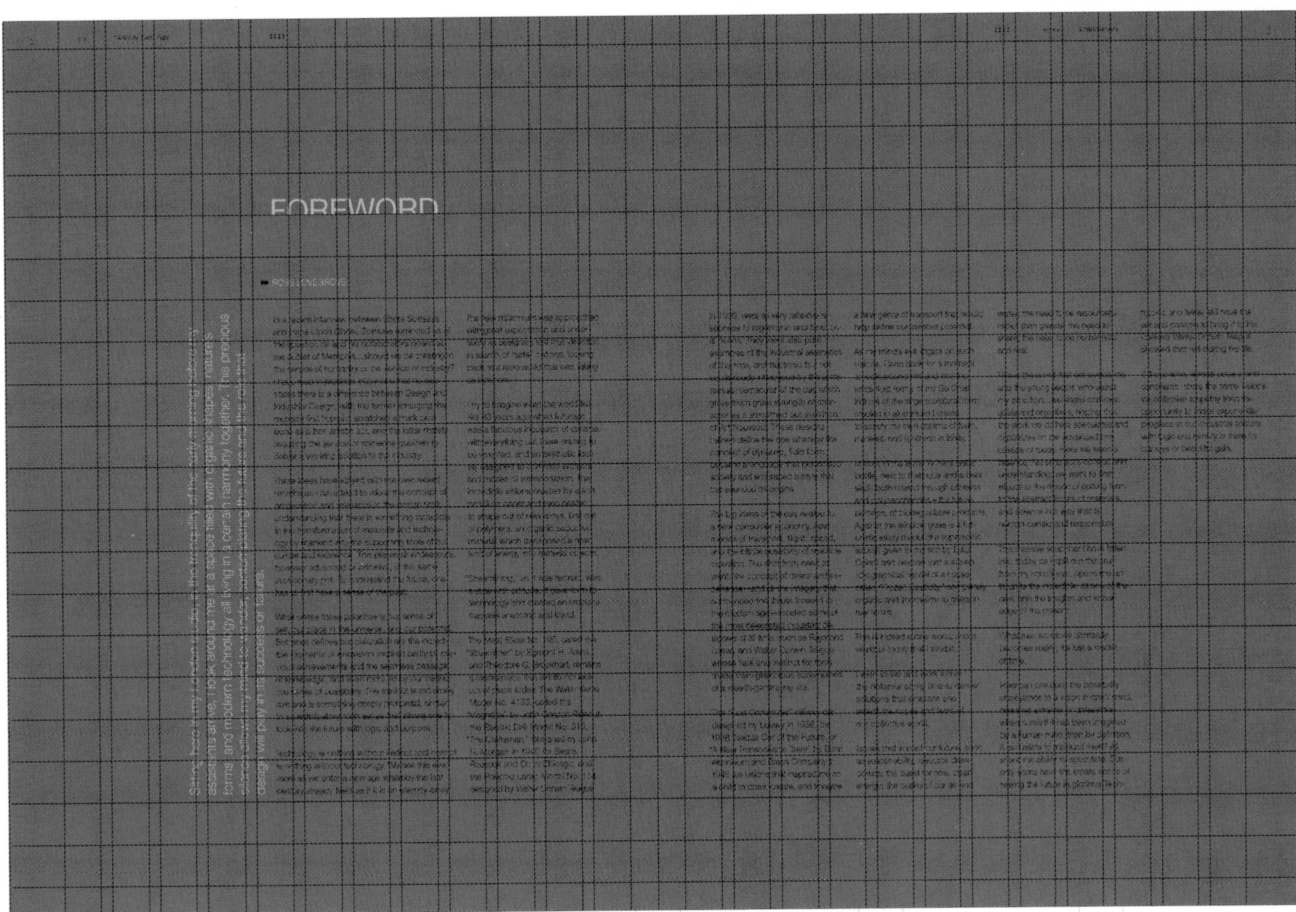

designers of the 1950s and 1960s, their 12-column grid is divided into 20 horizontal fields. The book is not just a showcase of Teague's finished work—it gives context by drawing on their initial ideas and methods of working, as well as showing the work of their design heroes. This provided an opportunity for Turnstyle to vary the visual pace of the book and introduce different paper stocks to make this a tactile as well as a visual experience.

GRID SPECIFICATIONS

Page size (trimmed)	228.6 x 304.8mm
Top margin	9.525mm
Bottom margin	9.525mm
Outside margin	9.525mm
Inside margin	19.05mm
Number of columns	12
Gutter width	4.064mm
Extras	Baseline grid, 0.706mm starting at 9.525mm; 20 horizontal fields

DESIGN THIS DAY
06.6
Citroën DS
1955
Designers
Manufacturer
Unveiled at the Paris Motor Show, the Citroën DS became an instant automotive classic. The futuristic, aerodynamic design is as well-known for its aesthetic appeal as it is for its innovative technology. Boasting sleek lines, self-leveling suspension, and a curve-hugging design—not to mention its ultra-modern interior detailing—the Citroën set a new bar for automobile design the world over. An avant-garde design with mass appeal, we're not alone in our absolute adoration for this distinctly modern automobile design.
06.7
Zero-In Low Table
2005
Designers
Manufacturer
Photography

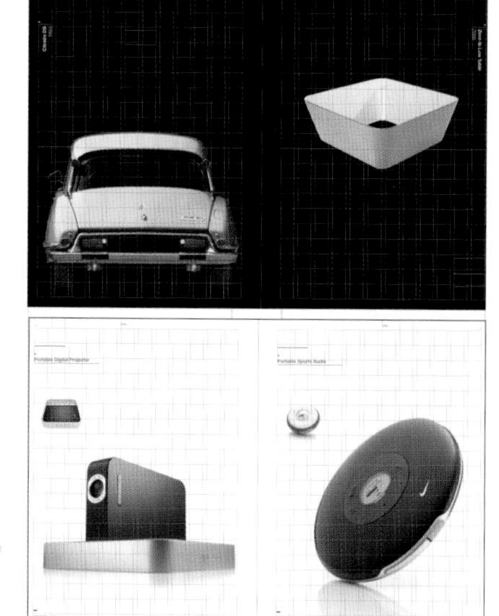

62
DESIGN THIS DAY
Client
Samsung Electronics
04.1
Portable Digital Projector
The compact and ultra portable projector was designed specifically for the highly mobile professional. Created to fit easily into today's busy schedule—not to mention a small bag or purse—the Samsung Portable Digital Projector is no larger than a digital camera. Utilizing laser diode technology to offer an integrated and seamless display experience, users interact with and control the extremely versatile projector via their mobile phone.
SAMSUNG
Date
2004
Award
2005 iF
Award
2006 IDEA
Silver

RECENT TEAGUE INNOVATIONS
63
Client
Nike
04.2
Portable Sports Audio
Teague worked with Nike's in-house team on all design aspects of this lightweight, rugged, and sophisticated family of products. Designed for the serious athlete, the MP3 Run's wireless features include a distance and speed sensor, as well as skip-free audio and FM radio that keeps athletes in tune with their music and their workout. The complementary MP3 CD's shock-resistant technology, no-look control belt, and strobe light all cater to the athlete who wants an uninterrupted workout experience.
Date
2003

IGNITE A COLLECTIVE PASSION
Aspire to a loftier goal than creating inspirational design. Aspire to creating an environment where the collaborative experience of working together is as inspirational as the results. Design work should be challenging, it should be emotional and passionate and exhilarating. And so should the collaboration. Enjoy the process and you'll almost always enjoy the results.
Chapter 3
TEAGUE CLASSICS

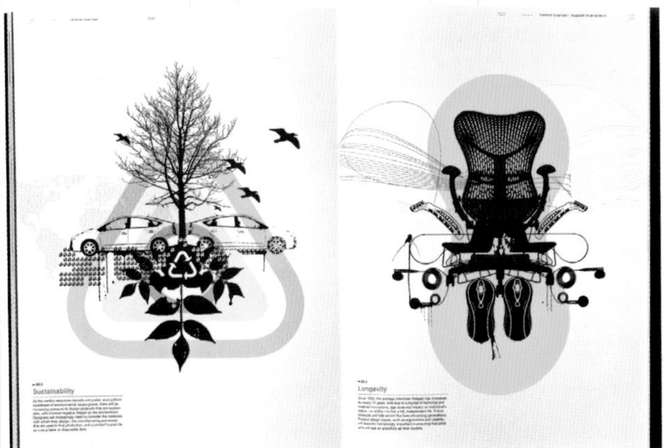
Sustainability
Longevity

747
757

Charles + Ray Eames
Ross Lovegrove

FOREWORD

GIAN LORENZO BERNINI
Apollo and Daphne
1622–1625
marble

I. THE MYTH OF ER

In the tremendous vision of transmigration which closes Plato's *Republic,* the dead are able to choose their fate in their future lives: Socrates describes how a warrior called Er was taken for dead and entered the other world, but came back to life on his funeral pyre; **after he had returned from the other world, he described how he saw there, in** "a certain demonic place," **the souls of Homeric heroes taking on their next existence—in the form of a new daimon. The dead were told,** "A demon will not select you, but you will choose a demon. Let him who gets the first lot make the first choice of a life to which he will be bound by necessity."[1] **As Er watches the redistribution of lives after death, he recognizes Orpheus who chooses to become a swan, Ajax who singles out the life of a lion, and Agamemnon who** decides to become an eagle. **The heroes' future** metamorphoses **in some ways correspond to their past character, sometimes ironically. Atalanta, the swift runner, chooses to become a male athlete, for example; Epeius, who made the Trojan horse, opts to become** a female

53

METAMORPHOSIS

METAMORPHOSIS

MARINA WARNER

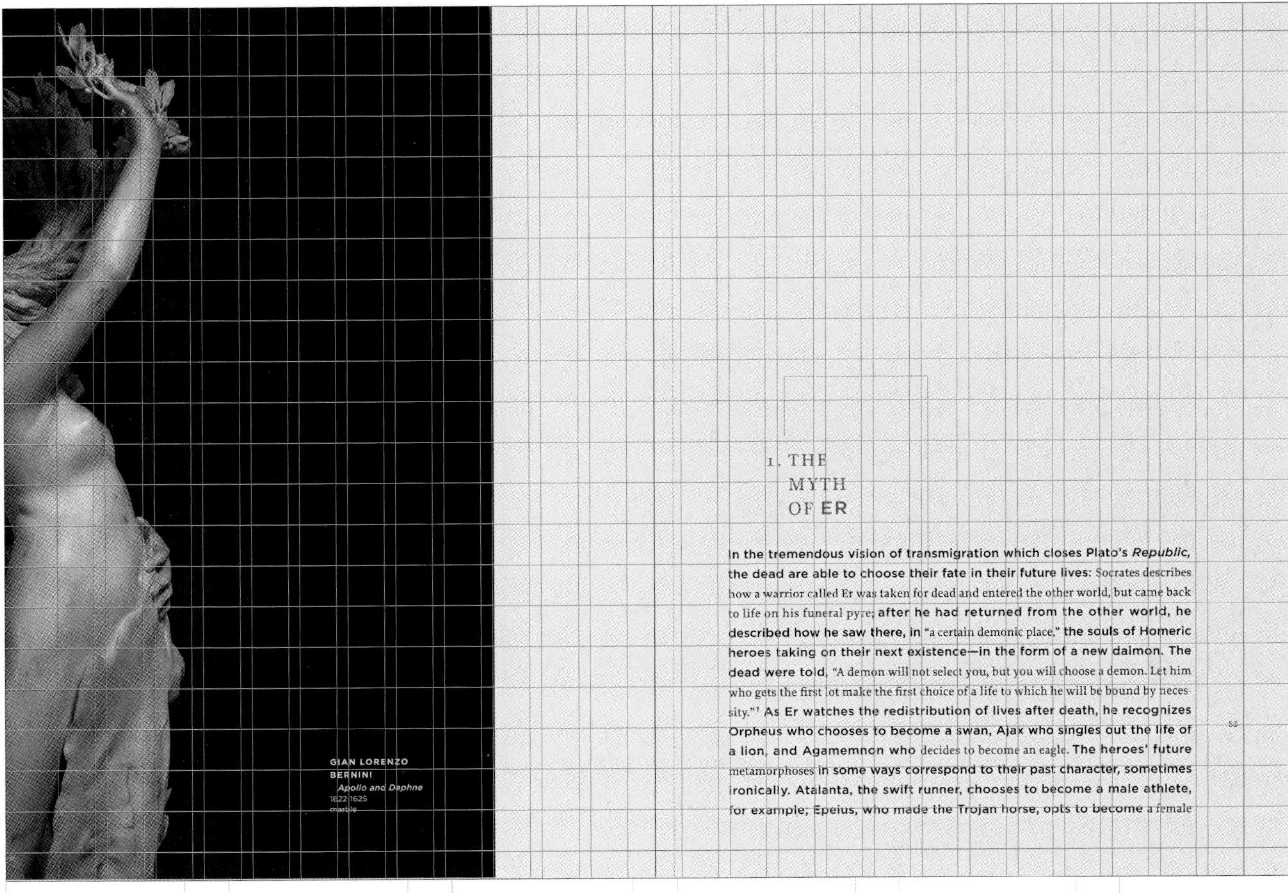

GIAN LORENZO
BERNINI
Apollo and Daphne
1622–1625
marble

1. THE MYTH OF ER

In the tremendous vision of transmigration which closes Plato's *Republic,* the dead are able to choose their fate in their future lives: Socrates describes how a warrior called Er was taken for dead and entered the other world, but came back to life on his funeral pyre; after he had returned from the other world, he described how he saw there, in "a certain demonic place," the souls of Homeric heroes taking on their next existence—in the form of a new daimon. The dead were told, "A demon will not select you, but you will choose a demon. Let him who gets the first lot make the first choice of a life to which he will be bound by necessity."[1] As Er watches the redistribution of lives after death, he recognizes Orpheus who chooses to become a swan, Ajax who singles out the life of a lion, and Agamemnon who decides to become an eagle. The heroes' future metamorphoses in some ways correspond to their past character, sometimes ironically. Atalanta, the swift runner, chooses to become a male athlete, for example; Epeius, who made the Trojan horse, opts to become a female

GRID SPECIFICATIONS

Page size (trimmed)	152.4 x 203.2mm
Top margin	19.05mm
Bottom margin	12.7mm
Outside margin	19.05mm
Inside margin	12.7mm
Number of columns	9
Gutter width	3.81mm
Extras	N/A

UNEASY NATURE

Design: Eric Heiman, Amber Reed, and Madhavi Jagdish at Volume Inc.

This exhibition catalog was produced for Weatherspoon Art Museum. The designers explored ideas of mutation by juxtaposing the natural and the unnatural in their design. They started with the cover, on which all the images from the show are overlaid digitally to create a single composite image. The typographic grid uses the golden section, however, the designers break this grid repeatedly, with various typographic mutations that often bleed off the pages. The body text changes from sans serif to serif throughout the essays, and on the whole, text and image are not integrated. The cover and essay pages are printed in two colors on uncoated cream stock, while the images are contained within a full-color section on coated white paper.

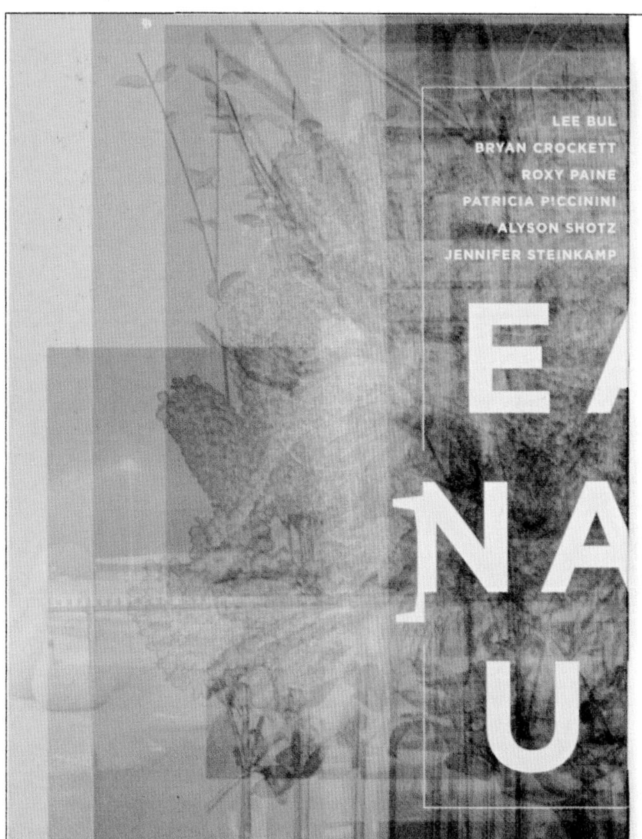
LEE BUL
BRYAN CROCKETT
ROXY PAINE
PATRICIA PICCININI
ALYSON SHOTZ
JENNIFER STEINKAMP

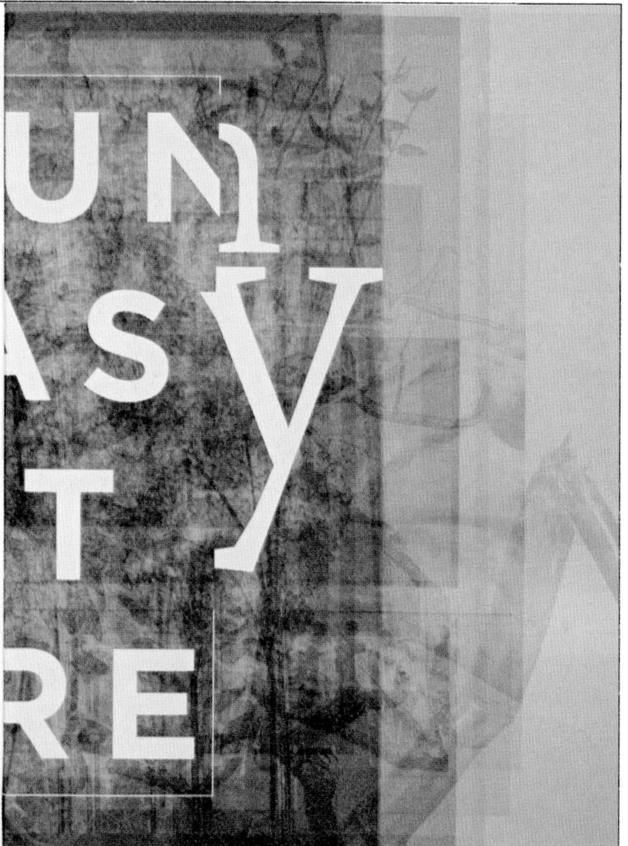
UN

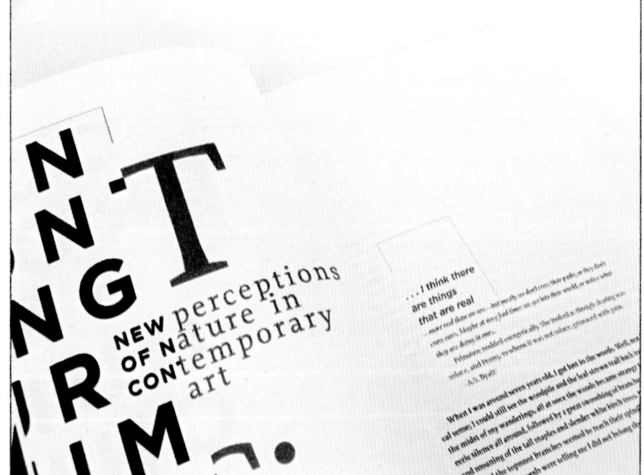
NEW perceptions
OF Nature in
CONtemporary
art
. . . I think there
are things
that are real
—A.S. Byatt

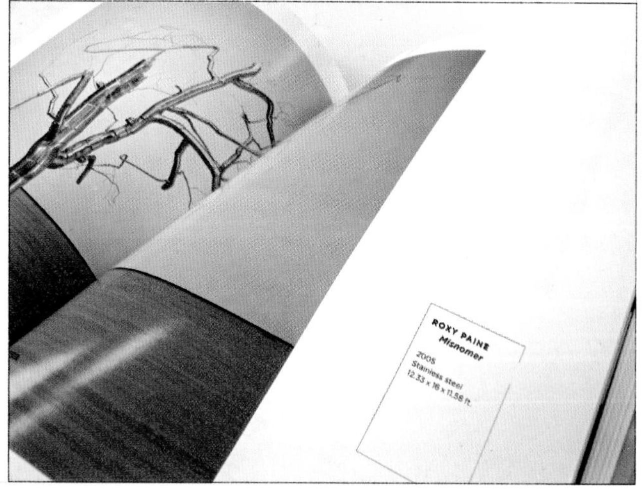
ROXY PAINE
Misnomer
2005
Stainless steel
12.33 x 16 x 11.58 ft.

LEE BUL
Ein Hungerkunstler

2004
Hand-cut polyurethane panels on aluminum armature, acrylic paint, epoxy coating, crystal and glass beads on nickel-chrome and stainless steel wires
38 x 75 x 197 in.

designs for small spaces

Jennifer Hudson

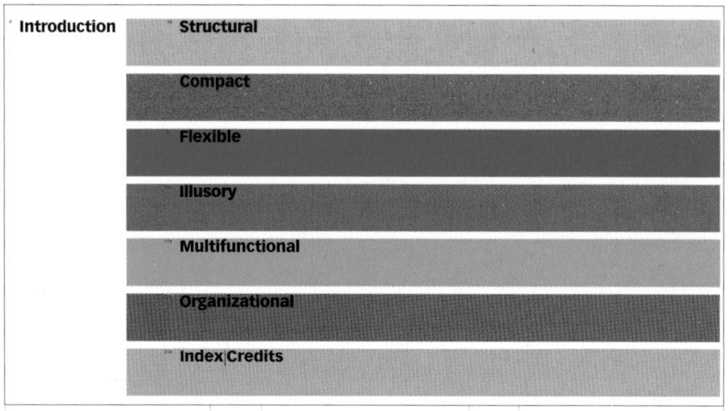

Introduction

Structural

Compact

Flexible

Illusory

Multifunctional

Organizational

Index|Credits

Introduction

Introduction
10|11

family home is becoming increasingly outdated as the high cost of accommodation, particularly in cities, forces many people to rethink the amount of space they actually need. If the current trend persists then buy-to-let investors will have to take note of the kind of accommodation they will need to provide. The increase in websites, books and magazines about small houses reflects the movement's growth and architects and builders are now providing smaller housing alternatives. The next step is to maximize their potential.

Downsizing involves a lot of creativity and a few simple design essentials but it's not rocket science. The bulk of this book is dedicated to products you can use to enhance the area you have available, and tips about their use are given in the relevant chapter introductions. On the following pages is a list of just some of the more general pointers you should consider when moving to a smaller home. Most you can do yourself but it's important to be aware that any structural alterations should be carried out with the collaboration of a surveyor or architect and may need planning permission.

↑ → The Mini Loft was designed by the Slovenian architectural practice OFIS for a bachelor living in Ljubljana. Their idea was to exploit as much of the 30m² (323 sq ft) floor space as possible for living. The functional areas – entrance, kitchenette, workspace, bathroom and bedroom – are displaced around the edges of the room to form a sort of enclosed cupboard. When not in use they are concealed behind semi-transparent Perspex panels that during the day appear as an opaque solid wall but at night transform the space into a bright, atmospheric lightbox.

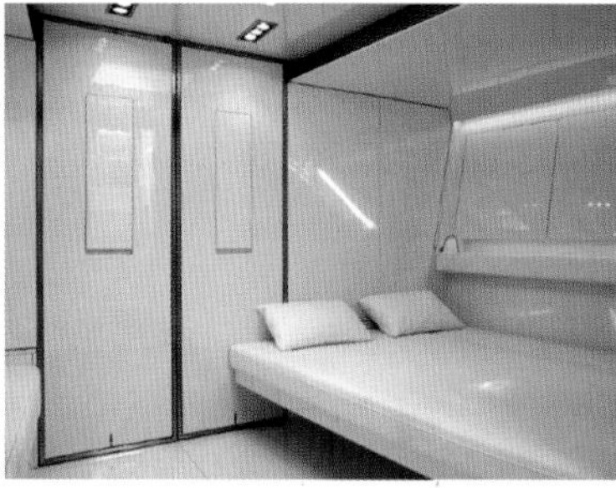

↑ → Interior design of the 18m (60ft) Magnum fast open speedboat by Rome-based Lazzerini Pickering Architetti. When creating or thinking about how best to organize a small apartment it is helpful to take a look at nautical design, where space-saving ideas are requisite. All furniture and fittings usually have more than one function and are flexible, and every 'useless' space doubles as storage. In the Magnum interior, for example, the doors that separate the living area from the bedroom/dining area also flip down to create a table, and the bed slides back to form a banquette.

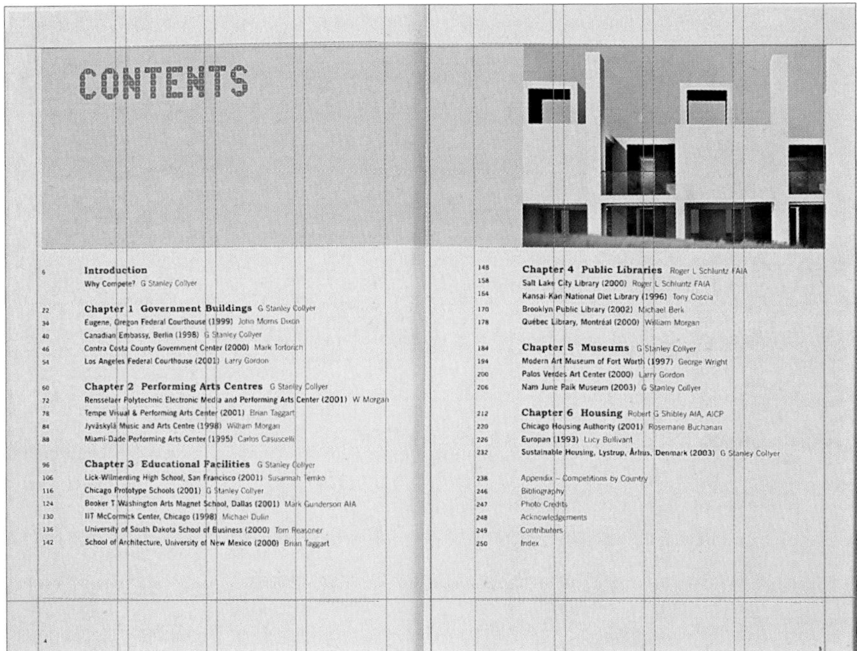

CONTENTS

6 Introduction
Why Compete? G Stanley Collyer

22 Chapter 1 Government Buildings G Stanley Collyer
34 Eugene, Oregon Federal Courthouse (1999) John Morris Dixon
40 Canadian Embassy, Berlin (1998) G Stanley Collyer
46 Contra Costa County Government Center (2000) Mark Tortorich
54 Los Angeles Federal Courthouse (2001) Larry Gordon

60 Chapter 2 Performing Arts Centres G Stanley Collyer
72 Rensselaer Polytechnic Electronic Media and Performing Arts Center (2001) W Morgan
78 Tempe Visual & Performing Arts Center (2001) Brian Taggart
84 Jyväskylä Music and Arts Centre (1998) William Morgan
88 Miami-Dade Performing Arts Center (1995) Carlos Casuscelli

96 Chapter 3 Educational Facilities G Stanley Collyer
106 Lick-Wilmerding High School, San Francisco (2001) Susannah Temko
116 Chicago Prototype Schools (2001) G Stanley Collyer
124 Booker T Washington Arts Magnet School, Dallas (2001) Mark Gunderson AIA
130 IIT McCormick Center, Chicago (1998) Michael Dulin
136 University of South Dakota School of Business (2000) Tom Reasoner
142 School of Architecture, University of New Mexico (2000) Brian Taggart

148 Chapter 4 Public Libraries Roger L Schluntz FAIA
158 Salt Lake City Library (2000) Roger L Schluntz FAIA
164 Kansai-Kan National Diet Library (1996) Tony Coscia
170 Brooklyn Public Library (2002) Michael Berk
178 Québec Library, Montréal (2000) William Morgan

184 Chapter 5 Museums G Stanley Collyer
194 Modern Art Museum of Fort Worth (1997) George Wright
200 Palos Verdes Art Center (2000) Larry Gordon
206 Nam June Paik Museum (2003) G Stanley Collyer

212 Chapter 6 Housing Robert G Shibley AIA, AICP
220 Chicago Housing Authority (2001) Rosemarie Buchanan
226 Europan (1993) Lucy Bullivant
232 Sustainable Housing, Lystrup, Århus, Denmark (2003) G Stanley Collyer

238 Appendix – Competitions by Country
246 Bibliography
247 Photo Credits
248 Acknowledgements
249 Contributors
250 Index

GRID SPECIFICATIONS

Page size (trimmed)	195 x 215mm
Top margin	8mm
Bottom margin	8mm
Outside margin	10mm
Inside margin	15mm
Number of columns	6
Gutter width	4mm
Extras	N/A

DESIGNS FOR SMALL SPACES

Design: Roger Fawcett-Tang at Struktur

As available space continues to become a premium commodity and global property prices soar, living in small spaces has become an increasingly necessary proposition for many urban dwellers. This book showcases the functional products that serve to maximise space efficiency and help those who live in restricted spaces to make the most of their living environment. Each of the six chapters are colour coded and have their own horizon line built into the grid. All caption text hangs from each of the vertical divisions of the grid, and relates to the coloured tabs that are visible at the edge of the page.

structural

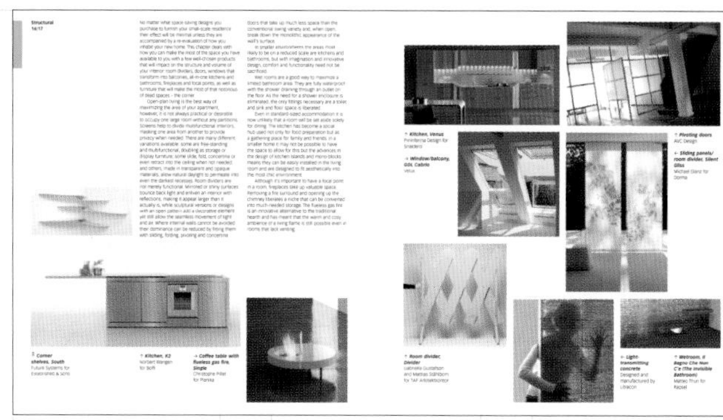

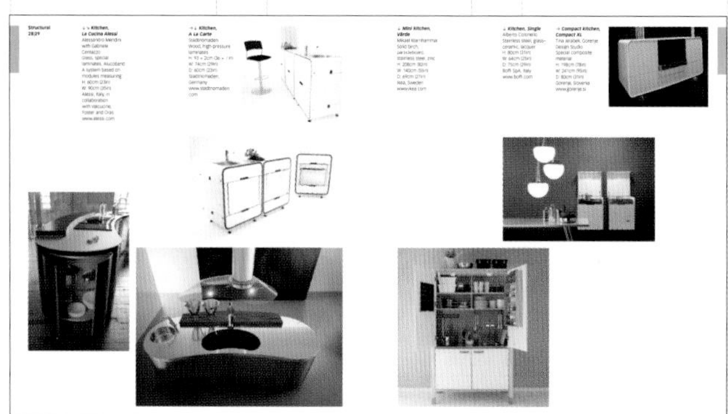

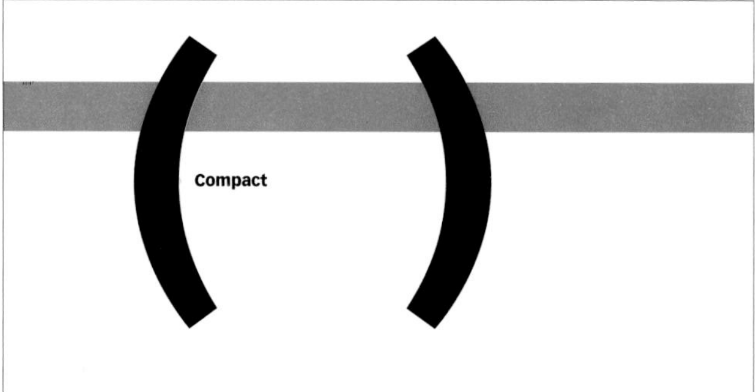
Compact

Compact
58|59

↓ Armchair, OM
Martín Azúa
Polyethylene
H: 75cm (29in)
H (seat): 45cm (17¾in)
W: 57cm (22in)
D: 54cm (21in)
Mobles 114, Spain
www.mobles114.com

A single block polyethylene seat for both interiors and exteriors, the Om chair is small on the outside but comfortable and generous on the inside. It is exceptionally light and can be easily transported from one environment to another.

→ Armchair, Lotus
Simon Pengelly
Fabric, foam, metal
H: 79cm (31in)
H (seat): 48cm (18⅞in)
W: 61cm (24in)
D: 59cm (23in)
Montis, the Netherlands
www.montis.nl

↓ Mini rocking chair, Mini Dada
Claudio Colucci
Foam, wood, fabric
H: 59cm (23in)
W: 40cm (15¾in)
D: 58cm (22in)
Ligne Roset, France
www.ligneroset.fr

↓ Armchair, Mermaid
Tokujin Yoshioka
Polyethylene
H: 83.5cm (33in)
H (seat): 43.5cm (17⅛in)
W: 70cm (27in)
D: 65cm (25in)
Driade, Italy
www.driade.com

→↓ Armchair, Rosebud
Ilkka Suppanen
10mm steel rod, fabric
H: 77cm (30in)
W: 72cm (28in)
D: 66cm (26in)
Vivero Oy, Finland
www.vivero.fi

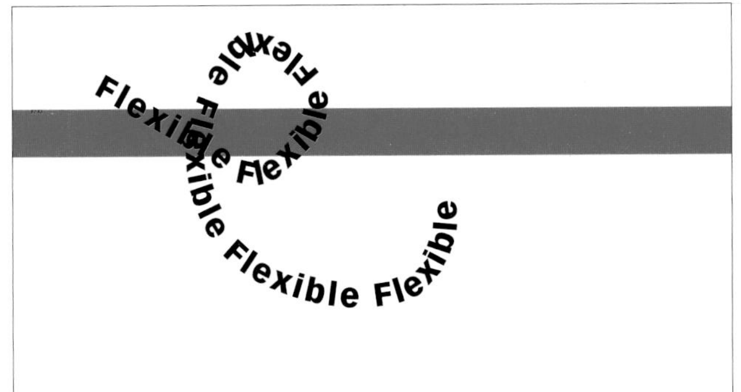

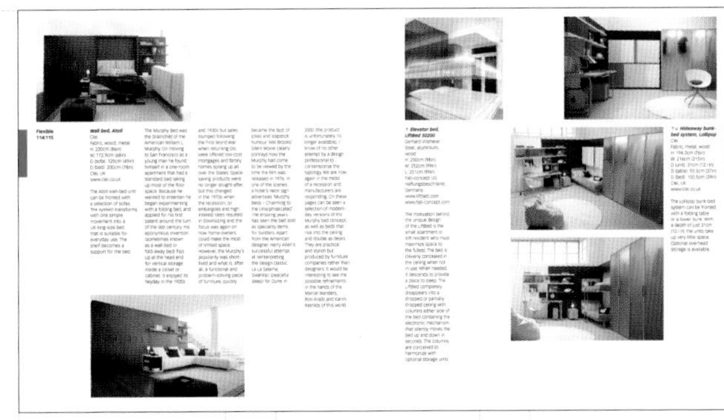

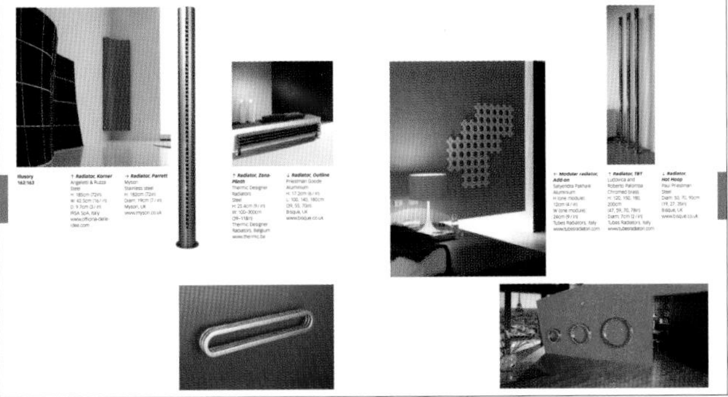

Multifunctional
188|189

↑ ***Chair, Peg chair***
Alex Hellum
Beech, clear lacquer
H: 166cm (65in)
H (seat): 40cm (15¾in)
W: 43cm (16⅞in)
D: 50cm (19in)
Ercol, UK
www.ercol.com
www.heals.co.uk

↘ ***Chair, Hanger Chair***
Philippe Malouin
Russian plywood
H: 87.8cm (34in)
W: 45cm (17¾in)
Philippe Malouin, UK
www.philippemalouin.com

↑ ***Armchair/pouffe/cushion, Joele***
Riccardo Giovannetti
Fabric
H: 86cm (33in)
Diam: 72cm (28in)
Flou, Italy
www.flou.it

↑ ***Multifunctional seating/table units, X Series***
Graeme Massie Architects
Treated exterior-grade birch-faced plywood
L: 60/120/150cm (23/47/59in)
Outgang, UK
www.outgang.com

Series X is the first range of furniture being developed for Outgang Ltd, a Scottish-based producer of high-quality contemporary furniture. The continuous 'loop' forms can be rotated into a number of positions to provide differing seat positions and table heights. Manufactured by laminating CNC-cut plywood sections and finished with a clear lacquer, the products are for use both internally and externally.

↙ ***Small tables with trays and storage, Fat Fat-Lady Fat***
Patricia Urquiola
Metal, polyurethane, PET
H: 45, 35cm (17¾, 13¾in)
Diam: 66, 86cm (26, 33in)
B&B Italia SpA, Italy
www.bebitalia.it

Identities

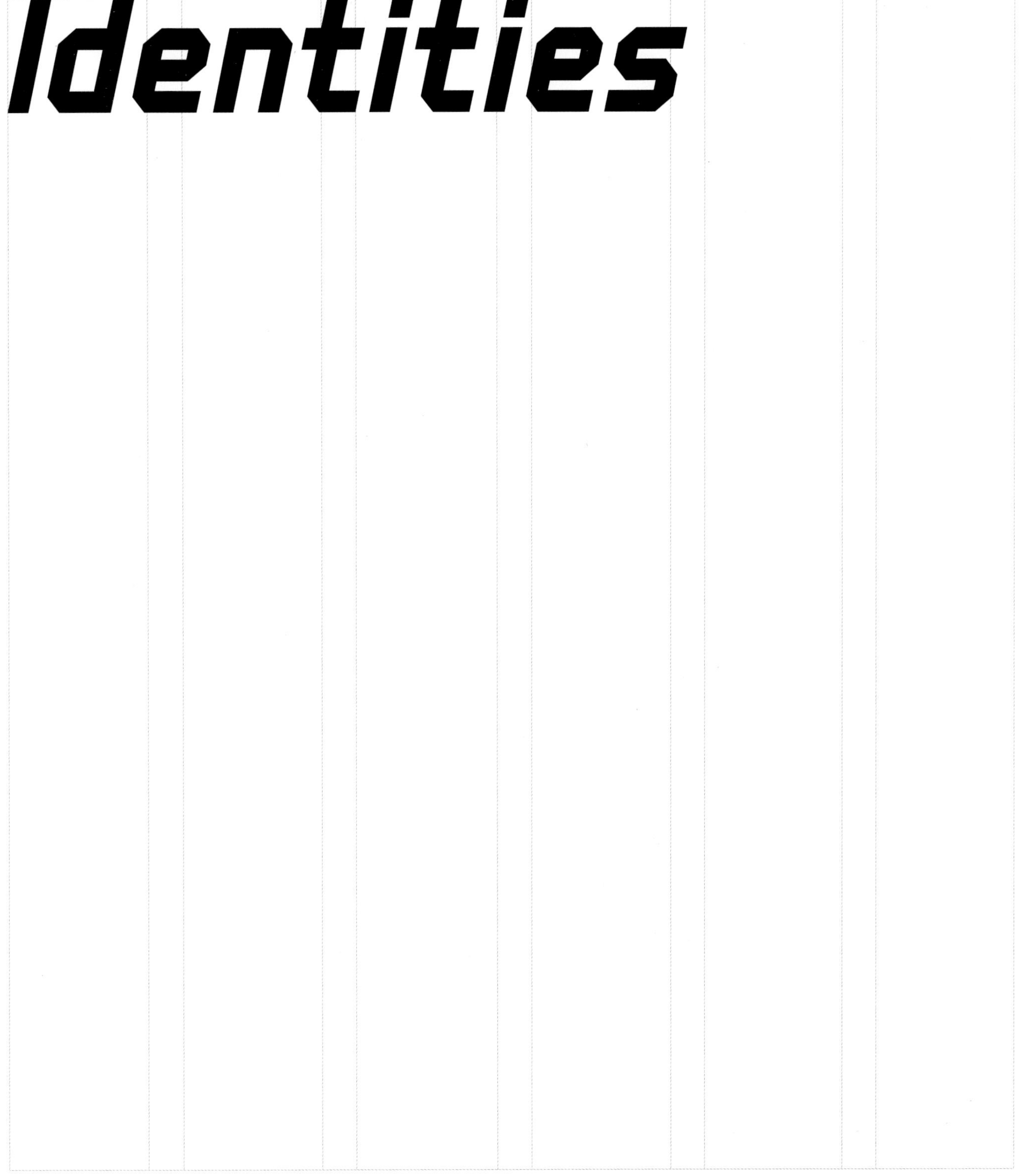

365
Pages
BB/
Saunders

GRID SPECIFICATIONS

Page size (trimmed)	210 x 170mm
Top margin	5mm
Bottom margin	5mm
Outside margin	5mm
Inside margin	15mm
Number of columns	6
Gutter width	5mm
Extras	Baseline grid 5mm; 6 horizontal fields

365 PAGES

Design: BB/Saunders

Every week, members of design and branding consultancy BB/Saunders produce a diary for inclusion on its website. The brief is open; it might be a map of somebody's last seven days or a manifesto calling to save the world. The initial idea behind *365 Pages* was to catalog these and create a journal of diaries. Based on the assumption that designers love to doodle in sketchbooks, BB/Saunders went on to create a book that included inventive and unusual multicolumn and field-based grids as backgrounds to the pages—the objective was to encourage readers to record their own daily experiences, observations, or thoughts. Using its in-house technical drafting grids as a starting point, 12 new grids were created for this book.

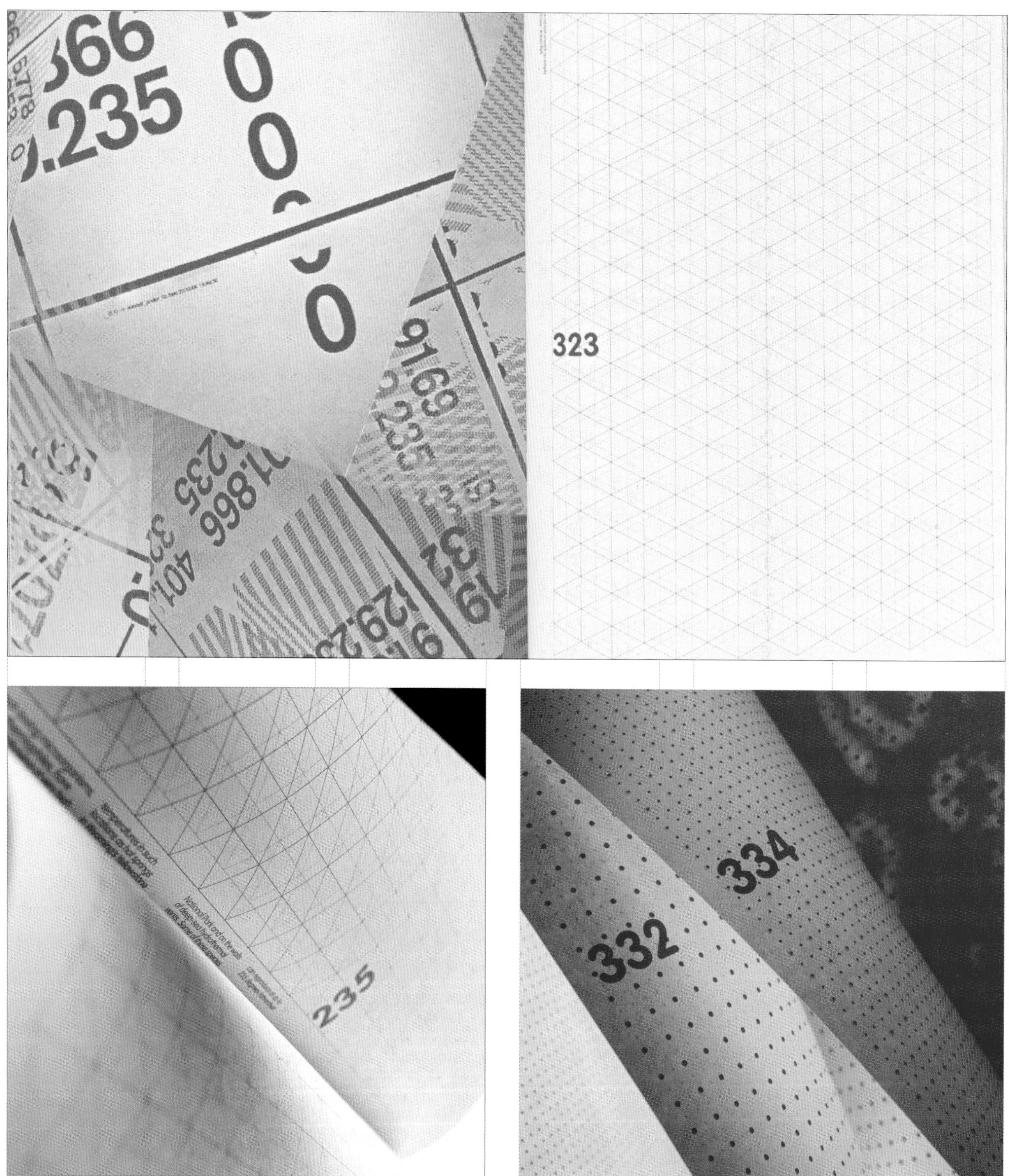

2yrs.mar'04—mar'06

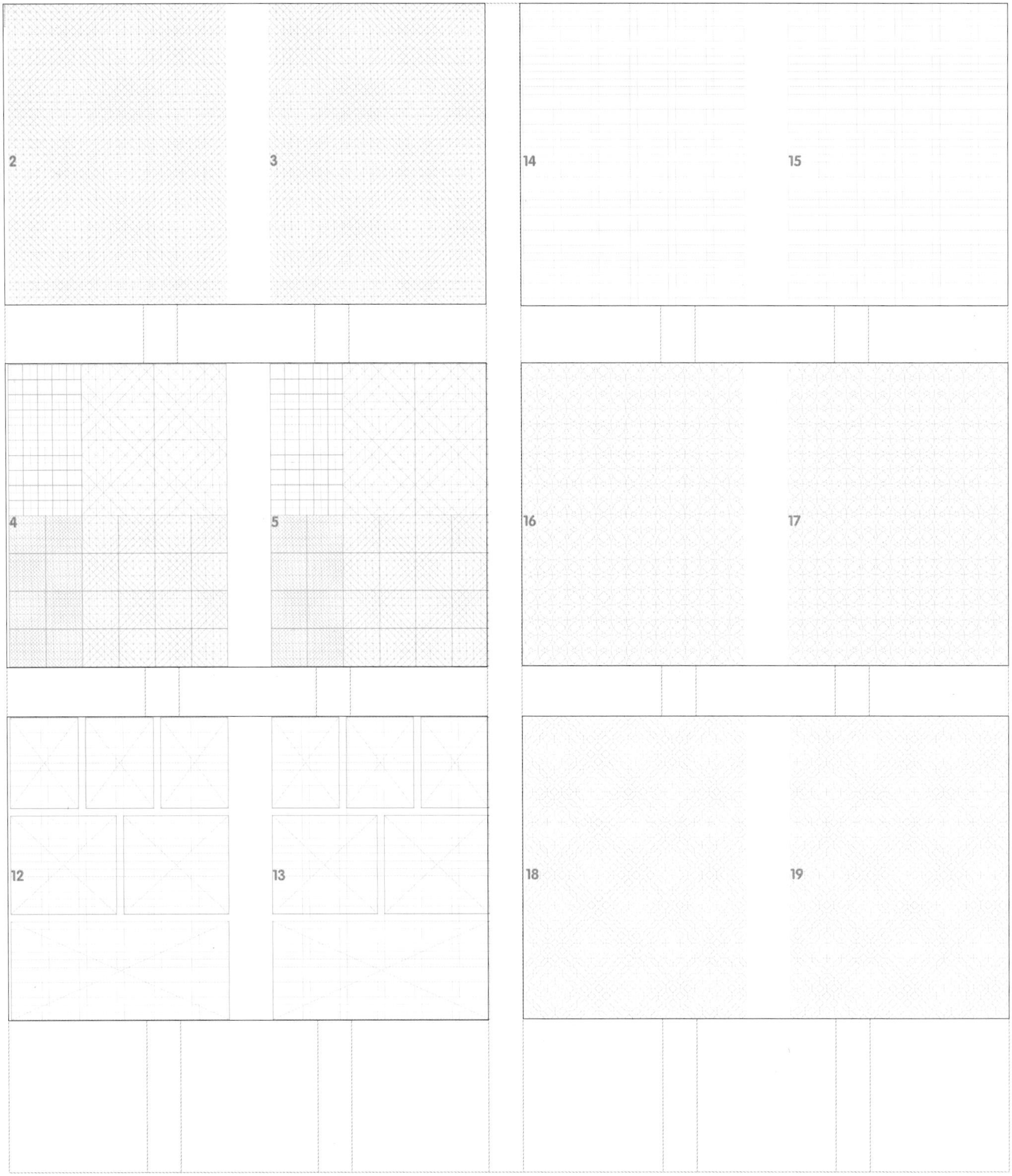

2 3 14 15

4 5 16 17

12 13 18 19

22

23

32

33

24

25

34

35

30

31

36

37

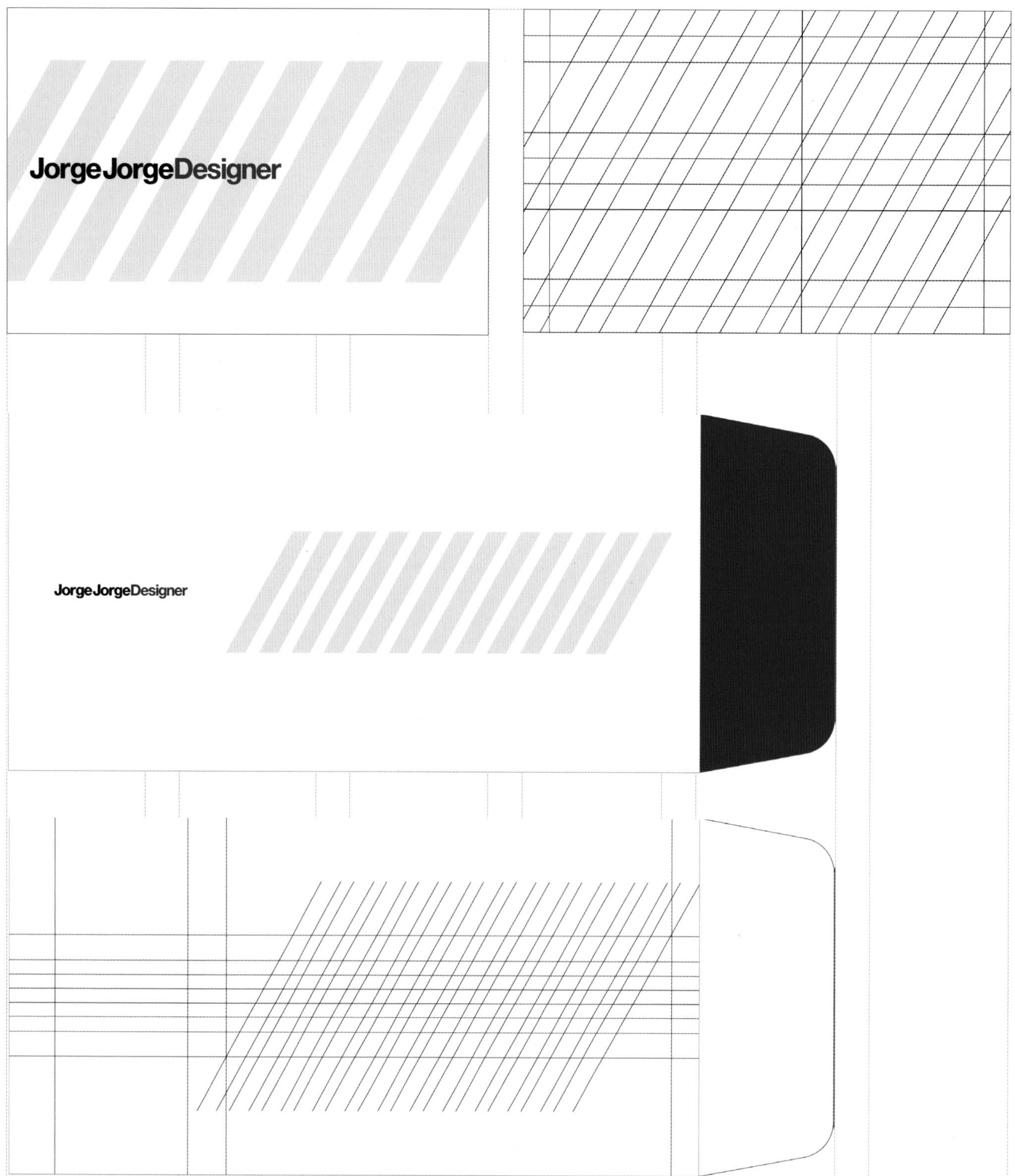
JorgeJorgeDesigner
JorgeJorgeDesigner

JORGE JORGE DESIGN IDENTITY

Design: Jorge Jorge at Jorge Jorge Design

Jorge Jorge's aim was to create a simple and contemporary identity that would work across a range of graphic applications and formats, and communicate his personality and potential to clients. He achieved this through economic means; the diagonal rules and use of limited color distinguish a considered and minimal layout. Although grids are used most prevalently in multipage documents, they can also be used very effectively across a range of related single-page items. Here Jorge Jorge's grid ensures consistency. It determines hanging heights and alignments across each element of the stationery.

Fax

For: Dr. João Soares
Company: Brand Y
Fax nº: 225 876 987
Subject: Something

From: Jorge Jorge
Pages: 1/2
Date: 22/02/07
Reply to: JorgeJorge / 225 899 645

JorgeJorgeDesigner

Porto, 14 Janeiro 2007

Olá João Soares!
Lorem ipsum dolor sit amet, consectetuer adipiscing elit, sed diam nonummy nibh euismod tincidunt ut laoreet dolore magna aliquam erat volutpat. Ut wisi enim ad minim veniam, quis nostrud exerci tation ullamcorper suscipit lobortis nisl ut aliquip ex ea commodo consequat. Duis autem vel eum iriure dolor in hendrerit in vulputate velit esse molestie consequat, vel illum dolore eu feugiat nulla facilisis at vero eros et accumsan et iusto odio dignissim qui blandit praesent luptatum zzril delenit augue duis dolore te feugait nulla facilisi. Lorem ipsum dolor sit amet, consectetuer adipiscing elit, sed diam nonummy nibh euismod tincidunt ut laoreet dolore magna aliquam erat volutpat. Ut wisi enim ad minim veniam, quis nostrud exerci tation ullamcorper suscipit lobortis nisl ut aliquip ex ea commodo consequat.
Duis autem vel eum iriure dolor in hendrerit in vulputate velit esse molestie consequat, vel illum dolore eu feugiat nulla facilisis at vero eros et accumsan et iusto odio dignissim qui blandit praesent luptatum zzril delenit augue duis dolore te feugait nulla facilisi. Nam liber tempor cum soluta nobis eleifend option congue nihil imperdiet doming id quod mazim placerat facer possim assum. Lorem ipsum dolor sit amet, consectetuer adipiscing elit, sed diam nonummy nibh euismod tincidunt ut laoreet dolore magna aliquam erat volut

Aguardo contacto seu!
Cumprimentos,

Jorge Jorge

+351 934 201 420
mail@jorgejorge.com
www.jorgejorge.com

Internal Memo Subject: New Briefing

JorgeJorgeDesigner

Subject 01
Lorem ipsum dolor sit amet, consectetuer adipiscing elit, sed diam nonummy nibh euismod tincidunt ut laoreet dolore magna aliquam erat volutpat. Ut wisi enim ad minim veniam, quis nostrud exerci tation ullamcorper suscipit lobortis nisl ut aliquip ex ea commodo consequat. Duis autem vel eum iriure dolor in hendrerit in vulputate velit esse molestie consequat, vel illum dolore eu feugiat nulla facilisis at vero eros et accumsan et iusto odio dignissim qui blandit praesent luptatum zzril delenit augue duis dolore te feugait nulla facilisi. Lorem ipsum dolor sit amet, consectetuer adipiscing elit, sed diam nonummy nibh euismod tincidunt ut laoreet dolore magna aliquam erat volutpat. Ut wisi enim ad minim veniam, quis nostrud exerci tation ullamcorper suscipit lobortis nisl ut aliquip ex ea commodo consequat.

Subject 02
Duis autem vel eum iriure dolor in hendrerit in vulputate velit esse molestie consequat, vel illum dolore eu feugiat nulla facilisis at vero eros et accumsan et iusto odio dignissim qui blandit praesent luptatum zzril delenit augue duis dolore te feugait nulla facilisi. Nam liber tempor cum soluta nobis eleifend option congue nihil imperdiet doming id quod mazim placerat facer possim assum. Lorem ipsum dolor sit amet, consectetuer adipiscing elit, sed diam nonummy nibh euismod tincidunt ut laoreet dolore magna aliquam erat volut

+351 934 201 420
mail@jorgejorge.com
www.jorgejorge.com

Subject:

JorgeJorgeDesigner

Porto, 14 Janeiro 2007

Olá João Soares!

Lorem ipsum dolor sit amet, consectetuer adipiscing elit, sed diam nonummy nibh euismod tincidunt ut laoreet dolore magna aliquam erat volutpat. Ut wisi enim ad minim veniam, quis nostrud exerci tation ullamcorper suscipit lobortis nisl ut aliquip ex ea commodo consequat. Duis autem vel eum iriure dolor in hendrerit in vulputate velit esse molestie consequat, vel illum dolore eu feugiat nulla facilisis at vero eros et accumsan et iusto odio dignissim qui blandit praesent luptatum zzril delenit augue duis dolore te feugait nulla facilisi. Lorem ipsum dolor sit amet, consectetuer adipiscing elit, sed diam nonummy nibh euismod tincidunt ut laoreet dolore magna aliquam erat volutpat. Ut wisi enim ad minim veniam, quis nostrud exerci tation ullamcorper suscipit lobortis nisl ut aliquip ex ea commodo consequat.

Duis autem vel eum iriure dolor in hendrerit in vulputate velit esse molestie consequat, vel illum dolore eu feugiat nulla facilisis at vero eros et accumsan et iusto odio dignissim qui blandit praesent luptatum zzril delenit augue duis dolore te feugait nulla facilisi. Nam liber tempor cum soluta nobis eleifend option congue nihil imperdiet doming id quod mazim placerat facer possim assum. Lorem ipsum dolor sit amet, consectetuer adipiscing elit, sed diam nonummy nibh euismod tincidunt ut laoreet dolore magna aliquam erat volut

Aguardo contacto seu!

Cumprimentos,

Jorge Jorge

+351 934 201 420
mail@jorgejorge.com
www.jorgejorge.com

Subject:

JorgeJorgeDesigner

Porto, 14 Janeiro 2007

Olá João Soares!
Lorem ipsum dolor sit amet, consectetuer adipiscing elit, sed diam nonummy nibh euismod tincidunt ut laoreet dolore magna aliquam erat volutpat. Ut wisi enim ad minim veniam, quis nostrud exerci tation ullamcorper suscipit lobortis nisl ut aliquip ex ea commodo consequat. Duis autem vel eum iriure dolor in hendrerit in vulputate velit esse molestie consequat, vel illum dolore eu feugiat nulla facilisis at vero eros et accumsan et iusto odio dignissim qui blandit praesent luptatum zzril delenit augue duis dolore te feugait nulla facilisi. Lorem ipsum dolor sit amet, consectetuer adipiscing elit, sed diam nonummy nibh euismod tincidunt ut laoreet dolore magna aliquam erat volutpat. Ut wisi enim ad minim veniam, quis nostrud exerci tation ullamcorper suscipit lobortis nisl ut aliquip ex ea commodo consequat.
Duis autem vel eum iriure dolor in hendrerit in vulputate velit esse molestie consequat, vel illum dolore eu feugiat nulla facilisis at vero eros et accumsan et iusto odio dignissim qui blandit praesent luptatum zzril delenit augue duis dolore te feugait nulla facilisi. Nam liber tempor cum soluta nobis eleifend option congue nihil imperdiet doming id quod mazim placerat facer possim assum. Lorem ipsum dolor sit amet, consectetuer adipiscing elit, sed diam nonummy nibh euismod tincidunt ut laoreet dolore magna aliquam erat volut

Aguardo contacto seu!
Cumprimentos,

Jorge Jorge

+351 934 201 420
mail@jorgejorge.com
www.jorgejorge.com

GRID SPECIFICATIONS

Page size (trimmed)	Card: 850 x 550mm Letterhead: 210 x 297mm Envelope: 110 x 220mm
Top margin	Card: 90mm Letterhead: 270mm Envelope: 350mm
Bottom margin	Card: 90mm Letterhead: 250mm Envelope: 350mm
Outside margin	Card: 9mm Letterhead: 27mm Envelope: 35mm
Inside margin	Card: 9mm Letterhead: 25mm Envelope: 35mm
Number of columns	Card: 4 Letterhead: 5 Envelope: 5
Gutter width	N/A
Extras	Card and envelope: 9 horizontal fields Letterhead: 20 horizontal fields

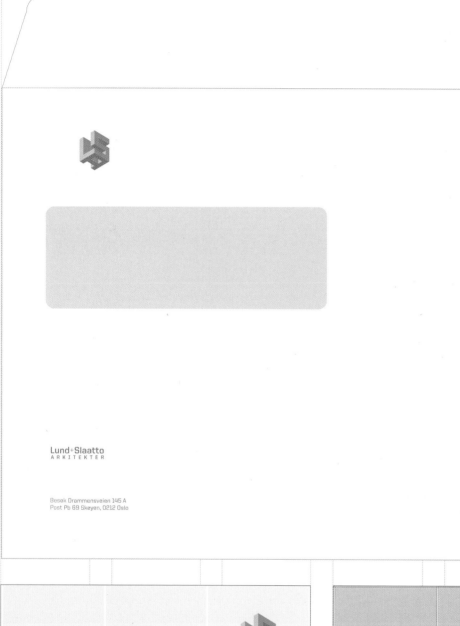

Espen Pedersen
Sivilarkitekt MNLA / Partner

Besøk Drammensveien 145 A
Post Pb 69 Skøyen, 0212 Oslo

Dir +47 22 12 29 15
Mob +47 90 72 24 25
Email pedersen@lsa.no

Tel +47 22 12 29 00
Fax +47 22 12 29 99
Web www.lsa.no

Lund+Slaatto
ARKITEKTER

Espen Pedersen
Sivilarkitekt MNLA / Partner

Besøk Drammensveien 145 A
Post Pb 69 Skøyen, 0212 Oslo

Dir +47 22 12 29 15
Mob +47 90 72 24 25
Email pedersen@lsa.no

Tel +47 22 12 29 00
Fax +47 22 12 29 99
Web www.lsa.no

Lund+Slaatto
ARKITEKTER

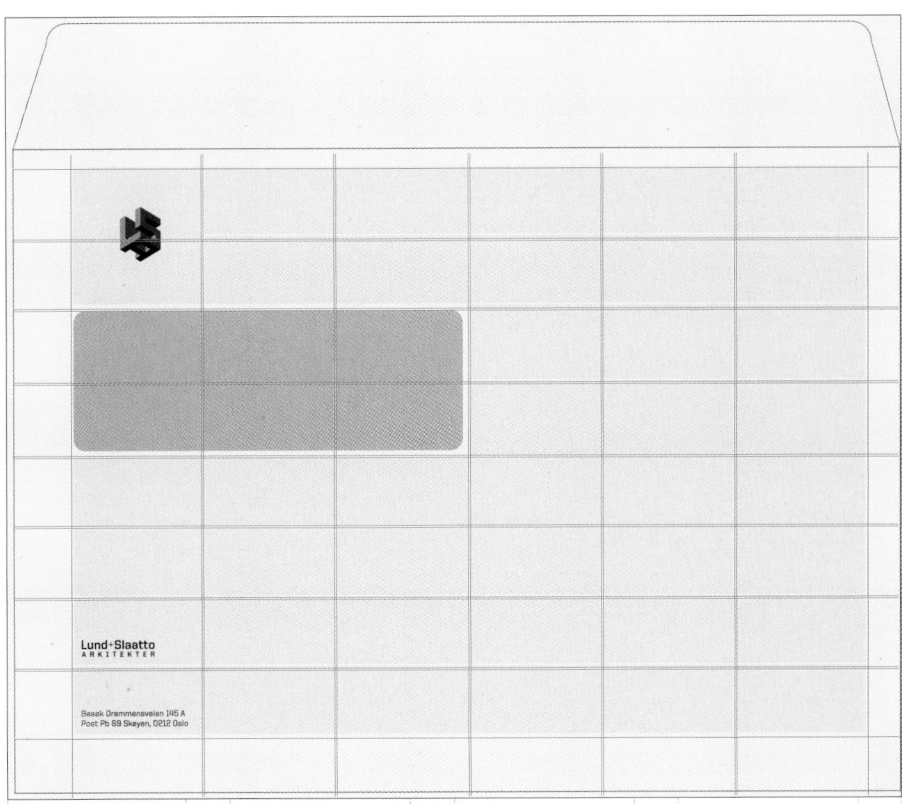

GRID SPECIFICATIONS

Page size (trimmed)	Envelope: 228 x 161mm Card: 45.5 x 89mm
Top margin	Envelope: 4mm/Card: 0.5mm
Bottom margin	Envelope: 14mm/Card: 0.5mm
Outside margin	Envelope: 15mm/Card: 0.5mm
Inside margin	Envelope: 8mm/Card: 0.5mm
Number of columns	Envelope: 6/Card: 3
Gutter width	Envelope: 0.5mm/Card: 0.5mm
Extras	Base unit—landscape rectangle with a ratio of 2:1; baseline grid, 7pt; Envelope: 9 horizontal fields/ Card: 3 horizontal fields

LUND+SLAATTO STATIONERY

Design: Karl Martin Saetren at Mission Design

Mission Design developed this identity for leading Norwegian architects Lund+Slaatto. The pared down, clean design reflects the attention to detail and architectural style for which the client is known. The layout is based on a grid using fields that have a ratio of 2:1. To ensure consistency between small items, such as business cards, and larger pieces of print, this proportion is used in all the grids, although the overall size of each field does change. For large items, more fields are added to the overall grid. In this way the grid works across a range of scales and formats.

DAMIAN HEINISCH\PHOTOGRAPHER

01 —

02 —

DAMIAN MICHAL HEINISCH
GRENSEVEIEN 11F
0571 OSLO, NORWAY
TLF +47 45 02 43 71
CONTACT@DAMIANHEINISCH.COM
WWW.DAMIAN HEINISCH
ORG.NR. 983 587 305

GRID SPECIFICATIONS

Page size (trimmed)	210 x 297mm
Top margin	7.5mm
Bottom margin	8mm
Outside margin	N/A
Inside margin	N/A
Number of columns	34
Gutter width	1mm
Extras	Baseline grid, 24pt

DAMIAN HEINISCH STATIONERY

Design: Karl Martin Saetren at Mission Design

Most grids need both horizontal and vertical subdivisions, but this identity, for photographer Damian Heinisch, uses just a series of horizontal stripes that relate to the body height of the type. The smallest type equates to this unit of measurement and fits within the height of one of the grid's units, while the larger type fits within two. The muted color palette and strict systematic design create a distinctive look, while the dark and controlled atmosphere the design exudes echoes the stark and graphic photographs of the client.

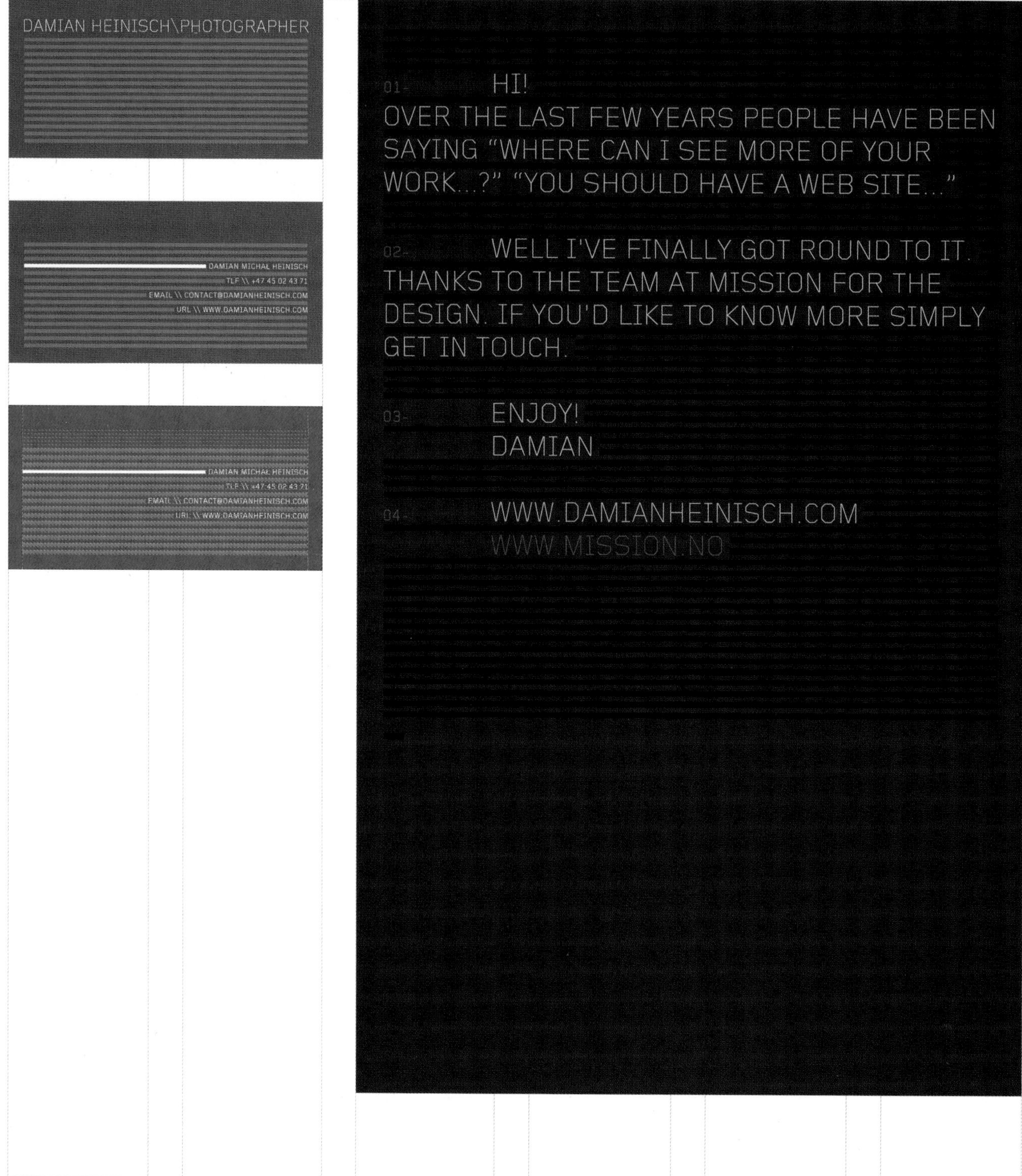
DAMIAN HEINISCH\PHOTOGRAPHER
DAMIAN MICHAŁ HEINISCH
TLF \\ +47 45 02 43 71
EMAIL \\ CONTACT@DAMIANHEINISCH.COM
URL \\ WWW.DAMIANHEINISCH.COM
DAMIAN MICHAŁ HEINISCH
TLF \\ +47 45 02 43 71
EMAIL \\ CONTACT@DAMIANHEINISCH.COM
URL \\ WWW.DAMIANHEINISCH.COM
01- HI!
OVER THE LAST FEW YEARS PEOPLE HAVE BEEN SAYING "WHERE CAN I SEE MORE OF YOUR WORK...?" "YOU SHOULD HAVE A WEB SITE..."
02- WELL I'VE FINALLY GOT ROUND TO IT. THANKS TO THE TEAM AT MISSION FOR THE DESIGN. IF YOU'D LIKE TO KNOW MORE SIMPLY GET IN TOUCH.
03- ENJOY!
DAMIAN
04- WWW.DAMIANHEINISCH.COM
WWW.MISSION.NO

01 HI!
OVER THE LAST FEW YEARS PEOPLE HAVE BEEN SAYING "WHERE CAN I SEE MORE OF YOUR WORK...?" "YOU SHOULD HAVE A WEB SITE..."

02 WELL I'VE FINALLY GOT ROUND TO IT THANKS TO THE TEAM AT MISSION FOR THE DESIGN. IF YOU'D LIKE TO KNOW MORE SIMPLY GET IN TOUCH.

03 ENJOY!
DAMIAN

04 WWW.DAMIANHEINISCH.COM
WWW.MISSION.NO

GRID SPECIFICATIONS	
Page size (trimmed)	176.4 x 282.2mm
Top margin	8.8mm
Bottom margin	91.72mm
Outside margin	7.05mm
Inside margin	7.05mm
Number of columns	1
Gutter width	N/A
Extras	Baseline grid, 24pt; 460 horizontal rows, 1.4mm apart

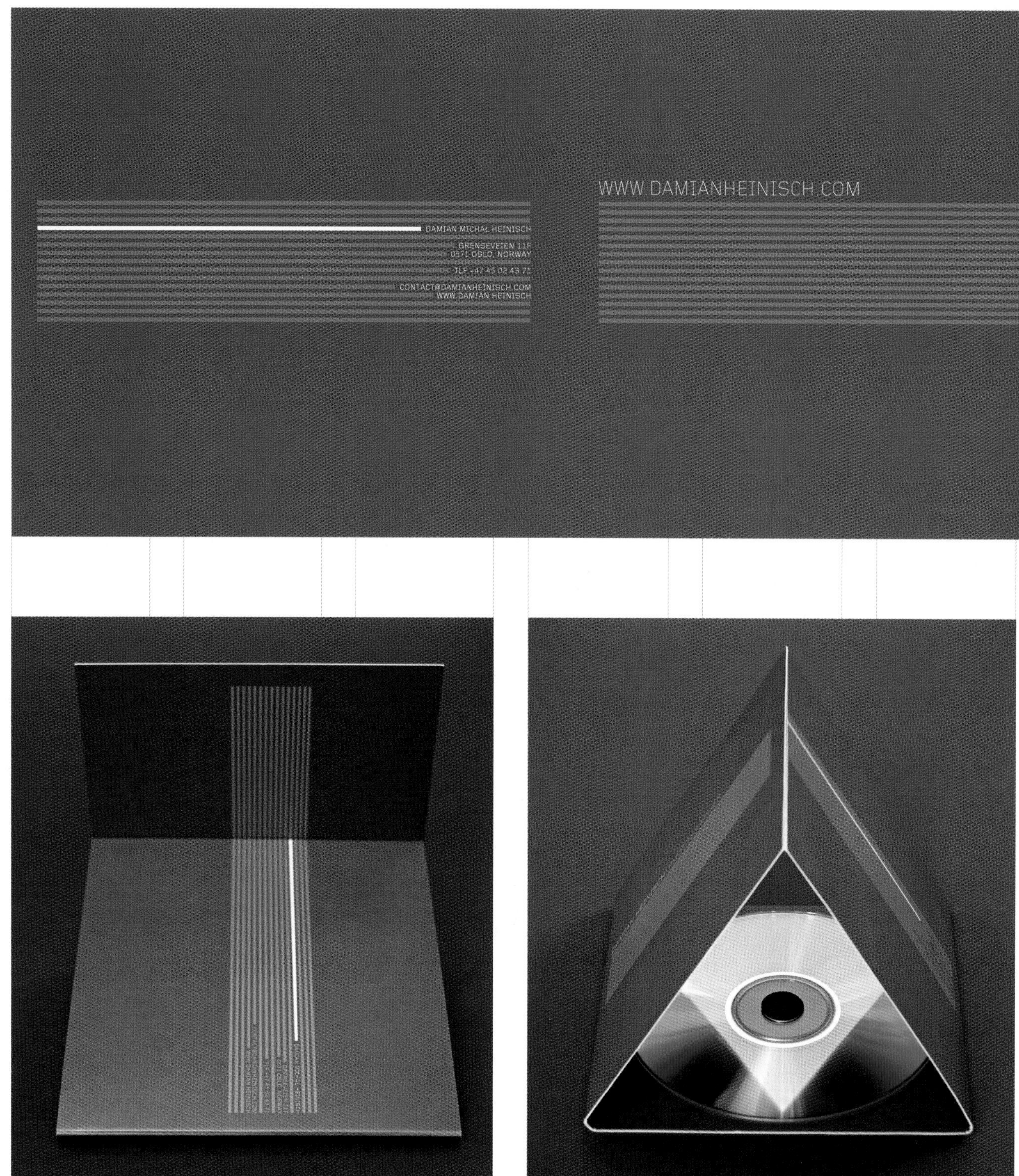
WWW.DAMIANHEINISCH.COM
DAMIAN MICHAŁ HEINISCH
GRENSEVEIEN 11F
0571 OSLO, NORWAY
TLF +47 45 02 43 71
CONTACT@DAMIANHEINISCH.COM
WWW.DAMIAN HEINISCH

DAMIAN HEINISCH\PHOTOGRAPHER

GRID SPECIFICATIONS

Page size (trimmed)	404 x 130mm
Top margin	N/A
Bottom margin	N/A
Outside margin	6.5mm
Inside margin	6.5mm
Number of columns	1
Gutter width	N/A
Extras	30 horizontal rows, 1mm apart

WWW.DAMIANHEINISCH.COM

DAMIAN HEINISCH\PHOTOGRAPHER

DAMIAN HEINISCH\PHOTOGRAPHER

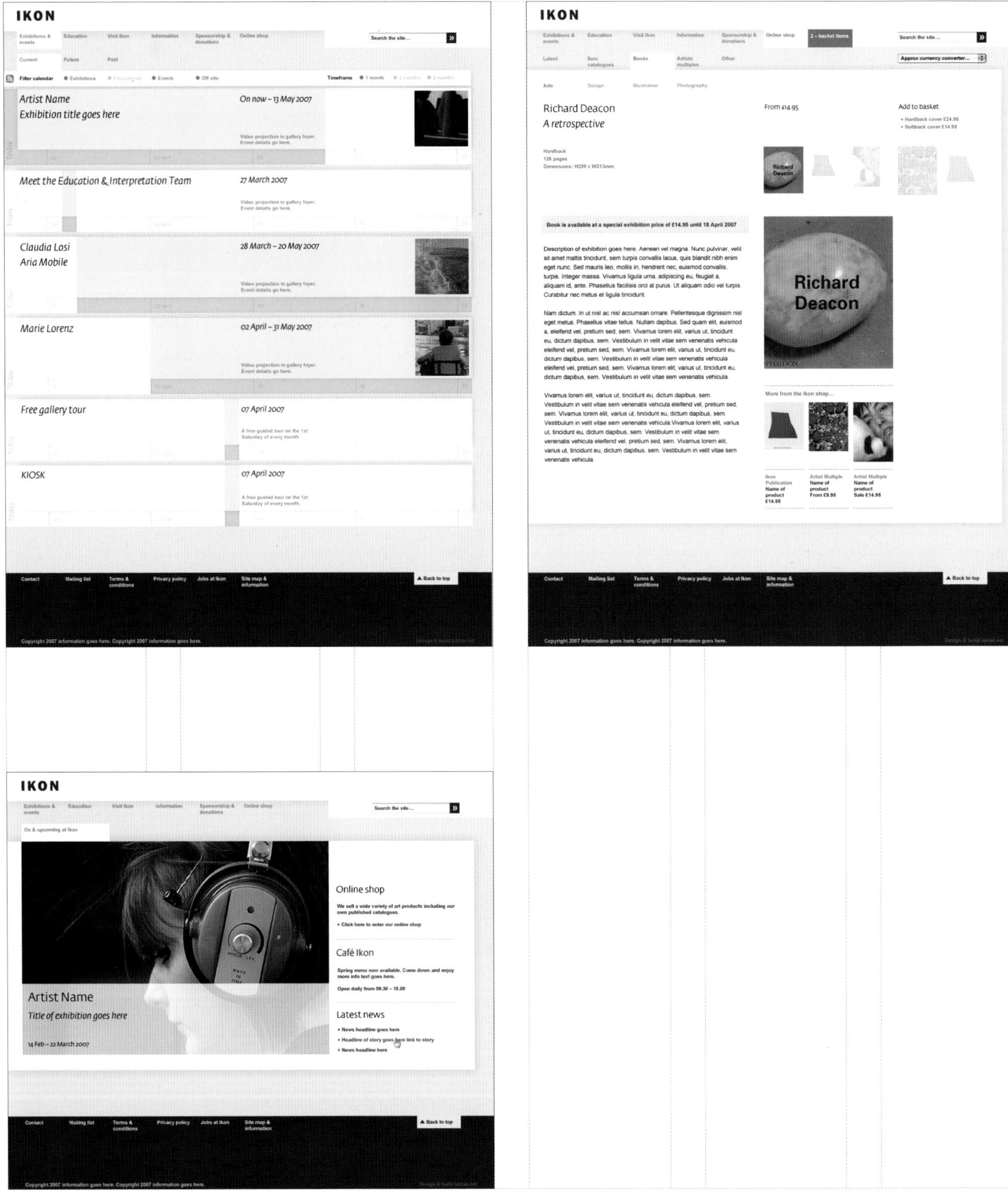
IKON
Artist Name
Exhibition title goes here
On now – 13 May 2007
Meet the Education & Interpretation Team
27 March 2007
Claudia Losi
Aria Mobile
28 March – 20 May 2007
Marie Lorenz
02 April – 31 May 2007
Free gallery tour
07 April 2007
KIOSK
07 April 2007
Richard Deacon
A retrospective
From £14.95
Add to basket
Book is available at a special exhibition price of £14.95 until 18 April 2007
Richard Deacon
Online shop
Café Ikon
Latest news
Artist Name
Title of exhibition goes here
14 Feb – 22 March 2007

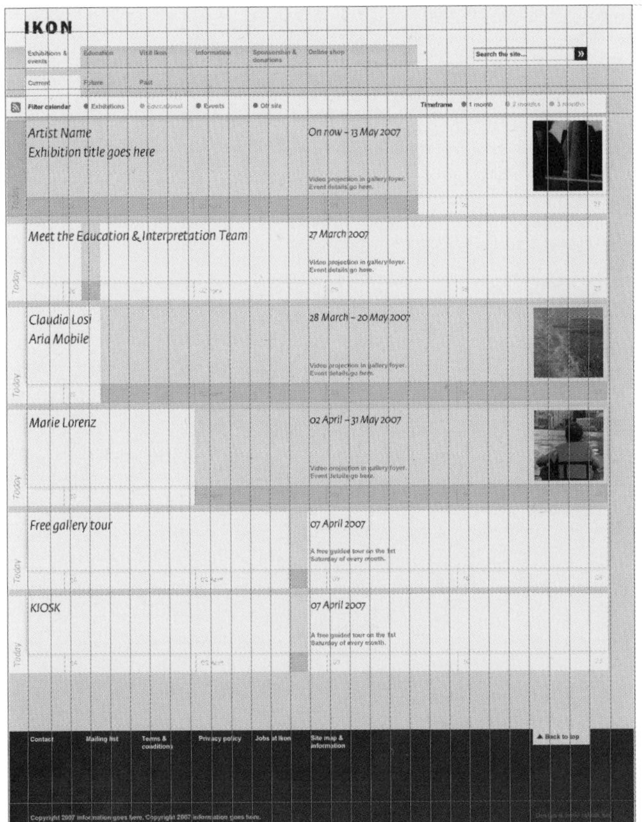

GRID SPECIFICATIONS

Page size (trimmed)	270.933 x 361.244mm
Top margin	10.583mm
Bottom margin	10.583mm
Outside margin	10.583mm
Inside margin	10.583mm
Number of columns	15
Gutter width	8.5mm
Extras	4 horizontal fields

IKON GALLERY WEBSITE

Design: Dom Murphy at TAK!

Although the unit of measurement is different, grids are as relevant to web design as they are to print. The grid for this redesign of the Ikon Gallery website is based around its events calendar and monthly overview. The page is divided into 30-pixel units. This grid determines the position of all elements of the design, from navigation to the placement of information. The grid is most apparent on the events page where the area on the left represents "today," and each block represents a subsequent day. The blue/green panels show the time frame of events over the coming month, and therefore change each day.

Magazines, newspapers & newsletters

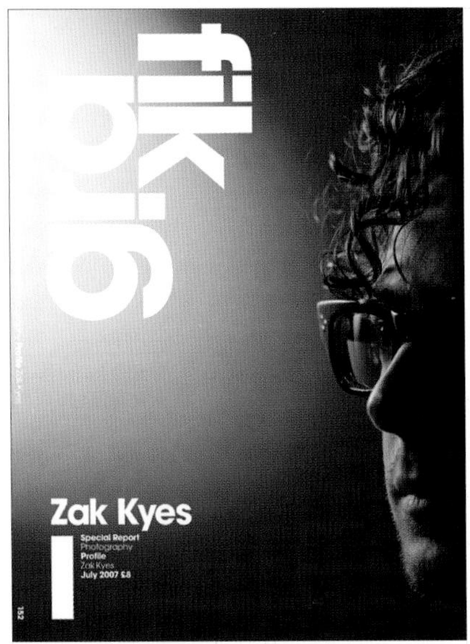

Zak Kyes
Special Report
Photography
Profile
Zak Kyes
July 2007 £8

22
Talent
Dont Panic
23
Talent

12
Roughs
01st
Park Life
Take it from us, there's no better way to spend a sunny Yorkshire day than picnicking in the county's idyllic Sculpture Park. And this month you can do so with the added lure of a new series of exhibitions courtesy of the Arts Council. Between now and January, Catch This will showcase the work of four UK-based artists all characterised by their use of new media and technology. Head down this summer to enjoy new film works by Hayley Newman and Mark Lewis, and don't forget to pack the Factor Twenty. Find out more at www.ysp.co.uk.
15th
Pen and Caper
For those of you who missed it the first time round, Felt-Tip is back, and this time it's brandishing a passport. Grafik's own exhibition of hand-penned posters (courtesy of thirty top designers including Alan Fletcher and Frauke Stegman) will land this month at Cape Town's What If the World gallery. Celebrating the simple charms of felt pen on paper, not to mention the power of the imagination, Felt-Tip opens on 15 June... Next stop Namibia. Go to www.whatiftheworld.com for the lowdown.

13
Roughs
PRINT RUN
FOR CHARITY
NO. 1046854
PRINT RUN:
10/05/07
PRIVATE:
07/06/07
DISPLAY:
design
makes me sick
design
makes me better
design
makes me
complete.
08th
Picture of Health
Does design make you sick? Or, perhaps, is it the only thing worth getting up for in the morning? See how a selection of the world's top designers and studios responded to the conundrum of design's health-giving properties thanks to a new poster exhibition at London's Kemistry Gallery this month. Print Run will feature twenty A1 screenprinted creations from the likes of Experimental Jetset, Spin and North—and what's more, all entries will be on sale, with proceeds going to the Roy Castle Lung Cancer Foundation. Healthy consciences all round. Check out www.print-run.org for further information.
15th
Great Expectations
It's been quite some time since the legendary Great Exhibition of 1851. This summer, however, prepare to be transported back in time as the Royal College of Art stages its own version to celebrate 150 years at its current South Kensington location. Bringing together all of its graduate shows for the very first time, the RCA will erect an enormous tent in Kensington Gardens alongside a simultaneous exhibition at the College Galleries. With the work of over 400 students on display, they'll certainly be giving Prince Albert a run for his money. Full details are available at www.rca.ac.uk.

GRID SPECIFICATIONS

Page size (trimmed)	225 x 311mm
Top margin	7mm
Bottom margin	11mm
Outside margin	11mm
Inside margin	20mm
Number of columns	12
Gutter width	2.5mm
Extras	N/A

GRAFIK

Design: SEA

Designing for your peers always brings added pressures. *Grafik*'s readership had been predominantly student based, but SEA's brief was to redesign the magazine to appeal to a broader demographic. Its solution rationalized the existing design, retaining its energy within a functional and accessible structure. Developing a flexible grid was the key to this. The grid is multicolumn and also divides the page into a series of small horizontal fields. This structure supports various typographic devices—large indents and staggered text, along with continuous text, captions, standfirsts, and titling—and full-bleed, squared-up, and cut-out images.

28
Showcase

June Showcase

29
Showcase

01
Jonny Enegvist, Anton Östholm and Vieter Pyk
Distance, A Conversation

02
HarrimanSteel
Lost Souls

03
Mode
Bernie Grant Arts Centre

04
Sara de Bondt and James Goggin
DJ Simpson

05
Shin Tanaka
Chitsuka Tiger

06
This Studio
Kirsten Whittle

07
Klaus Haapaniemi
Iittala

08
ODD
Casarotto Ramsay

09
Work in Progress
Self Service magazine

10
Rachel Thomas
ACNE Paper

43
Case Study

Case Study Plastique

New London-based fashion glossy Plastique struts on to the scene this month, sporting a ballsy look courtesy of Studio8. **Matt Willey** reveals how rubberstamps, monochrome, metallics and a healthy disregard for the grid helped him achieve a spirited design to match the mag's editorial brio.

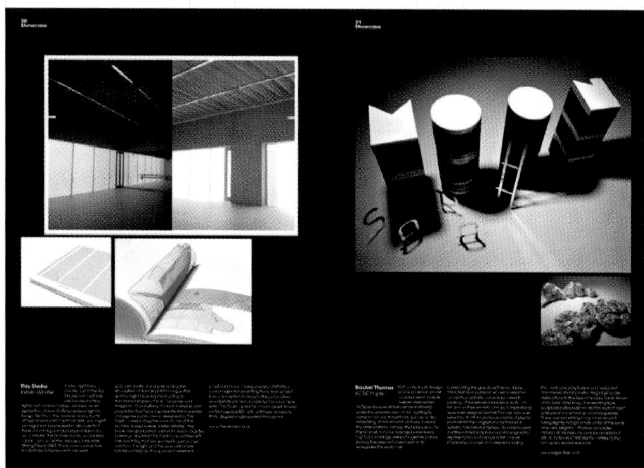

30
Showcase

31
Showcase

This Studio

Rachel Thomas

56
Special Report

Dark Arts

Alongside his much-admired commercial work, photographer Richard Learoyd has been working on a time-consuming personal project that has produced some strikingly beautiful results. Originating from his long-standing obsession with the idea of creating a photograph by the simplest means possible, here he talks to **Jonathan Bell** about creating a modern-day camera obscura.

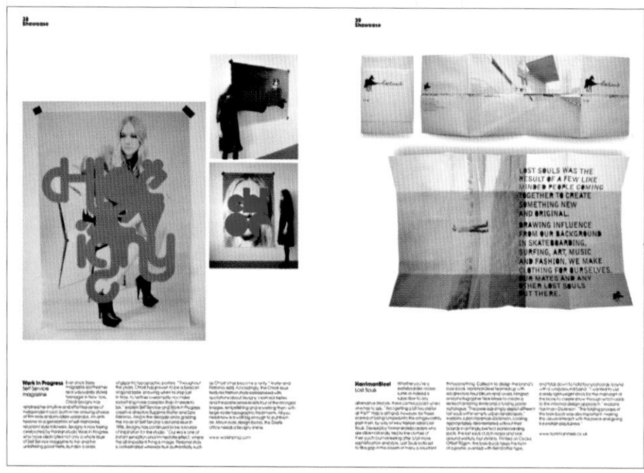

28
Showcase

29
Showcase

Work in Progress
Self Service magazine

HarrimanSteel
Lost Souls

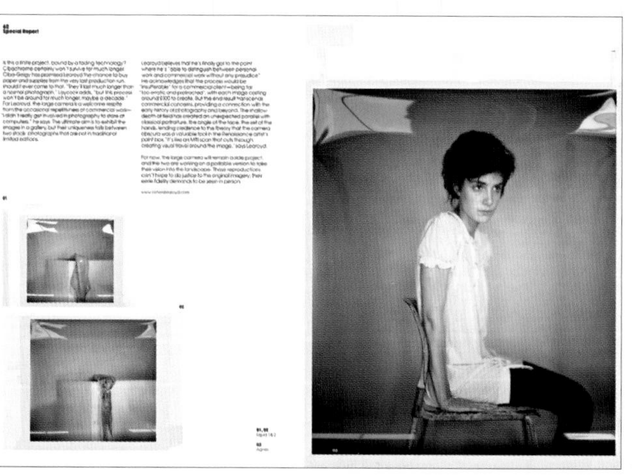

60
Special Report

Six Books
CAMOUFLAGE
FURNISH
100 years of Fashion Illustration
OPTIC NERVE
Mies van der Rohe

Insight
Always reaching for the same paper samples? Then maybe it's time to try something new. We asked the paper experts to give us the lowdown on their hottest new products, and this is what they came up with.

FAC 1 to MCR, AA Lecture, 30 November 2006

FAC1–MCR
Lecture poster designed by AA Print Studio

THERE IS AN EXPECTANCY OF MANCHESTER

Peter Saville is a designer whose practice spans the fields of graphics, creative direction and art. Past clients have included Yohji Yamamoto, Christian Dior, Givenchy, and the Whitechapel Gallery.

I invited him to speak at the AA, a place that he hadn't visited for around 20 years, but he told me he hated preparing lectures. This isn't surprising. Saville's resume is both extensive and complex, a testament to his creative restlessness and dogged desire for ultimate independence. So I struck a deal with him. I offered to put together an image-trawl through three decades of his work, the exact results of which he wasn't to find out until the conversation began that November evening.

My reasons to get Saville to talk at the AA were twofold. On the one hand, for a certain generation (often in their 30s and 40s) Saville's sumptuous visualisations were synonymous with the best of British pop culture: Joy Division, New Order, Factory Records to name a few. Beyond the nostalgia, though, Saville continues to inspire through his inimitable capacity to disown his status as a 'graphic designer' (a label he finds limiting) while being one of the most famous graphic designers living today. It's one of the reasons Manchester awarded him the job of 'art directing' its future cultural image. Here are a few highlights from our conversation.

Shumon Basar, AACP Director

On being a graphic designer: 'I became a mercenary, a hired killer. I tried to work for clients who I didn't think were too bad. You have to work, to earn money and you just have to find a way to cope with that.'

On Joy Division's Unknown Pleasures: 'I hated the idea of things looking like record covers. If you put the name of the group on the front and put the title on the front it looks like a record cover. I did what I could with the elements – Joy Division gave me the wave pattern – but I didn't know anything, I had just left college...I wasn't even sure how you prepared artwork for print. I could only trust black and white....'

On New Order: 'The most enthusiastic reaction I got to any of the covers was "They don't much mind it." The worst was for Low-Life. When they saw it they all said, in unison, "You fucking bastard". Regret they liked because it was glossy and sexy ... Bernard said, "We might fucking sell something with this one, Peter. How long has it taken?" But they never asked me about any of them, they weren't interested.'

On Yohji Yamamoto's 1991 menswear collection: 'He said, "I don't want to see the clothes. I don't want models." In other words, "I am sick of this ... It doesn't make sense anymore." So I made a campaign that said as much. The company panicked, "This is financial suicide. We have to stop Peter, we have to stop Yohji, we have to stop it!".'

On Adidas limited edition Adicolor trainers: 'Adidas told me "Do what you want" but all of these brand partnerships are a lie... The brief made the truth plain to see, dictating the meaning of the word green. On page 1 they say I'm a "preeminent image-maker of my generation" and on page 5 they

Peter Saville logos
Various logos used in the early years of Saville's practice

AArchitecture – Issue 3 News from the Architectural Association 14

AArchitecture – Issue 3 We Have To Stop Peter 15

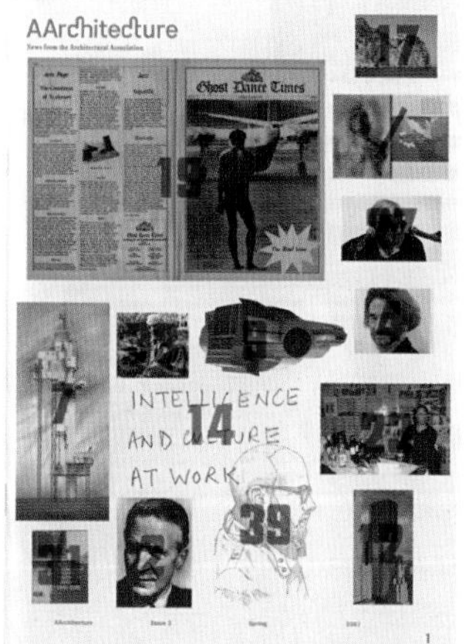

AArchitecture ISSUE 3 / SPRING 2007

CRISTIANO TORALDO DI FRANCIA: SUPERSTUDIO PG 4
MIKE WEINSTOCK ON AAIR PG 7
GOT A NEW MOTOR? PG 9
ANNEX #4 PG 11
NEW BIG BUILDINGS PG 13
WE HAVE TO STOP PETER PG 14
RUMOURS OF CAPRI PG 17
EES RESEARCH CLUSTER PG 19
BOB MAXWELL'S LAST LECTURE PG 21
KOSHIRAKURA LANDSCAPE PROJECT: A MODEL OF RURAL REJUVENATION PG 28
AA PUBLICATIONS PG 32
DENIS CLARKE HALL PG 33
AA MEMBERS PG 35
AA NEWS BRIEFS PG 36
GUESS THE BUILDING PG 38

DESIGN IS A METHOD OF DOCUMENTING REALITY RATHER THAN MAKING SOMETHING NEW. WITH THE MATERIALS AVAILABLE, BUILDING IS NOT ABOUT MAKING THE OBJECT ITSELF. IT IS THE TIME, PATIENCE AND ATTENTION GIVEN TO A PLACE – THE REVELATION OF ORDINARY THINGS – THAT IS OF VALUE SHORIKASHORA PG 28

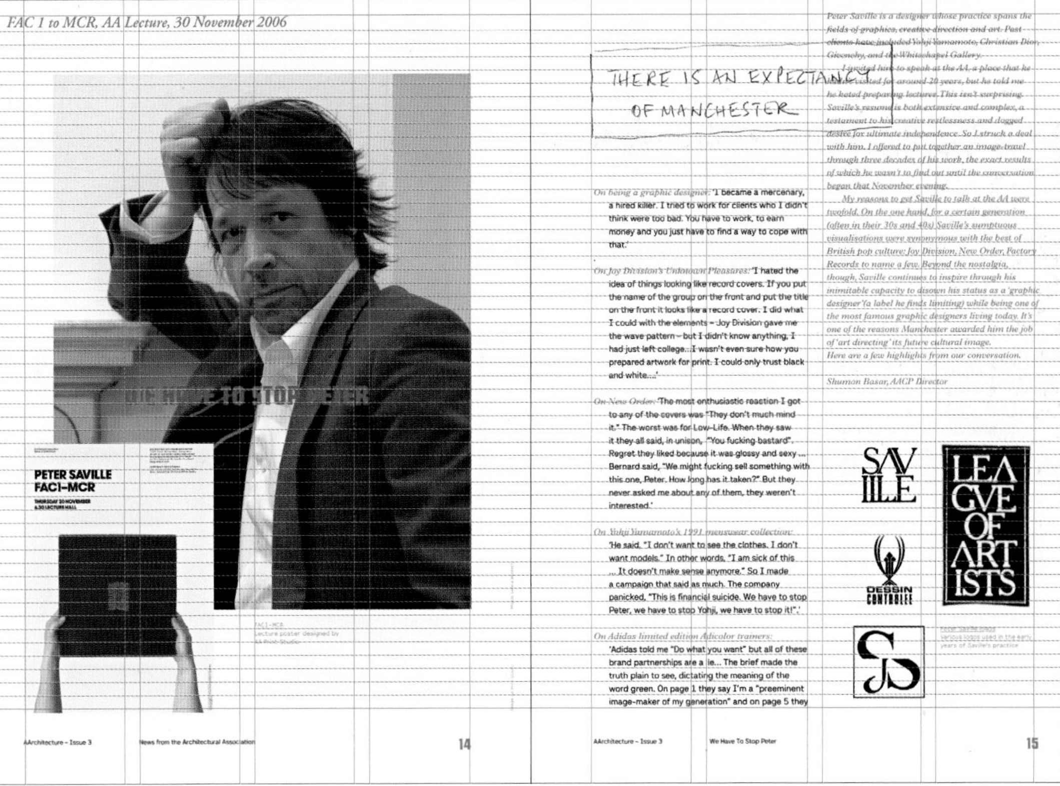

FAC 1 to MCR, AA Lecture, 30 November 2006

PETER SAVILLE
FAC1-MCR

THERE IS AN EXPECTANCY OF MANCHESTER

On being a graphic designer: 'I became a mercenary, a hired killer. I tried to work for clients who I didn't think were too bad. You have to work, to earn money and you just have to find a way to cope with that.'

On Joy Division's Unknown Pleasures: 'I hated the idea of things looking like record covers. If you put the name of the group on the front and put the title on the front it looks like a record cover. I did what I could with the elements – Joy Division gave me the wave pattern – but I didn't know anything, I had just left college... I wasn't even sure how you prepared artwork for print. I could only trust black and white....'

On New Order: 'The most enthusiastic reaction I got to any of the covers was "They don't much mind it." The worst was for Low-Life. When they saw it they all said, in unison, "You fucking bastard". Regret they liked because it was glossy and sexy ... Bernard said, "We might fucking sell something with this one, Peter. How long has it taken?" But they never asked me about any of them, they weren't interested.'

On Yohji Yamamoto's 1991 menswear collection: 'He said, "I don't want to see the clothes. I don't want models." In other words, "I am sick of this ... It doesn't make sense anymore." So I made a campaign that said as much. The company panicked, "This is financial suicide. We have to stop Peter, we have to stop Yohji, we have to stop it!".'

On Adidas limited edition Adicolor trainers: 'Adidas told me "Do what you want" but all of these brand partnerships are a lie... The brief made the truth plain to see, dictating the meaning of the word green. On page 1 they say I'm a "preeminent image-maker of my generation" and on page 5 they

Peter Saville is a designer whose practice spans the fields of graphics, creative direction and art. Past clients have included Yohji Yamamoto, Christian Dior, Givenchy, and the Whitechapel Gallery.

I invited him to speak at the AA, a place that he hasn't visited for around 20 years, but he told me he hated preparing lectures. This isn't surprising. Saville's resume is both extensive and complex, a testament to his creative restlessness and dogged desire for ultimate independence. So I struck a deal with him. I offered to put together an image-trawl through three decades of his work, the exact results of which he wasn't to find out until the conversation began that November evening.

My reasons to get Saville to talk at the AA were twofold. On the one hand, for a certain generation (often in their 30s and 40s) Saville's sumptuous visualisations were synonymous with the best of British pop culture: Joy Division, New Order, Factory Records to name a few. Beyond the nostalgia, though, Saville continues to inspire through his inimitable capacity to disown his status as a 'graphic designer' (a label he finds limiting) while being one of the most famous graphic designers living today. It's one of the reasons Manchester awarded him the job of 'art directing' its future cultural image.

Here are a few highlights from our conversation.

Shumon Basar, AACP Director

AArchitecture – Issue 3 News from the Architectural Association 14

AArchitecture – Issue 3 We Have To Stop Peter 15

GRID SPECIFICATIONS

Page size (trimmed)	176 x 250mm
Top margin	5mm
Bottom margin	24mm
Outside margin	10mm
Inside margin	20mm
Number of columns	4
Gutter width	5mm
Extras	Baseline grid, 12pt

AARCHITECTURE

Design: Wayne Daly and Grégory Ambos at AA Print Studio with Zak Group

AArchitecture is a "news-zine" published quarterly by the Architectural Association School of Architecture and designed by Wayne Daly and Grégory Ambos. The content is broad and designed to encourage debate. Sometimes spreads show a book-within-a-book, sometimes texts are indented and staggered, sometimes full-bleed color pages are used as part of the navigation. This playful layering of information reflects the purpose of the publication—to provide a discursive forum for students, tutors, and professionals to scrutinize and shape their subject. The four-column text grid appears to be only one of the publication's defining structures.

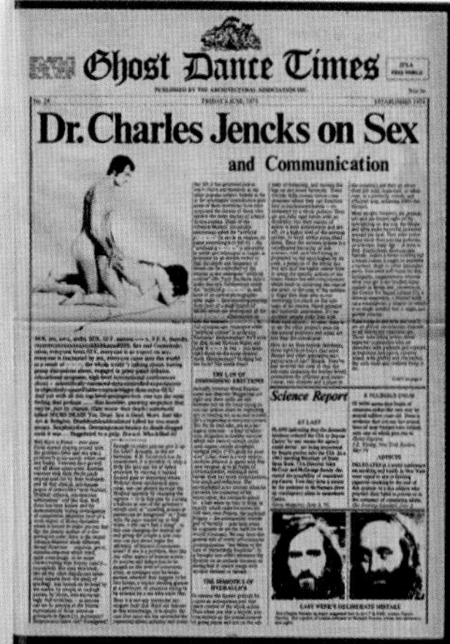
Ghost Dance Times

Dr. Charles Jencks on Sex

and Communication

Science Report

mance goals, fosters innovation in construction.[6] Yet the role of architectural design within this context remains open to question. The latest update of the building regulations made performance evaluation more complex by introducing plant and equipment into the building's 'system performance'. This could potentially lead to environmental design principles being abandoned and the responsibility for 'making it work' being handed over to the building services engineer. Architecture could lose or give up its responsibility to perform if we no longer have environmental achievement 'per form' but only 'per system'.

An example of this scenario is apparent in the Thames Gateway, one of the UK's most celebrated 'sustainable' developments. Here architecture was used as a starting point, but the results disappointed the ambitious developer. The at times restrictive and limiting architectural features did not prove as effective at reducing carbon emissions as other on-site initiatives, such as those designed to reduce car usage. The developer has now changed approach, and in more recent projects has concentrated on embedded efficiency and low and zero carbon technologies (LZC), in physical as well as service infrastructures, to facilitate sustainable lifestyles.

Dialogue

The above examples demonstrate that many interpretations of environment and environmental performance are possible. The research cluster's ambition is to harness each group's engagement, knowledge and enthusiasm for research into EES design. In order not to be biased, the curators set out to develop a methodology that would identify research topics that address issues of interest to the design community but are also of scientific relevance. This ensures the interpretation of 'environment' matches the scale against which its performance is measured.

Cluster Activity

To gain an overview of current EES design activity the cluster organised an open competition. No specific subjects or categories were defined by the organising committee. The submissions document a self-assessment of our profession's ability to respond to environmental, ecological and sustainability-related challenges. Of particular interest are the definitions of 'environment' and 'environmental performance' of the individual entries.

The outcome of the competition and accompanying survey resulted in an exhibition preview hosted at the Architectural Association from 8 to 11 November 2006. The validity and importance of differing strands was examined during the event and recommendations were made for future research activities. The winning and shortlisted entries were exhibited, and a book is forthcoming.

During the academic year the EES Research Cluster also facilitated open and informal roundtable discussions with participants from all realms of the built environment. The aim was to communicate the different stakeholders' views on performance-related issues to EES. Participants ranged from investors and developers, architects and engineers, planners and government officials to scientists, educators and students of all levels. The complexity of addressing multiple, often contradictory demands of performance was highlighted by the contrasting views.

Conclusion

The work of the EES Research Cluster has so far revealed that the terms 'environment' and 'performance' are used vaguely and are not defined rigorously enough to evaluate design performance. The survey information taken from the submissions to the Call for Projects awaits further investigation.

The intentions of the research cluster have been presented along with the methodology employed. Gathering and identifying these relevant research strands has been the main subject of the cluster's work to date, and it is hoped that this study will stimulate an ongoing discussion involving a wide audience that stretches beyond the educational setting and the architectural profession.

Acknowledgements

The authors would like to thank Brett Steele for his encouragement and the idea of creating the research clusters at the AA. The contributions of all discussion members, judges and participants are duly acknowledged.

This text is adapted from a paper published in 'PLEA Conference Proceedings 2006', the publication accompanying the 23rd Conference on Passive and Low Energy Architecture, Geneva, Switzerland, September 2006.

Werner Gaiser is a course tutor on the Sustainable Environmental Design MA programme and a Curator of the EES Research Cluster.
Steve Hardy is Unit Master of Diploma 16 and a Curator of the EES Research Cluster.

AArchitecture – Issue 3 News from the Architectural Association 26

BOB MAXWELL'S LAST LECTURE

On Wednesday 22 November, an evening event was held to mark the decision of Bob Maxwell to give up his teaching on the Histories and Theories MA programme. He marked the occasion with a lecture entitled 'Maxwell's Last Lecture'. The lecture hall was packed with students, teachers and above all with several generations of professional colleagues and friends. He opened his lecture with a melancholy roll-call of all those who were absent by reason of death. Foremost in his mind was the figure of James Stirling. The evening was full of the memory of friends.

The lecture itself must have surprised some of his audience, who perhaps were expecting a more purely architectural topic. But the teacher in him was still passionately concerned with educating his fellow architects by introducing aspects of the human sciences which could illuminate architecture, and which could provide architects with an understanding of how all objects present meaning. Most of the lecture was devoted to an outline of subjects as it was understood by de Saussure and Roland Barthes. The concerns reflected on Bob's teaching, both while he had been Dean at Princeton University and in his teaching at the AA in the last two decades.

After the lecture tributes were paid to Bob by Ed Jones and Rick Mather, who spoke warmly of Bob as an architect and a friend. From his lecture the audience were again made aware of the striking force of his complex character in which the twin aspects of Ulster Protestantism and Francophile Hedonism were intertwined. Above all the audience was aware of his underlying humanity, which has always shaped his students' experience of him.

By Mark Cousins, Director of Histories and Theories programme.

Bob Maxwell
Places were reserved long in advance for Bob Maxwell's last lecture

AArchitecture – Issue 3 Bob Maxwell's Last Lecture 27

SATELLITE is an ad-hoc magazine, colonising the architecture of other AA publications, in this case AArchitecture No. 3, to create an autonomous space for editorial and curatorial projects.

There are no limitations, but possible subjects may include: student work, fictions, satrical reviews, essays, independent projects...

The idea behind this selection of Second and Third Year projects is to show some of the diversity of student work created here at the weird and remarkable Architectural Association. I am myself part of the Intermediate School; every day I see and hear about my fellow students' projects, and the richness and the creativity of the work never cease to amaze me. Everyone brings ideas and emotions into the school, producing the recipe for this glowing soup we all swim in. This is a taster – a small sample of the AA's collective creativity – that I hope you will enjoy.
– FH

Satellite 1
Guest-edited by Fredrik Hellberg
Hosted by AArchitecture Issue 3
Published by the Architectural Association
Designed by Wayne Daly/Zak Kyes

To guest-edit please write to:
contribute@aaschool.ac.uk

Azri Syazwan – Inter One

The vitrine is required to hold and unfold information about a specific product. In this case a football was the subject of interest. While the first layer of the vitrine communicates the history of developing the 'modern' football, the next layer reveals the true nature of football production, including its darker side and the nature of the construction itself. The user deconstructs the components of the football on the wired vitrine placed onto specified areas on the board, and in the process reveals video information through a computer and projector located elsewhere.

AArchitecture
News from the Architectural Association

I DO NOT WANT TO TALK TO YOU ABOUT ARCHITECTURE. I DETEST TALK ABOUT ARCHITECTURE.

VERSO

AArchitecture
News from the Architectural Association
Issue 4 / Summer 2007
aaschool.net

Published by Architectural Association,
36 Bedford Square, London WC1B 3ES.

Contact:
contribute@aaschool.ac.uk
Nicola Quinn +44 (0) 207 887 4000

To send news briefs:
news@aaschool.ac.uk

EDITORIAL TEAM
Brett Steele, Editorial Director
Nicola Quinn, Managing Editor
Zak Kyes / Zak Group, Art Director
Wayne Daly, Graphic Designer
Alex Lorente
Fredrik Hellberg

ACKNOWLEDGEMENTS
Valerie Bennett
Pamela Johnston
Marilyn Sparrow
Hinda Sklar
Russell Bestley

Printed by Cassochrome, Belgium

CONTRIBUTORS

Rosa Ainley
<eventslist@aaschool.ac.uk>

Edward Bottoms
<edward@aaschool.ac.uk>

Mark Cousins
<markcousins@aaschool.ac.uk>

Wayne Daly
<daly_wa@aaschool.ac.uk>

Margaret Dewhurst
<margiedewhurst@hotmail.com>

Zak Kyes
<z@zak.to>

Aram Mooradian
<aram.mooradian@gmail.com>

Harmony Murphy
<harmonymurphy@gmail.com>

Joel Newman
<joel@aaschool.ac.uk>

Kitty O'Grady
<ogrady_ki@aaschool.ac.uk>

Mark Prizeman

Simone Sagi
<simone@aaschool.ac.uk>

Vasilis Stroumpakos
<vasi@00110.org>

COVER

Front Cover:
Le Corbusier, AA after-dinner speech
1 April 1953

Front inner cover: Hans Scharoun's Staatsbibliothek
Back inner cover: Peter Eisenman's Memorial to the Murdered Jews of Europe
Photos: Timothy Deal, on AA Members' trip to Berlin, 19–22 April 2007

* * * *

PEIGNOT

MARY TYLER MOORE
MARY TYLER MOORE

Headlines in the issue are set in Peignot, a geometrically constructed sans-serif display typeface designed by A. M. Cassandre in 1937. It was commissioned by the French foundry Peignot et Deberny. The typeface is notable for not having a traditional lower-case, but in its place a 'multi-case' combining traditional lower-case and small capital characters. The typeface achieved some popularity in poster and advertising publishing from its release through the late 1940s. Use of Peignot declined with the growth of the International Typographic Style which favoured less decorative, more objective typeface. Peignot experienced a revival in the 1970s as the typeface used on *The Mary Tyler Moore Show*. While often classified as 'decorative', the face is a serious exploration of typographic form and legibility.
Taken from:
http://en.wikipedia.org/wiki/Peignot

Body text is set in Sabon Bold.

Architectural Association (Inc.), Registered Charity No. 311083. Company limited by guarantee. Registered in England No. 171402. Registered office as above.

AArchitecture ISSUE 4 / SUMMER 2007

PATRICK BOUCHAIN:
KNOW-HOW/SAVOIR FAIRE PG 4
AA MEMBERS' VISIT: BERLIN PG 8
NORMAN KLEIN:
THE SPACE BETWEEN 1975–2050 PG 9
NEW MEDIA RESEARCH INITIATIVE PG 13
EVERYTHING YOU'VE EVER WANTED
TO KNOW ABOUT ORNAMENT PG 16
STREET FARMER PG 19
CORB AT THE AA PG 23
MARK COUSINS: THE UGLY PG 26
JOHN MACLEAN: BRASILIA PG 28
AA SUMMER PAVILION 2007 PG 30
DALE BENEDICT /
AA SECRETARY'S OFFICE PG 32
SOM AWARD / AA MEMBERS PG 33
AA NEWS BRIEFS PG 34

WE DO NOT KNOW EACH OTHER BUT WE READ EACH OTHER AS SIGNS, WE BUILD UP A CODE OF RECOGNITION THAT ENABLES US TO IDENTIFY PEOPLE AND OBJECTS THROUGH THEIR ATTRIBUTES. MARK COUSINS PG 27

PATRICK BOUCHAIN
KNOW-HOW/SAVOIR FAIRE
ARCHITECTURAL ASSOCIATION
SCHOOL OF ARCHITECTURE
icon
THE BUILDING SITE IS
THE IDEAL PLACE
TO SHARE DESIRES
AND KNOWLEDGE
AND BUILD A RELEVANT
VISION FOR THE
FUTURE, IN THE INTEREST
OF EVERYONE

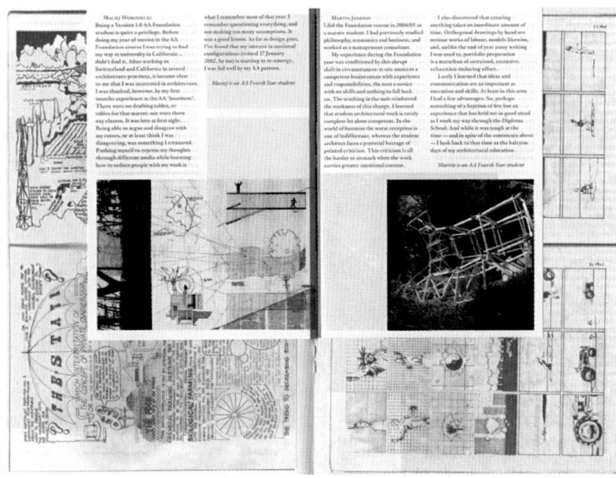

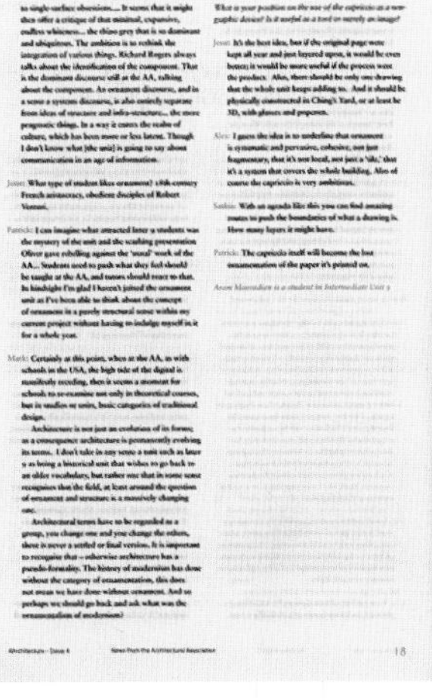

Street Farmer 2

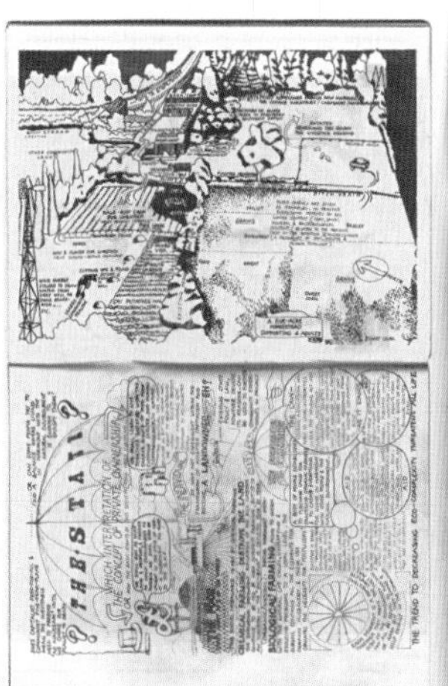

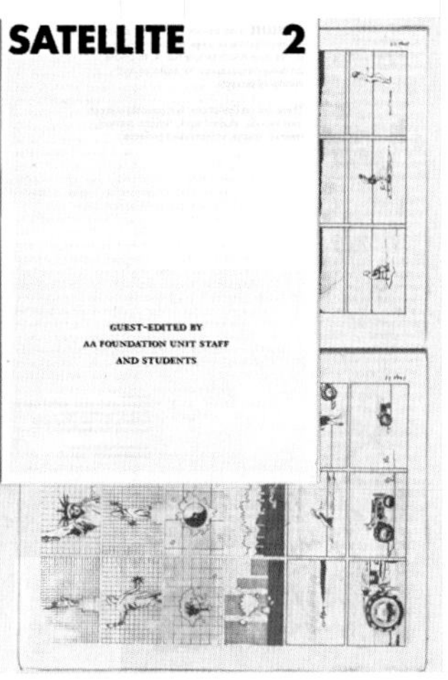
SATELLITE 2
GUEST-EDITED BY
AA FOUNDATION UNIT STAFF
AND STUDENTS

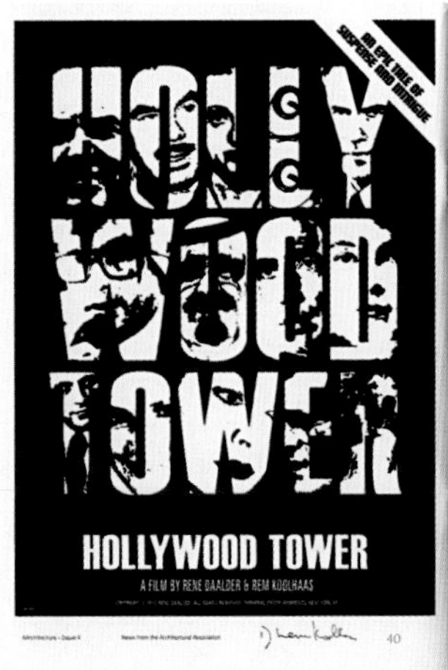
AN EPIC TALE OF SUSPENSE AND INTRIGUE
HOLLYWOOD TOWER
A FILM BY RENE DAALDER & REM KOOLHAAS
40

Photography by Pete Moss

Type designer Matthew Carter (facing page) was born in England in the 1930s. He trained as a punch cutter in the Netherlands before working as typography consultant for Crosfield electronics. He later worked for Mergenthaler-Linotype in New York before becoming typography consultant to Her Majesty's Stationery Office in the 1980s. In 1981 he set up Bitstream Inc with Mike Parker in Massachusetts, the first independent American company to manufacture digital type. In 1992 he founded Carter & Cone Type Inc with Cherie Cone. Matthew Carter was named a Royal Designer for Industry in 1981. In his recent visit to London, Carter gave a talk at the Design Museum: for future events and exhibitions see www.designmuseum.org

Simon Esterson is a magazine and newspaper designer. He has been art director of The Guardian in London and creative director of Domus in Milan.

With thanks to the St Bride Printing Library

SIMON ESTERSON: You are one of the very few type designers to have worked with metal type-setting, then photosetting, through the digital revolution, and then on to screen-based, non-print media. How do you feel about what has happened to typeface design in the last 25 years?

MATTHEW CARTER: [laughs] It's been 50 years, by the way, since I left school and started working in type. I'm happy to have had a traditional training, although even by the late 1950s making type by hand was obsolete commercially speaking. It never really had a commercial application for me. It's been very interesting to live through these various changes in technology. Through most of type's history, sons, grandsons, great grandsons came and went and the technology never changed. The opposite has been true in the last 50 years: the technology has changed faster than the typefaces if anything. So it's been interesting.

My own feeling about it: if you took all of the things that go into making a typeface, and you gave them a score out of ten, I would say that the technical part of it is worth one or two on that scale. In other words, however the type is made, about at least 80 per cent of it is still the same, whatever tools you use. There are exceptions to that. When I worked on Bell Centennial for the United States phonebooks, where the environment it's used in is rather hostile, the technology played a larger part. For phone books, we're talking about six point type on newsprint. When I did the screen fonts for Microsoft, I think more than 20 percent of that was technical influence. So that's my feeling about it. A lot of people disagree and believe that type cut in steel has different qualities, and I can look at beautiful letterpress printing from metal type and I can see that things have been lost. But in my opinion the gains in digital type far outweigh the losses.

It's a fatuous thing to say in a way, but if I had my choice of period in which to have worked in this business I would choose exactly the one that I happen to have lucked into, precisely because of all these changes. I'm endlessly glad to have survived into the digital era because I regard that as the best technology we've ever had. There are some drawbacks, there have been some losses, but for me, it's just a dream.

SE: I suppose designers who are used to working on a Mac, take being able to track and kern type for granted, when actually tracking and kerning with metal type-setting was very difficult, if not sometimes impossible.

MC: Kerning is a good example: strictly speaking, there was kerning in the latter days of film composition, there were some refinement programmes and so on, but essentially it became part of type with the coming of Type 1 PostScript fonts, True Type and so on. I regard kerning tables as a great blessing for typography.

SE: Once, the making of type was almost like a secret society: there was the mystique of being a punch-cutter and type-maker. Then it became quite an industrial process and Monotype and Linotype seemed to rule the world in composition terms: if they didn't make a typeface then it wasn't going to be made. Now, there's this incredible blossoming, where it seems as if everybody can be a type designer if they want to.

MC: I'm entirely happy about that. I'm sometimes a bit nostalgic about the time when it was a tiny club, when you had to go through painful initiations in order to be a type designer, but on balance, I'm glad the whole thing got blown wide open by the computer and particularly the coming of open font formats in the late 80s. There was a huge flow of interest in type design and it got democratised. There was no longer just a priesthood, but a sort of laity as well. I think a huge amount of very interesting work was done then, and some continues. What there is much more of, of course, are people who are primarily graphic designers or typographers, who occasionally make a typeface as a labour of love. This would have never happened in the old regime because it was just too hard to get started. Now, it's not uncommon to see student portfolios with typefaces they've designed and I'm completely delighted by that. It doesn't mean to say that everything made under those conditions are things that I like, but cream rises, and out of that ferment come very good things.

SE: Type design is quite stratified – even in the Victorian era you had display type and text type, and there's been a lot of activity in recent years in exuberant display typography. While you do some of these things too, a lot of your work is about what I'd call industrial-strength text typesetting.

MC: Yes, I think in my case there isn't a moral issue there, it's just a matter of temperament. Because I made my start in type founding, I never went to design school. I think that I've always been interested in these rather thorny, problem-solving projects, which are largely text faces. I have done a few display faces as well, but I seem to have mostly been asked to work in the text field, and I'm very happy with that. I don't think you're ever going to be a type designer unless you accept that you have to work within certain constraints.

SE: How does it work? Do you sit at home and wait for the phone to ring, with somebody saying 'we've got a problem,' or do you wake up in the morning thinking 'I have this beautiful idea for a lower case A, now I just need to do the rest of the alphabet?'

MC: I suppose both things happen. In an ideal world, life would be a nice balance between speculative projects and commissions. In fact I'm not good at bright ideas. If you sat me down in front of a blank computer screen on a Monday it would still be blank on the Friday. But if you said to me 'we have this typeface and it's a bit too heavy and too wide, fix it up,' I'd have something for you.

I tend not to get bolts from the blue very often although for example, a typeface like Mantinia was the direct result of going into an exhibition at the Royal Academy in 1992 and looking at some lettering there. I wish that happened more often, I wish I could say 'I'm going down the road now, I'm going to see a piece of vernacular lettering which is going to turn me on and become a wonderful typeface,' it doesn't normally happen.

SE: So it's not the case that you walk down the street and see so much inspiring typography...

MC: Obviously, I do see things I like, walking down the street, looking at books and so on. A good proportion of the faces that I've done have been based, to some degree, on historical models, and I'm interested in the history of typeface design, but, as you say, a lot of my faces do come about because somebody calls me up with a particular problem. ▶

A Life in Type

(Part One)

Matthew Carter is the world's leading type designer. In the apt setting of the St Bride Printing Library, editorial designer Simon Esterson talks to him about his 50 years in the industry. Continued next month

GRID SPECIFICATIONS

Page size (trimmed)	280 x 280mm
Top margin	8mm
Bottom margin	18mm
Outside margin	8mm
Inside margin	18mm
Number of columns	15
Gutter width	4.5mm
Extras	N/A

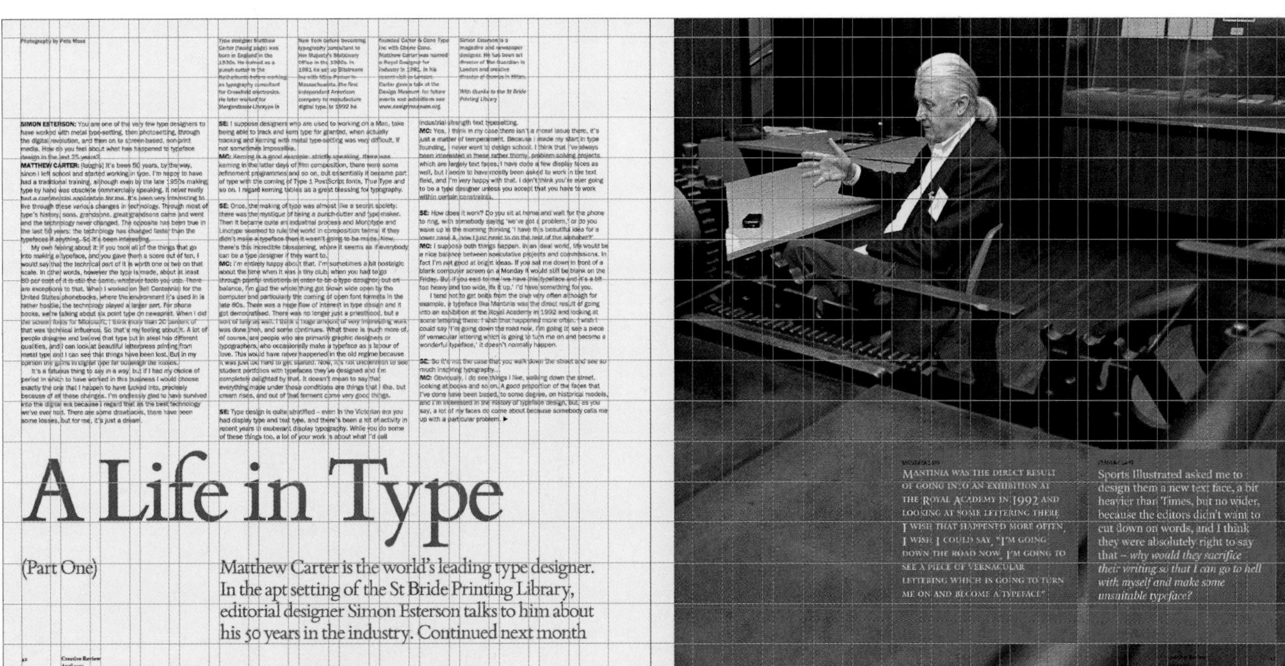

Photography by Pete Moss

Type designer Matthew Carter (facing page) was born in England in the 1930s. He trained as a punch cutter in the Netherlands before working as typography consultant for Crosfield electronics. He later worked for Mergenthaler-Linotype in New York before becoming typography consultant to Her Majesty's Stationery Office in the 1980s. In 1981 he set up Bitstream Inc with Mike Parker in Massachusetts, the first independent American company to manufacture digital type. In 1992 he founded Carter & Cone Type Inc with Cherie Cone. Matthew Carter was named a Royal Designer for Industry in 1981. In his recent visit to London, Carter gave a talk at the Design Museum; for future events and exhibitions see www.designmuseum.org

Simon Esterson is a magazine and newspaper designer. He has been art director of The Guardian in London and creative director of Domus in Milan.

With thanks to the St Bride Printing Library

SIMON ESTERSON: You are one of the very few type designers to have worked with metal type-setting, then photosetting, through the digital revolution, and then on to screen-based, non-print media. How do you feel about what has happened to typeface design in the last 25 years?

MATTHEW CARTER: [laughs] It's been 50 years, by the way, since I left school and started working in type. I'm happy to have had a traditional training, although even by the late 1950s making type by hand was obsolete commercially speaking. It never really had a commercial application for me. It's been very interesting to live through these various changes in technology. Through most of type's history, sons, grandsons, great grandsons came and went and the technology never changed. The opposite has been true in the last 50 years: the technology has changed faster than the typefaces if anything. So it's been interesting.

My own feeling about it: if you took all of the things that go into making a typeface, and you gave them a score out of ten, I would say that the technical part of it is worth one or two on that scale. In other words, however the type is made, about at least 80 per cent of it is still the same, whatever tools you use. There are exceptions to that. When I worked on Bell Centennial for the United States phonebooks, where the environment it's used in is rather hostile, the technology played a larger part. For phone books, we're talking about six point type on newsprint. When I did the screen fonts for Microsoft, I think more than 20 percent of that was technical influence. So that's my feeling about it. A lot of people disagree and believe that type cut in steel has different qualities, and I can look at beautiful letterpress printing from metal type and I can see that things have been lost. But in my opinion the gains in digital type far outweigh the losses.

It's a fatuous thing to say in a way, but if I had my choice of period in which to have worked in this business I would choose exactly the one that I happen to have lucked into, precisely because of all these changes. I'm endlessly glad to have survived into the digital era because I regard that as the best technology we've ever had. There are some drawbacks, there have been some losses, but for me, it's just a dream.

SE: I suppose designers who are used to working on a Mac, take being able to track and kern type for granted, when actually tracking and kerning with metal type-setting was very difficult, if not sometimes impossible.

MC: Kerning is a good example: strictly speaking, there was kerning in the latter days of film composition, there were some refinement programmes and so on, but essentially it became part of type with the coming of Type 1 PostScript fonts, True Type and so on. I regard kerning tables as a great blessing for typography.

SE: Once, the making of type was almost like a secret society: there was the mystique of being a punch-cutter and type-maker. Then it became quite an industrial process and Monotype and Linotype seemed to rule the world in composition terms: if they didn't make a typeface then it wasn't going to be made. Now, there's this incredible blossoming, where it seems as if everybody can be a type designer if they want to.

MC: I'm entirely happy about that. I'm sometimes a bit nostalgic about the time when it was a tiny club, when you had to go through painful initiations in order to be a type designer, but on balance, I'm glad the whole thing got blown wide open by the computer and particularly the coming of open font formats in the late 80s. There was a huge flow of interest in type design and it got democratised. There was no longer just a priesthood, but a sort of laity as well. I think a huge amount of very interesting work was done then, and some continues. What there is much more of, of course, are people who are primarily graphic designers or typographers, who occasionally make a typeface as a labour of love. This would have never happened in the old regime because it was just too hard to get started. Now, it's not uncommon to see student portfolios with typefaces they've designed and I'm completely delighted by that. It doesn't mean to say that everything made under those conditions are things that I like, but cream rises, and out of that ferment come very good things.

SE: Type design is quite stratified – even in the Victorian era you had display type and text type, and there's been a lot of activity in recent years in exuberant display typography. While you do some of these things too, a lot of your work is about what I'd call industrial-strength text typesetting.

MC: Yes, I think in my case there isn't a moral issue there, it's just a matter of temperament. Because I made my start in type founding, I never went to design school. I think that I've always been interested in these rather thorny, problem-solving projects, which are largely text faces. I have done a few display faces as well, but I seem to have mostly been asked to work in the text field, and I'm very happy with that. I don't think you're ever going to be a type designer unless you accept that you have to work within certain constraints.

SE: How does it work? Do you sit at home and wait for the phone to ring, with somebody saying 'we've got a problem,' or do you wake up in the morning thinking 'I have this beautiful idea for a lower case A, now I just need to do the rest of the alphabet?'

MC: I suppose both things happen. In an ideal world, life would be a nice balance between speculative projects and commissions. In fact I'm not good at bright ideas. If you sat me down in front of a blank computer screen on a Monday it would still be blank on the Friday. But if you said to me 'we have this typeface and it's a bit too heavy and too wide, fix it up,' I'd have something for you.

I tend not to get bolts from the blue very often although for example, a typeface like Mantinia was the direct result of going into an exhibition at the Royal Academy in 1992 and looking at some lettering there. I wish that happened more often. I wish I could say 'I'm going down the road now, I'm going to see a piece of vernacular lettering which is going to turn me on and become a wonderful typeface,' it doesn't normally happen.

SE: So it's not the case that you walk down the street and see so much inspiring typography...

MC: Obviously, I do see things I like, walking down the street, looking at books and so on. A good proportion of the faces that I've done have been based, to some degree, on historical models, and I'm interested in the history of typeface design, but, as you say, a lot of my faces do come about because somebody calls me up with a particular problem. ►

A Life in Type

(Part One)

Matthew Carter is the world's leading type designer. In the apt setting of the St Bride Printing Library, editorial designer Simon Esterson talks to him about his 50 years in the industry. Continued next month

MANTINIA WAS THE DIRECT RESULT OF GOING INTO AN EXHIBITION AT THE ROYAL ACADEMY IN 1992 AND LOOKING AT SOME LETTERING THERE. I WISH THAT HAPPENED MORE OFTEN. I WISH I COULD SAY, "I'M GOING DOWN THE ROAD NOW, I'M GOING TO SEE A PIECE OF VERNACULAR LETTERING WHICH IS GOING TO TURN ME ON AND BECOME A TYPEFACE"

Sports Illustrated asked me to design them a new text face, a bit heavier than Times, but no wider, because the editors didn't want to cut down on words, and I think they were absolutely right to say that – *why would they sacrifice their writing so that I can go to hell with myself and make some unsuitable typeface?*

CREATIVE REVIEW

Design: Nathan Gale at Creative Review

When the design magazine *Creative Review* was redesigned, it gave art director Nathan Gale an opportunity to introduce one grid that was flexible enough to accommodate all the different material the magazine shows. Previously it had used more than one grid, and Gale thought this was an opportune time to rationalize the design system. The new grid is multicolumn and divided into small horizontal fields. By combining columns and fields, text can run to the three different widths the magazine needs, and images of different sizes and scales can be positioned easily and flexibly.

ABRAM GAMES MAXIMUM MEANING FROM MINIMUM MEANS

By Carmen Martínez-López

Abram Games (1914-96) was one of the great poster designers of the 20th century. His contribution to the development of graphic communication was even more remarkable for having been made within the constricts of propaganda communication during World War II. Images such as *Your Talk May Kill Your Comrades* or *Don't Crow About What You Know About* applied modern design sophistication to the primary messages of wartime in a witty and effective way. Although Games' career coincided with the demise of his original trade as a graphic artist, as the promotional power of posters diminished in the face of television and colour supplements, he remained productive throughout. Following Games' death in 1996, the illustrator David Gentleman FCSD wrote that: **"All Abram Games' designs were recognisably his own. They had vigour, imagination, passion and individuality ... And he was lucky—and clever—in contriving, over a long and creative working life, to keep on doing what he did best."**

SELECTED ILLUSTRATIONS LEFT TO RIGHT

Festival of Britain, 1951
© Estate of Abram Games

British Railways poster to promote tourism in Blackpool, 1952
© Estate of Abram Games

London Underground, 1937
© Transport for London

20

The Designer October & November '03 21

The Designer
The Magazine of The Chartered Society of Designers

OUR SOCIETY 3
4
THE WORKS 4
NEWS & EVENTS 6
CSD INTERNATIONAL 8
THE MODERN JOURNEY 10
14
DARE TO BE DIFFERENT 14
BOOK REVIEWS 17
GOING FREELANCE 18
BATTLE FOR THE MIDDLE GROUND 20
23
STUDENT & GRADUATE 22
CAREER LONG LEARNING 24

ABRAM GAMES MAXIMUM MEANING FROM MINIMUM MEANS

By Carmen Martínez-López

Abram Games (1914–96) was one of the great poster designers of the 20th century. His contribution to the development of graphic communication was even more remarkable for having been made within the constricts of propaganda communication during World War II. Images such as *Your Talk May Kill Your Comrades* or *Don't Crow About What You Know About* applied modern design sophistication to the primary messages of wartime in a witty and effective way. Although Games' career coincided with the demise of his original trade as a graphic artist, as the promotional power of posters diminished in the face of television and colour supplements, he remained productive throughout. Following Games' death in 1996, the illustrator David Gentleman RCSD wrote that:

"All Abram Games' designs were recognisably his own. They had vigour, imagination, passion and individuality ... And he was lucky—and clever—in contriving, over a long and creative working life, to keep on doing what he did best."

SELECTED ILLUSTRATIONS LEFT TO RIGHT

The Designer

GRID SPECIFICATIONS	
Page size (trimmed)	297 x 210mm
Top margin	12mm
Bottom margin	21.1mm
Outside margin	10mm
Inside margin	10mm
Number of columns	6
Gutter width	5mm
Extras	Baseline grid, 11pt starting at 12mm

THE DESIGNER

Design: Brad Yendle at Design Typography

The Designer is a 32-page magazine produced every month by the Chartered Society of Designers. Given its readership, any redesign would be a tough brief, particularly as the objective was to increase appeal by injecting visual excitement. Inspired by the work of Willy Fleckhaus and Simon Esterson, designer Brad Yendle introduced a simple six-column grid. By combining columns, this could accommodate text and a variety of picture sizes. Yendle paid particular attention to typographic detailing, making sure that the choice of font, type sizes, and leading gave optimum legibility in his three-column text structure.

CONTINUOUS PROFESSIONAL DEVELOPMENT CSD COURSES

BRASIL!
BRASIL!

Millions on the planet know, Brazil is 'Campeao do mundo' – the reigning world champion of futébol – itself the world's greatest sport …
By Robert L Peters FCDC

AS

INSTITUTO BRASIL LEITOR

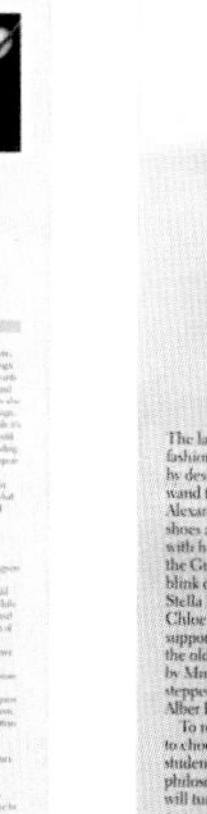

Former Vice-President of Corporate Communications at Herman Miller for sixteen years John R. Berry has worked closely with Eames Office, George Nelson and other major designers, here he describes the philosophy behind the company founded in 1936 by D.J. De Pree who committed Herman Miller to 'modern' furniture.

HERMAN MILLER THE PURPOSE OF DESIGN

IS THE DESIGNER LEADING?

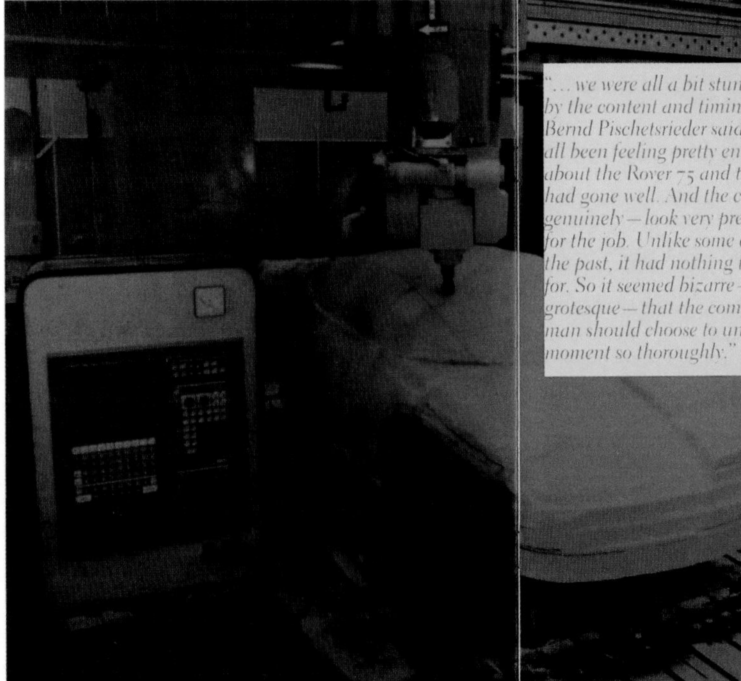

"… we were all a bit stunned, both by the content and timing of what Bernd Pischetsrieder said. We had all been feeling pretty enthusiastic about the Rover 75 and the unveiling had gone well. And the car did—quite genuinely—look very pretty and right for the job. Unlike some creations of the past, it had nothing to apologise for. So it seemed bizarre—even grotesque—that the company's top man should choose to undermine the moment so thoroughly."

The Designer Issue 25

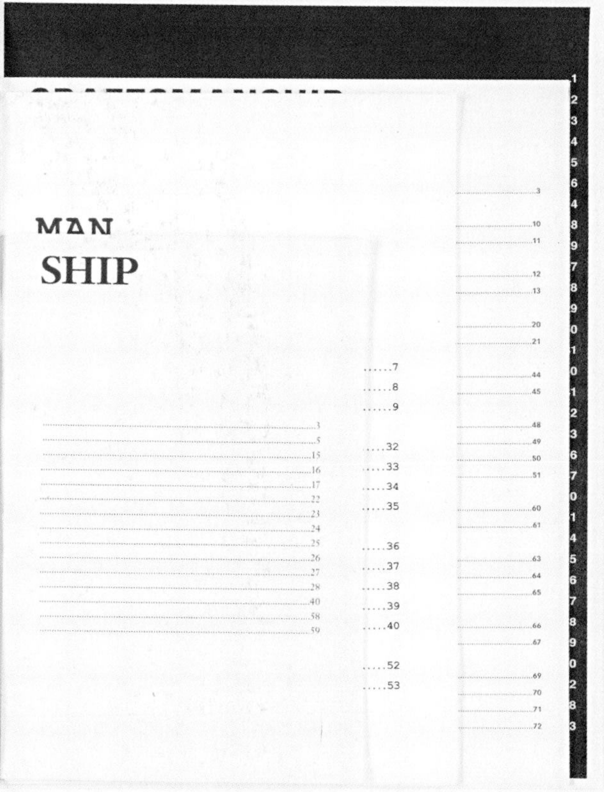

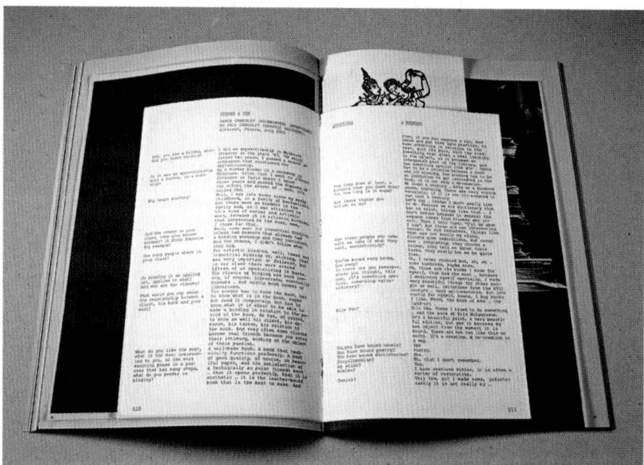

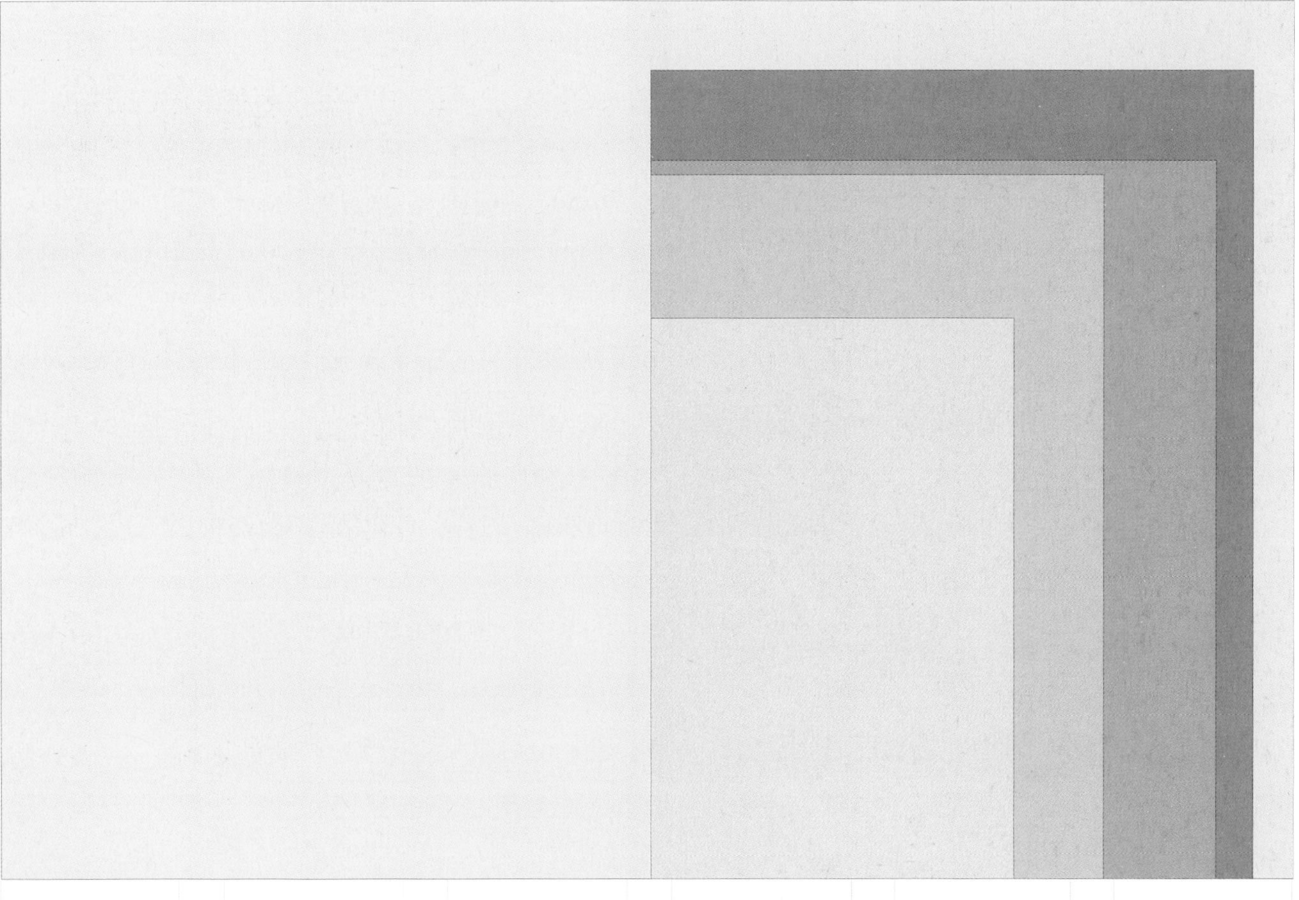

GRID SPECIFICATIONS

Page size (trimmed)	210 x 297mm
Format/Grid 1	200 x 270mm
Format/Grid 2	185 x 239mm
Format/Grid 3	146 x 234mm
Format/Grid 4	115 x 185mm
Number of columns	N/A
Gutter width	N/A
Extras	N/A

GRAY MAGAZINE

Design: Clare McNally, Lane Gry, and Risto Kalmre

GRAy is the official magazine of the Gerrit Rietveld Academy in Amsterdam. An annual publication, it is designed, edited, and produced by graduating graphic design students. The three designers, Clare McNally, Lane Gry, and Risto Kalmre, wanted *GRAy* to reflect its theme—craftsmanship—partly through its precision, but also through their hands-on skill in putting it together. They evolved two approaches to the grid.

The first grid was derived from the different formats of various types of publication: the novel, the art book, technical manuals, and A4 (210 x 297mm [c. 8⅛ x 11⅝in]) magazines. These four formats were amalgamated to form the underlying structure governing the placement text and images.

A test scan using the reprographic scanner.

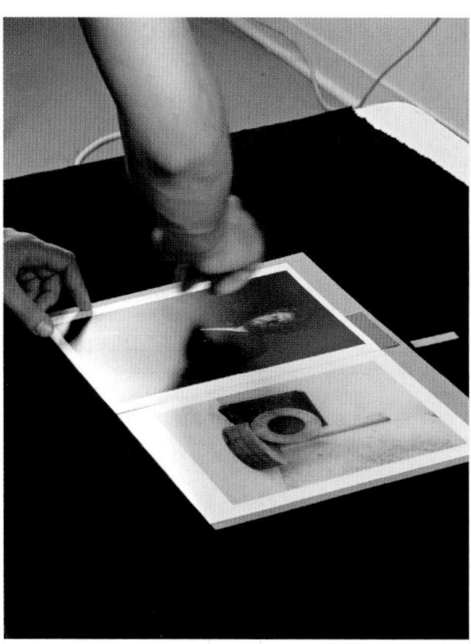

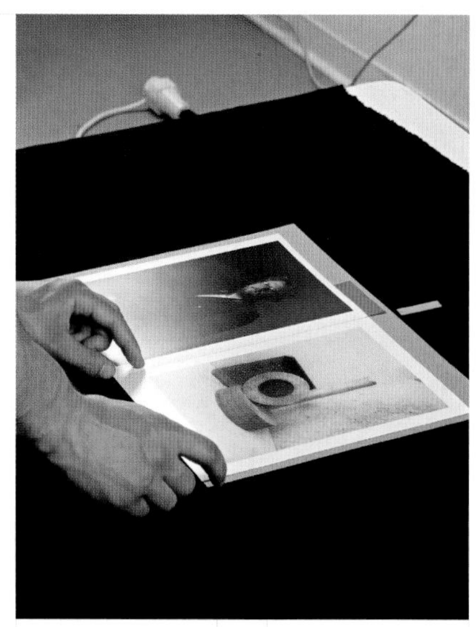

Each spread was laid out by hand as an "image."

The day of scanning.

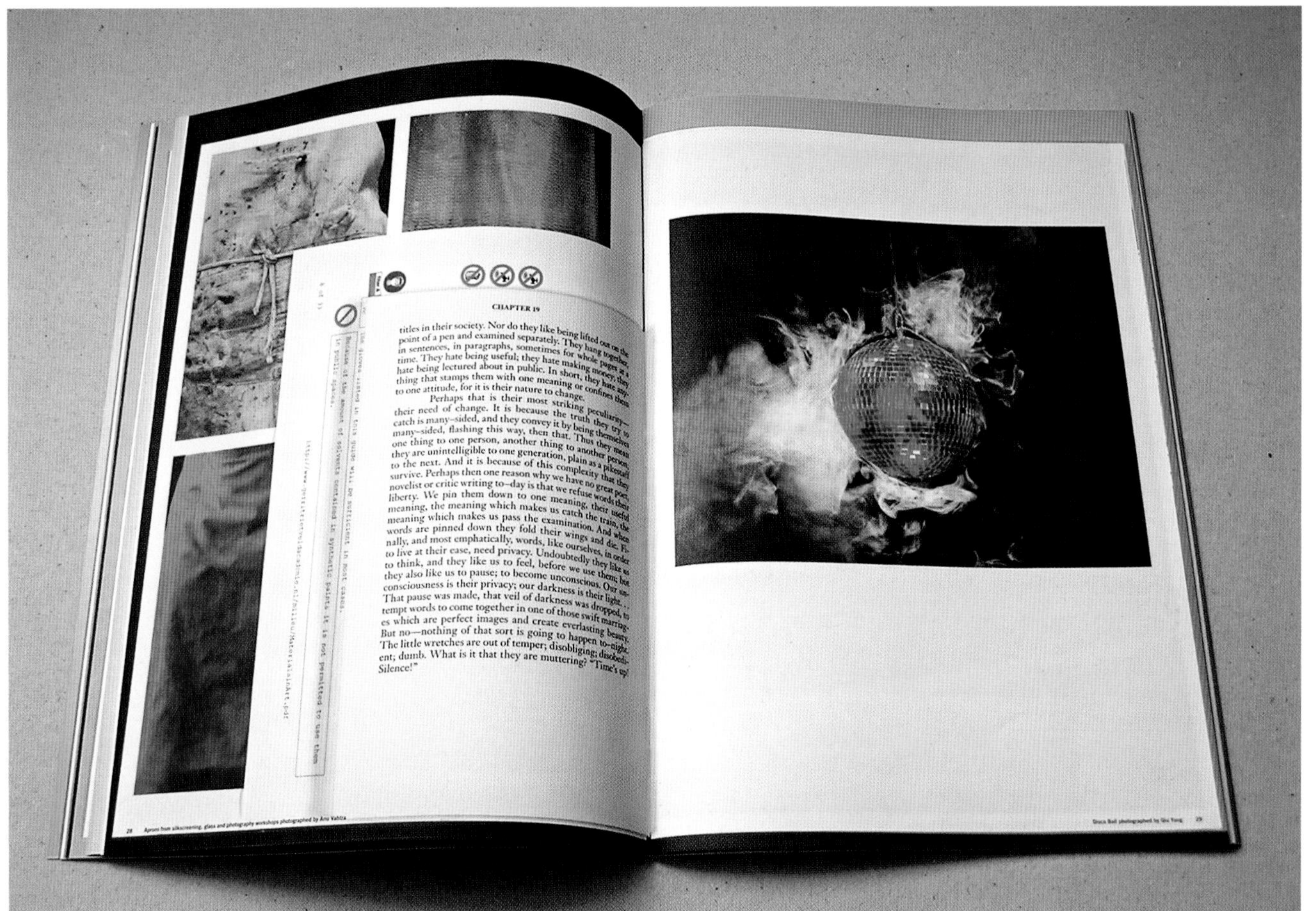

CHAPTER 19

titles in their society. Nor do they like being lifted out on the point of a pen and examined separately. They hang together, in sentences, in paragraphs, sometimes for whole pages at a time. They hate being useful; they hate making money; they hate being lectured about in public. In short, they hate anything that stamps them with one meaning or confines them to one attitude, for it is their nature to change.

Perhaps that is their most striking peculiarity—their need of change. It is because the truth they try to catch is many-sided, and they convey it by being themselves many-sided, flashing this way, then that. Thus they mean one thing to one person, another thing to another person; they are unintelligible to one generation, plain as a pikestaff to the next. And it is because of this complexity that they survive. Perhaps then one reason why we have no great poet, novelist or critic writing to-day is that we refuse words their liberty. We pin them down to one meaning, their useful meaning, the meaning which makes us catch the train, the meaning which makes us pass the examination. And when words are pinned down they fold their wings and die. Finally, and most emphatically, words, like ourselves, in order to live at their ease, need privacy. Undoubtedly they like us to think, and they like us to feel, before we use them; but they also like us to pause; to become unconscious. Our unconsciousness is their privacy; our darkness is their light. . . That pause was made, that veil of darkness was dropped, to tempt words to come together in one of those swift marriages which are perfect images and create everlasting beauty. But no—nothing of that sort is going to happen to-night. The little wretches are out of temper; disobliging; disobedient; dumb. What is it that they are muttering? "Time's up! Silence!"

The scan of pages 2 and 3.

The second grid was generated in InDesign to give a consistent position for folios and running feet. Each section of the magazine was printed and cut out according to the various formats. These spreads were then positioned by hand according to the InDesign grid, then scanned and reprinted, making the final design process interactive in a totally physical way.

SHIP

"I LOVE
THE MEISSEN PROJECT

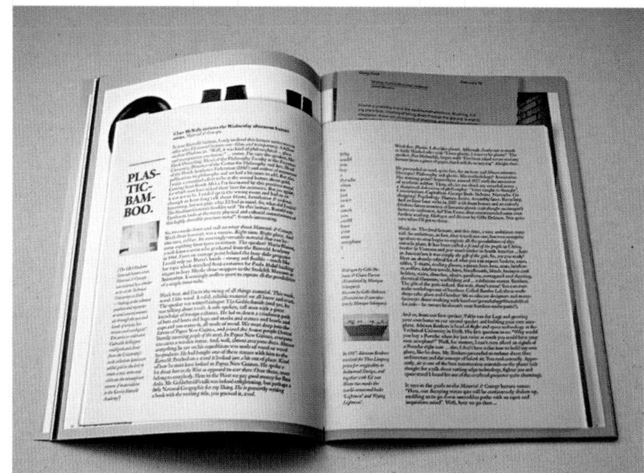
PLAS-
TIC-
BAM-
BOO.

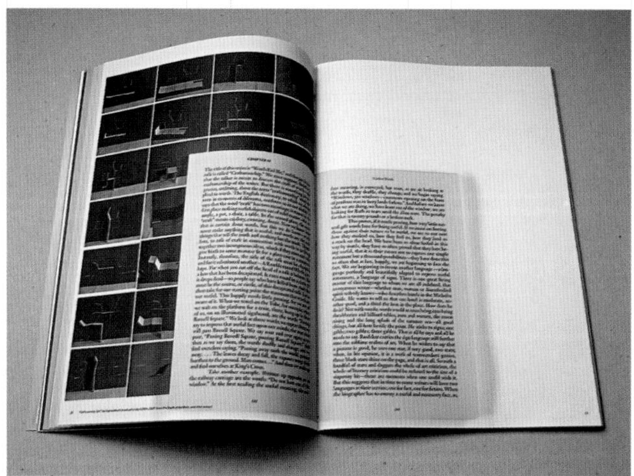

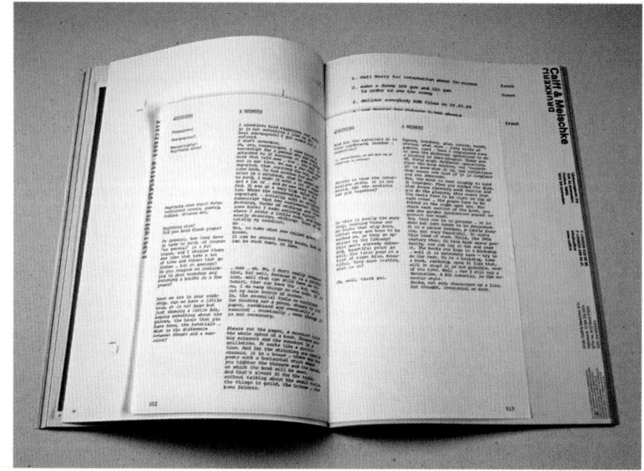
Calff & Meischke

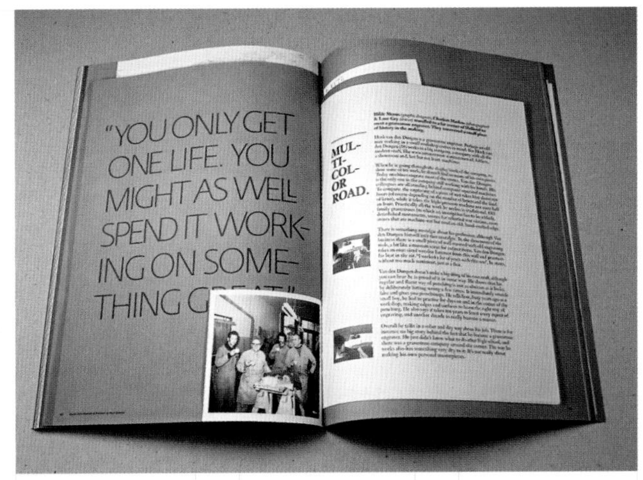
"YOU ONLY GET ONE LIFE. YOU MIGHT AS WELL SPEND IT WORK-ING ON SOME-THING G
MUL-TI-COL-OR ROAD.

THE HON-ESTY OF KING M.
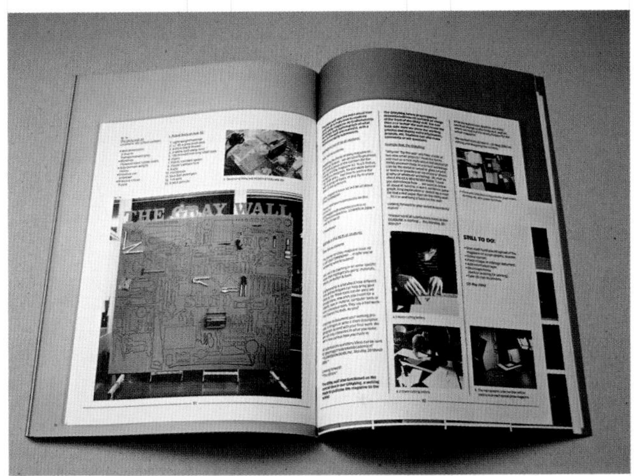
THE GRAY WALL
STILL TO DO!

CLARE MCNALLY, LANE GRY & RISTO KALMRE
FINAL YEAR GRAPHIC DESIGN
THE GRAY WALL
ELEMENTS:
GRAY

EDITORIAL
STEP-BY-STEP

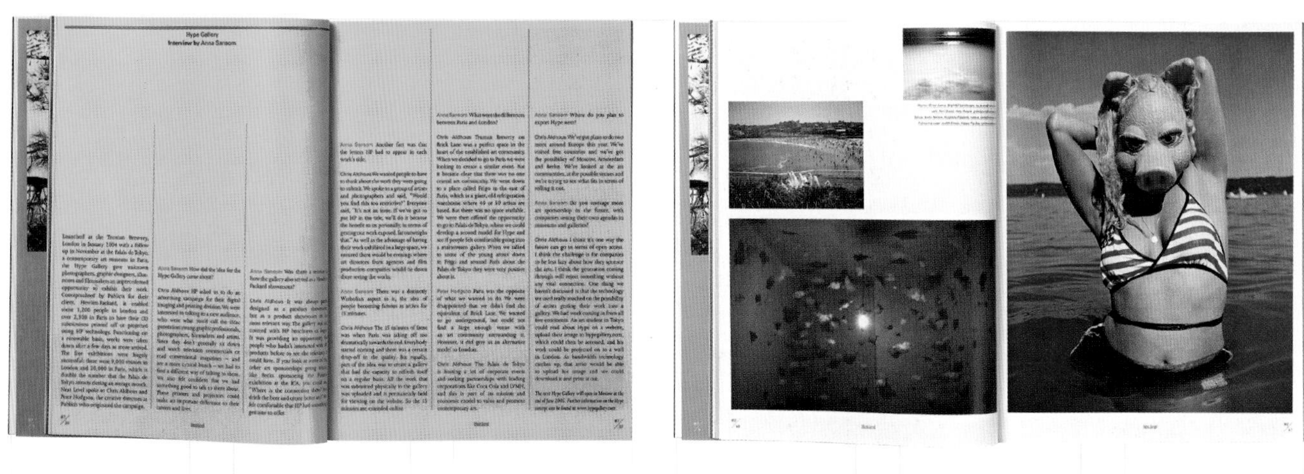

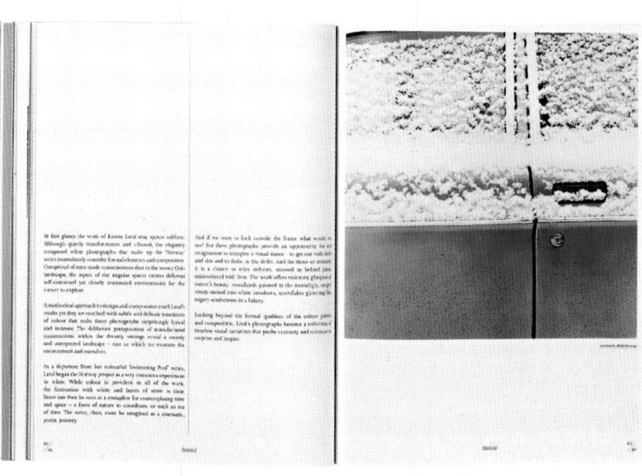

GRID SPECIFICATIONS

Page size (trimmed)	235 x 304mm
Top margin	9mm
Bottom margin	30mm
Outside margin	9mm
Inside margin	15mm
Number of columns	5
Gutter width	7mm
Extras	N/A

NEXT LEVEL: IF...

Design: Nick Steel at Harriman Steel

Next Level, a themed photography, arts, and ideas magazine, is produced twice a year. Each theme calls for a different design. This issue was inspired by the idea of simplification. Designer Nick Steel wanted the publication to be visually naive. He introduced larger-than-standard type for the body copy, and alternates between very simple two- and three-column grids. Space is introduced where possible, and images are generally squared up as determined by the grid.

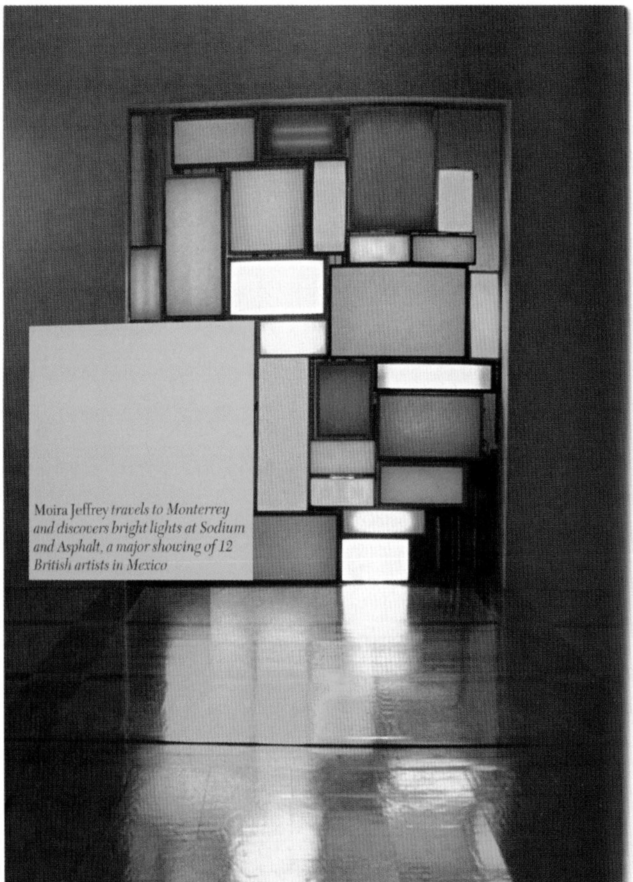

I arrive in Monterrey, north Mexico, after dark. To get there I have flown into and out of Mexico City by night. Thirty million people below me and I haven't seen one of them – just an infinite pattern of sodium light. I try to translate that into some kind of human presence: for every streetlight, say, a household. It's like looking at the night sky and trying to imagine each distant star as populous and as complex as planet Earth.

There is no seat belt in my taxi and I try to work up the courage to complain. I don't or can't. I'm weak-willed through lack of sleep. Feeling weirdly untethered I look outside at the view from the highway. A shabby industrial zone gives way to neon signs, billboards, a run of burger bars, car showrooms, low density housing, and a car wash chain that is styled as an African village, complete with a canopy that imitates grass huts.

The taxi driver pulls down a screen above the front passenger's seat: Jennifer Lopez in concert. She is wearing a bright red dress, but I don't recognise the song. He drives me to my hotel, paying more attention to the TV screen than the view through the windscreen. I'm thankful it is late on a Sunday night and the roads seem deserted. I arrive at my hotel, a neat tower at the heart of a downtown grid. They have never heard of me.

The texture of the city, its visual cues, the distinctive way we move through it, the familiarity and the strangeness of the urban fabric, these were the themes of *Sodium and Asphalt, Contemporary British Art in Mexico*. Curated by Ann Gallagher of the British Council and Tobias Ostrander, of the Tamayo Museum, Mexico City, it opened in July 2004 before transferring to MARCO, Monterrey until February 2005.

Sodium and Asphalt could not be described as a survey, nor as a generational show, but it does mark a number of significant developments in British art of the last decade or so. Some of these are age and stage-related, some geographic. Four of the 12 selected artists were Glasgow-based or trained. The youngest artists, Oliver Payne and Nick Relph, are based in New York City. Melanie Smith lives and works in Mexico City.

The exhibition, which grew out of a seminar series on colour and the city at the Tamayo Museum attended by artists David Batchelor and Melanie Smith, also marks a more collaborative structure for exhibition-making at the British Council and coincides with an increased synergy between artists in two countries without any emphatic historical or colonial ties. The last year or two has seen a number of significant shows of Mexican artists in London. In April Mexican collecting gets an airing when a number of works from the Jumex collection will be shown at Glasgow's Tramway as part of Glasgow International, 2005.

What distinguishes *Sodium and Asphalt* from any number of recent themed shows on cities and urbanism is its particular, although not exclusive, emphasis on formal qualities alongside social realities: on the distinctive visual vocabulary of the urban environment, and its relationship to the history of art, architecture, music and literature.

In the formal spaces of MARCO, a pristine modern concrete building designed by Ricardo Legoretta, the exhibition unfolds as a Baudelarian stroll through a series of different urban environments.

Melanie Smith's installation acts as a kind of transitional zone: a shop front for urban sensations. A series of vibrating striped paintings in acrylic colours of lime green, bright pink – rosa mexicana – and concrete, lean against the gallery wall as though just unpacked. A series of video pieces are shown on televisions sitting on their cardboard boxes. Her paintings form a kind of background hum, a Broadway boogie-woogie, to the more intimate structures of the films. In one of these the camera peers through a fluorescent-lettered window into a downtown aerobics class, the rhythm of pumping bodies, a kind of fleshy parody of the machine age. Above these elements, suspended from the ceiling, is a knot of fluorescent nylon string. An image of the city itself, perhaps, not as a coherent grid but as a tangle.

Nigel Cooke's landscape paintings, with their urban sublime of contemporary ruin and decay, form a kind of exterior wall, albeit one that is characteristically cracked and graffiti-strewn. Jim Lambie's 'Zobop' provides a disco interior, and the film 'Gentlemen' by Payne and Relph, a kind of psychological inner space for the city-dweller.

From David Batchelor's stack of lightboxes to Richard Wright's work 'Untitled (31.3.04)' – a painting of a simulated wooden surface, over which is floated a series of disconnected geometric shapes like ribbons – the language of signage, of simulation and stimulation is a persistent presence.

Kathrin Bohm's installation is part of her ongoing artwork, 'and millions and millions', in which graphic prints are flyposted onto the gallery walls and stacked up on shelves, freely available for visitors to take away.

Mark Titchner and Melanie Smith also contribute billboard projects, posted on commercial plots on the fringes of the city's highway. A set of Richard Wright's delicately modulated posters is slapped up on city walls in an insouciant manner that might make collectors weep (in Mexico City they were flyposted by a crack team specialising in Mexican wrestling posters) and allowed to deteriorate in wind, sun and competition.

Although in many ways some of the artworks selected apparently conform to formal abstraction or minimalism, many emphasise a deliberate disruption of conceptions of purity once associated with it. Mark Titchner's rhythmic billboard-sized piece, 'Y and Y', shown in the gallery, conceals complex coded content derived from industrial punch cards within its geometric patterning.

Opposite
'The Magic Hour'
David Batchelor, 2004

23

Issue 1/Spring 2005/**MAP**

MAP

You are here: Journeys in Contemporary Art

FRANCIS ALYS / NATHAN COLEY / SIMON STARLING / GRAHAM FAGEN / BEAGLES AND RAMSAY / JERUSALEM / MEXICO / ARGYLL

Issue 1 / Spring 2005
£4.95

9 771745 448013 01

The new international art magazine from Scotland

Certain of **NOTHING:**

MAP Issue 1/Spring 2005

Issue 1/Spring 2005/**MAP**

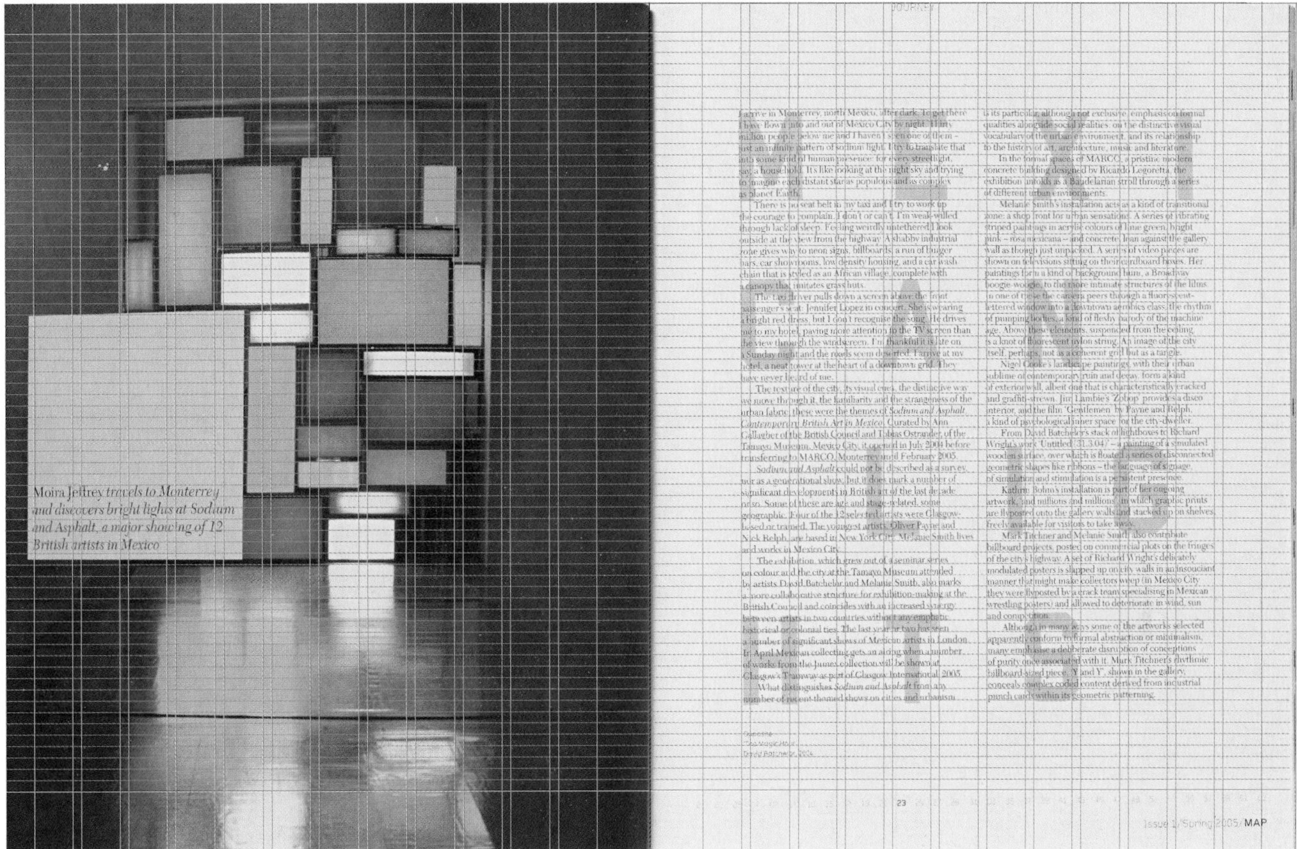

Moira Jeffrey *travels to Monterrey and discovers bright lights at Sodium and Asphalt, a major showing of 12 British artists in Mexico*

I arrive in Monterrey, north Mexico, after dark. To get there I have flown into and out of Mexico City by night. Thirty million people below me and I haven't seen one of them – just an infinite pattern of sodium light. I try to translate that into some kind of human presence: for every streetlight, say, a household. It's like looking at the night sky and trying to imagine each distant star as populous and as complex as planet Earth.

There is no seat belt in my taxi and I try to work up the courage to complain. I don't or can't. I'm weak-willed through lack of sleep. Feeling weirdly untethered I look outside at the view from the highway. A shabby industrial zone gives way to neon signs, billboards, a run of burger bars, car showrooms, low density housing, and a car wash chain that is styled as an African village, complete with a canopy that imitates grass huts.

The taxi driver pulls down a screen above the front passenger's seat: Jennifer Lopez in concert. She is wearing a bright red dress, but I don't recognise the song. He drives me to my hotel, paying more attention to the TV screen than the view through the windscreen. I'm thankful it is late on a Sunday night and the roads seem deserted. I arrive at my hotel, a neat tower at the heart of a downtown grid. They have never heard of me.

The texture of the city, its visual cues, the distinctive way we move through it, the familiarity and the strangeness of the urban fabric; these were the themes of *Sodium and Asphalt, Contemporary British Art in Mexico*. Curated by Ann Gallagher of the British Council and Tobias Ostrander, of the Tamayo Museum, Mexico City, it opened in July 2004 before transferring to MARCO, Monterrey until February 2005.

Sodium and Asphalt could not be described as a survey, nor as a generational show, but it does mark a number of significant developments in British art of the last decade or so. Some of these are age and stage-related, some geographic. Four of the 12 selected artists were Glasgow-based or trained. The youngest artists, Oliver Payne and Nick Relph, are based in New York City. Melanie Smith lives and works in Mexico City.

The exhibition, which grew out of a seminar series on colour and the city at the Tamayo Museum attended by artists David Batchelor and Melanie Smith, also marks a more collaborative structure for exhibition-making at the British Council and coincides with an increased synergy between artists in two countries without any emphatic historical or colonial ties. The last year or two has seen a number of significant shows of Mexican artists in London. In April Mexican collecting gets an airing when a number of works from the Jumex collection will be shown at Glasgow's Tramway as part of Glasgow International 2005.

What distinguishes *Sodium and Asphalt* from any number of recent themed shows on cities and urbanism is its particular, although not exclusive, emphasis on formal qualities alongside social realities: on the distinctive visual vocabulary of the urban environment, and its relationship to the history of art, architecture, music and literature.

In the formal spaces of MARCO, a pristine modern concrete building designed by Ricardo Legoretta, the exhibition unfolds as a Baudelarian stroll through a series of different urban environments.

Melanie Smith's installation acts as a kind of transitional zone: a shop front for urban sensations. A series of vibrating striped paintings in acrylic colours of lime green, bright pink – rosa mexicana – and concrete, lean against the gallery wall as though just unpacked. A series of video pieces are shown on televisions sitting on their cardboard boxes. Her paintings form a kind of background hum, a Broadway boogie-woogie, to the more intimate structures of the films. In one of these the camera peers through a fluorescent-lettered window into a downtown aerobics class, the rhythm of pumping bodies, a kind of fleshy parody of the machine age. Above these elements, suspended from the ceiling, is a knot of fluorescent nylon string. An image of the city itself, perhaps, not as a coherent grid but as a tangle.

Nigel Cooke's landscape paintings, with their urban sublime of contemporary ruin and decay, form a kind of exterior wall, albeit one that is characteristically cracked and graffiti-strewn. Jim Lambie's 'Zobop' provides a disco interior, and the film 'Gentlemen' by Payne and Relph, a kind of psychological inner space for the city-dweller.

From David Batchelor's stack of lightboxes to Richard Wright's work 'Untitled (31.3.04)' – a painting of a simulated wooden surface, over which is floated a series of disconnected geometric shapes like ribbons – the language of signage, of simulation and stimulation is a persistent presence.

Kathrin Bohm's installation is part of her ongoing artwork, 'and millions and millions', in which graphic prints are flyposted onto the gallery walls and stacked up on shelves, freely available for visitors to take away.

Mark Titchner and Melanie Smith also contribute billboard projects, posted on commercial plots on the fringes of the city's highway. A set of Richard Wright's delicately modulated posters is slapped up on city walls in an insouciant manner that might make collectors weep (in Mexico City they were flyposted by a crack team specialising in Mexican wrestling posters) and allowed to deteriorate in wind, sun and competition.

Although in many ways some of the artworks selected apparently conform to formal abstraction or minimalism, many emphasise a deliberate disruption of conceptions of purity once associated with it. Mark Titchner's rhythmic billboard-sized piece, 'Y and Y', shown in the gallery, conceals complex coded content derived from industrial punch cards within its geometric patterning.

GRID SPECIFICATIONS

Page size (trimmed)	221 x 277mm
Top margin	10mm
Bottom margin	20mm
Outside margin	10mm
Inside margin	18mm
Number of columns	12
Gutter width	3mm
Extras	Baseline grid, 10.5pt

MAP MAGAZINE

Design: Matt Willey and Zoë Bather

MAP is an international art magazine published in Scotland. From the outset, designers Matt Willey and Zoë Bather felt a duty to display the work in a visually arresting, yet respectful and clear way. Willey and Bather took the rich, but functional language of cartography as their visual starting point. The grid on the cover divides the space so that the masthead can occupy any of six possible positions, depending upon its relationship to the image behind. The same grid determines the position of the standfirsts that announce each article. The grid on the review pages is plotted using cross-marks that borrow from the language of maps, while the navigation system uses blue vertical lines positioned next to the folios like lines of longitude.

Right: AnTobar/Highland renewal project, Ursula Ziegler, 2004
Photo by Dom Morgan

Still, all is well, because we are each given the beautifully designed catalogue of Morrison's most recent show, and the paintings of slate quarries and cottages in the Easdale area, with the sea and islands looming, do make a positive impact. Apparently, Jolomo has had a couple of exhibitions organised by Kranenburg and Fowler on the Caledonian MacBrayne ferry. But there is no such luck for us, and our boat to Mull does not even have 'WE ARE NOT AFRAID OF THE INNER HEBRIDES' emblazoned along its flank. Nevertheless, we travel across the water in good spirits, with me wearing a brand new Oban-bought t-shirt that sports the slogan 'BOOTY FUN CLUB'. We give Mull a good going over. At least we

a primary blue job overprinted in red with the words 'NODDY GOES TO TOYLAND'. I switch on my mobile. Shit, there is no message from the director of Cove Park, which means I won't be bailing out of the bus journey back to Glasgow in order to visit that Open Studios site – just outside the territory of the Highlands and Islands development agency and so not scheduled into our tour. Never mind, because on a future journey I will explore Cove Park and investigate its seven annual residencies and close links with Glasgow School of Art. Never mind also, because I still have the present day at my disposal.

On one wall of my Tobermory Hotel bedroom is a recent oil by Jolomo whose nightscape – a dramatically moonlit bay – neatly complements the view through the window. The real Tobermory Bay presents a placid sunrise, with red infusing the otherwise pale blue sky. The wash of pink above the horizon takes me back to the very thing that started me off on this journey – the pink poster advertising the Chris Johanson show at the Modern Institute. Let me recall it in detail: from the mouth of a crudely drawn figure with the letters 'CONTEMPORARY' running

A N D M U L L

drive backwards and forwards along the coastal road that surrounds the great lump of a place. Our jaunt culminates in a visit to the arts centre, An Tobar (Gaelic for the well), in the island's capital of Tobermory. Again it's lottery funding that's responsible for the building itself, which contains studio space for both artists and musicians, a café and a gallery. And again, a shortage of revenue funding leaves the gallery scrabbling to make the most of its potential. The island's population is only 2,500, so perhaps it's not surprising that Lee Hendrick – the person we first met this morning in her Workshop Gallery nearby, whose prominent piece we came across on the island's sculpture trail, and who is responsible for the set design for the production of Jekyll and Hyde we will be seeing this evening – is here to greet us in her role as An Tobar's visual arts officer. One head, myriad hats. Isn't that how it goes in the film *Local Hero*?

Anyway, she introduces us to the gallery installation 'Passing', by Ursula Ziegler. This is a straight transfer of the artist's 2004 degree show from Glasgow School of Art. Every day for a month, Ziegler pushed a wheelbarrow through a circular route in the city centre, the flat-tyred, rusty old vehicle supporting a pane of glass in which the artist watched the world pass by upside down. The perversity, delicacy and tenacity of her viewing experience are captured in the photographs and slides that make up the uncompromising installation. German-born Ziegler, formerly a resident of Mull, was artist-in-residence at An Tobar for a month in 2004 in which period she developed further her ideas of self-consciously walking and looking by 'invigilating the land' with the use of the frame of a chair stripped of its furnishings. She both sat on the object and used it as a frame in which to regard the Mull landscape at different times of the day and in the endlessly varying weather conditions. An attempt is being made to get funding so that a future show in the gallery can bring together Ziegler's field-work for the people of the island to mull over.

When I awake on the last morning of the tour, conscious that the long drinking evenings and the early cooked breakfasts haven't been leaving much time for sleep, I feel surprisingly fresh. I pull on my second new t-shirt,

through him or her, is the observation, 'Gradually systems are breaking down'. A figure with a cube-shaped head replies via a voice-bubble of its own, 'Problem does not compute'. When in Glasgow, I appreciated the concern of the despairing city dweller. But now, after my – admittedly privileged – journey, and from a non-urban perspective, things simply don't look the same. To my mind it's the cube-headed modernist who laments, 'Gradually systems are breaking down'. The reply from the upright organic figure, whom I see as an amalgam of Benny Nesbit, Joseph Beuys, and Ursula Ziegler, is a resoundingly confident, 'Problem does not compute.'

M

Duncan McLaren is an author and arts writer. He has recently contributed to Infallible: In Search of the Real George Elliot, *published by ARTicle Press*

www.themoderninstitute.com
www.somewhere.org.uk Nina Pope, Karen Guthrie and their Bata-ville coach trip
www.kilmartin.org
www.blinkred.com Demarco and Beuys
www.kranenburg-fowler.com
www.antobar.co.uk

48

MAP/Issue 1/Spring 2005

LASGOW
ONDON
ARIS
ASHI
INBU
REVIEW

Focus
São Paolo Bienal.................50

Glasgow
Torsten Lauschmann.........52
Michael Fullerton..............52
Kate Davis..........................53

Paris
Thomas Hirschhorn..........54

Stirling
Rings of Saturn..................55

Washington DC
Dan Flavin..........................56

Edinburgh
Mat Collishaw....................57
Andy Warhol......................57
Ellen Gallagher..................58
Holbein to Hockney...........59

Aberdeen
Urban Atlas........................59

London
Camilla Løw.......................60
Faces in the Crowd...........61

Issue 1/Spring 2005/MAP

'Once there was a man who … pushed a block of ice across a vast city until it melted and disappeared; an artist who sent a peacock to take his place in an important gathering of his peers; a man who persuaded a small army of workers to move an immense sand dune armed only with shovels; a solitary walker who one day emerged from a shop holding a loaded pistol…'

SAO
PAULO

S T U D I O
Ruth Hedges talks to artist Jim Lambie in his Glasgow studio. Portrait by Luke Watson

grotesque visions of railway architecture, a mish-mash of Otto Wagner urbanity and bizarre Gothick fantasy, complete with verbose quotes from an unknown source. Whether capricious or designed, both this and 'Mama, I got burned', on the opposite wall, are funny in a *Big Night Out* kind of way – a marriage of the avant-garde and kitsch.

At the back of the first room, Piper's 'Double Door' divides the usually open-plan (or at least open door) gallery into two separate spaces by means of swinging saloon doors. The centre of the doors is pierced by a cut-out star shape, which serves to frame the fixed, smiling face of the endlessly hula-hooping woman in 'Loop', Maurice Doherty's double-sided video projection in the room beyond. The doors, unmistakably celluloid-inspired, are such that the temptation to burst, rather than walk through, is hard to resist, and gallery etiquette is put at risk by the potential actions of wannabe cowboys.

This feast of Saturnalia may not be as licentious as its Roman precedent, but it's similarly impious, peppered with visual raillery and, like W G Sebald's book which shares its title, the *Rings of Saturn* might well be a meditation on the possibly restorative powers of art.

Susannah Thompson is an art writer and lecturer at Glasgow School of Art

Changing Room Gallery
3 Nov – 10 Dec 2004

Dan Flavin Washington DC

Dan Flavin's was once reputed a difficult art – a fact difficult to grasp retrospectively when it can be seen for its sheer beauty. Should we now try to recapture the old sense of obduracy and negation, or rather give ourselves over to the visual fascination exercised by Flavin's bundles of light? Walking through the National Gallery, where Flavin's retrospective premiered before moving on to Fort Worth, then an international tour set to continue through 2007, it's easy to decide on the second course. The installation is ravishing, and the artist's ever-increasing mastery of his chosen medium, white and coloured fluorescent light in real architectural space, becomes patent as one follows his progress: from the early 'icons' (Johnsian painted monochrome boxes mounted with fluorescent or, more often, incandescent bulbs) through the inaugural pure fluorescent piece, 'the diagonal of May 25, 1963 (to Constantin Brancusi)' – a eureka point in Flavin's story comparable to, say, 'Onement I' (1948), in Barnett Newman's, marking the moment of greatest conceivable reduction or contraction (the Kabalistic *zimzum* that gave its name to one of Newman's sculptures) in which it momentarily seemed that 'little artistic craft could be possible' but from which all further creation would proceed. And then the polychromatic mixes with which Flavin began experimenting in 1964 but which really took off in richness and complexity around 1970, when Flavin made 'untitled (to Barnett Newman to commemorate his simple problem, red, yellow, and blue)'. As shown by this corner construction with its vertical red and blue lights facing away from the open space and back toward the wall while the horizontal yellow fluorescent tubes face outward, the 'simple' combination of three primary colours as they interfuse in space becomes something almost ungraspable, and indeed escapes language altogether with resulting colour combinations no longer nameable red, yellow, or blue.

What this indicates is that difficulty remains secreted within the suave beauty of Flavin's 'propositions' – an intellectual rather than an emotional difficulty, at least for the viewer. All the more curious, then, that it should have taken such an irascible character to produce this work. Although Flavin famously wrote of his material as 'common light repeated effulgently across anybody's wall' and of his subject as 'a neutral pleasure of seeing known to everyone', he was in fact notably possessive, one might even say illiberally close-fisted about the *notion* of his art, compulsively but always eloquently 'deflecting away from the methodological comprehension of his work,' as Jack Burnham put it. Whereas most artists seem to believe that their work will unfold itself through time to reveal unforeseeable meaning, Flavin mused of leaving 'a will and testament to declare everything void at my death . . . because only I know this work as it ought to be. All posthumous interpretations are less.' Robert Morris, of course, had already made 'Statement of Aesthetic Withdrawal' (1963) removing 'all esthetic quality and content' from a previous work of his but the result was the addition of a new work, not the subtraction of an existing one from what Arthur C. Danto was about to dub 'the art world' – meaning, not the social milieu of artists, dealers, collectors, and so on, but the realm of things accepted at a given point in history as belonging to art. No more could Flavin have asserted the ultimate control over the artistic existence of his work by the supreme and sovereign act of disowning it, yet he needed to believe in such control in order to produce something fine enough to escape it. His art's posthumous existence cannot be switched off like an electric light; despite all the situational uncertainties that surround the effort to represent the effects he sought, the work continues to shine forth, expansively.

Barry Schwabsky is an art critic and author of The Widening Circle: Consequences of Modernism in Contemporary Art *(Cambridge University Press) and Opera:* Poems 1981-2002 *(San Francisco: Meritage Press)*

National Gallery of Art Washington DC
3 Oct 2004 – 9 Jan 2005

Left: 'The diagonal of May 25, 1963 (to Constantin Brancusi)'
Dan Flavin, 1963

Mat Collishaw Edinburgh

Mat Collishaw flatters to deceive. His best known work takes the form of exquisite photographs of flowers whose petals, on closer inspection, have been electronically replaced by close-ups of human skin diseases. Alongside these are his video installations: in one example, a video projection onto an ornate free-standing vanity mirror, depicting a beautiful young girl brushing her long blonde locks, fades into an image of what might well be the same girl 75 years later, still brushing, brushing, brushing her hair. Elsewhere, it's the deceptive power of the medium itself that interests Collishaw: an image of prisoners at the Abu Ghraib prison camp in Iraq is rendered in the form of a room-sized mosaic – in which a highly pixellated internet image provides the pattern for a craft form that originated in Persia, and provided the spoils of war in a different age.

Collishaw's largest solo exhibition to date is located in the beautifully restored Inverleith House, and it comes at an important time for an artist who – amazingly – emerged from the epicentre of Young British Art without having been ripped apart by the media. How could Tracey Emin's (now ex) long-term lover have avoided the same tabloid mauling that was the daily grind for Tracey, Damien, Sarah and Gillian for so much of the past decade? Maybe it is precisely because the work is so hard to pin down. It can be so wilfully artificial that it feels resistant, even at times slippery.

Looking at a projection of blurry photos of victims of Operation Barbarossa lying dead in the frozen Russian winter, you steel yourself for some grim thoughts about the atrocities of the German-Russian war in the early 1940s. But no sooner have you prepared yourself for this emotional onslaught than the image literally fizzles and melts away, as if the transparency inside the slide projector has just been destroyed by the heat. Again and again a grimly fuzzy image bubbles into oblivion, just as its content is becoming clear. It is hard to trust your judgement in Collishaw's work, because there's always a sense that, once you succumb to the sheer power or beauty of what you first see, that emotional response will be undermined by the realisation that things are definitely not what they first seemed.

In the end Collishaw's work frustrates because, despite its often very powerful ideas, it doesn't allow the viewer enough room in the work to engage with the artist's vision. Certainly, there's a sense that Collishaw's interests are sharply political. Yet by dickering about with the medium, he undermines the complexity of his message. Again and again he reminds us that what we see may not actually be the whole truth – but in the process each time he gives the impression that, when we get anywhere near his heartfelt convictions, he doesn't in fact hold them at all.

Staring at the 'Infectious Orchid' photographs with their skin-diseased petals, I found myself trying to think of something other than the trite aphorism, 'beauty is only skin deep', and wishing I could get to an understanding of his passions that went a little deeper.

Nick Barley is editor of The List

Inverleith House
15 Jan – 13 Mar 2005

Andy Warhol: Self Portraits Edinburgh

'He was always such a strong, strong man/ I saw him go to pieces/ I saw him go to pieces'

'Pieces of a Man' – Gil Scott Heron's 1971 hymn to his disenfranchised father could well have been penned after wandering the rooms housing this remarkably complete collection of Warhol's self portraits. Following a trajectory of gauche vulgarity, enthusiasm and playfulness through a tunnel of darkness into vanity and morbidity, his portraits move to a final reduction of form that, like the man himself in his later years, is almost translucent. At his best and worst Warhol was gifted and truly godless in his experimentation and this superb exhibition runs the gamut of the pope of pop art's (self) reflections and creativity.

Opening with Warhol's early childish but oddly effective graphite on paper sketches, his influence on future artists, even as a boy, can be identified in a drawing of Clint Hamilton, Nathan Gluck and himself (nicely stained with what looks like coffee). This graphite and coloured pencil sketch on Strathmore paper can now be seen as the reference point for a composition to which fellow artists David Hockney and Dennis Hopper (as photographer) frequently returned.

What follows next serves to illustrate what a funny, silly and joyful artist Warhol could be. His youthful visage bursts out of blue, pink and yellow acrylic screen prints: in some he looks like the Jackal, in others like blonde

Above left: 'Burning Flower'
Mat Collishaw, 2004
Left: Early Self-Portrait
Andy Warhol, 1964

Certain of **NOTHING:**

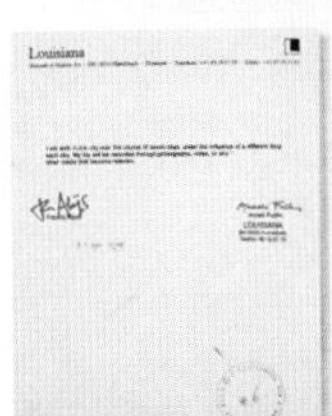

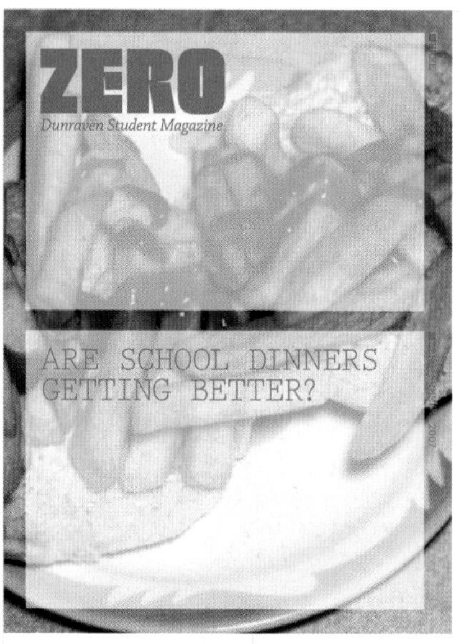

ZERO
Dunraven Student Magazine
ARE SCHOOL DINNERS GETTING BETTER?

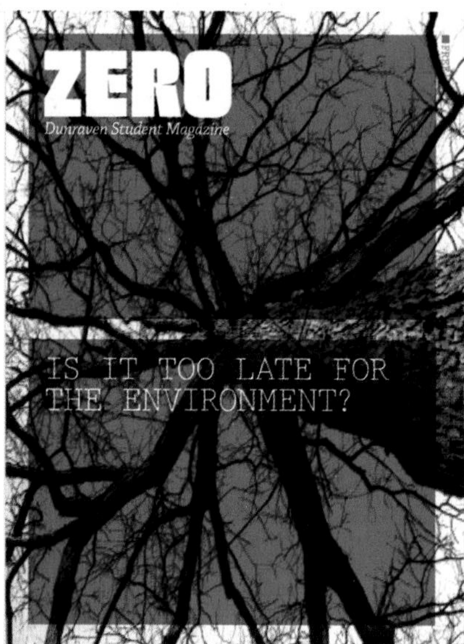

ZERO
Dunraven Student Magazine
IS IT TOO LATE FOR THE ENVIRONMENT?

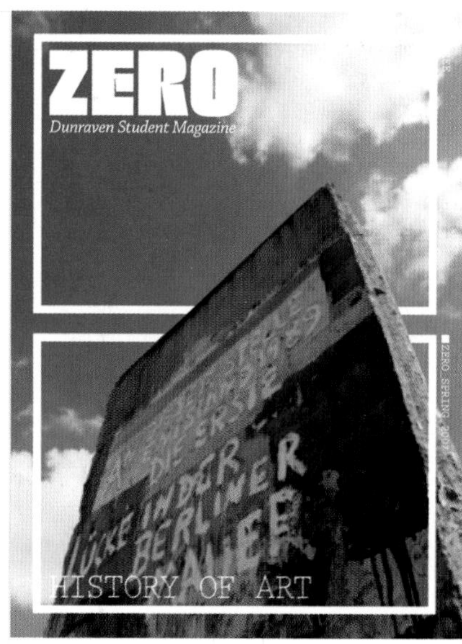

IN THIS ISSUE

Welcome to Zero, issue one of our new magazine. Within these pages are the opinions, ideas and interests of the students of this fine institution. We hope you will also be contributing, at: **zeromagazine@duravenschool.org.uk**

The project itself is the brainchild of previous students of the school and was conceived almost three years ago as part of the joinedupdesignforschools programme, a national project. In late 2006 the editorial and design teams that have worked so hard to bring this magazine to you were formed.

Studio8 Design worked with the student design team and have come up with an original and professional concept which gave us the name "Zero". As you can see the page numbers form the layout of the page and the front cover was page "Zero".

This issue of the magazine feature articles on Chinese New Year, a feature on size zero models and the obscure, intense, Afgan sport of Buzkashi.

Truman Wright, Yr 10

ZERO_SUMMER_2007

EVENTS
02 Around Town
TREND
03 Size Zero Tolerance
04 Who Is King Karl?
05 PS3 Vs WII
INSIGHT
06 Explore Spitafields
07 Debate: Vegetarianism
FEATURE
08 On Beauty
09 Live By The Gun
11 Showcase
13 Environmental Change
CULTURE
15 Interviews with Caroline Lawrence and Michael Morpurgo, plus Poetry Slammers
17 The latest music and film, plus Swap Shop
19 Buzkashi: The fierce Afghani game, plus Chinese New Year
SPORT
21 The UK Athletics Crisis: Why aren't there enough young Athletes?

EVENTS

AROUND TOWN

Places to go on your days off

Friday 30th March 2007
Gilbert & George exhibition at Tate modern

Monday 16th April 2007
Fortnum & Masons Tea

Monday 7th May 2007
Bloomsbury Bowling Alley

30th March 2007
Gilbert and George bring their large scale controversial work to the Tate Modern. Don't be put however, by the bad press: even if you think its s**t the work is worth seeing for the sheer power of the images. www.tate.org.uk/modern

Monday 16th April
Well, how about a spot of tea at Fortnum & Mason? Fortnum & Mason you say? But that's for archdukes and wealthy Cypriots or those who get fifty million pound Christmas bonuses. Correct if one is wishing to purchase a three course meal with Beluga Caviar and a one hundred and ten pound bottle of 1977 Tailor Vintage Port, but, if you only want an ice cream sundae it will not dent your pocket by more than about 23 pounds. www.fortnumandmason.com

Monday 7th May 2007
Situated in the classy center of London, the Bloomsbury Bowling Alley provides an experience well above the of the grotty Megabowl. With authentic imported American furnishings, a vintage cinema and shoes worthy of any 50s sitcom, a great atmosphere fill the place. It's cheap to (on Mondays) and the food is deliciously authentic. www.bloomsburybowling.com

And Weekends
Don't be alarmed, there are more than three days off for the entirity of next year, so we have come up with a list of other choses faire. Here they are: Brick Lane for bric-a-brac, records and the heigth of fashion. Go to the countryside, a coach trip to Oxford can cost as little as £1 and as a large number of people in the school have never experienced the joys of out-of-city life it is a fantastic thing to do. Brighton by train, includes shops, markets and fish and chips.
www.visitbricklane.com; www.eastlondonmarkets.com
www.oxfordcity.co.uk; www.nationalexpress.com
www.brighton.co.uk

Oscar Taylor & William Elliott, Yr 10

ZERO_SUMMER_2007

Above: Brighton's attractions exert their pull

Below: Gilbert and George, a menacing epic

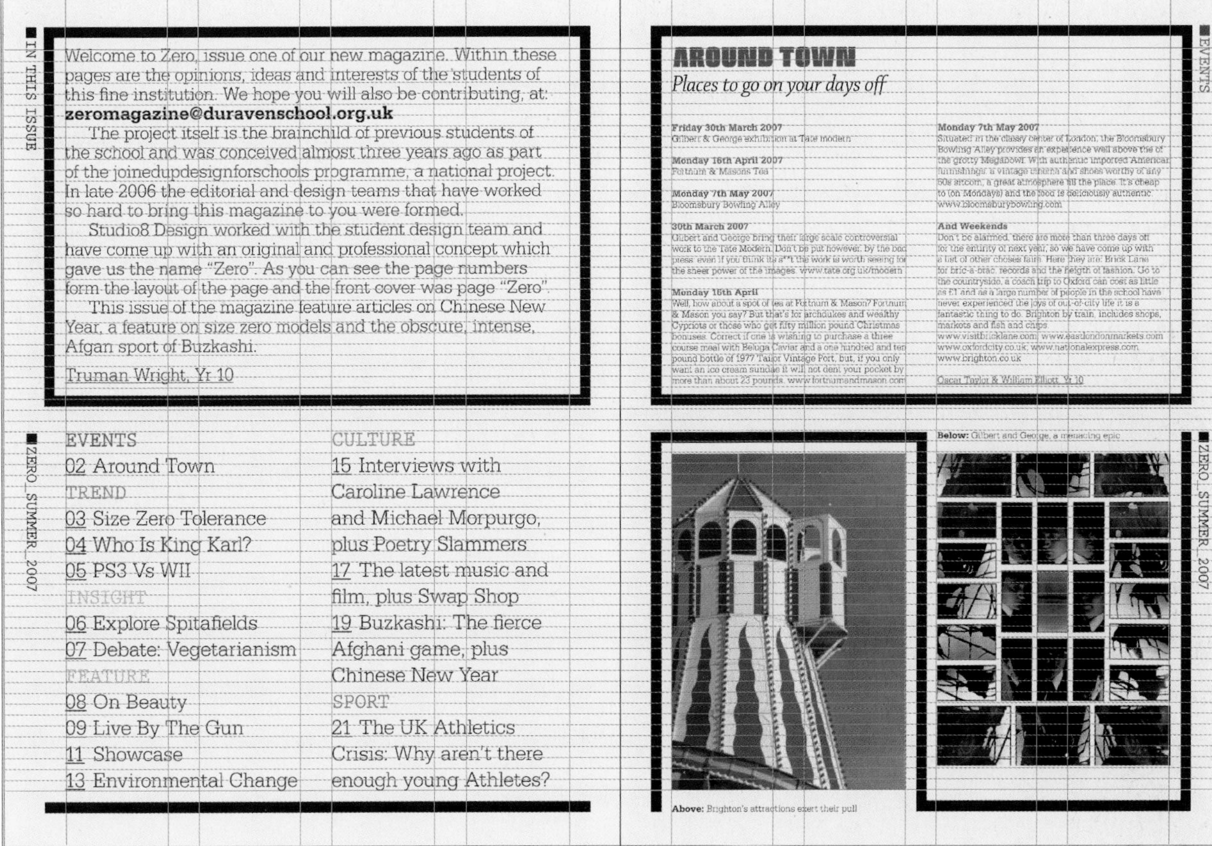

IN THIS ISSUE

Welcome to Zero, issue one of our new magazine. Within these pages are the opinions, ideas and interests of the students of this fine institution. We hope you will also be contributing, at:
zeromagazine@duravenschool.org.uk

The project itself is the brainchild of previous students of the school and was conceived almost three years ago as part of the joinedupdesignforschools programme, a national project. In late 2006 the editorial and design teams that have worked so hard to bring this magazine to you were formed.

Studio8 Design worked with the student design team and have come up with an original and professional concept which gave us the name "Zero". As you can see the page numbers form the layout of the page and the front cover was page "Zero".

This issue of the magazine feature articles on Chinese New Year, a feature on size zero models and the obscure, intense, Afgan sport of Buzkashi.

Truman Wright, Yr 10

ZERO_SUMMER_2007

EVENTS
02 Around Town
TREND
03 Size Zero Tolerance
04 Who Is King Karl?
05 PS3 Vs WII
INSIGHT
06 Explore Spitafields
07 Debate: Vegetarianism
FEATURE
08 On Beauty
09 Live By The Gun
11 Showcase
13 Environmental Change
CULTURE
15 Interviews with Caroline Lawrence and Michael Morpurgo, plus Poetry Slammers
17 The latest music and film, plus Swap Shop
19 Buzkashi: The fierce Afghani game, plus Chinese New Year
SPORT
21 The UK Athletics Crisis: Why aren't there enough young Athletes?

EVENTS

AROUND TOWN

Places to go on your days off

Friday 30th March 2007
Gilbert & George exhibition at Tate modern

Monday 16th April 2007
Fortnum & Masons Tea

Monday 7th May 2007
Bloomsbury Bowling Alley

30th March 2007
Gilbert and George bring their large scale controversial work to the Tate Modern. Don't be put however, by the bad press: even if you think its s**t the work is worth seeing for the sheer power of the images. www.tate.org.uk/modern

Monday 16th April
Well, how about a spot of tea at Fortnum & Mason? Fortnum & Mason you say? But that's for archdukes and wealthy Cypriots or those who get fifty million pound Christmas bonuses. Correct if one is wishing to purchase a three course meal with Beluga Caviar and a one hundred and ten pound bottle of 1977 Tailor Vintage Port, but, if you only want an ice cream sundae it will not dent your pocket by more than about 23 pounds. www.fortnumandmason.com

Monday 7th May 2007
Situated in the classy center of London, the Bloomsbury Bowling Alley provides an experience well above the of the grotty Megabowl. With authentic imported American furnishings, a vintage [illegible] and shoes worthy of any 50s sitcom, a great atmosphere fill the place. It's cheap to (on Mondays) and the food is deliciously authentic. www.bloomsburybowling.com

And Weekends
Don't be alarmed, there are more than three days off for the entirity of next year, so we have come up with a list of other choses faire. Here they are: Brick Lane for bric-a-brac, records and the heigth of fashion. Go to the countryside, a coach trip to Oxford can cost as little as £1 and as a large number of people in the school have never experienced the joys of out-of-city life it is a fantastic thing to do. Brighton by train, includes shops, markets and fish and chips.
www.visitbricklane.com; www.eastlondonmarkets.com
www.oxfordcity.co.uk; www.nationalexpress.com
www.brighton.co.uk

Oscar Taylor & William Elliott, Yr 10

Below: Gilbert and George, a menacing epic

Above: Brighton's attractions exert their pull

ZERO_SUMMER_2007

GRID SPECIFICATIONS

Page size (trimmed)	205 x 275mm
Top margin	17mm
Bottom margin	18.06mm
Outside margin	20.492mm
Inside margin	17mm
Number of columns	4
Gutter width	10.5mm
Extras	Baseline grid, 10pt

ZERO: DUNRAVEN STUDENT MAGAZINE

Design: Matt Willey and Zoë Bather at Studio8 Design

Zero is the Dunraven Secondary School termly magazine. It was commissioned by the Sorrell Foundation, which links designers and students in collaborative projects to improve the quality of life in schools. Designers Matt Willey and Zoë Bather worked closely with the pupils, to create a template that would be easy for them to use as editorial content was developed. The system is based around large folio numbers which fill each page. These count up from zero on the front cover, and create a set of different-shaped spaces into which the students drop the content. This rigid and explicit grid ensures that the students' layouts are consistent and professional, and gives a strong identity to the magazine.

20

CONTEMPORARY KALEIDOSCOPE

Kathy Battista surveys autumn highlights from the energetic British contemporary art scene

WILDER WEST
Rumours of the demise of the West End, long a bastion of the art trade, have been exaggerated. Recently, something of a renaissance has been taking place, with galleries such as Sprüth Magers Lee, Riflemaker, Blow de la Barra, Waddington Galleries and Annely Juda fighting back with an impressive array of exhibitions this autumn. Catch painters Richard Patterson at Timothy Taylor Gallery, and Federico Herrero at Blow de la Barra, and installation artist Jason Rhoades at Hauser & Wirth.

Not to be missed is Haunch of Venison's show of the late American artist Edward Kienholz and his wife Nancy Reddin Kienholz (7 Oct–9 Nov), known for their disturbing sculptural installations (below). The show features pieces from their recent joint retrospective at Baltic, including anti-war works, and new work previously unseen in the UK.

FRANCIS ALYS
The peripatetic artist Francis Alÿs has turned walking into an art form. Born in Antwerp, and now working in Mexico City, Alÿs sees the city as a huge open-air studio and makes work, such as animations, poetic films and paintings, that map cities in elusive ways. Over the past five years, he has walked the streets of London to create a new project for Artangel, called 'Seven Walks' (28 Sep–20 Nov), which explores the everyday rituals of the metropolis – from Coldstream Guards (below) to London's commuters. The show also provides a rare glimpse of one of London's most stunning buildings: Robert Adam's eighteenth-century townhouse in Portman Square, now a private club.

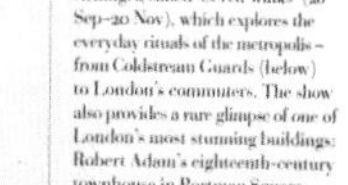

BRITISH ART SHOW 6
The British Art Show, which takes place every five years, provides an important opportunity to take the pulse of contemporary art in the UK. Each show selects a group of artists to represent the diversity and range of British art. This year, the show starts at Baltic (24 Sep–8 Jan 2006), the revamped flourmill in Gateshead that has changed the face of the contemporary art scene in the North.

Organised by London's Hayward Gallery and selected by independent curators Andrea Schlieker and Alex Farquharson, the exhibition features 49 of the most important emerging artists now working in Britain. Look out for Haluk Akakçe (below) and Saskia Olde Wolbers, both masters of digital and video installation. Other highlights include Juneau/Projects, an artists' collective who examine technology's role in consumer culture, and French-born Zineb Sedira, an artist with Algerian roots, who explores cultural identity. If you miss the Baltic show, there is still a chance to see it as it tours to Manchester, Nottingham and Bristol.

This page, clockwise from left
'The Bronze Pinball Machine with Woman Affixed Also', 1980, by Ed & Nancy Kienholz; 'Seven Walks', 2005, by Francis Alÿs; 'The Birth of Art', 2003, by Haluk Akakçe and 'It was hard to believe that just 24 hours earlier I had been sitting at my desk wrestling with the next round of deadlines', 2004, by Matthew Houlding (both in British Art Show 6)

Opposite, clockwise from left
'True North Series', 2004, by Isaac Julien; 'Whiteout, implant, spike', 2004, by Anish Kapoor RA; 'Untitled', 2004, by Cindy Sherman; 'Roundup – An Entomological Endeavour for the Smart Museum of Art', 2000, by Mark Dion; 'Work no. 329 – Half the Air in a Given Space', 2004, by Martin Creed

RA // Autumn 2005

Preview 21

WAY OUT EAST
London's East End has become an established hub of contemporary art. With a combination of existing venues such as White Cube – showing the Chapman brothers' new work this autumn (19 Oct–3 Dec) – and newcomers such as Herald Street and David Risley, East London offers endless opportunities for seeing new art. Highlights this autumn include paintings by the duo Muntean/Rosenblum at Maureen Paley's Interim Art, and Susanne Kühn at a new space called Fred. At Paul Stolper's gallery (13 Oct–19 Nov), Damien Hirst creates a chapel-like installation where religion meets pharmaceuticals, with an altar, a cedar cross and 40 newly commissioned silkscreen prints.

A particular highlight this autumn is a show of Isaac Julien's films at Victoria Miro Gallery (14 Oct–12 Nov). Julien is a master of creating impeccably crafted, lush film installations that focus on the impact of location – both cultural and physical. Victoria Miro Gallery will also host the UK premiere of two new films: *True North* (below), about Matthew Henson, the first African-American to reach the North Pole; and *Fantôme Afrique*, shot in the arid spaces of rural Burkina Faso, and features rich imagery of urban Ouagadougou, the centre for cinema in Africa.

FRIEZE (AND OTHER) ART FAIRS
The Frieze Art Fair (21–24 Oct), established two years ago, has become one of the most important events in London's contemporary art calendar. It hosts 150 galleries (selected from a field of over 450) from around the world in an elaborate tent in Regent's Park, designed by the young British architect David Adjaye. In addition to providing the opportunity to see and buy cutting-edge art, Frieze also hosts events, including talks, a music programme and high-profile public arts commissions. Peckish art-lovers are also well-catered for – the café menu has been created by Mark Hix, of The Ivy and Le Caprice.

Last year saw the birth of two satellite events around Frieze – Zoo Art Fair, located in Regent's Park Zoo, and ScopeLondon in the Meliá White House hotel just outside the park. Limited to UK-based galleries less than three years old, Zoo presents more experimental work than the grown-up fair and is an opportunity to see up-and-coming talent. Look out for RA graduate Francesca Lowe's exquisite and delicate paintings at Riflemaker's stand.

Meanwhile, ScopeLondon, a fair that also takes place in Miami, New York and LA, has had the bright idea of asking galleries to set up shop in their hotel rooms. By combining the costs of travel and exhibiting, international galleries can take the work of relatively young and affordable, emerging artists on the road.

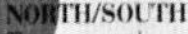

NORTH/SOUTH
This autumn, art lovers need to cross the Thames for two shows that are not to be missed. The South London Gallery presents 'Microcosmographia' by American artist Mark Dion (until 30 Oct), a fantastic nature-inspired sculptural world inhabited by gigantic creatures, including a life-size replica of an Ichthyosaur, a prehistoric aquatic animal, considered to be the Tyrannosaurus rex of the sea.

In North London, Camden Arts Centre presents Runa Islam and Roderick Buchanan (23 Sep–13 Nov). The show includes Islam's *First Day of Spring*, a film featuring rickshaw drivers in Dhaka, and Buchanan's *History Painting*, which looks at soldiers in North Yorkshire and Madras. Elsewhere in North London, dealer Simon Gillespie has turned his Georgian townhouse in Islington into a contemporary art gallery, Rollo. This autumn he shows the atmospheric landscape work of Korean photographer Bae Bien-U (29 Sep–3 Nov).

RA // Autumn 2005

20

CONTEMPORARY KALEIDOSCOPE

Kathy Battista surveys autumn highlights from the energetic British contemporary art scene

WILDER WEST
Rumours of the demise of the West End, long a bastion of the art trade, have been exaggerated. Recently, something of a renaissance has been taking place, with galleries such as Sprüth Magers Lee, Riflemaker, Blow de la Barra, Waddington Galleries and Annely Juda fighting back with an impressive array of exhibitions this autumn. Catch painters Richard Patterson at Timothy Taylor Gallery and Federico Herrero at Blow de la Barra, and installation artist Jason Rhoades at Hauser & Wirth.

Not to be missed is Haunch of Venison's show of the late American artist Edward Kienholz and his wife Nancy Reddin Kienholz (5 Oct–9 Nov), known for their disturbing sculptural installations (below). The show features pieces from their recent joint retrospective at Baltic, including anti-war works, and new work previously unseen in the UK.

FRANCIS ALYS
The peripatetic artist Francis Alÿs has turned walking into an art form. Born in Antwerp, and now working in Mexico City, Alÿs sees the city as a huge open-air studio and makes work, such as animations, poetic films and paintings, that map cities in elusive ways. Over the past five years, he has walked the streets of London to create a new project for Artangel, called 'Seven Walks' (28 Sep–20 Nov), which explores the everyday rituals of the metropolis – from Coldstream Guards (below) to London's commuters. The show also provides a rare glimpse of one of London's most stunning buildings: Robert Adam's eighteenth-century townhouse in Portman Square, now a private club.

BRITISH ART SHOW 6
The British Art Show, which takes place every five years, provides an important opportunity to take the pulse of contemporary art in the UK. Each show selects a group of artists to represent the diversity and range of British art. This year, the show starts at Baltic (24 Sep–8 Jan 2006), the revamped flourmill in Gateshead that has changed the face of the contemporary art scene in the North.

Organised by London's Hayward Gallery and selected by independent curators Andrea Schlieker and Alex Farquharson, the exhibition features 49 of the most important emerging artists now working in Britain. Look out for Haluk Akakçe (below) and Saskia Olde Wolbers, both masters of digital and video installation. Other highlights include Juneau/Projects, an artists' collective who examine technology's role in consumer culture, and French-born Zineb Sedira, an artist with Algerian roots, who explores cultural identity. If you miss the Baltic show, there is still a chance to see it as it tours to Manchester, Nottingham and Bristol.

This page, clockwise from left 'The Bronze Pinball Machine with Woman Affixed Also', 1980, by Ed & Nancy Kienholz; 'Seven Walks', 2005, by Francis Alÿs; 'The Birth of Art', 2003, by Haluk Akakçe; and 'It was hard to believe that just 24 hours earlier I had been sitting at my desk wrestling with the next round of deadlines', 2004, by Matthew Houlding (both in British Art Show 6)

Opposite, clockwise from left 'True North Series', 2004, by Isaac Julien; 'Whiteout, indiant, spire', 2004, by Anish Kapoor RA; 'Untitled', 2004, by Cindy Sherman; 'Roundup – An Entomological Endeavour for the Smart Museum of Art', 2000, by Mark Dion; 'Work no. 329 – Half the Air in a Given Space', 2004, by Martin Creed

Preview 21

WAY OUT EAST
London's East End has become an established hub of contemporary art. With a combination of existing venues such as White Cube – showing the Chapman brothers' new work this autumn (19 Oct–3 Dec) – and newcomers such as Herald Street and David Risley, East London offers endless opportunities for seeing new art. Highlights this autumn include paintings by the duo Muntean/Rosenblum at Maureen Paley's Interim Art, and Susanne Kühn at a new space called Fred. At Paul Stolper's gallery (13 Oct–19 Nov), Damien Hirst creates a chapel-like installation where religion meets pharmaceuticals, with an altar, a cedar cross and 40 newly commissioned silkscreen prints.

A particular highlight this autumn is a show of Isaac Julien's films at Victoria Miro Gallery (14 Oct–12 Nov). Julien is a master of creating impeccably crafted, lush film installations that focus on the impact of location – both cultural and physical. Victoria Miro Gallery will also host the UK premiere of two new films: *True North* (below), about Matthew Henson, the first African-American to reach the North Pole; and *Fantôme Afrique*, shot in the arid spaces of rural Burkina Faso, and features rich imagery of urban Ouagadougou, the centre for cinema in Africa.

FRIEZE (AND OTHER) ART FAIRS
The Frieze Art Fair (21–24 Oct), established two years ago, has become one of the most important events in London's contemporary art calendar. It hosts 150 galleries (selected from a field of over 450) from around the world in an elaborate tent in Regent's Park, designed by the young British architect David Adjaye. In addition to providing the opportunity to see and buy cutting-edge art, Frieze also hosts events, including talks, a music programme and high-profile public arts commissions. Peckish art-lovers are also well-catered for – the café menu has been created by Mark Hix, of The Ivy and Le Caprice.

Last year saw the birth of two satellite events around Frieze – Zoo Art Fair, located in Regent's Park Zoo, and Scope London in the Meliá White House hotel just outside the park. Limited to UK-based galleries less than three years old, Zoo presents more experimental work than the grown-up fair and is an opportunity to see up-and-coming talent. Look out for RA graduate Francesca Lowe's exquisite and delicate paintings at Riflemaker's stand.

Meanwhile, Scope London, a fair that also takes place in Miami, New York and LA, has had the bright idea of asking galleries to set up shop in their hotel rooms. By combining the costs of travel and exhibiting, international galleries can take the work of relatively young and affordable, emerging artists on the road.

NORTH/SOUTH
This autumn, art lovers need to cross the Thames for two shows that are not to be missed. The South London Gallery presents 'Microcosmographia' by American artist Mark Dion (until 30 Oct), a fantastic nature-inspired sculptural world inhabited by gigantic creatures, including a life-size replica of an Ichthyosaur, a prehistoric aquatic animal, considered to be the Tyrannosaurus rex of the sea.

In North London, Camden Arts Centre presents Runa Islam and Roderick Buchanan (23 Sep–13 Nov). The show includes Islam's *First Day of Spring*, a film featuring rickshaw drivers in Dhaka, and Buchanan's *History Painting*, which looks at soldiers in North Yorkshire and Madeira. Elsewhere in North London, dealer Simon Gillespie has turned his Georgian townhouse in Islington into a contemporary art gallery, Rollo. This autumn he shows the atmospheric landscape work of Korean photographer Bae Bien-U (29 Sep–3 Nov).

RA // Autumn 2005

RA // Autumn 2005

GRID SPECIFICATIONS

Page size (trimmed)	230 x 300mm
Top margin	20mm
Bottom margin	16mm
Outside margin	10mm
Inside margin	18mm
Number of columns	12
Gutter width	4mm
Extras	Baseline grid, 11pt

RA MAGAZINE

Design: Matt Willey and Zoë Bather at Studio8 Design

The redesign of the *RA Magazine* was a particularly challenging job. It was established 25 years ago, has the largest circulation of any art magazine in Europe, and represents a major institution. The readership of the magazine demands clear navigation with clean, elegant design, but designer Matt Willey also wanted "to put time and craft into making pages that were dynamic and expressive." Willey believes that grids can be restrictive and, especially within editorial design, can prevent pages from looking interesting if followed too religiously. In this design he employs a flexible multi-column structure so that his designs are respectful of content, yet a little playful as well.

China

ENTER THE DRAGON

On a visit to the Forbidden City to discover the world of the Three Emperors, *Sarah Greenberg* is surprised to find a much earthier place than the poetic vision she had imagined. But the more she searches for the emperors, the more she loses herself in their endless labyrinth of beauty

Ruisdael

A NATURAL PHENOMENON

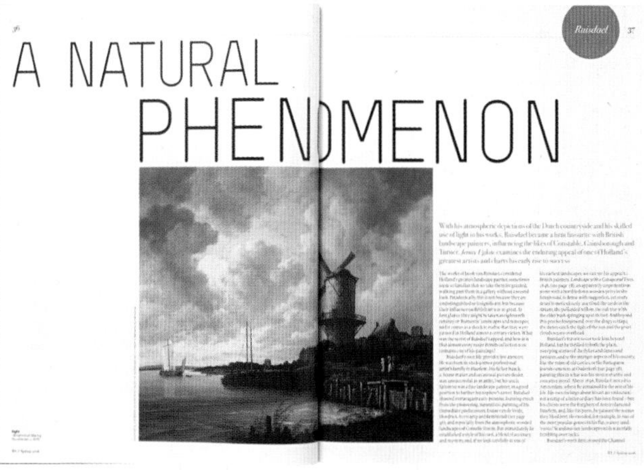

With his atmospheric depictions of the Dutch countryside and his skilled use of light in his works, Ruisdael became a firm favourite with British landscape painters, influencing the likes of Constable, Gainsborough and Turner. *James Upton* examines the enduring appeal of one of Holland's greatest artists and charts his early rise to success

Americans in Paris

WE'LL ALWAYS HAVE PARIS

Americans artists and writers flocked to the French capital in the late nineteenth century. The novelist *David Lodge* considers this phenomenon – celebrated in a new exhibition – and wonders why Americans never depicted the sexier side of the city they so adored

Academy

MAN OF MYSTERY

Painter Humphrey Ocean RA is a rather cryptic character. As he treats *Sarah Greenberg* to tales of his rock and roll past and love of Raymond Chandler, he reveals clues to his art and life. Photograph by *Julian Anderson*

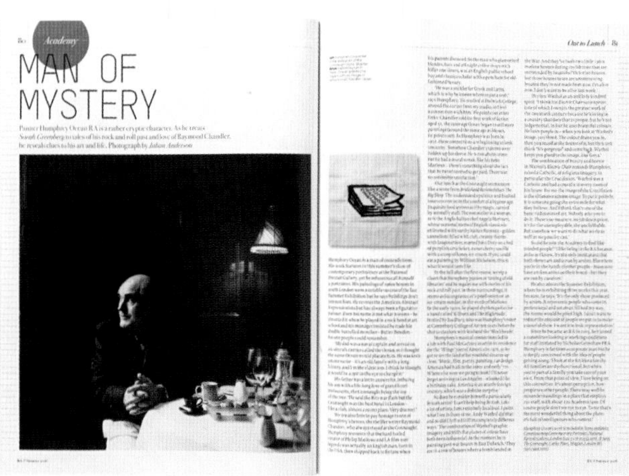

Academy

TO BE PERFECTLY FRANK

Newly elected Academician Frank Bowling prefers to let his painting do the talking, learns *Louisa Gascoigne* as she meets the artist in his south London studio. Photograph by *Eamonn McCabe*

Modigliani

NAKED AMBITION

Amedeo Modigliani's sensuous nudes and portraits are as captivating as the artist's legendary life story, argues *Kenneth Wayne*

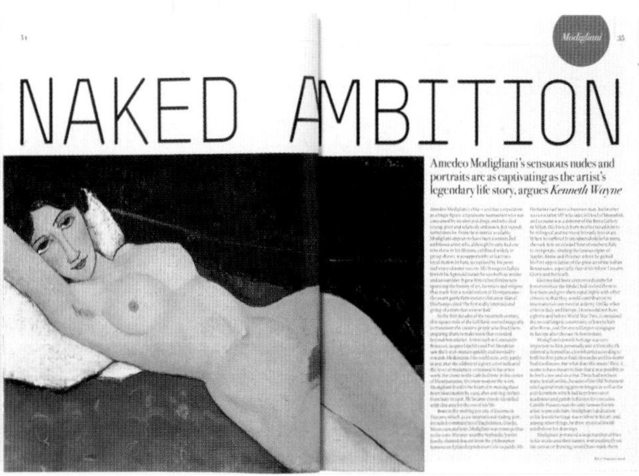

33

In a class of their own The RA Schools final-year students showcase their art this summer. On the following pages, photographer *Nick Cunard* visits their studios to capture the spirit of the young artists at work. Here *Maurice Cockrill RA*, Keeper of the RA Schools, explains what makes the place so special and praises the outgoing graduates

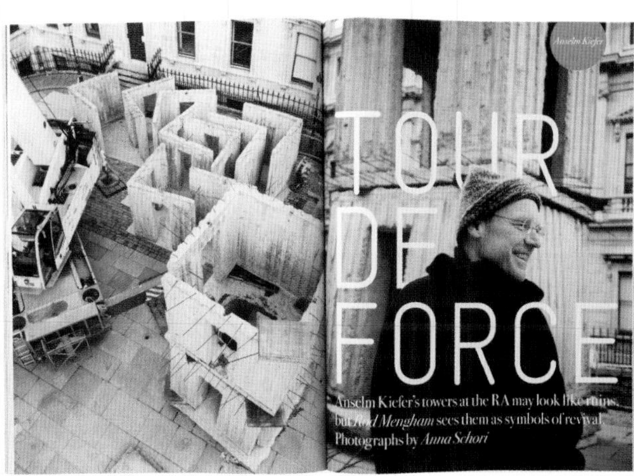

Anselm Kiefer
TOUR
DE
FORCE
Anselm Kiefer's towers at the RA may look like ruins, but *Rod Mengham* sees them as symbols of revival.
Photographs by *Anna Schori*

PREMIUM DENIM

86 years is a long time to perfect the art of jean craftsmanship. Fortunately 1921 Premium Denim have mastered it and are now bringing their cult LA jeans to London. Denim brand fads are often more fleeting than runway trends themselves, but as one of the oldest family-owned denim manufacturers in the world, heritage and endurance is something they clearly understand. Using Italian or Japanese denim, each piece is handcrafted, treated, washed and then finished with a special abrasion technique ensuring every pair is unique, and characterised by a vintage style finish. Not just lovingly crafted, but with a conscience too, all denim is spun from ecologically sound cottons ■

NEWS

SANDRA BACKLUND

Swedish knitwear genius, Sandra Backlund incorporated human hair into her first collection of architectural, madcap knits. That phase has passed and she is now using only the richest red wools instead. A knitwear couturier, Backlund plays with structure, creating outlandish tulip skirts, massive shoulders and kooky headgear. Not a Purl knit in sight, thank God, just futuristic sculptures that manage to retain romance and femininity in their shapes. Her inventiveness has earnt her a place in knitting's renaissance ■

BALENCIAGA

If the metal leggings are just a little *too Tron* for you, one can still indulge in Nicholas Ghesquire's feminine, android futurism, with Balenciaga's first ever eyewear range. Echoing the space-cadet look for his spring/summer '07 ready-to-wear collection, the eyewear line is a first for Ghesquire at the Parisian house.

Large transparent framed wrap-arounds, house grey or yellow reflective lenses with giant chrome studs on the arms. Cyber-goggles they're not, but being bug-eyed has never been so chic.

Influenced heavily by sci-fi, this was Ghesquire's first full-on flirtation with the future – spurning plundering the archives of Cristobal like he's done in previous seasons. Decidedly creating his own legacy at Balenciaga, rather than just seizing the Spanish designers' radically formed silhouettes.

Think today, tomorrow, and what may be. Are the days of designers pilfering the past for inspiration gone? The future is now ■

TOM FORD

The tanned Texan responsible for putting the sex back into Gucci is launching his first solo store in New York. 845 Madison Avenue, Manhattan is to be the home of the new TOM FORD signature menswear collection, which will include, RTW, footwear and eyewear. "My aim is to address an extremely discerning luxury customer who demands the highest quality product and service," claims Ford.

Fortunately for disciples of his suave and polished chic, he's plans to spread his wings over the next few years – opening stores in Milan, London, LA and Tokyo ■

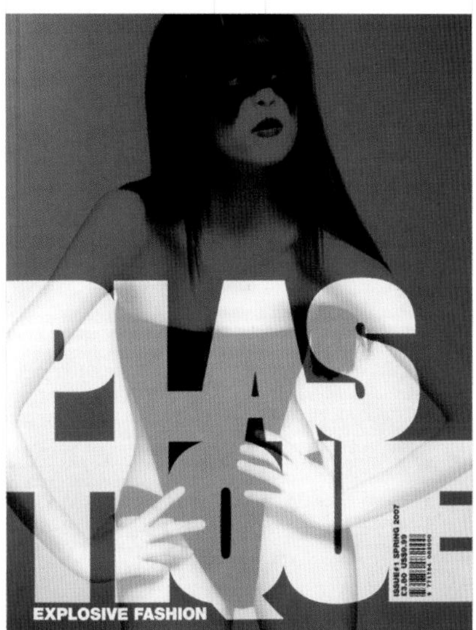

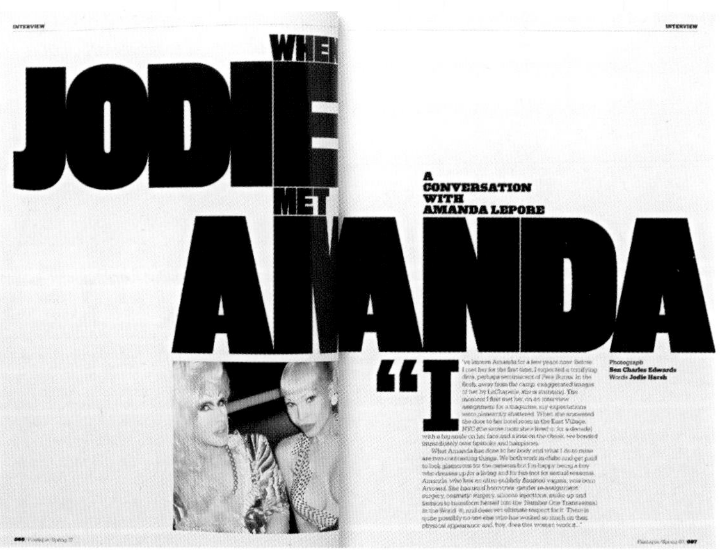

INTERVIEW
INTERVIEW
WHEN
JODIE
MET
AMANDA
A CONVERSATION WITH AMANDA LEPORE
"I
Photograph Ben Charles Edwards
Words Jodie Harsh

GRID SPECIFICATIONS

Page size (trimmed)	220 x 285mm
Top margin	15mm
Bottom margin	15mm
Outside margin	10mm
Inside margin	20mm
Number of columns	12
Gutter width	4mm
Extras	Baseline grid, 11pt

PLASTIQUE

Design: Matt Willey and Matt Curtis at Studio8 Design

Plastique is a quarterly women's fashion magazine. The basic elements of its design are very simple. There are two headline fonts; one text font, also used for the captions; and a 12-column grid that is frequently ignored! Designers Matt Willey and Matt Curtis wanted to work with as few rules as possible so that pages are designed as much through instinct as preconceived logic. The largely monochromatic color scheme was chosen to suit the ballsy and unapologetic nature of the magazine. As Willey says, "we didn't want anything too clinical, too fluffy, too saccharine, too girly."

NEWS

GIL CARVALHO

"Never under estimate the power of the stiletto," says Gil Carvalho. Given that he's followed the career route of Mr. Ford, who also gave up architecture for fashion design, Carvalho's ethos is on a par with his vigorous, towering platforms. Covered in vivid python and crocodile skins, with metallic feathers, they epitomize empowerment.

His architectural background is not entirely wasted however: like skyscrapers for the feet, Carvalho has produced a concept collection of soaring, polished steel stilettos – hand-laced elastic string, or satin cord that's woven to mould the foot – unmistakably requiring his construction precision and skill.

For something closer to the ground, Carvalho produces flat-of-foot sandals with slashed-leather fronts. Alternatively why not try his made-to-order black rubber and leather thigh-highs? ■

Todd Lynn is that kid at school that nobod noticed until parents' evening, where his mum and dad were unnecessarily cool a his report card gleamed, despite him being quie rebellious. With a bespoke-tailor CV reading like a rock 'n' roll-call of the last 40 years in music, it was no surprise his former mentor, Roland Mou looked on admiringly in the front row. Lynn's collection was rife with androgynous tailoring a fluid lines that effortlessly sexed up waistcoats, tuxedo jackets, and cropped trousers, which we swapped between the girls and the boys. ■

TODD LYNN

ALEXANDER WANG

Thank goodness he left his San Francisco frat boy beginnings at the door when joining Marc Jacobs as an intern. It no doubt ensured that despite being only 23, his own collection is one of hot sophistication and understatement. Sticking with the cashmere roots planted in his very first 2004 collection with some tasty cardigans and sweaters, Wang also channelled his NYC street cred' via sporty playsuits and sexy micro shorts. Think Debbie Harry circa 1977. ■

034/Plastique/Spring 07

Plastique/Spring 07/035

81

GREAT EASTERN STREET

PHOTOGRAPHY DAVID DUNAN

EDITORS ADDRESS
THIS IS IT.
CREATIVITY.
BRAVERY.
FEARLESSNESS.
LIFE IS A JOURNEY.
SO IS PLASTIQUE.
THINK
FOR
YOURSELF.
BRYLIE QUINN FOWLER
PAULE K

OSMAN YOUSEFZADA
KIM JONES
LAGERFELD RANGE

THE MAKING OF McQ
MYSPACE: CASTING AGENCY OF THE FUTURE?

A MARRIAGE OF CULTURAL HISTORY & MODERN DESIGN
SEX DRUGS & TURKISH RUGS

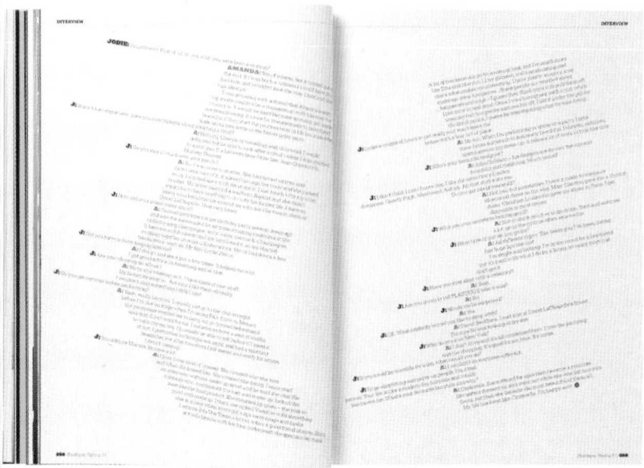

BOBS & BOY CUTS
THE SCISSORS ARE OUT AGAIN. THE BOB IS MOVING FORWARD INTO THE SPRING, REMAINING A STRONG TREND BUT WITH ADDED BITE. LOP A BIT MORE OFF AND GO WITH A BOY CUT

ZERO
DEGREES

KILLAH KOLOR
PHOTOGRAPHY
JOHN LINDGUIST
K

AGGR
ESSO
RIES
URBAN ARMOUR – FASHIONISTAS ARM THEMSELVES FOR EVERYDAY BATTLE

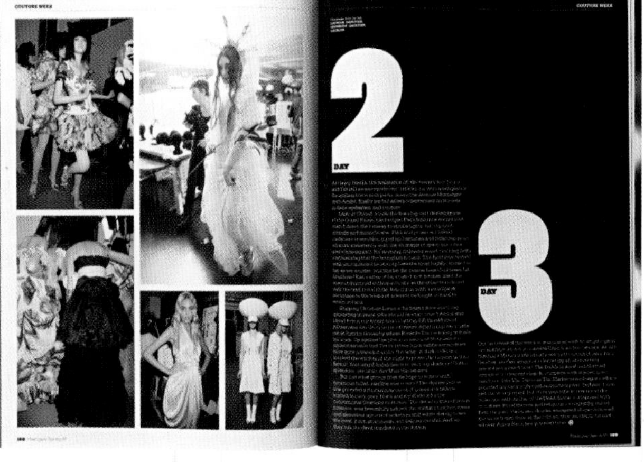
2
DAY
3
DAY

GO TO WWW.PLASTIQUEMAGAZINE.COM

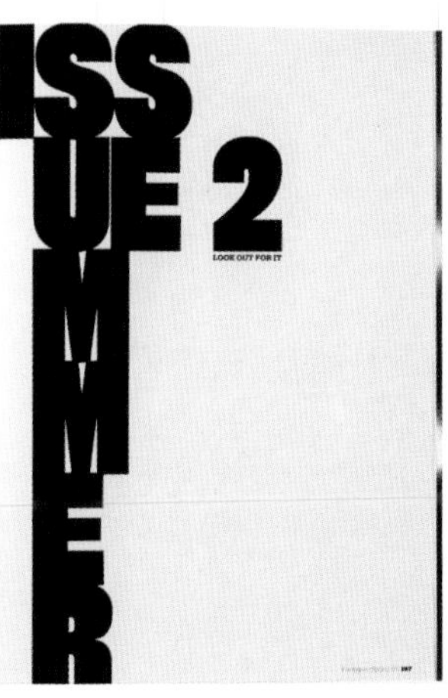
ISS
UE 2
SUMMER
LOOK OUT FOR IT

CANADIAN
EXPORT
DRAGONETTE BRINGS PLASTIQUE INTO THEIR WORLD OF ELECTRO-POP ORGIES

AJ
13.10.05
RIBA STIRLING
PRIZE
THE ARCHITECTS' JOURNAL WWW.AJPLUS.CO.UK
ISSN 0003-8466
£3.25

BUILDING STUDY
THE FASCINATION WITH
SURFACE GIVES THIS MOST
BASIC OF BUILDING TYPES
AN INTELLIGENCE AND
ENQUIRY THAT IS PALPABLE

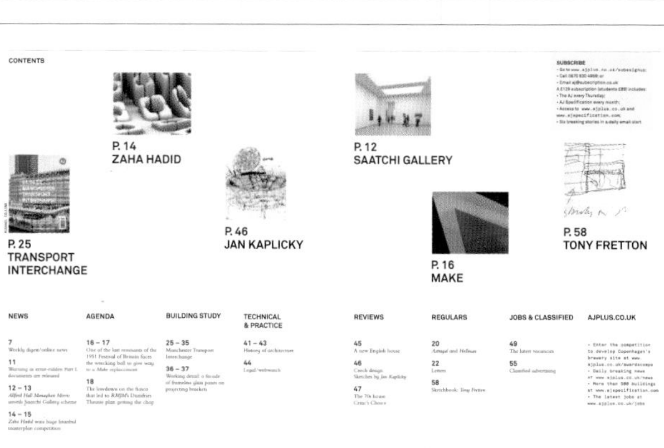
CONTENTS
P. 14
ZAHA HADID
P. 12
SAATCHI GALLERY
P. 25
TRANSPORT
INTERCHANGE
P. 46
JAN KAPLICKY
P. 58
TONY FRETTON
P. 16
MAKE
NEWS
AGENDA
BUILDING STUDY
TECHNICAL
& PRACTICE
REVIEWS
REGULARS
JOBS & CLASSIFIED
AJPLUS.CO.UK

CONTENTS

P. 14
ZAHA HADID

P. 25
TRANSPORT
INTERCHANGE

P. 46
JAN KAPLICKY

P. 12
SAATCHI GALLERY

P. 16
MAKE

P. 58
TONY FRETTON

SUBSCRIBE
• Go to www.ajplus.co.uk/subssignup;
• Call 0870 830 4959; or
• Email aj@subscription.co.uk
A £129 subscription (students £89) includes:
• The AJ every Thursday;
• AJ Specification every month;
• Access to www.ajplus.co.uk and www.ajspecification.com;
• Six breaking stories in a daily email alert

NEWS

7
Weekly digest/online news

11
Warning as error-ridden Part L documents are released

12 – 13
Allford Hall Monaghan Morris unveils Saatchi Gallery scheme

14 – 15
Zaha Hadid wins huge Istanbul masterplan competition

AGENDA

16 – 17
One of the last remnants of the 1951 Festival of Britain faces the wrecking ball to give way to a *Make* replacement

18
The lowdown on the fiasco that led to *RMJM*'s Dumfries Theatre plan getting the chop

BUILDING STUDY

25 – 35
Manchester Transport Interchange

36 – 37
Working detail: a facade of frameless glass panes on projecting brackets

TECHNICAL & PRACTICE

41 – 43
History of architecture

44
Legal/webwatch

REVIEWS

45
A new English house

46
Czech design.
Sketches by *Jan Kaplicky*

47
The 70s house.
Critic's Choice

REGULARS

20
Astragal and *Hellman*

22
Letters

58
Sketchbook: *Tony Fretton*

JOBS & CLASSIFIED

49
The latest vacancies

55
Classified advertising

AJPLUS.CO.UK

• Enter the competition to develop Copenhagen's brewery site at www.ajplus.co.uk/awardscomps
• Daily breaking news at www.ajplus.co.uk/news
• More than 500 buildings at www.ajspecification.com
• The latest jobs at www.ajplus.co.uk/jobs

4 AJ 06.04.06 AJ 06.04.06 5

GRID SPECIFICATIONS

Page size (trimmed)	210 x 265mm
Top margin	12mm
Bottom margin	12mm
Outside margin	12mm
Inside margin	12mm
Number of columns	4
Gutter width	4mm
Extras	Baseline grid, 3.883mm

AJ: THE ARCHITECTS' JOURNAL

Design: APFEL (A Practice for Everyday Life) with Sarah Douglas

APFEL redesigned *The Architects' Journal* in collaboration with Sarah Douglas. Together they developed a clean and simple design so that architectural process and progress are foregrounded. The grid is a simple four-column structure, and is used discreetly. Spreads look considered without being precious so that layouts can happily accommodate ephemeral content and at the same time showcase finished work. Images can be full bleed or squared up, and at times overlap or appear to hang from a top rule as though pinned on a wall. Folios, running feet, and rules at the top and bottom of each page quietly establish the overall page architecture.

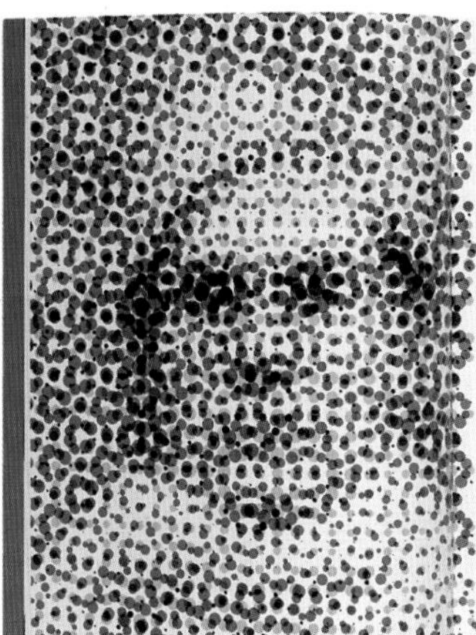

ART AND POLITICS

R O G E R · C O O K

THE LOVE THAT DARES TO SPEAK ITS NAME

Claire Portelli

THE PRINCE

CHAPTER —VI—

THE PRINCE CHAPTER VI

The drawing room of the Prince was hidden away beyond the great red walls of the armoury, the entrance a secret doorway that sheltered behind the tapestry of the hunting unicorn. In a corner amongst the shadows of the dusty room, lined by the books of time sat an old withered man of loathsome visage, whose nostrils would flare at the fragrance of the dying thorn impregnating its musty decay into the remembrance of his walls. He was seated in front of his portrait, which hung on an easel half uncovered with a purple velvet throw. It had been painted as a portal, which in turn preserved the impurities of his soul. All of a sudden he drew himself up from his throne and declared to the room:

"I am the Prince of an ancient bloodline whose forefathers walked the path of the righteous through the valley of darkness. My species evolved through time by crafts of virtue, understanding the evolution of our inherited principalities of power. Mine is a kingdom not of this world", he paused licking his lips, the curves of which once rewrote history, and tasted the distinct flavour of nutmeg mixed with the metallic of blood, and with saliva running down his chin he spat out, "I do not fear, I do not love".

The elderly Prince sat back in his throne, his many children closely huddled beside him whispering in a rasping unison 'Father, that is not dead that can eternal lie' and with long tongues they licked the wounds of his portrait that still wept from the scars of virtue and evil. The Prince had once woven the rich tapestry of shapes that had haunted all those that stood before him, for he was the keeper of the brotherhood and struck down with great vengeance and fury all those who attempted to poison or destroy. He knew the cave of time was cracked and blackened, shrouded in scarlet rose, the stain of his sin. His physical and intellectual distinction was destined to continually bare witness to his fascination with rebellion, a charming disobedience that flirted with the morning star of evil. To be feared, or to be loved was the compassion of his cruelty.

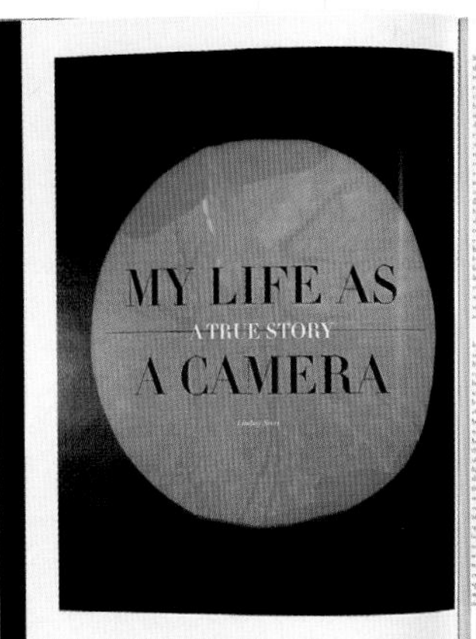

MY LIFE AS A CAMERA

A TRUE STORY

MERLIN JAMES

FICTIONS OF REPRESENTATION

The work of Merlin James (along with that of some of his near contemporaries) offers an opportunity to examine some pressing issues within representational painting as perceived in the current climate of contemporary art. James's paintings are interesting because they appeal to some generality of perception of what a painting practice should be, and while acknowledging a developmental modernist lineage, refuse to sit comfortably within this.

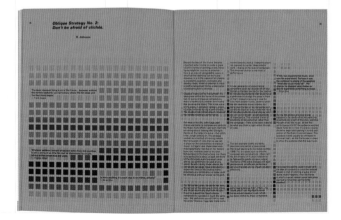

Oblique Strategy No. 2: Don't be afraid of clichés.

R. Johnson

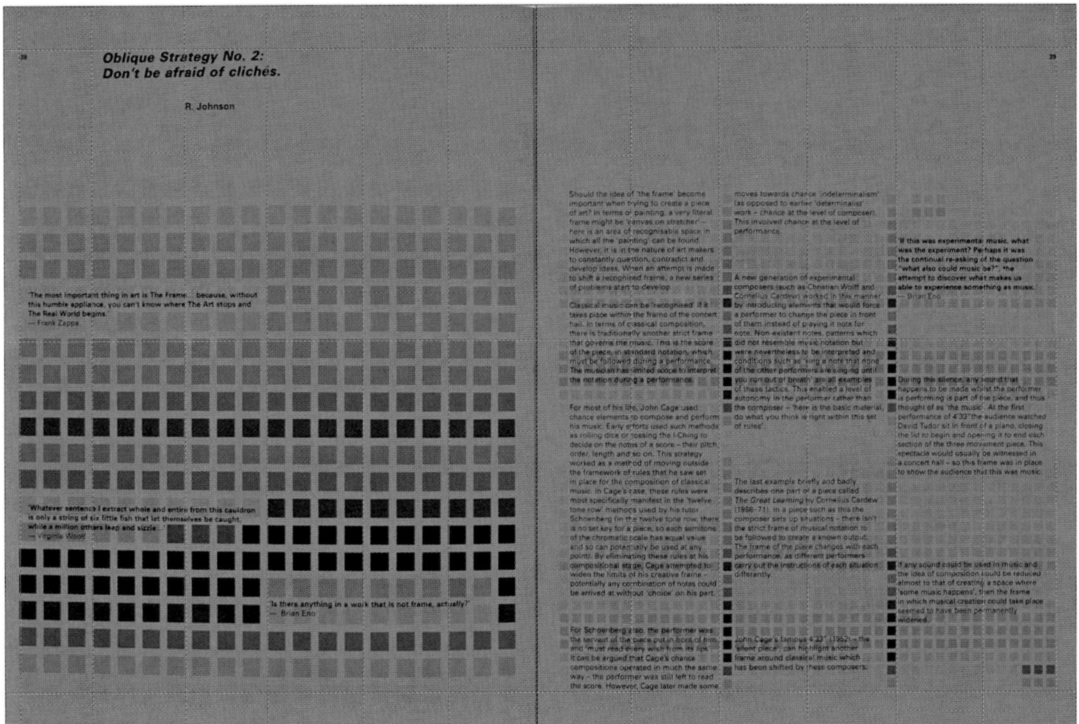

Oblique Strategy No. 2: Don't be afraid of clichés.

R. Johnson

'The most important thing in art is The Frame... because, without this humble appliance, you can't know where The Art stops and The Real World begins.'
— Frank Zappa

'Whatever sentence I extract whole and entire from this cauldron is only a string of six little fish that let themselves be caught, while a million others leap and sizzle...'
— Virginia Woolf

'Is there anything in a work that is not frame, actually?'
— Brian Eno

Should the idea of 'the frame' become important when trying to create a piece of art? In terms of painting, a very literal frame might be 'canvas on stretcher' – here is an area of recognisable space in which all the 'painting' can be found. However, it is in the nature of art makers to constantly question, contradict and develop ideas. When an attempt is made to shift a recognised frame, a new series of problems start to develop.

Classical music can be 'recognised' if it takes place within the frame of the concert hall. In terms of classical composition, there is traditionally another strict frame that governs the music. This is the score of the piece, in standard notation, which must be followed during a performance. The musician has limited scope to interpret the notation during a performance.

For most of his life, John Cage used chance elements to compose and perform his music. Early efforts used such methods as rolling dice or tossing the I-Ching to decide on the notes of a score – their pitch, order, length and so on. This strategy worked as a method of moving outside the framework of rules that he saw set in place for the composition of classical music. In Cage's case, these rules were most specifically manifest in the 'twelve tone row' methods used by his tutor Schoenberg (in the twelve tone row, there is no set key for a piece, so each semitone of the chromatic scale has equal value and so can potentially be used at any point). By eliminating these rules at his compositional stage, Cage attempted to widen the limits of his creative frame – potentially any combination of notes could be arrived at without 'choice' on his part.

For Schoenberg also, the performer was the servant of the piece put in front of him, and 'must read every wish from its lips'. It can be argued that Cage's chance compositions operated in much the same way – the performer was still left to read the score. However, Cage later made some moves towards chance 'indeterminalism' (as opposed to earlier 'determinalist' work – chance at the level of composer). This involved chance at the level of performance.

A new generation of experimental composers (such as Christian Wolff and Cornelius Cardew) worked in this manner by introducing elements that would force a performer to change the piece in front of them instead of playing it note for note. Non-existent notes, patterns which did not resemble music notation but were nevertheless to be interpreted and conditions such as 'sing a note that none of the other performers are singing until you run out of breath' are all examples of these tactics. This enabled a level of autonomy in the performer rather than the composer – 'here is the basic material, do what you think is right within this set of rules'.

The last example briefly and badly describes one part of a piece called *The Great Learning* by Cornelius Cardew (1968–71). In a piece such as this the composer sets up situations – there isn't the strict frame of musical notation to be followed to create a known output. The frame of the piece changes with each performance, as different performers carry out the instructions of each situation differently.

John Cage's famous 4'33" (1952) – the 'silent piece' – can highlight another frame around classical music which has been shifted by these composers.

'If this was experimental music, what was the experiment? Perhaps it was the continual re-asking of the question "what also could music be?", the attempt to discover what makes us able to experience something as music.'
— Brian Eno

During this silence, any sound that happens to be made whilst the performer is performing is part of the piece, and thus thought of as 'the music'. At the first performance of 4'33" the audience watched David Tudor sit in front of a piano, closing the lid to begin and opening it to end each section of the three movement piece. This spectacle would usually be witnessed in a concert hall – so this frame was in place to show the audience that this was music.

If any sound could be used in music and the idea of composition could be reduced almost to that of creating a space where 'some music happens', then the frame in which musical creation could take place seemed to have been permanently widened.

GRID SPECIFICATIONS

Page size (trimmed)	210 x 265mm
Top margin	18.8mm
Bottom margin	18.8mm
Outside margin	7.8mm
Inside margin	5.6mm
Number of columns	6
Gutter width	N/A
Extras	N/A

MISER & NOW

Design: Hannah Dumphy at CHK Design

Miser & Now (an anagram of the publishers' first names—Simon and Andrew) is an occasional visual arts magazine published by the Keith Talent Gallery. Art director Christian Küsters took banknote design as a starting point—a subliminal reminder of the relationship between the finance and fine art markets. Küsters and designer Hannah Dumphy respond to the editorial content of each issue and design accordingly—sometimes there isn't a conventional grid, sometimes each article is designed to fit its page using a flexible grid system, and sometimes opening pages are designed to read more like a poster.

Packaging

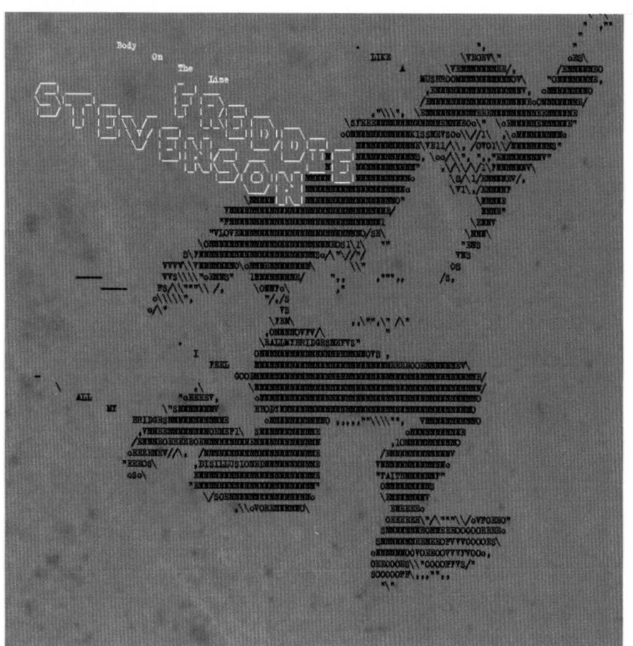

And my heart is like a wrinkled up balloon
When I see the love light in her eyes
Now that we're apart
It's a like a mushroom in the dark
Money has been spent
your demands
see for all this gloom
When I came too soon
He's a wonderful recording artist too
Thunder in the skies
Milan
As she walks in to the room
She says 'Just a sec'
So, keep on reaffirming my faith my fellow man
And how she always seems so
genuinely surprised
And your fake St Tropez tan
So I go to kiss her neck
peculiar
I try not to gag on her cheap perfume
I think I'm feeling good
If you don't kiss me soon
mood
I need more than just holding hands
surprise
Winters really taking hold
Then I'll kiss you

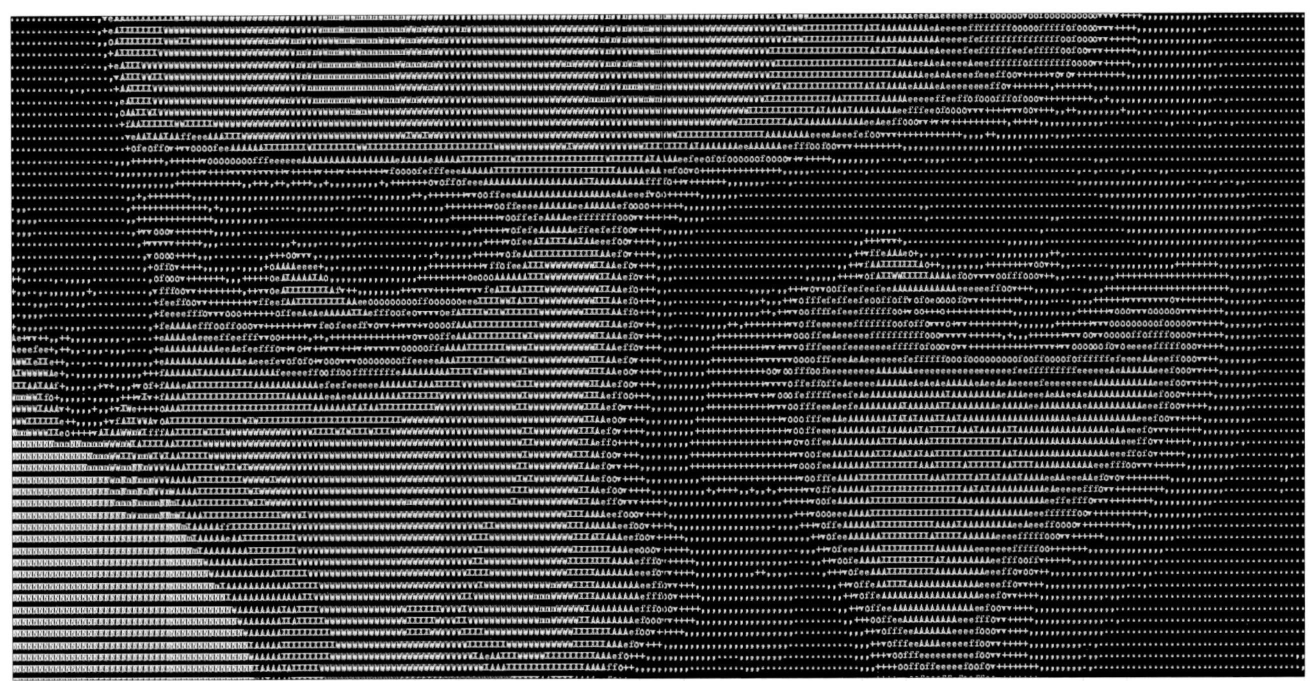

GRID SPECIFICATIONS

Page size (trimmed)	CD inlay: 150 x 117.5mm Booklet: 120.65 x 119.89mm
Top margin	N/A
Bottom margin	N/A
Outside margin	N/A
Inside margin	N/A
Number of columns	1
Gutter width	N/A
Extras	Baseline grid, as set by typerwriter; 56 horizontal rows

FREDDIE STEVENSON: A BODY ON THE LINE

Design: Rian Hughes at Device

Although the artwork was, in fact, put together on a Mac, with images created using an ASCII-art program, the overall impression of Rian Hughes' design for this CD packaging is that it is mechanically produced and generally low-tech. Hughes' intention was to echo Stevenson's music visually. Stevenson's music is made with little modern studio equipment, and without the aid of computer trickery. While there is no column grid employed, the type and images utilize a tightly packed series of horizontal lines that give a repetitive structure to the overall design, and increase its mechanical feel.

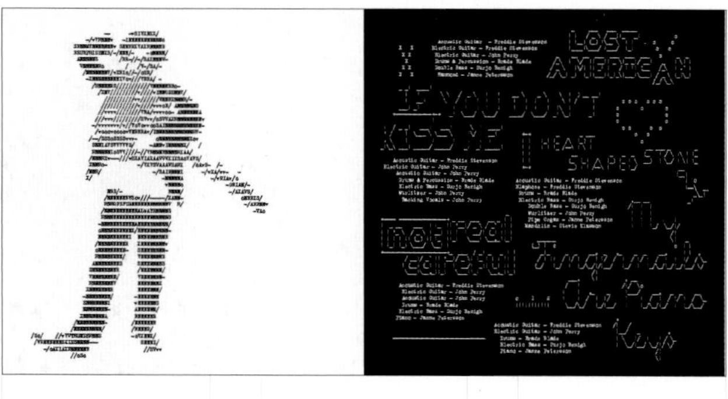

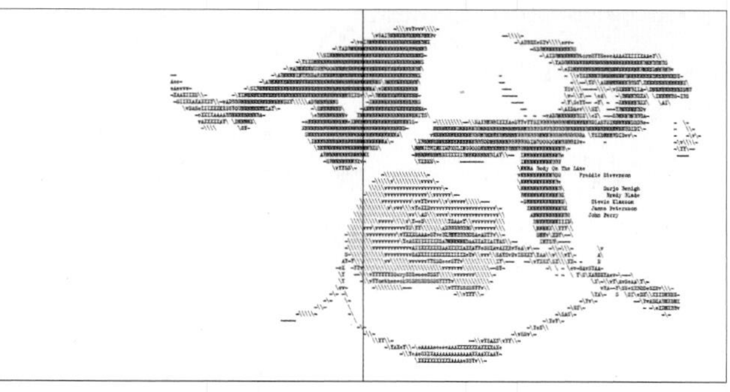

All songs written by FS
Freddie Stevenson

Produced by
John Perry
Mixed by Jason Glover at Vinylizor Productions
Engineered by Conny Wall
at Gig Studio, Stockholm
and Matthew Pleydell-Bouverie at Juicy Musical Creations, London
Mastered by
Ted Jensen at Sterling Sound, New York
Management by Juicy Musical Creations
Booking by Alex Nightingale and Jack Notman at EC1 Music Agency

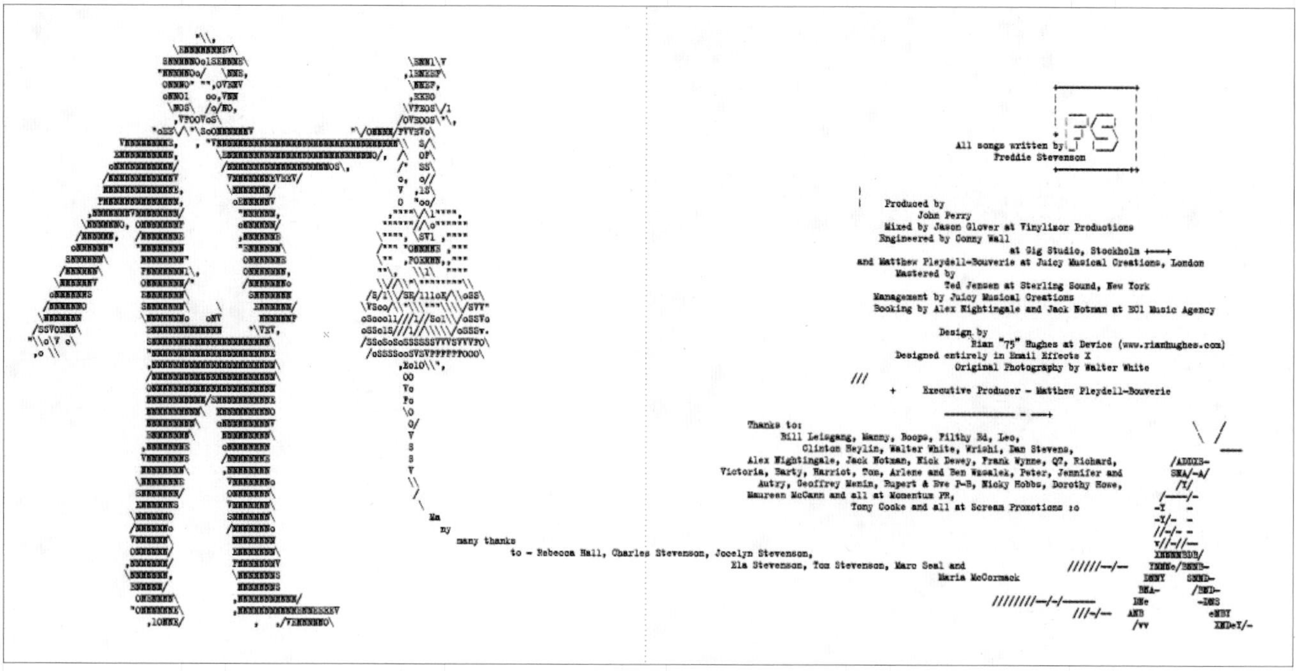

Design by
Rian "75" Hughes at Device (www.rianhughes.com)
Designed entirely in Email Effects X
Original Photography by Walter White

Executive Producer – Matthew Pleydell-Bouverie

Thanks to:
Bill Leisgang, Manny, Boops, Filthy Ed, Leo,
Clinton Heylin, Walter White, Wrishi, Dan Stevens,
Alex Nightingale, Jack Notman, Nick Dewey, Frank Wynne, Q7, Richard,
Victoria, Barty, Harriot, Tom, Arlene and Ben Wasalek, Peter, Jennifer and
Autry, Geoffrey Menin, Rupert & Eve P-B, Nicky Hobbs, Dorothy Howe,
Maureen McCann and all at Momentum PR,
Tony Cooke and all at Scream Promotions :o

Ma
ny
many thanks
to – Rebecca Hall, Charles Stevenson, Jocelyn Stevenson,
Ela Stevenson, Tom Stevenson, Marc Seal and
Maria McCormack

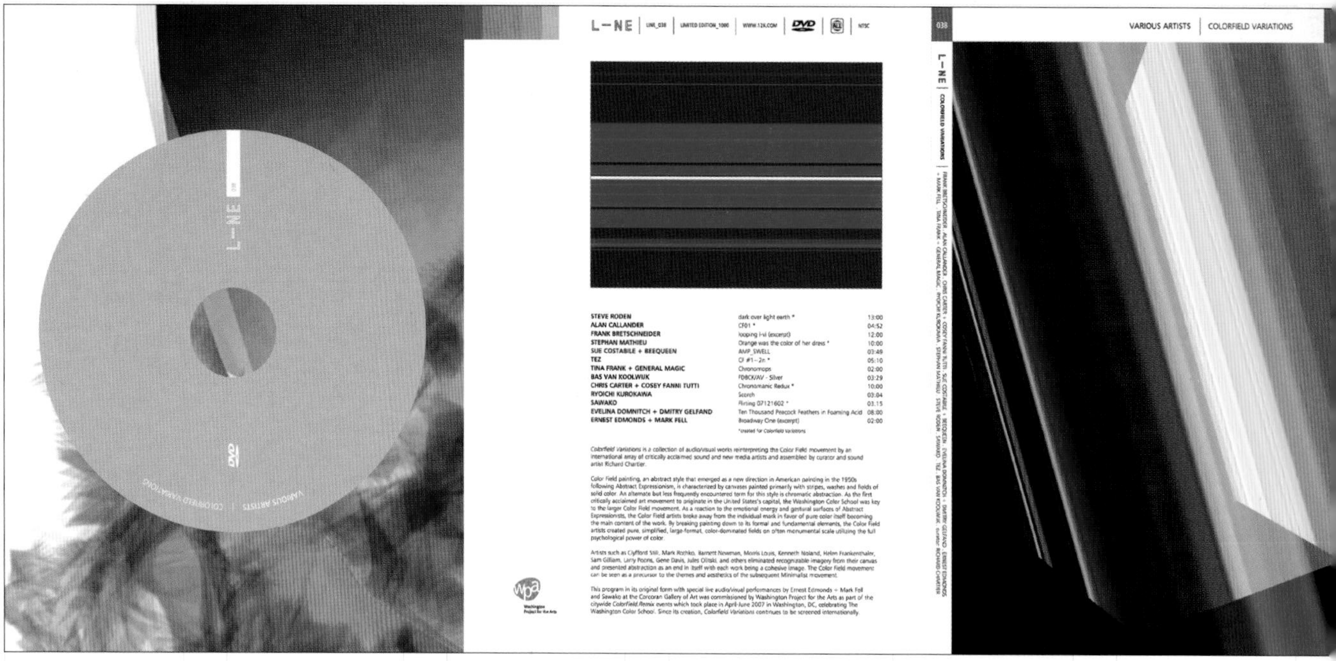

L—NE | LINE_038 | LIMITED EDITION_1000 | WWW.12K.COM | DVD | ALL | NTSC

038 | VARIOUS ARTISTS | COLORFIELD VARIATIONS

L—NE | COLORFIELD VARIATIONS

STEVE RODEN	dark over light earth *	13:00
ALAN CALLANDER	CF01 *	04:52
FRANK BRETSCHNEIDER	looping i-vi (excerpt)	12:00
STEPHAN MATHIEU	Orange was the color of her dress *	10:00
SUE COSTABILE + BEEQUEEN	AMP_SWELL	03:49
TEZ	CF #1–2n *	05:10
TINA FRANK + GENERAL MAGIC	Chronomops	02:00
BAS VAN KOOLWIJK	FDBCK/AV - Silver	03:29
CHRIS CARTER + COSEY FANNI TUTTI	Chronomanic Redux *	10:00
RYOICHI KUROKAWA	Scorch	03:04
SAWAKO	Flirting 07121602 *	03:15
EVELINA DOMNITCH + DMITRY GELFAND	Ten Thousand Peacock Feathers in Foaming Acid	08:00
ERNEST EDMONDS + MARK FELL	Broadway Cine (excerpt)	02:00

*created for Colorfield Variations

Colorfield Variations is a collection of audio/visual works reinterpreting the Color Field movement by an international array of critically acclaimed sound and new media artists and assembled by curator and sound artist Richard Chartier.

Color Field painting, an abstract style that emerged as a new direction in American painting in the 1950s following Abstract Expressionism, is characterized by canvases painted primarily with stripes, washes and fields of solid color. An alternate but less frequently encountered term for this style is chromatic abstraction. As the first critically acclaimed art movement to originate in the United States's capital, the Washington Color School was key to the larger Color Field movement. As a reaction to the emotional energy and gestural surfaces of Abstract Expressionists, the Color Field artists broke away from the individual mark in favor of pure color itself becoming the main content of the work. By breaking painting down to its formal and fundamental elements, the Color Field artists created pure, simplified, large-format, color-dominated fields on often monumental scale utilizing the full psychological power of color.

Artists such as Clyfford Still, Mark Rothko, Barnett Newman, Morris Louis, Kenneth Noland, Helen Frankenthaler, Sam Gilliam, Larry Poons, Gene Davis, Jules Olitski, and others eliminated recognizable imagery from their canvas and presented abstraction as an end in itself with each work being a cohesive image. The Color Field movement can be seen as a precursor to the themes and aesthetics of the subsequent Minimalist movement.

This program in its original form with special live audio/visual performances by Ernest Edmonds + Mark Fell and Sawako at the Corcoran Gallery of Art was commissioned by Washington Project for the Arts as part of the citywide *Colorfield.Remix* events which took place in April-June 2007 in Washington, DC, celebrating The Washington Color School. Since its creation, *Colorfield Variations* continues to be screened internationally.

wpa Washington Project for the Arts

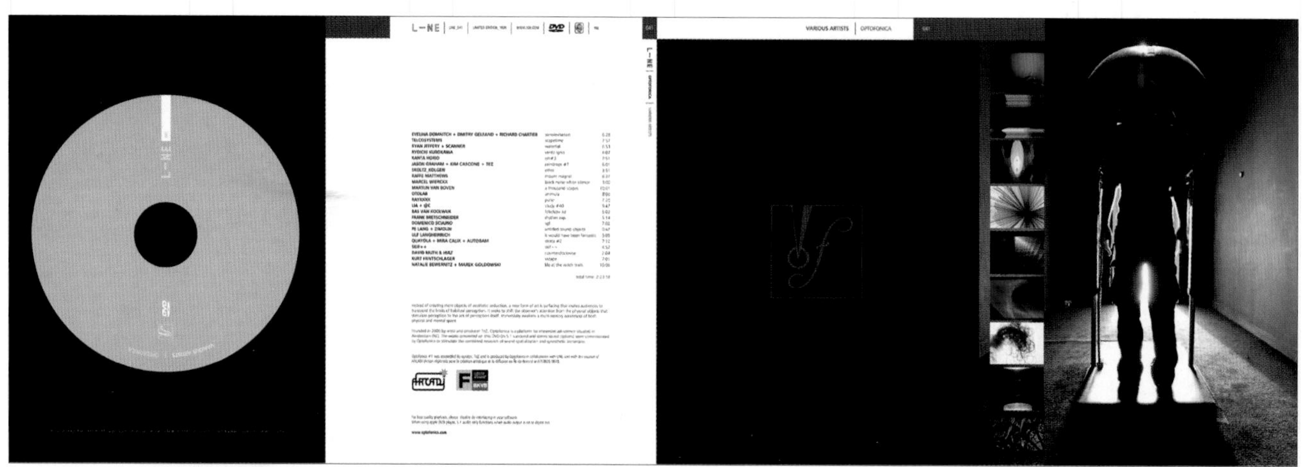

STEVE RODEN . "dark over light earth" (2007) was composed using electronics and harmonium played by Roden and violin played by Jacob Danzinger. Intended to act as a smaller ninth painting it was discreetly installed and created for the Los Angeles Museum of Contemporary Art's exhibit of eight paintings by Mark Rothko. Roden, using the colors in the eight paintings to generate a score for his own parts asked Danzinger to listen to Morton Feldman's *Rothko Chapel* on headphones and attempt to play along without a previous rehearsal. The video version was created using the same score with Roden finding each color in a catalog of 1940's house paint. Each swatch was a single frame in sequence and layered through simple dissolves. audio+video by Steve Roden, cello by Jacob Danzinger. www.inbetweennoise.com / **ALAN CALLANDER** . "CF01" (2007) is based on a meticulous visual analysis of the basic shapes and color palettes found in Mark Rothko's paintings. It generates approximately 200 individual rectilinear forms. audio+video by Alan Callander. / **FRANK BRETSCHNEIDER** . "looping i-vi" (2004-5) is an excerpt from the larger work *Looping I-VI (And Other Assorted Love Songs)* (12k, US). The video piece was created to accompany live performances. Published by Freibank, 2004. audio+video by Frank Bretschneider ©2005. www.frankbretschneider.de / **STEPHAN MATHIEU** . "Orange was the color of her dress" (2007) was created using processed shortwave radio signals and a visual ride through 256 colors. The audio is an early version of "Michael" originally released on *Radioland* (Die Schachtel, Italy). Published by Touch Music (MCPS). audio+video by Stephan Mathieu. www.bitsteam.de / **SUE COSTABILE + BEEQUEEN** . "AMP_SWELL" (2005) is a handmade video and employs backlighting to photographs and other translucent materials, a digital animation technique created by Costabile. Sound is translated into animated images of black and white photograms of fabrics, textured papers, and watercolors on tracing paper. Originally produced for *triMIX: Installation Soundtracks Deconstructed* (Innova Recordings, US). video by Sue Costabile, audio by Beequeen. www.sue-c.net + www.beequeen.nl / **TEZ** . "CF#1—2n" (2007) is part of a continuing series of works generated using software developed by the artist. These ever-changing video-paintings composite two layers of algorithmic color gradients with photo maps and react in real-time to dual-channel sound compositions. audio+video by Tez. www.tez.it / **TINA FRANK + GENERAL MAGIC** . "Chronomops" (2006) was generated by five rotating cubes moving through space—an abstract architecture of vertical color bars set in endless rotation. video by Tina Frank, audio by General Magic. www.frank.at / **BAS VAN KOOLWIJK** . "FDBCK/AV - Silver" (2007) is produced with software applications developed for the live performance *FDBCK/AV*. A feedback control circuit is created between audio and video signals which become two facets of a self-sustaining data stream. audio+video by Bas Van Koolwijk. www.basvankoolwijk.com / **CHRIS CARTER + COSEY FANNI TUTTI** . "Chronomanic Redux" (2007) Copyright Control 2007. audio+video by Chris Carter and Cosey Fanni Tutti. www.cartertutti.com / **RYOICHI KUROKAWA** . "Scorch" (2005) abstractly represents the act of scorching. It uses digitally generated images and sounds derived from fragments of field recordings. audio+video by Ryoichi Kurokawa. www.ryoichikurokawa.com / **SAWAKO** . "Flirting 07121602" (2007) is from a series of improvisational sketches based on color data from Helen Frankenthaler's painting, *Flirt*. video+audio by Sawako, cello by Jacob Kirkegaard. www.troncolon.com / **EVELINA DOMNITCH + DMITRY GELFAND** . In "Ten Thousand Peacock Feathers in Foaming Acid" (2007), Domnitch and Gelfand use laser light to scan the surfaces of nucleating and dissipating soap bubble clusters. Unlike ordinary light, the laser's focused beam is capable of crawling through the micro and nano structures within a bubble's skin. When aimed at specific angles, this penetrating light generates a large-scale projection of molecular interactions as well as mind-boggling phenomena of non-linear optics recently detected at the Lebedev Physics Institute (Moscow). Viewed in such proximity, the ionic innards of a bubble membrane evoke the dynamics of living cells. audio+video by Evelyn Domnitch and Dmitry Gelfand with additional audio by Andy Graydon and Kenneth Kirschner. www.portablepalace.com / **ERNEST EDMONDS + MARK FELL** . "Broadway One (excerpt)" (2004-5), part of an ongoing *Broadway* series, explores pure color, tone, and the harmonic relationships between those elements combined with the often simple systems that govern how they change and evolve. www.ernestedmonds.com + www.markfell.com / **RICHARD CHARTIER** (curator) www.3particles.com

Digital coding/mastering by Tez.

Thank you to all the artists involved in this project and Washington Project for the Arts (wpadc.org) as well as Keiichi Sugimoto, ExRealm, Volume, The Hammer Museum, Cimatics AV Festival, Leptopia, Decibel, The Henry Art Gallery, Issue Project Room, G Fine Art, Corcoran Gallery of Art, and the Ellipse Art Center.

LARGE IMAGES: Tina Frank (cover), Frank Bretschneider (back), Ryoichi Kurokawa (interior)

GRID SPECIFICATIONS

Page size (trimmed)	556.5 x 190.5mm
Top margin	9.5mm
Bottom margin	12.7mm
Left margin	0mm
Right margin	0mm
Number of columns	N/A
Gutter width	N/A
Extras	

LINE SERIES 3 CD/DVD PACKAGING

Design: Richard Chartier

The LINE imprint was born from the desire to take the tactile qualities of audio installations to listeners' living rooms. Since 2000 the imprint, curated and art directed by Richard Chartier, has continued to publish documents of compositional and installation work by international sound artists and composers, exploring the aesthetics of contemporary and digital minimalism in the form of limited edition Compact Discs and DVDs. The inspiration for this system came from the idea of the sleeve as a limited edition folder for the sound it contained, with extraneous design elements kept to a minimum.

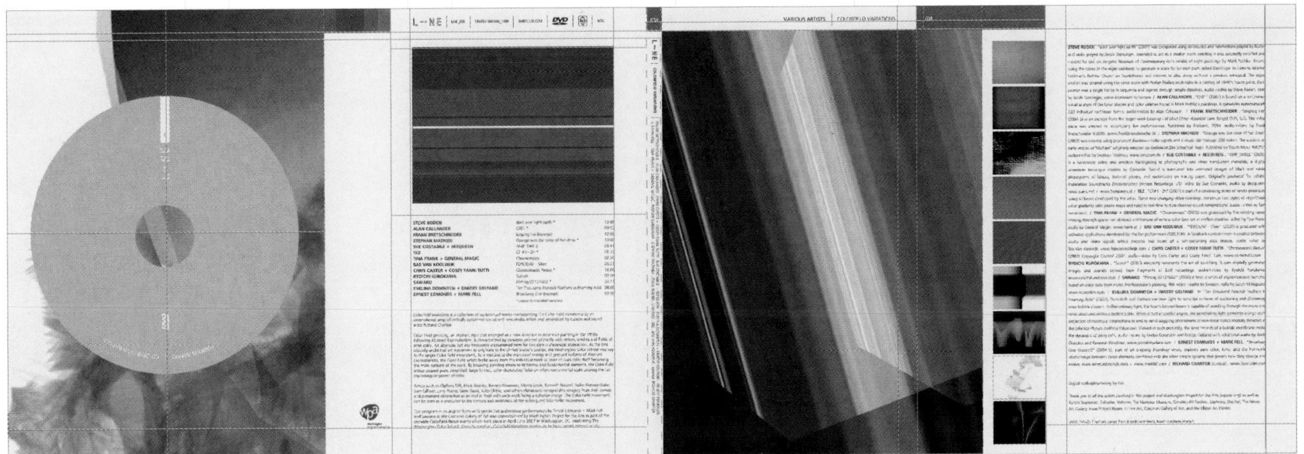

L–NE | LINE_036 | LIMITED EDITION_600 | WWW.12K.COM

JANEK SCHAEFER | EXTENDED PLAY [triptych for the child survivors of war and conflict] 036

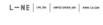

Extended Play - Vinyl Cello Duo	12:00
Extended Play - Vinyl Piano Trio	14:00
Extended Play - Vinyl Violin Duo	10:00
Extended Play - Acoustic Ensemble	24:00
Extended Play - Radio Jodoform	04:00

Red is the colour of Life, of Death, and of Love. Scarlett, my first child, was born in 2005, and since then I have been very aware of how lucky we all are. I have been constantly comparing this to the fact that my mother was born in Warsaw in 1942 - the epicentre of World War II. How opposite can two beginnings be? This inspired me to produce the Extended Play installation, which continuously and positively celebrates hope and new beginnings, for child survivors in all situations around the world.

The original idea for the composition, came from learning about the 'Jodoform' system of secret musical messages, that were broadcast by the BBC World Service, during World War II. The music they played was given a particular meaning, which was interpreted by The Polish Underground. I discovered from the original Jodoform log book, that the lovely Polish folk song 'Tango tyczakowskie', was broadcast on the day my mother was born. The song describes how children in 1918, had been forced to take up arms, in defense of their town. From this tune, I chose a short rising musical phrase, and with my arranger Michael Jennings, developed a ten minute score. Each of the three solo parts was then recorded separately, edited, and cut onto vinyl. In the gallery, 3 x Cello EP's, 3 x Piano EP's, and 3 x Violin EP's are played at either 33, 45, or 78rpm using nine retro record players. These play continuously, and each was modified to stop playing briefly in response to the audience moving around the exhibition. This has the effect of changing and extending the composition, so that it is never the same again.

For the album, Tracks 1, 2, and 3 were recorded using these record players, with all the character of hearing their mechanisms, and time passing within the dusty grooves. Track 4 creates a nine part ensemble, layering the acoustic recordings of the instruments at various speeds. Track 5 is a collage incorporating 'Tango tyczakowskie', recorded using a 1940's radio.

Commissioned by The Huddersfield Contemporary Music Festival 2007.
Performed by Michael Jennings [Piano], Simon Hewitt Jones [Violin], Thomas Hewitt Jones [Cello].
Thanks to Mary, Scarlett, Graham, Michael, Simon, Tom, Nikki, Andrew, Nirmal, Ty, Richard, and Catherine.
Thanks to The Polish Underground Movement Study Trust for their assistance in researching Jodoform Music.
Record Players produced & sponsored by Crosley USA.

Composed by Janek Schaefer. Copyright of audiOh! Recordings. Published by 12kmusicdascapo 2008.

www.audiOh.com

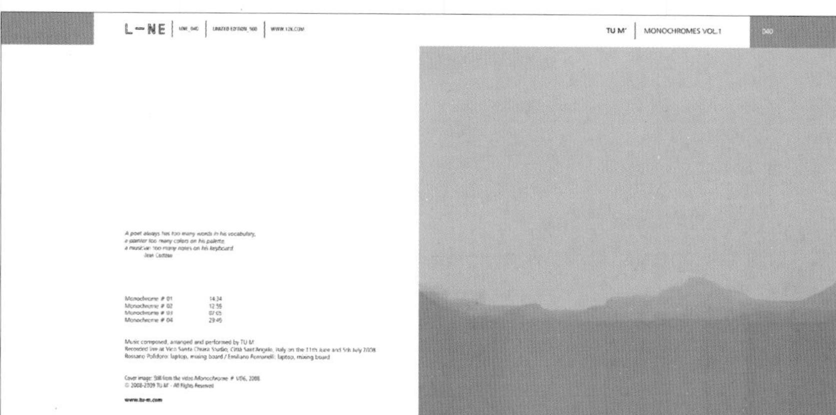

L–NE | LINE_040 | LIMITED EDITION_500 | WWW.12K.COM

TU M' | MONOCHROMES VOL.1 040

A poet always has too many words in his vocabulary,
a painter too many colors on his palette,
a musician too many notes on his keyboard.
Jean Cocteau

Monochrome # 01	14:34
Monochrome # 02	12:59
Monochrome # 03	07:05
Monochrome # 04	29:45

Music composed, arranged and performed by TU M'
Recorded live at Vico Santa Chiara Studio, Città Sant'Angelo, Italy on the 11th June and 5th July 2008
Rossano Polidoro: laptop, mixing board / Emiliano Romanelli: laptop, mixing board

Cover image: Still from the video *Monochrome # V06*, 2008
© 2008-2009 TU M' - All Rights Reserved

www.tu-m.com

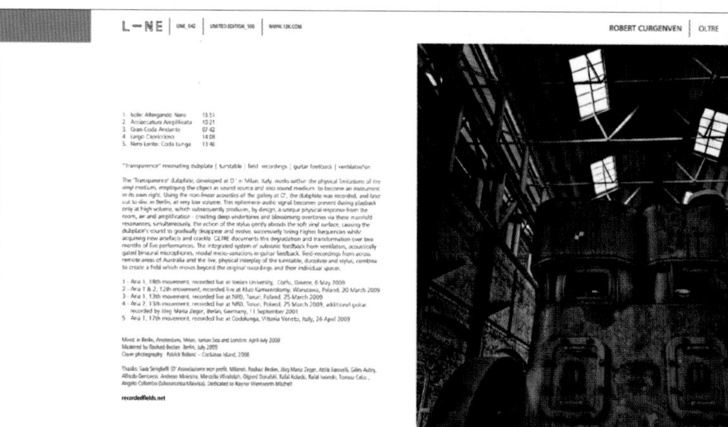

L–NE | LINE_042 | LIMITED EDITION_500 | WWW.12K.COM

ROBERT CURGENVEN | OLTRE 042

1.	Isole: Allargando Nero	13:51
2.	Acciaccatura Amplificata	10:21
3.	Gran Coda Andante	07:42
4.	Largo Capriccioso	14:08
5.	Nero Lento: Coda Lunga	13:46

"Transparence" resonating dubplate | turntable | field recordings | guitar feedback | ventilator/fan

The 'Transparence' dubplate, developed at O' in Milan, Italy, works within the physical limitations of the vinyl medium, employing the object as sound source and also sound medium, to become an instrument in its own right. Using the non-linear acoustics of the gallery at O', the dubplate was recorded, and later cut to disc in Berlin, at very low volume. This ephemeral audio signal becomes present during playback only at high volume, which subsequently produces, by design, a unique physical response from the room, air and amplification - creating deep undertones and blossoming overtones via these manifold resonances. Simultaneously, the action of the stylus gently abrades the soft vinyl surface, causing the dubplate's sound to gradually disappear and evolve, successively losing higher frequencies whilst acquiring new artefacts and crackle. OLTRE documents this degradation and transformation over two months of live performances. The integrated system of subsonic feedback from ventilators, acoustically gated binaural microphones, modal micro-variations in guitar feedback, field-recordings from across remote areas of Australia and the live, physical interplay of the turntable, dubplate and stylus, combine to create a field which moves beyond the original recordings and their individual spaces.

1 - Aria 1, 18th movement, recorded live at Ionian University, Corfu, Greece, 6 May 2009
2 - Aria 1 & 2, 12th movement, recorded live at Klub Kamieniołomy, Warszawa, Poland, 20 March 2009
3 - Aria 1, 13th movement, recorded live at NRD, Torun, Poland, 25 March 2009
4 - Aria 2, 13th movement, recorded live at NRD, Torun, Poland, 25 March 2009, additional guitar recorded by Jörg Maria Zeger, Berlin, Germany, 11 September 2001
5 - Aria 1, 17th movement, recorded live at Codalunga, Vittoria Veneto, Italy, 26 April 2009

Mixed in Berlin, Amsterdam, Milan, Ionian Sea and London: April-July 2009
Mastered by Rashad Becker, Berlin, July 2009
Cover photography: Patrick Boland – Cockatoo Island, 2008

Thanks: Sara Serighelli (O' Associazione non profit, Milano), Rashad Becker, Jörg Maria Zeger, Attila Faravelli, Gilles Aubry, Alfredo Genovesi, Andreas Maiestra, Marcello Wirabdeh, Olgierd Dokalski, Rafał Kołacki, Rafał Iwanski, Tomasz Cebo, Angelo Colombo (laboorontbartbovisa). Dedicated to Rayner Wentworth Mitchell

recordedfields.net

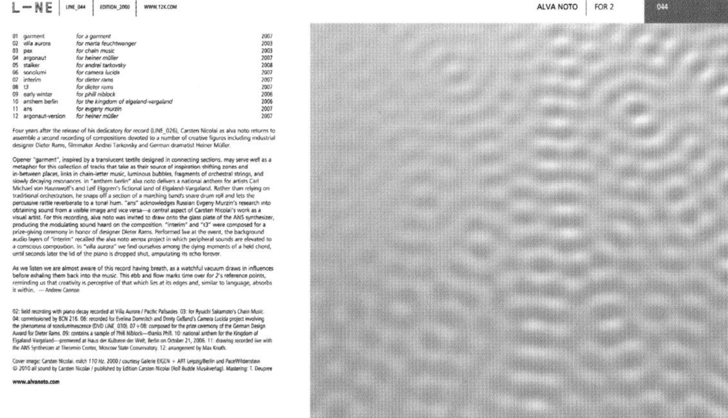

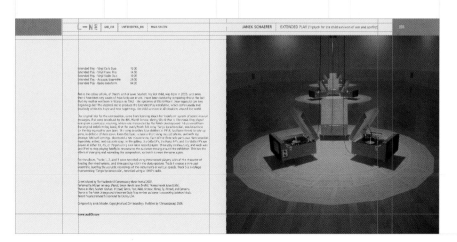

GRID SPECIFICATIONS

Page size (trimmed)	256.5 x 126mm
Top margin	9.5mm
Bottom margin	11.5mm
Outside margin	0mm
Inside margin	0mm
Number of columns	N/A
Gutter width	N/A

Abbeydale Grange
visual identity guidelines
and digital templates

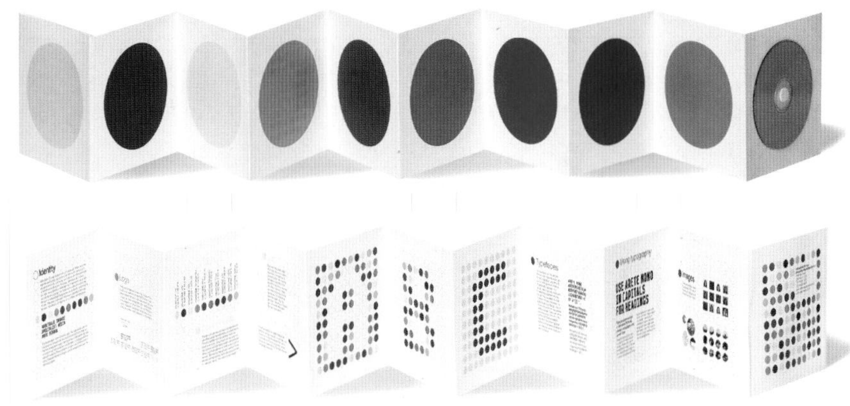

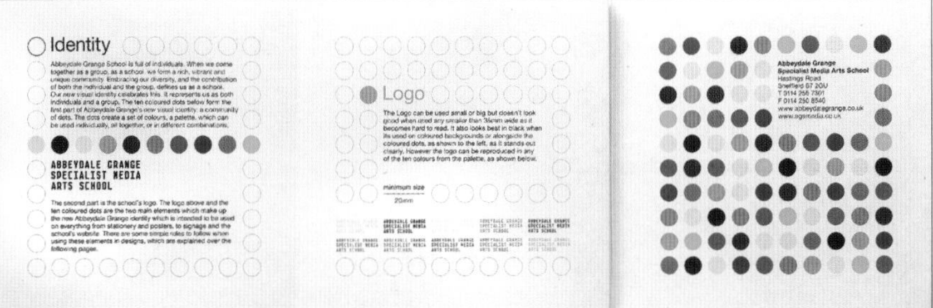
Identity
ABBEYDALE GRANGE
SPECIALIST MEDIA
ARTS SCHOOL
Logo
minimum size
20mm
Abbeydale Grange
Specialist Media Arts School
Hastings Road
Sheffield S7 2GU

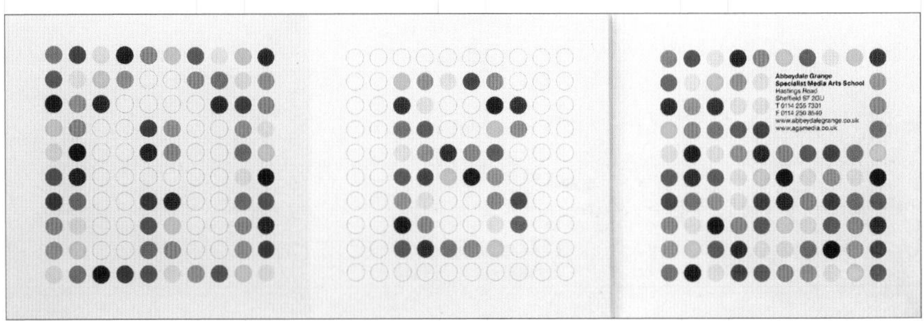

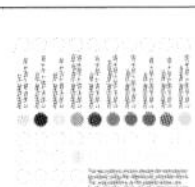

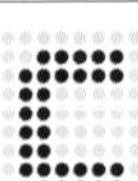

Using typography
USE ARETE MONO
IN CAPITALS
FOR HEADINGS

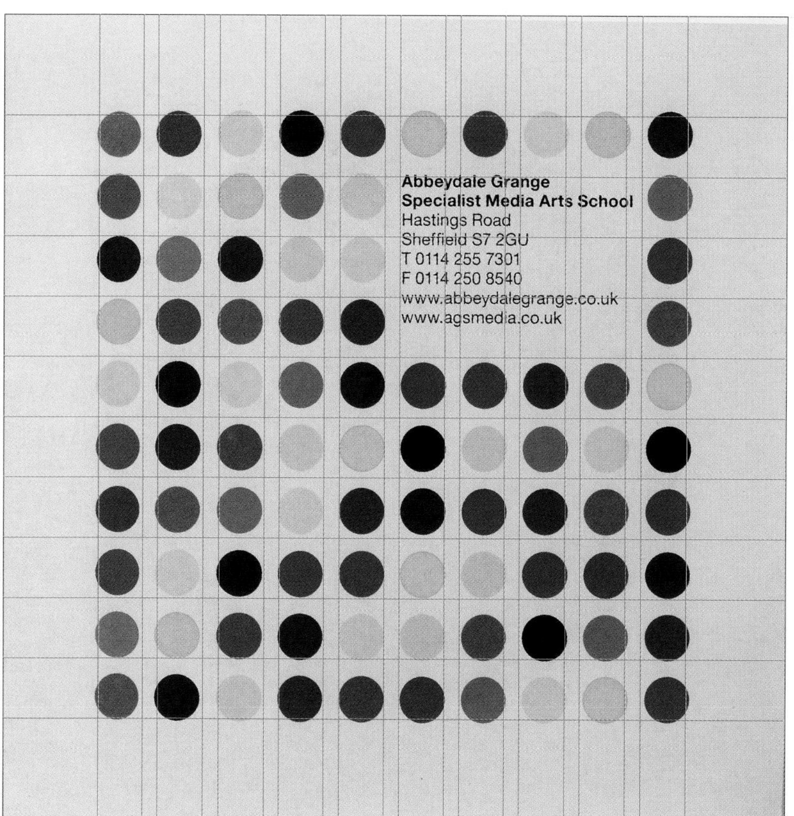

GRID SPECIFICATIONS

Page size (trimmed)	1,763 x 160mm
Top margin	20mm
Bottom margin	20mm
Outside margin	20mm
Inside margin	20mm
Number of columns	140
Gutter width	3.131mm
Extras	10 horizontal fields

ABBEYDALE GRANGE IDENTITY

Design: Zoë Bather at Studio8 Design

Abbeydale is one of a number of schools that are involved in the Joinedupdesignforschools initiative run by the Sorrell Foundation. This initiative links designers with schools where the pupils are the commissioning clients. Working closely with the students, Studio8 developed a new visual identity for the school, creating a logo, stationery, signage, posters, brochures, and design guidelines to guarantee effective implementation of the identity. To ensure flexibility and consistency, designer Zoë Bather employed a multi-column structure, further divided into a series of small fields, across the various items. The school's vibrant multiculturalism—over 50 different languages are spoken there—is celebrated in the bright, multicolored graphics.

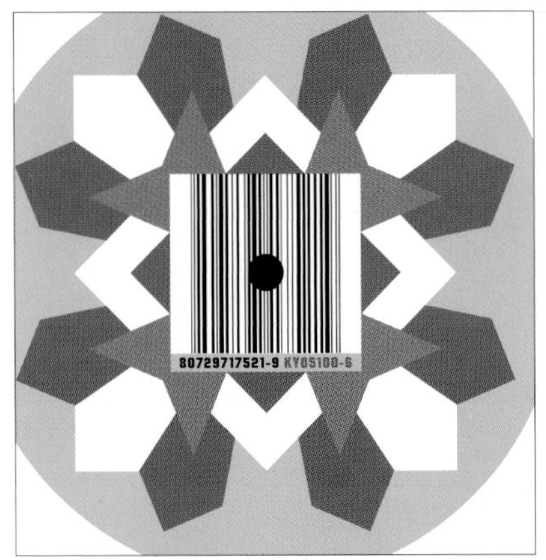

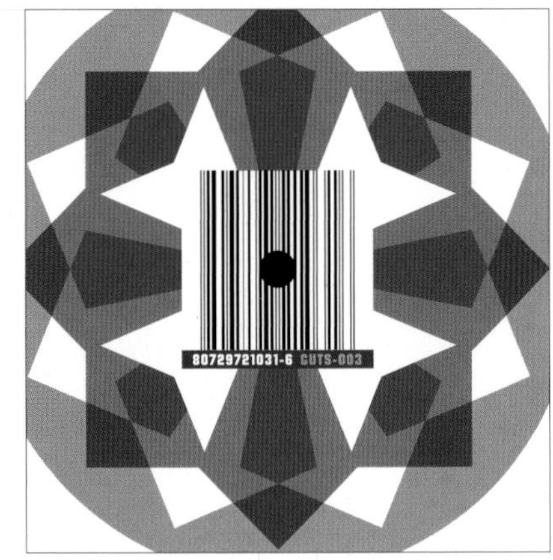

RAZ OHARA
HYMN MIXES

A1/JAHCOOZI REMIX//A2/RICHARD
DAVIS REMIX//B1/RICHARD DAVIS
ACID REPRISE//B2/LITWINENKO R
EMIX//33RPM

ALL TRACKS WRITTEN AND COMPOSED BY PATRICK RASMUSSEN//A1 REMI
XED BY ROBOT KOCH/MIXED DOWN BY OREN GERLITZ AT JAHCOOZI STUDIO
//A2 AND B1 REMIXES AND ADDITIONAL PRODUCTION BY RICHARD DAVIS//B
2 REMIX AND ADDITIONAL PRODUCTION BY LITWINENKO//ALL TRACKS PUB
LISHED BY EDITION BIATHLON/BUDDE MUSIKVERLAG//MASTERED BY HELMU
T ERLER AT DUBPLATES AND MASTERING/DESIGN BY ALORENZ BERLIN/MAN
UFACTURED BY HANDLE WITH CARE/WWW.HANDLEWITHCARE.DE/MADE IN
GERMANY/GEMA/LC02816//P AND C 2005 KITTY-YO/WWW.KITTY-YO.COM
//WORLDWIDE DISTRIBUTION BY INTERGROOVE/FAX 49(0)69-94547555/O
RDER NO. CUTS-003-6//THIS IS SIDE B

CHIKINKI
ETHER RADIO REMIXES

A1/ETHER RADIO JAN DRIVER & SIR
IUSMO – BOLT REMIX//A2/ASSASS
INATOR 13 ED LALIQ'S ALBION CALL
REMIX//B1/ETHER RADIO SERGE SA
NTIAGO VOCAL 45RPM

ALL TRACKS WRITTEN BY CHIKINKI/COPYRIGHT CONTROL//A1 REMIX AND A
DDITIONAL PRODUCTION BY JAN DRIVER AND SIRIUSMO/RECORDED AT THE
SUPER-SOUND-SUITE BERLIN/JAN DRIVER APPEARS COURTESY OF GRAND
PETROL RECORDINGS GERMANY/WWW.GRANDPETROL.INFO//A2 REMIX AN
D ADDITIONAL PRODUCTION BY E. BURDIS AND M. LANCASTER//B1 REMIX A
ND ADDITIONAL PRODUCTION BY SERGE SANTIAGO//MASTERED BY LUPO AT
DUBPLATES AND MASTERING//DESIGN BY ALORENZ BERLIN/MANUFACTURE
D BY HANDLE WITH CARE/MADE IN GERMANY/GEMA/LC02816//A1 AND A2
P AND C 2005 KITTY-YO/WWW.KITTY-YO.COM//B1 P AND C 2004 AND 2005
UNIVERSAL ISLAND RECORDS LTD. UNDER EXCLUSIVE LICENSE TO KITTY-YO
//WORLDWIDE DISTRIBUTION BY INTERGROOVE/FAX 49(0)69-94547555/O
RDER NO. CUTS-001-6//THIS IS SIDE B

SEX IN DALLAS AND BILADOLL
GRAND OPENING EP

A1/GRAND OPENING//A2/THREADS
//B1/THREADS KIDNAP'S PITCH BL
ACK LAKE MIX//B2/GRAND OPENIN
G KONDYLOM REMIX BY GUI.TAR//3
3RPM

ALL TRACKS WRITTEN AND COMPOSED BY ADRIEN WALTER/MIA VON MATT/
DAVID DUCAROGE//COPYRIGHT CONTROL//B1 ADDITIONAL REMIX PRODUCTI
ON BY KIDNAP/THORSTEN MINNING AND CORINNA VIGIC/WWW.THEKIDNA
P.NET//B2 ADDITIONAL REMIX PRODUCTION BY GUI.TAR WHO APPEARS COU
RTESY OF CARELESS//ALL TRACKS RECORDED MIXED AND PRODUCED BY KID
NAP/A2 COPRODUCED BY SEX IN DALLAS AND BILADOLL//MASTERED BY AN
DREAS AT SCHNITTSTELLE//DESIGN ALORENZ BERLIN/MANUFACTURED BY
HANDLE WITH CARE/MADE IN GERMANY/GEMA//P AND C KITTY-CUTS 2005
//WORLDWIDE DISTRIBUTION BY INTERGROOVE/FAX 0049(0)69-9454755
5/ORDER NO KYOS100-6//THIS IS SIDE B

LITWINENKO
REISEFIEBER EP

A1/REISEFIEBER//B1/KAUBEAT//B
2/OLTIMER//45RPM

ALL TRACKS WRITTEN AND PRODUCED BY LITWINENKO/TIMING MUSIC PUBL
ISHING/ARABELLA MUSIKVERLAG//MASTERED BY ANDREAS AT SCHNITTSTE
LLE//DESIGN ALORENZ BERLIN/MANUFACTURED BY HANDLE WITH CARE/M
ADE IN GERMANY/GEMA//P AND C KITTY-CUTS 2005//WORLDWIDE DISTRIB
UTION BY INTERGROOVE/FAX 0049(0)69-94 54 75 55/ORDER NO KYOS101-
6//THIS IS SIDE B

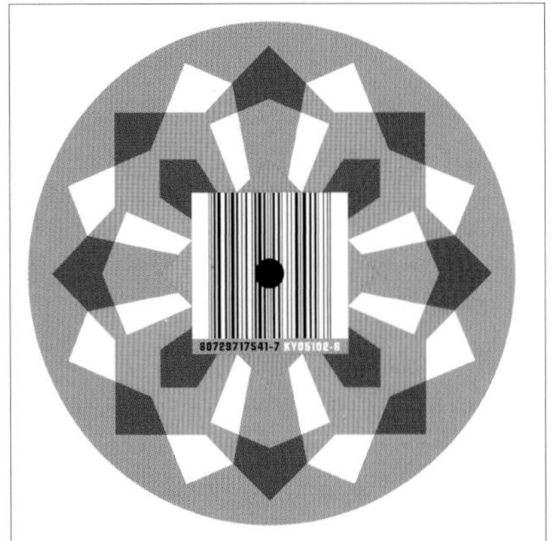

GOLD CHAINS & SUE CIE
CROWD CONTROL REMIXES

A1/CROWD CONTROL PHON.O REMI
X//A2/CROWD CONTROL TOPHER LA
FATA'S ALTERNATE VERSION//B1/C
ROWD CONTROL CB FUNK REMIX//3
3RPM

ALL TRACKS WRITTEN AND COMPOSED BY TOPHER LAFATA AND SUE COSTABI
LE/SEASIDE CITY MUSIC//A1 ADDITIONAL REMIX PRODUCTION BY PHON.O W
HO APPEARS COURTESY OF SHITKATAPULT WWW.SHITKATAPULT.COM//A2 A
DDITIONAL REMIX PRODUCTION BY TOPHER LA FATA//B1 ADDITIONAL REMIX
PRODUCTION BY CB FUNK WHO APPEARS COURTESY OF PUNKT MUSIC//PROD
UCED BY TOPHER LA FATA/VLADISLAV DELAY/SUE COSTABILE//RECORDED AT
ZOMBIE STUDIOS SAN FRANCISCO BY GCSC//MIXED BY VLADISLAV DELAY AN
D TOPHER LAFATA AT BASSDRESS BERLIN//MASTERED BY ANDREAS AT SCHNI
TTSTELLE//DESIGN ALORENZ BERLIN/MANUFACTURED BY HANDLE WITH CA
RE/MADE IN GERMANY/GEMA//UNDER EXCLUSIVE LICENSE OF KILL ROCK ST
ARS/P KILL ROCK STARS/C KITTY-CUTS 2005//WORLDWIDE DISTRIBUTION B
Y INTERGROOVE/FAX 49(0)69-94 54 75 55/ORDER NO KYOS102-6//SIDE B

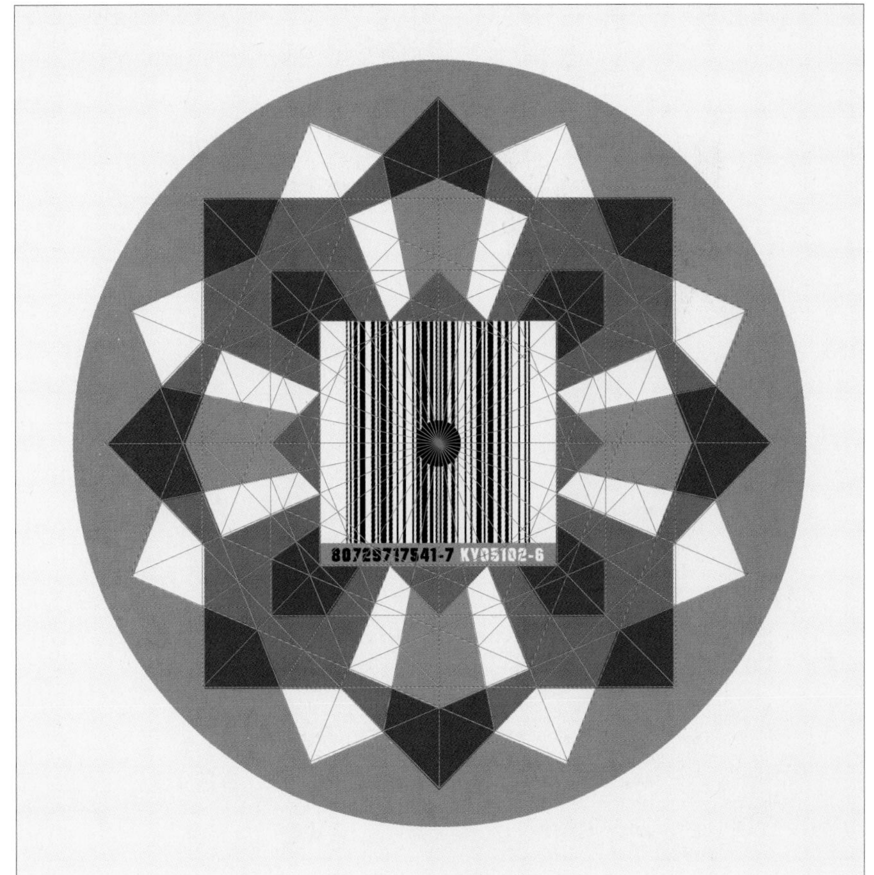

KITTY CUTS

Design: Angela Lorenz at alorenz, Berlin/Wien

Taking the name of the series at face value (in German "cut" is "Schnitt" and "intersection" is "Schnittmenge"), Angela Lorenz constructed the design for these 12in EP labels by appearing to cut into the central square that holds the bar code. Rotating, enlarging, and repeating this shape along its diagonal forms a star shape that resembles images created by a kaleidoscope or the cut of a jewel. Although Lorenz isn't working with a traditional horizontal/vertical grid, the resulting forms are repetitive and geometrically derived.

GRID SPECIFICATIONS	
Page size (trimmed)	100 x 100mm
Top margin	To bleed
Bottom margin	To bleed
Outside margin	To bleed
Inside margin	To bleed
Number of columns	N/A
Gutter width	N/A
Extras	Grid developed from base unit—
	32mm square

Komet »

I would not use the word minimal to describe my music. This is a fixed term for other music from other times. I'd rather call it economic...

Reciprocess + / vs.

reciprocal adj. + n. **1** in return. **2** mutual. **3** inversely correspondent; complementary.

process n. + v. **1** a course of action or procedure, esp. a series of stages in manufacture or some other operation. **2** the progress or course of something. **3** a natural or involuntary operation or series of changes. **4** (computing) operate on (data) by means of a program.

BiP-HOp in association with Fällt are pleased to present Reciprocess + / vs. A series of split CDs featuring the work(s) of two sound assemblers and documenting the process of musical reciprocality between them.

This first installment features two sound assemblers contributing a collaborative work; a series of independent works; and finally, contributing a remix of each other's work(s).

Reciprocess + / vs. is co-curated by Philippe Petit (BiP-HOp) and Christopher Murphy (Fällt) and features artwork by Fällt designers Feiler.

Introduction »

Bovine Life »

I was in a record shop in my home town of Edinburgh - Avalanche - when I first heard Frank Bretschneider's music.

I was in a record shop in my home town of Edinburgh - Avalanche - when I first heard Frank Bretschneider's music. I loved it.

I was struck by it's exacting tonal frequencies, mainly because they reminded me of a hearing test I underwent when I was fifteen. The shop's P.A. broadcasted this electronically fragile groove with some frequencies just on the border of my audible range and I found myself nodding gently to the pristine sound automatically...

At first, I didn't think the track was progressing much over the five minutes it lasted, but it soon occurred to me I had been engaged in a subtle form of electronic meditation for the duration of the track. I think the best way I can describe this music is that the track doesn't appear to go far in the traditional (compositional) sense, but the listener does .

That's not to say Frank's music isn't ever loose. I think one of the reasons I like this music is because it marries precise syncopation with the freedom of a penny rattling around in a jar.

There are boundaries, but it's as if the creator of the music has set up the track like a science project - tamed the chaos, and then put the lid on the sound.

All this (warm) military precision is the antithesis of my own forays into electronic music - they basically resemble scruffy, mutant and promiscuous audio-one-night-stands. I am not pure. I am messy and untidy - I think I may be diseased from my working practices. You can hear this evidence in my stuff - it can be impatient, rude, painful or playful. Even shambolic, so I reckoned it would be an interesting experiment to fuse our stuff together.

It would either discipline myself or disease Frank!

Because our styles are different, we had to be speaking some kind of similar tongue, albeit an electronic one. It wasn't an oil and water collaboration - I think that could have been disastrous, but I was nicely surprised by the opening track 'Riss' - Frank's remix of my material from my web site 'kit' of samples. It's got a sense of humour - and how much glitch/click/cut music has that?

I was very keen that this was going to be a collaboration forged strictly over the net, so we both sent each other economical .mp3 files to fashion into new material. While this method of working wasn't ground breaking, it was still exciting that I could sit in my studio and collaborate with someone in Berlin. I am the kind of person that still gets completely blown away by the fact that the telephone network exists and works.

I really enjoyed collaborating. Friends would wander into my studio (a cupboard in my flat) and ask me what I was doing. I would say, "Well right now... right this minute, I am making a track with a German guy. There's this guy in Berlin, right..." It felt very empowering. I have never met Frank Bretschneider, yet we've made an album!

I like the basic idea of the computer being a machine that works for you. My main applications are like organisms – living creatures. Once you've made friends with them you can rely on them and become a team.

I like precise impulsive sounds, sine waves and white noise, which are both simple and clear.

I'm a bit uncontrolled and easily distracted, but this allows my compositions to be guided by the circumstances of the moment.

I have a constant impatience with my own sound, seeking to devolve and simplify it, whilst leaving an emotional content.

Komet »

I would not use the word minimal to describe my music. This is a fixed term for other music from other times. I'd rather call it economic...

Introduction »

Bovine Life »

GRID SPECIFICATIONS

Page size (trimmed)	120 x 120mm
Top margin	12mm
Bottom margin	12mm
Outside margin	12mm
Inside margin	12mm
Number of columns	3
Gutter width	6mm
Extras	Baseline grid, 12.7mm; 3 horizontal fields

+/VS.

Design: Fehler

This series of CDs features soundworks by two different artists. Each contributes solo tracks as well as remixing the other's work, so the brief was to create a design that didn't privilege one artist over the other. A democratic solution was achieved by creating a grid that reads in four directions: right side up for one artist, right side down for the other, with the other two axes left to hold commentary and essays.

Posters & fliers

SUNSHINE
ICARUS II
MISSION STATEMENT
SUN'S COMPOSITION
CREW
TEAM PHOTO
SPACESUIT
TECHNICAL
SUN FACTS
MISSION BADGE
ICARUS II

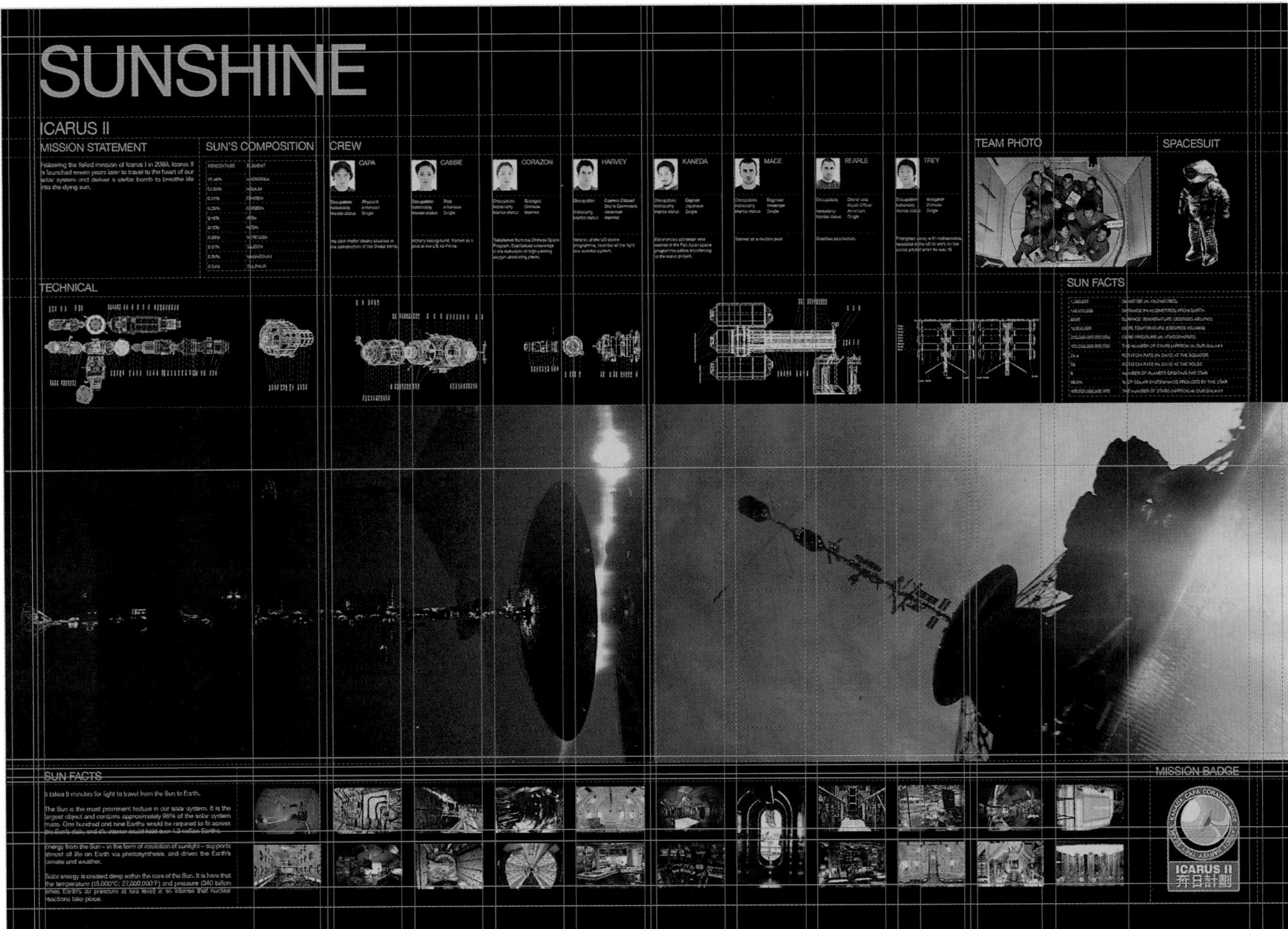

GRID SPECIFICATIONS

Page size (trimmed)	100 x 700mm
Top margin	21mm
Bottom margin	21mm
Outside margin	21mm
Inside margin	21mm
Number of columns	38
Gutter width	37mm
Extras	Front: 10 horizontal fields Back: 17 horizontal fields

SUNSHINE

Design: Airside

This foldout double-sided poster was designed for DNA Films as a gift for the crew involved in making the movie *Sunshine*. The back of the poster shows the crew listed as though members of a space mission. The grid wasn't determined by content and page size alone. It was planned so that images of over 400 crew members, and all relevant information, would fit on one side of the poster without any picture or text running over the three folds.

fad
la incubadora
del fad
PFC
Per Fi
Comencem!
el termòmetre
de la creativitat
emergent de catalunya
inauguració
dilluns 04.12.06
19:30 h.
L'exposició que, per primer cop i en un sol espai, recull els millors Projectes Final de Carrera 2005-2006 de les escoles de disseny, arquitectura, art i comunicació de Catalunya. També hi trobareu els projectes guanyadors de la
darrera edició dels premis per a estudiants organitzats per les associacions del FAD.
Exposició
05-22.12.06
De dilluns a divendres,
d'11:00 a 20:00 h.
Sala d'exposicions del FAD
FAD
Plaça dels Àngels 5-6
08001 Barcelona
T 93 443 75 20
F 93 329 60 79
fad@fadweb.org
www.fadweb.org
Amb la col·laboració de:
Generalitat de Catalunya
Departament
de Cultura
Institut de
cultura

fad
Contactes
Anuari
de la creativitat
del FAD 2007
Contactos
Anuario
de la creatividad
del FAD 2007
Socis professionals i estudiants
Socios profesionales y estudiantes
català > www.fadweb.org/contactos/
castellano > www.fadweb.org/contactos/CAST/
Empreses col·laboradores
Empresas colaboradoras
català > www.fadweb.org/contactos/empreses/ca
castellano > www.fadweb.org/contactos/empreses/es
Escoles
Escuelas
català > www.fadweb.org/contactos/escoles/ca
castellano > www.fadweb.org/contactos/escoles/es

mestres
la cadena del fad
Rosa Ventós
mestres
la cadena del fad
Oriol Bohigas
mestres
la cadena del fad
Albert
Ràfols-Casamada

N.05
gener
2007
agenda
del fad
fadzine
Foment
de les Arts
i del Disseny
fad
la mosca
del fad
altres
activitats

adi
fad
Associació de Disseny Industrial
Asociación de Diseño Industrial
Association of Industrial Design

fad
Foment de les Arts i del Disseny
Fomento de las Artes y del Diseño
Fostering Arts and Design
Plaça dels Àngels 5-6
08001 Barcelona
Tel. +34 93 443 75 20
Fax +34 93 329 60 79
fad@fadweb.org
www.fadweb.org
Amb el suport de
Con el apoyo de
Supported by
arquia

moda
fad
Associació d'Imatge i Moda
Asociación de Imagen y Moda
Association of Image and Fashion

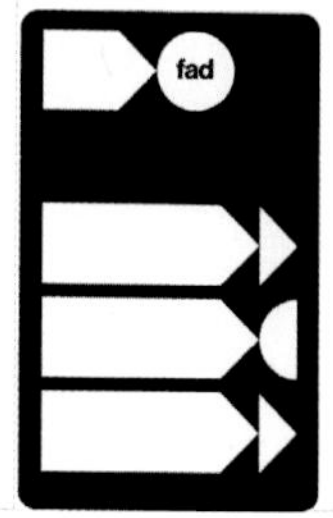
fad

GRID SPECIFICATIONS

Page size (trimmed)	Resizable, as required
Top margin	1 base unit
Bottom margin	1 base unit
Outside margin	1 base unit
Inside margin	1 base unit
Number of columns	Flexible
Gutter width	1 base unit
Extras	Grid developed from base unit—square

FAD GRAPHIC GUIDELINE

Design: BaseDESIGN

Three basic shapes—the square, the triangle, and the circle—form the core of the graphic system of BaseDESIGN's identity for FAD, a Spanish, not-for-profit cultural body promoting design, architecture, and art. The grid is determined by multiples of these forms, creating vertical and horizontal bands across the page. These bands are then used as columns and fields would be in a conventional grid.

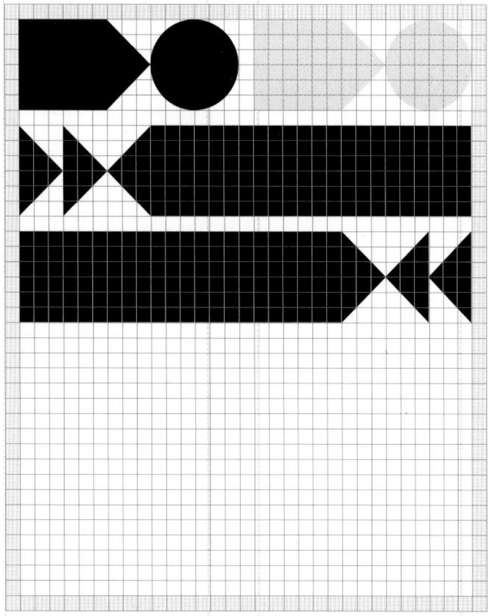

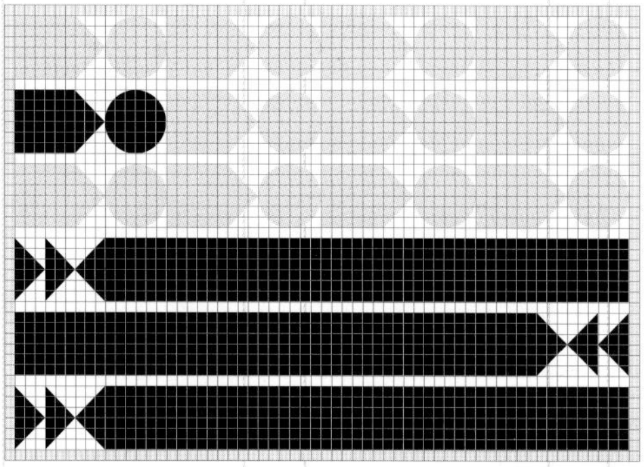

Exhibition
Convent dels Angels
August 2006

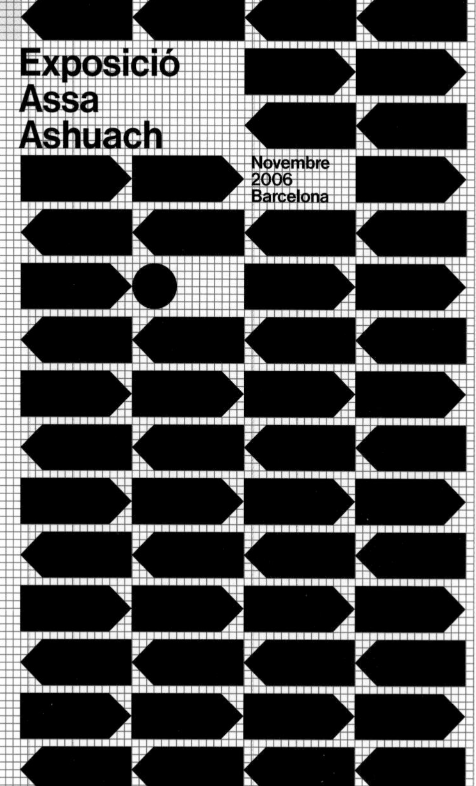
Exposició
Assa
Ashuach
Novembre
2006
Barcelona

Encuentros
Camper
FAD
Campana Brothers
Conferència
01.12 / 19:30h
FAD
CAMPER
fad

Encuentros
Camper
FAD
Campana Brothers
Conferència
01.12 / 19:30h
FAD
CAMPER
fad

01/11
02/11
03/11
04/11
05/11
06/11
07/11
I
WAS
THERE
YOU
ARE
HERE

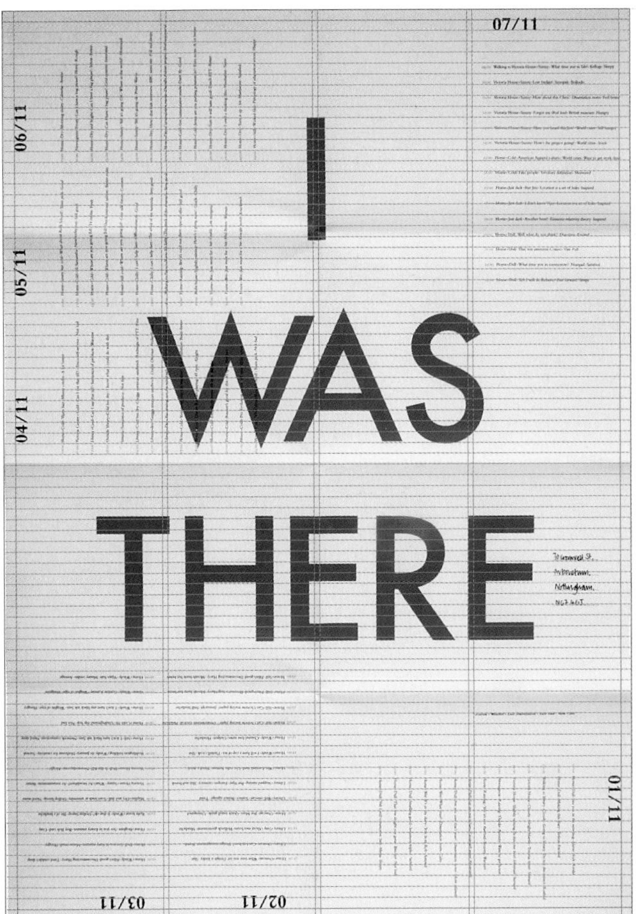

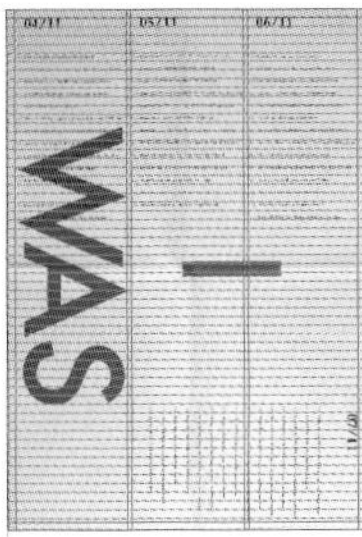

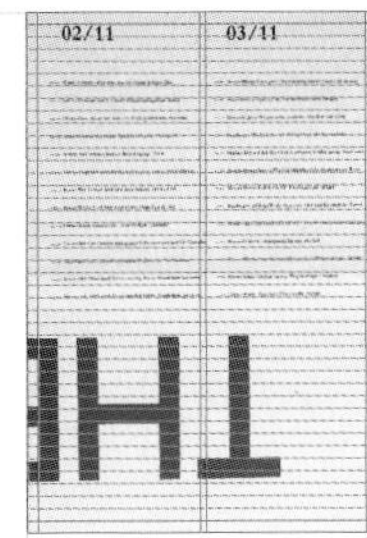

PERSONAL PROJECT

Design: George Adams

This is a personal project documenting a week in the life of designer George Adams. Every hour of the day is represented typographically, using categories such as "my location" and "my last conversation" to help the viewer navigate the piece. Adams was interested in how standard A paper sizes could be divided into areas that would represent units of time. When folded down to A4 (210 x 297mm [c. 8⅛ x 11⅝in]), only the first day is visible—the full week is revealed when the sheet is opened out to A1 (594 x 841mm [c. 23½ x 33in]).

GRID SPECIFICATIONS	
Page size (trimmed)	A1 (594 x 841mm [c. 23½ x 33in]) folded down to A4 (210 x 297mm [c. 8⅛ x 11⅝in])
Top margin	All sheets: 10mm
Bottom margin	All sheets: 10mm
Outside margin	A1, A2, and A3: 10mm/A4: 70mm
Inside margin	All sheets: 10mm
Number of columns	A1: 4/A2: 3/A3: 2/A4: 1
Gutter width	5mm
Extras	Baseline grid, 10mm

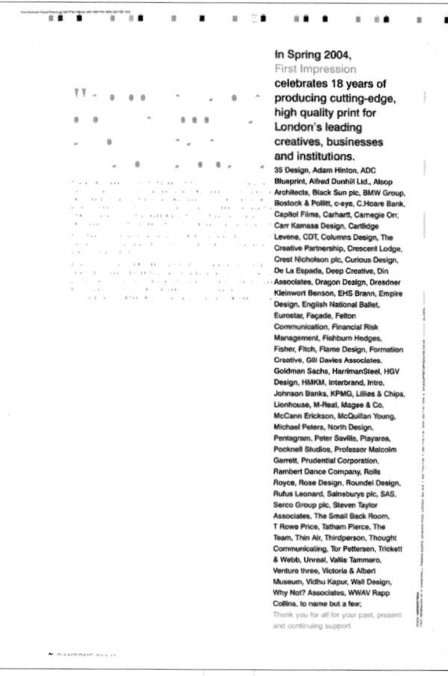

In Spring 2004,
First Impression
celebrates 18 years of producing cutting-edge, high quality print for London's leading creatives, businesses and institutions.
Thank you for all for your past, present and continuing support.

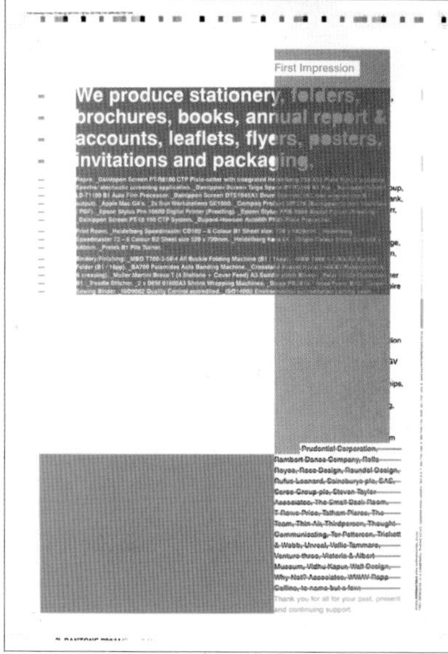

First Impression
We produce stationery, folders, brochures, books, annual report & accounts, leaflets, flyers, posters, invitations and packaging.

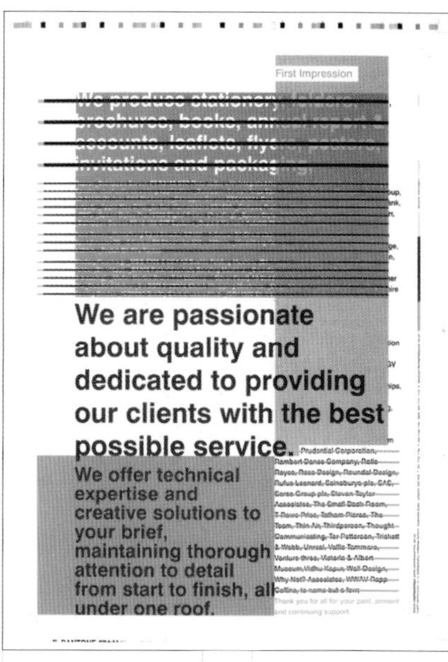

First Impression
We are passionate about quality and dedicated to providing our clients with the best possible service.
We offer technical expertise and creative solutions to your brief, maintaining thorough attention to detail from start to finish, all under one roof.

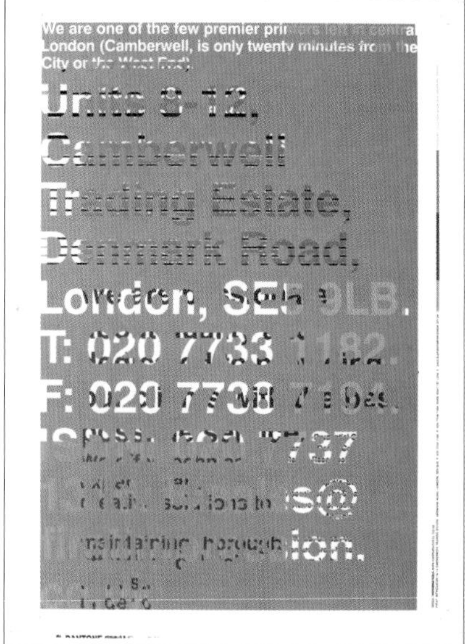

We are one of the few premier printers left in central London (Camberwell, is only twenty minutes from the City or the West End).
Units 8-12,
Camberwell
Trading Estate,
Denmark Road,
London, SE5 9LB.
T: 020 7733 1182.

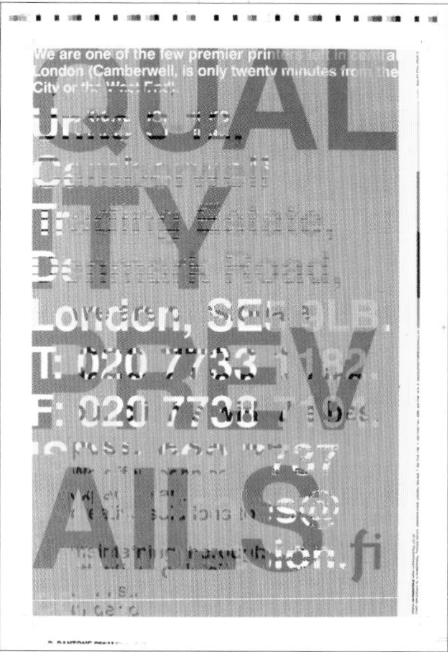

GRID SPECIFICATIONS

Page size (trimmed)	495 x 694mm
Top margin	67mm
Bottom margin	40mm
Outside margin	40mm
Inside margin	40mm
Number of columns	1
Gutter width	N/A
Extras	N/A

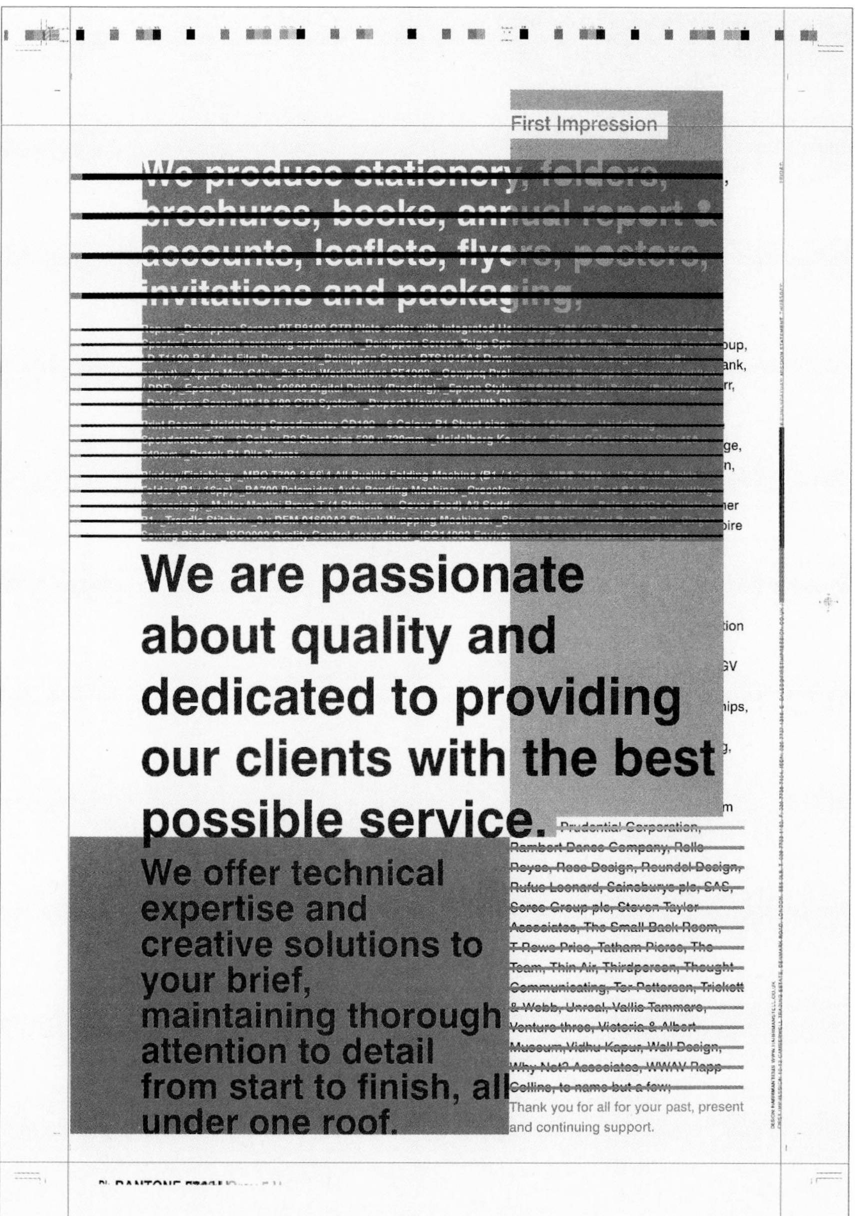

FIRST IMPRESSION

Design: Julian Harriman-Dickinson at Harriman Steel

When Julian Harriman-Dickinson was asked to design a new business mailer for a printing company, he decided to turn the brief into a challenge to create the most difficult print job the printers had ever worked on. These five posters use overprinting to showcase the high quality of registration and print. From the first print run of 5,000, 1,000 were sent out, and the remaining 4,000 were overprinted with more information; 1,000 of these were sent out, and so on, until all the mailers had been distributed. In this way, any underlying structure was gradually revealed.

Luke Wood is the Head of Design at the University of Canterbury and a practising designer. He designed and exhibited a typeface replicating the script of Colin McCahon's word paintings, and recently held a residency at Hatch Show Prints in Nashville.

Hamish Thompson is the author and designer of Paste-up: A Century of New Zealand Poster Art. Trained at the Basel School of Design in Switzerland, he has taught, written about and practised design for over 20 years.

Catherine Griffiths is an innovative typographer who designed the BEST Design Award-winning Wellington Writers Walk and gave a new meaning to concrete poetry. Design from her Wellington studio, Epitome, spans print and architecture.

OLD SCHOOL

NEW SCHOOL

TRUETYPE SCHOOL

3 DESIGNERS SPEAK

Hamish Thompson 'Poster Design'
Mon 15 Aug 12-1pm
St David 1

Catherine, Hamish & Luke Tues 16
Open Lecture Aug 6.30pm
Archway 3

Catherine & Luke 'Design & Typography'
seminar Wed 17 Aug 1-2pm
Design Studies CApSc 1.05

Brought to you by:
University of Otago
New Zealand Print Culture Area of Research Strength
DINZ (Designers Institute of New Zealand)
Design Studies | Te Toki a Rata

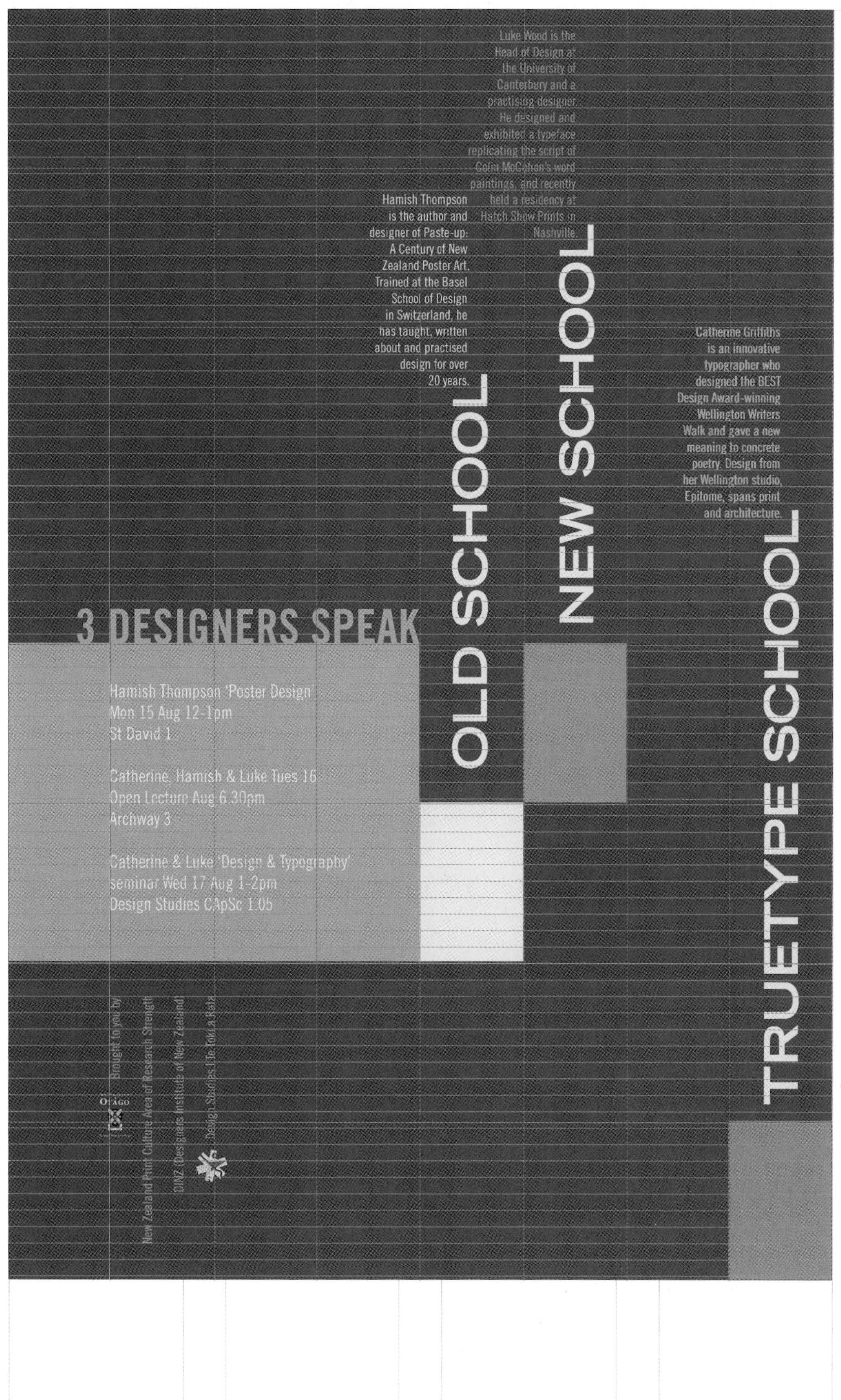

GRID SPECIFICATIONS

Page size (trimmed)	400 x 600mm
Top margin	N/A
Bottom margin	N/A
Outside margin	N/A
Inside margin	50mm
Number of columns	8
Gutter width	N/A
Extras	Grid developed from base unit—rectangle with ratio of 2:3; baseline grid, 22pt; 8 horizontal fields

OLD SCHOOL, NEW SCHOOL, TRUETYPE SCHOOL

Design: Lightship Visual

This poster was designed for a series of graphic design lectures at the University of Otago, New Zealand. The surface area of the poster is divided to form eight vertical and eight horizontal fields. The gray background provides a neutral ground for colored rectangular panels that correspond with this underlying system of organization and draw attention to the poster's structure. Designer Stuart Medley's decision to foreground the grid as an organizing principle was informed by the panel of speakers, which included designers taught by Emil Ruder and Wolfgang Weingart.

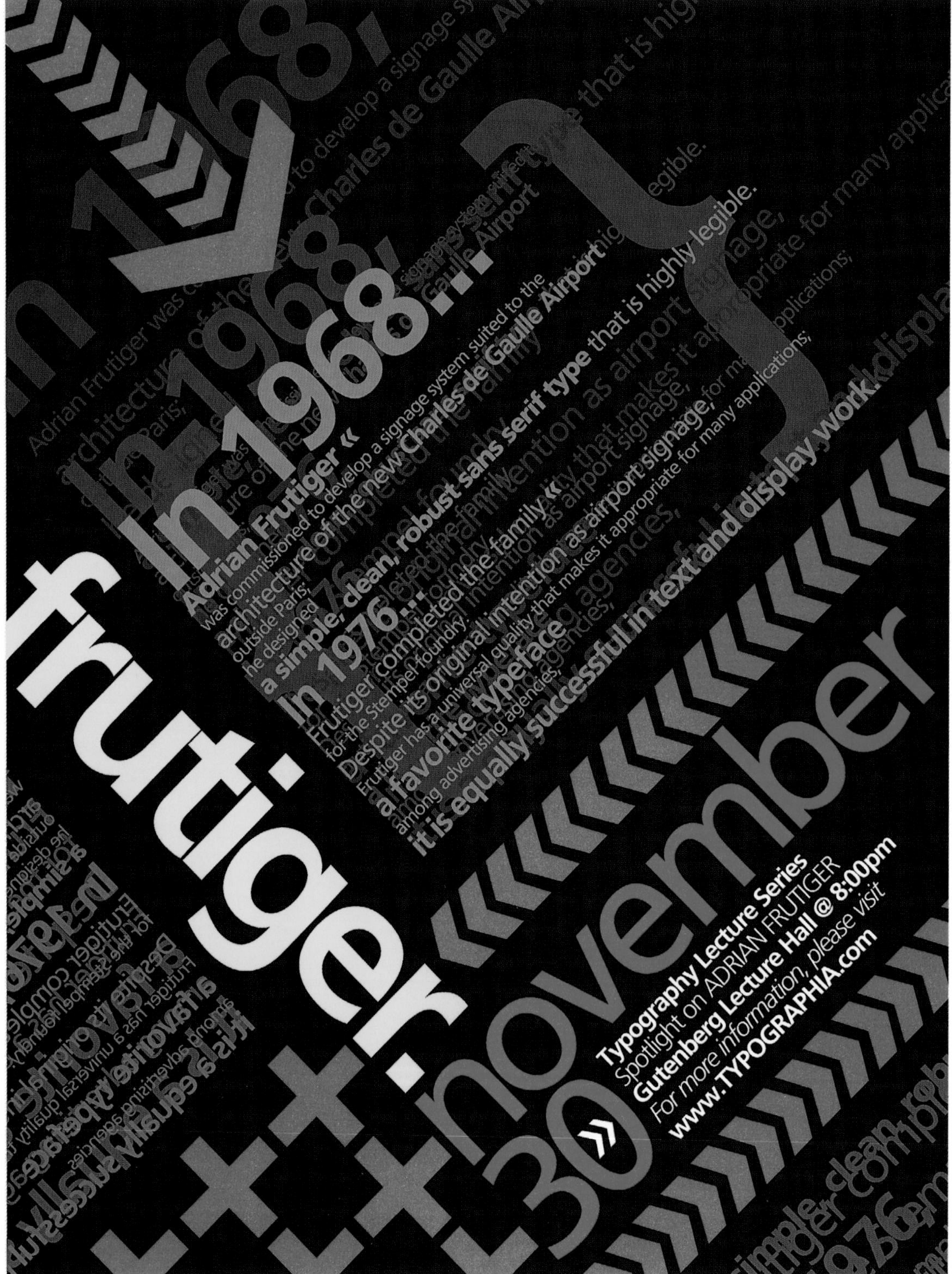

frutiger.
In 1968...
Adrian Frutiger «
was commissioned to develop a signage system suited to the
architecture of the new Charles de Gaulle Airport
outside Paris;
he designed
a simple, clean, robust sans serif type that is highly legible.
In 1976...
Frutiger completed the family «
for the Stempel foundry.
Despite its original intention as airport signage,
Frutiger has a universal quality that makes it appropriate for many applications;
a favorite typeface
among advertising agencies,
it is equally successful in text and display work.
november
30
Typography Lecture Series
Spotlight on ADRIAN FRUTIGER
Gutenberg Lecture Hall @ 8:00pm
For more information, please visit
www.TYPOGRAPHIA.com

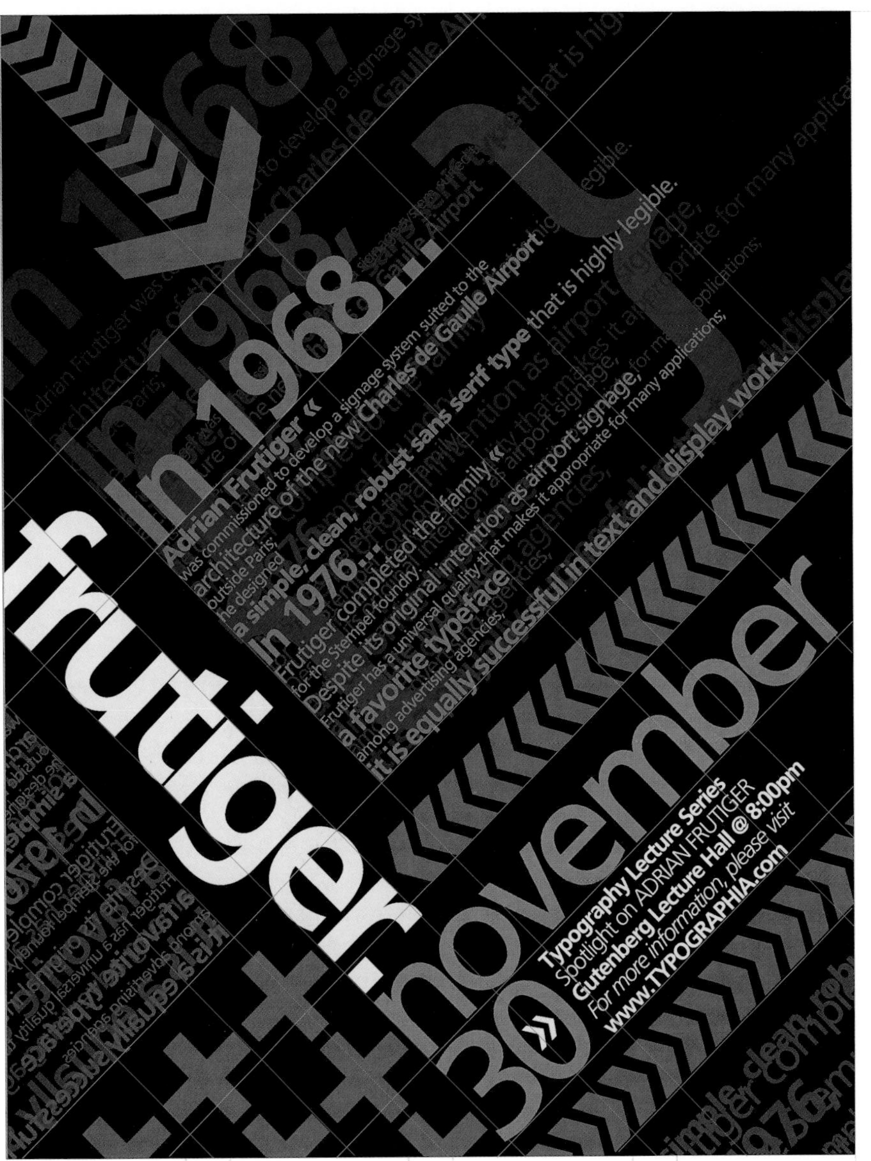

GRID SPECIFICATIONS

Page size (trimmed)	457.2 x 609.6mm
Top margin	To bleed
Bottom margin	To bleed
Outside margin	To bleed
Inside margin	To bleed
Number of columns	11
Column gutter	N/A
Extras	rotated grid; 8 horizontal fields

FRUTIGER POSTER

Design: Reggie Hidalgo at The Art Institute of California

This poster promotes a lecture series on typography, in particular, the work of Adrian Frutiger. It uses a series of angled alignments. The poster is divided into 11 columns and eight horizontal fields. Although this isn't a conventional grid, composed of equal columns or fields and gutters, it is reminiscent of the organizational approach followed by exponents of the Swiss school in the design of posters. Using these methods, art director Maggie Rossoni and designer Reggie Hidalgo have created a dynamic piece of design information that is easy to navigate.

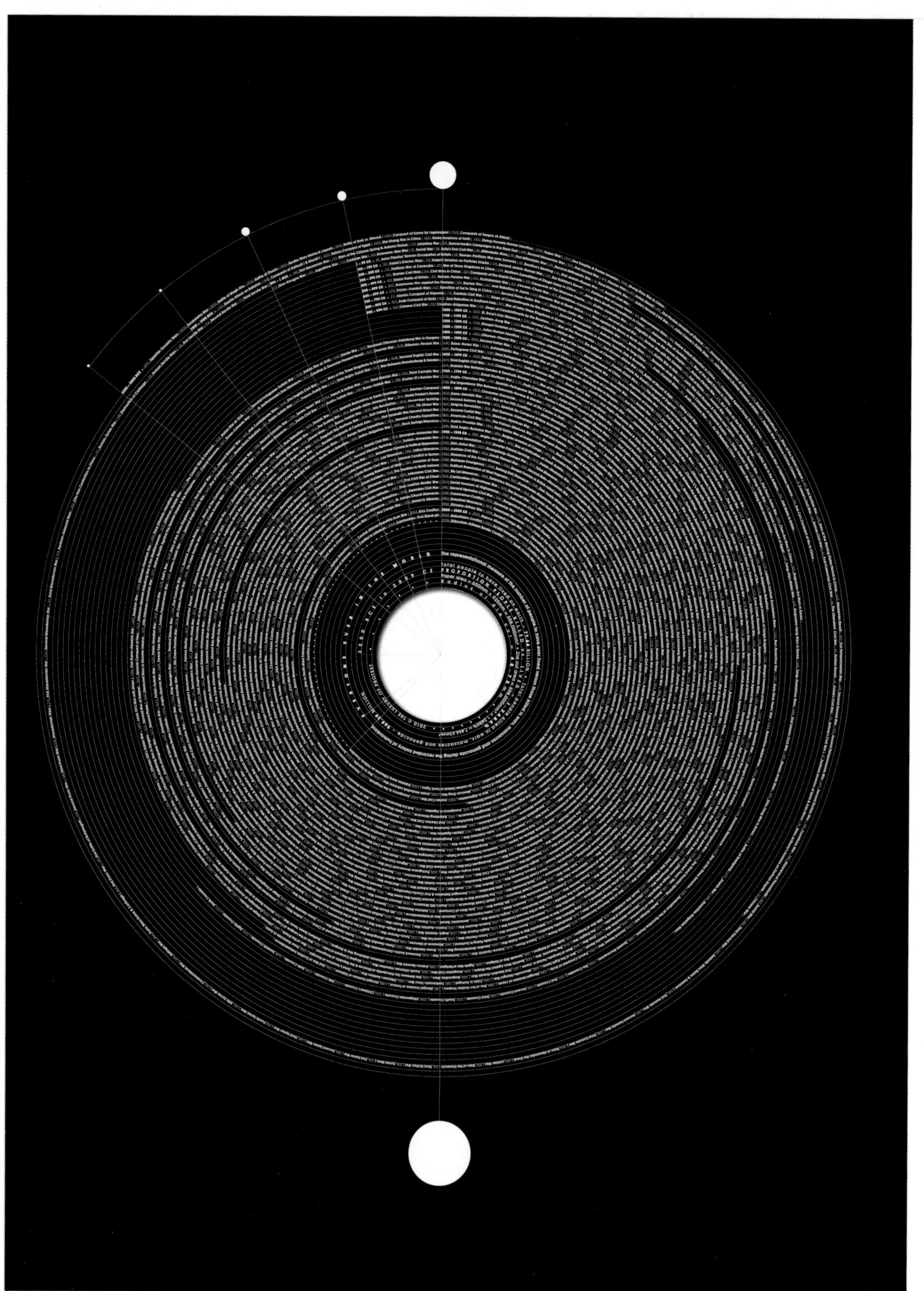

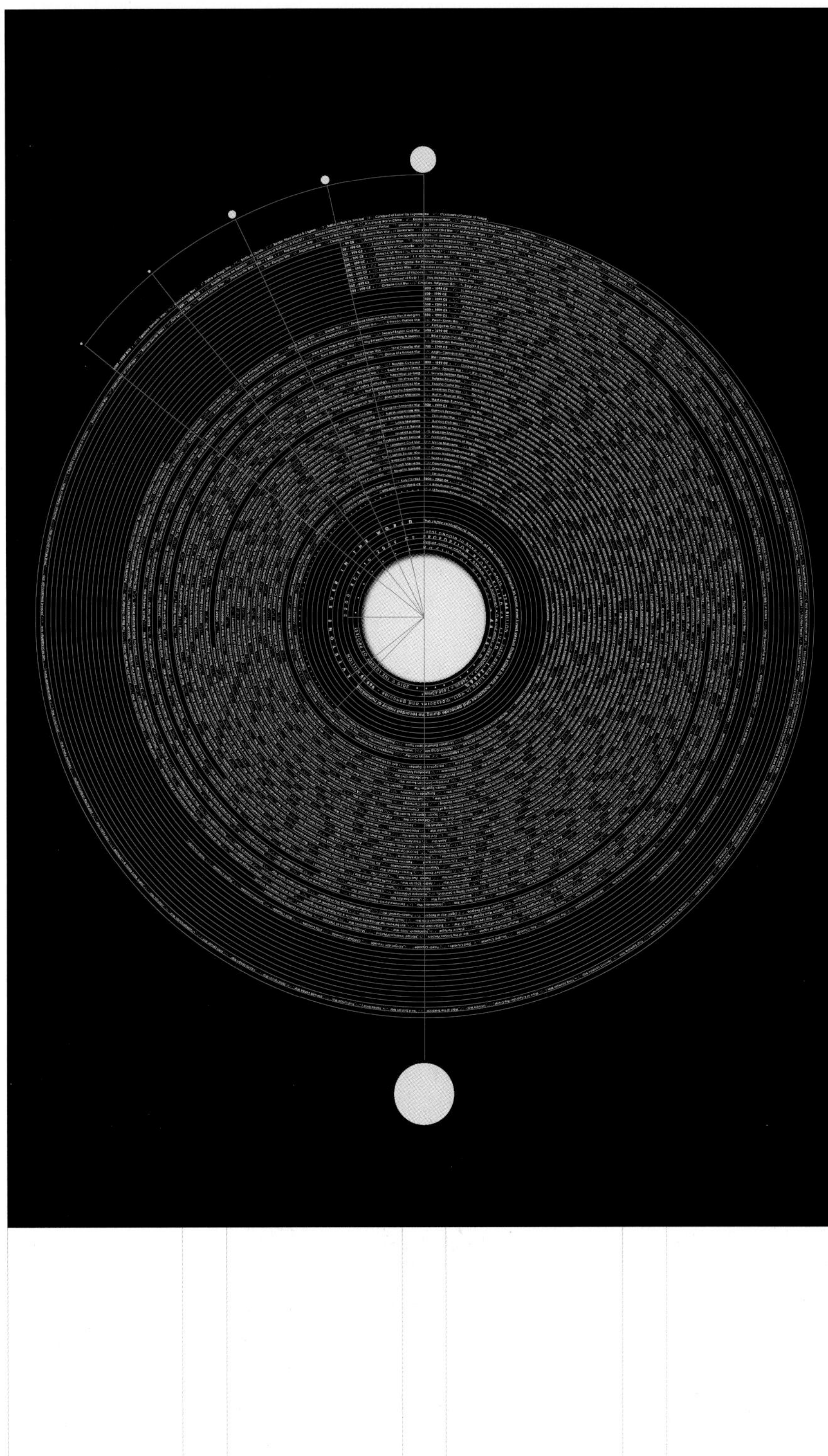

GRID SPECIFICATIONS	
Page size (trimmed)	650 x 920mm
Top margin	104mm
Bottom margin	77mm
Left margin	21mm
Right margin	21mm
Number of columns	64 radials
Number of rows	64 radials
Gutter width	N/A
Extras	N/A

EVERYONE EVER IN THE WORLD

Design: Peter Crnokrak at ±

Everyone Ever in the World is a visual representation of the number of people to have ever lived versus the number killed in wars, massacres, and genocide during the recorded history of humankind. Within the visualization, existing paper area and paper loss—a die-cut circle—are used to represent the concepts of life and death respectively. The sequence of dots to the top left of the graph shows the dramatic increase in the number of conflicts over the past five millennia, and the large dot below the graph represents a prediction of the 1000 years to come. Using a simple and intuitive graphic approach, the die-cut area symbolizes the total number of people killed, lending a direct poetry to the concept and affording the viewer an instantaneous assessment of the degree to which conflict has shaped human history.

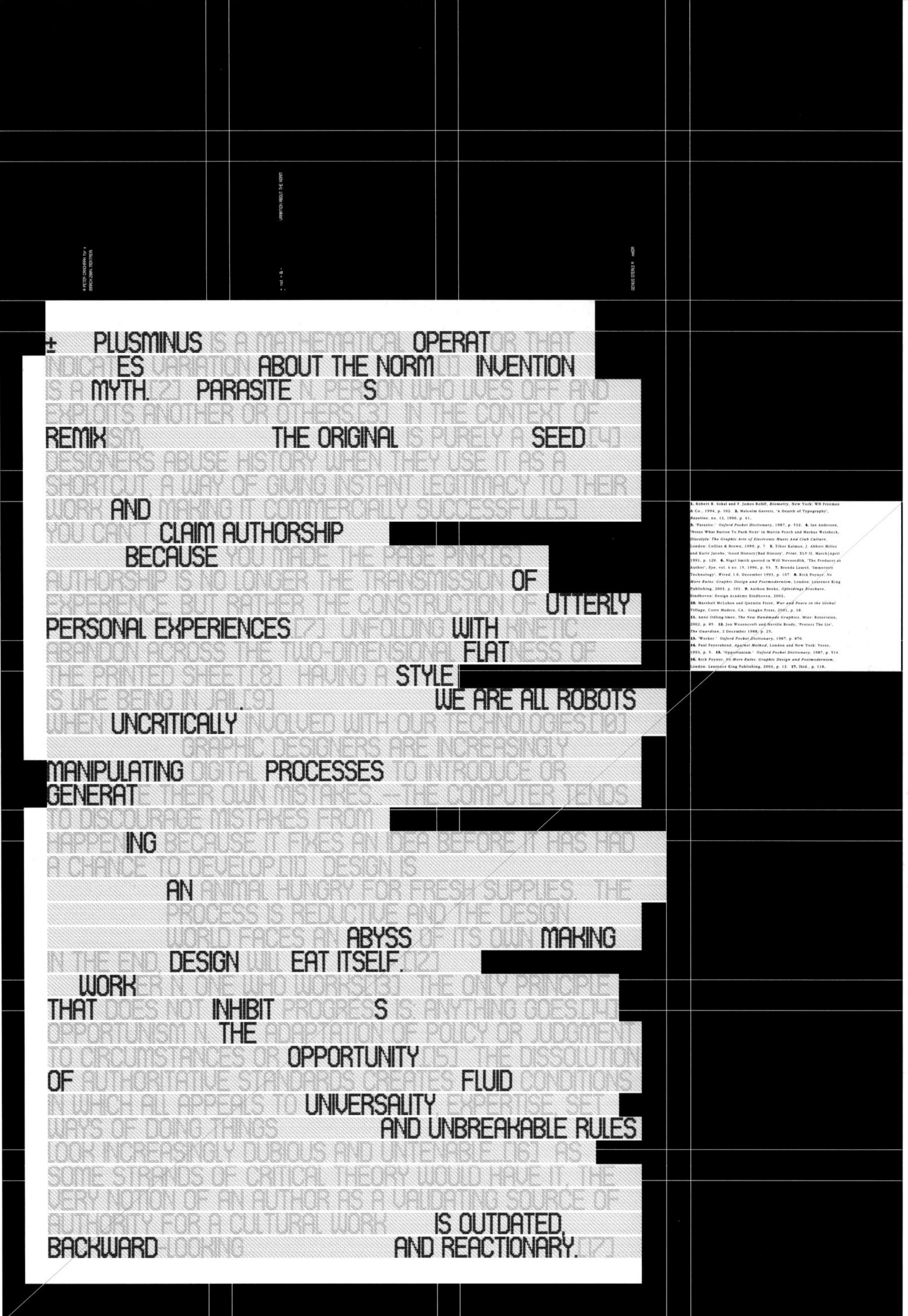
± PLUSMINUS IS A MATHEMATICAL OPERATOR THAT
INDICATES VARIATION ABOUT THE NORM[1] INVENTION
IS A MYTH.[2] PARASITE N. PERSON WHO LIVES OFF AND
EXPLOITS ANOTHER OR OTHERS.[3] IN THE CONTEXT OF
REMIXISM, THE ORIGINAL IS PURELY A SEED[4]
DESIGNERS ABUSE HISTORY WHEN THEY USE IT AS A
SHORTCUT, A WAY OF GIVING INSTANT LEGITIMACY TO THEIR
WORK AND MAKING IT COMMERCIALLY SUCCESSFUL[5]
YOU CAN'T CLAIM AUTHORSHIP
BECAUSE YOU MADE THE PAGE PINK[6]
AUTHORSHIP IS NO LONGER THE TRANSMISSION OF
EXPERIENCE, BUT RATHER THE CONSTRUCTION OF UTTERLY
PERSONAL EXPERIENCES[7] UNFOLDING WITH KINETIC
ABANDON ACROSS THE TWO-DIMENSIONAL FLATNESS OF
THE PRINTED SHEET[8] HAVING A STYLE
IS LIKE BEING IN JAIL[9]. WE ARE ALL ROBOTS
WHEN UNCRITICALLY INVOLVED WITH OUR TECHNOLOGIES[10]
GRAPHIC DESIGNERS ARE INCREASINGLY
MANIPULATING DIGITAL PROCESSES TO INTRODUCE OR
GENERATE THEIR OWN MISTAKES...THE COMPUTER TENDS
TO DISCOURAGE MISTAKES FROM
HAPPENING BECAUSE IT FIXES AN IDEA BEFORE IT HAS HAD
A CHANCE TO DEVELOP[11] DESIGN IS
AN ANIMAL HUNGRY FOR FRESH SUPPLIES. THE
PROCESS IS REDUCTIVE AND THE DESIGN
WORLD FACES AN ABYSS OF ITS OWN MAKING
IN THE END, DESIGN WILL EAT ITSELF.[12]
WORKER N. ONE WHO WORKS[13] THE ONLY PRINCIPLE
THAT DOES NOT INHIBIT PROGRESS IS: ANYTHING GOES.[14]
OPPORTUNISM N. THE ADAPTATION OF POLICY OR JUDGMENT
TO CIRCUMSTANCES OR OPPORTUNITY[15] THE DISSOLUTION
OF AUTHORITATIVE STANDARDS CREATES FLUID CONDITIONS
IN WHICH ALL APPEALS TO UNIVERSALITY, EXPERTISE, SET
WAYS OF DOING THINGS AND UNBREAKABLE RULES
LOOK INCREASINGLY DUBIOUS AND UNTENABLE.[16] AS
SOME STRANDS OF CRITICAL THEORY WOULD HAVE IT, THE
VERY NOTION OF AN AUTHOR AS A VALIDATING SOURCE OF
AUTHORITY FOR A CULTURAL WORK IS OUTDATED,
BACKWARD-LOOKING AND REACTIONARY.[17]
1. Robert R. Sokal and F. James Rohlf, Biometry, New York: WH Freeman & Co., 1994, p. 102. 2. Malcolm Garrett, 'A Dearth of Typography', Baseline, no. 13, 1990, p. 41.
3. 'Parasite.' Oxford Pocket Dictionary, 1987, p. 532. 4. Ian Anderson, 'Notes What Button To Push Next' in Martin Pesch and Markus Weisbeck, Discstyle: The Graphic Arts of Electronic Music And Club Culture, London: Collins & Brown, 1999, p. 7. 5. Tibor Kalman, J. Abbott Miller and Karie Jacobs, 'Good History|Bad History', Print, XLV:II, March|April 1991, p. 120. 6. Nigel Smith quoted in Will Novosedlik, 'The Producer as Author', Eye, vol. 4 no. 15, 1996, p. 53. 7. Brenda Laurel, 'Immersive Technology', Wired, 1.6, December 1993, p. 107. 8. Rick Poynor, No More Rules: Graphic Design and Postmodernism, London: Laurence King Publishing, 2003, p. 103. 9. Anthon Beeke, Opleidings Brochure, Eindhoven: Design Academy Eindhoven, 2003.
10. Marshall McLuhan and Quentin Fiore, War and Peace in the Global Village, Corte Madera, CA.: Gingko Press, 2001, p. 18.
11. Anne Odling-Smee, The New Handmade Graphics, Mies: Rotovision, 2002, p. 85. 12. Jon Wozencroft and Neville Brody, 'Protect The Lie', The Guardian, 2 December 1988, p. 25.
13. 'Worker.' Oxford Pocket Dictionary, 1987, p. 870.
14. Paul Feyerabend, Against Method, London and New York: Verso, 1993, p. 5. 15. 'Opportunism.' Oxford Pocket Dictionary, 1987, p. 514.
16. Rick Poynor, No More Rules: Graphic Design and Postmodernism, London: Laurence King Publishing, 2003, p. 12. 17. Ibid., p. 118.

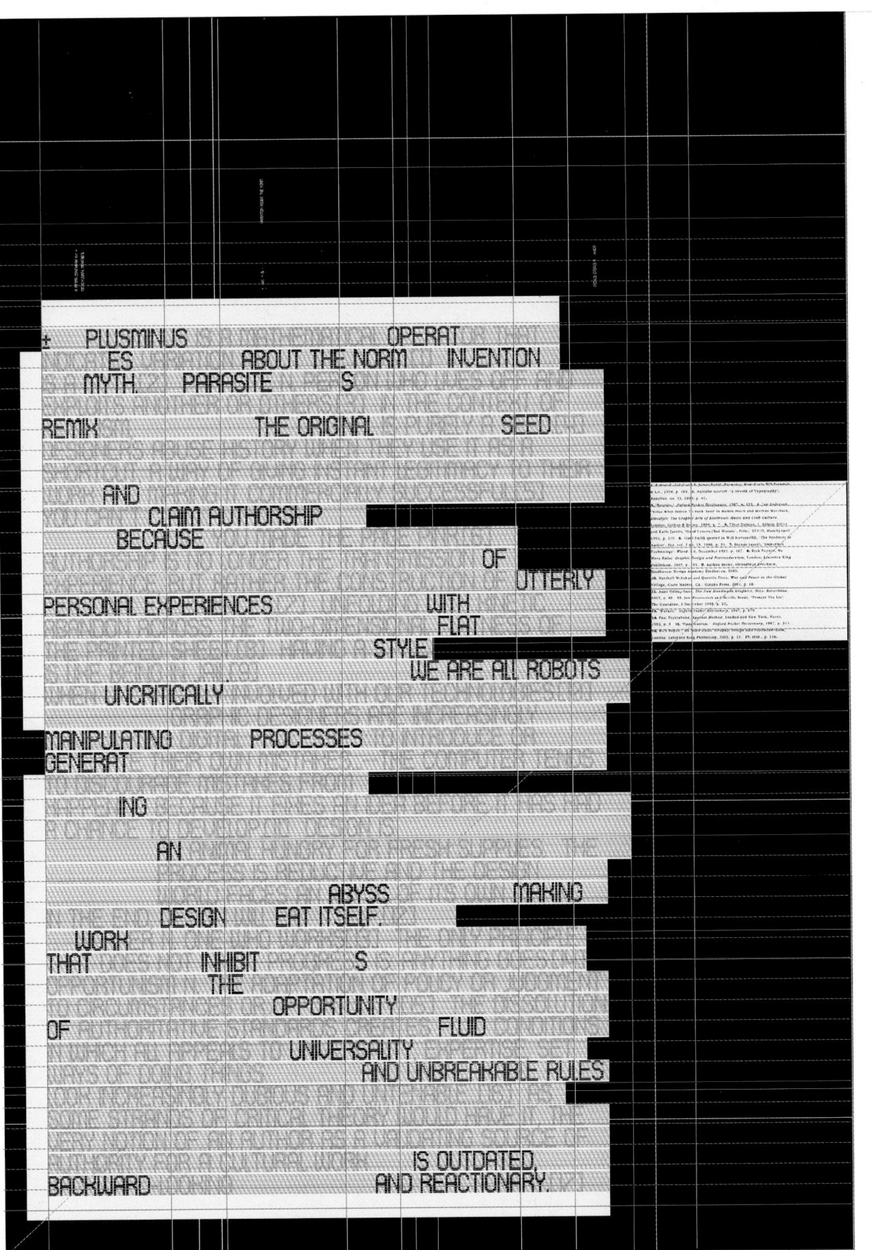
± PLUSMINUS OPERAT
ES ABOUT THE NORM INVENTION
MYTH. PARASITE S
REMIX THE ORIGINAL SEED
AND
CLAIM AUTHORSHIP
BECAUSE
OF
UTTERLY
PERSONAL EXPERIENCES WITH
FLAT
STYLE
WE ARE ALL ROBOTS
UNCRITICALLY
MANIPULATING PROCESSES
GENERAT
ING
AN
ABYSS MAKING
DESIGN EAT ITSELF.
WORK
THAT INHIBIT S
THE
OPPORTUNITY
OF FLUID
UNIVERSALITY
AND UNBREAKABLE RULES
IS OUTDATED,
BACKWARD AND REACTIONARY.

GRID SPECIFICATIONS

Page size (trimmed)	840 x 1,170mm
Top margin	193mm
Bottom margin	41mm
Outside margin	154mm
Inside margin	49mm
Number of columns	4
Gutter width	N/A
Extras	8 horizontal fields, 6 lines per field

WORKER/PARASITE MANIFESTO

Design: Peter Crnokrak at ±

The ± worker/parasite manifesto uses appropriated statements and graphics "remixed" by designer Peter Crnokrak. The original quotes all relate in some form to notions of originality, authorship, and rules (including the use of the grid) in graphic design. These are printed in light-gray horizontal lines that can only be read from a certain distance, while the ± manifesto text is highlighted in black, thereby making clear what is a paradox for Crnokrak.

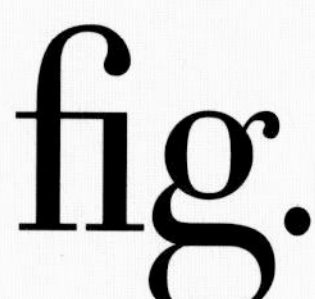

Research RCA : **Schools** - *Departments* - **Degrees**_Types (time) • ***Students*** (NATIONALITIES)

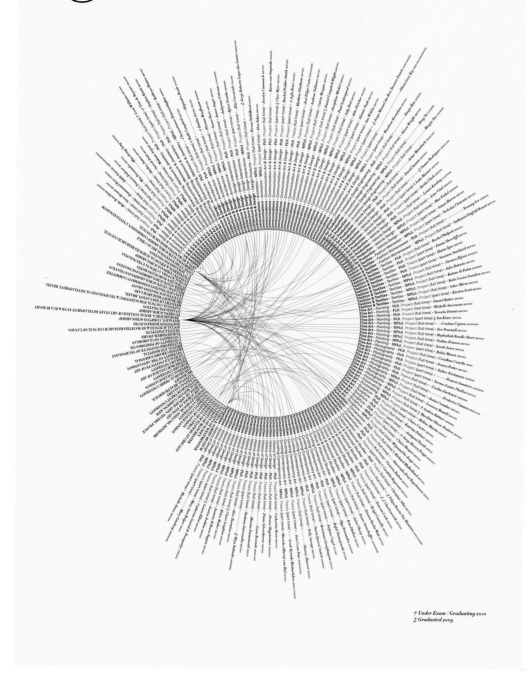

† *Under Exam / Graduating 2010*
‡ *Graduated 2009*

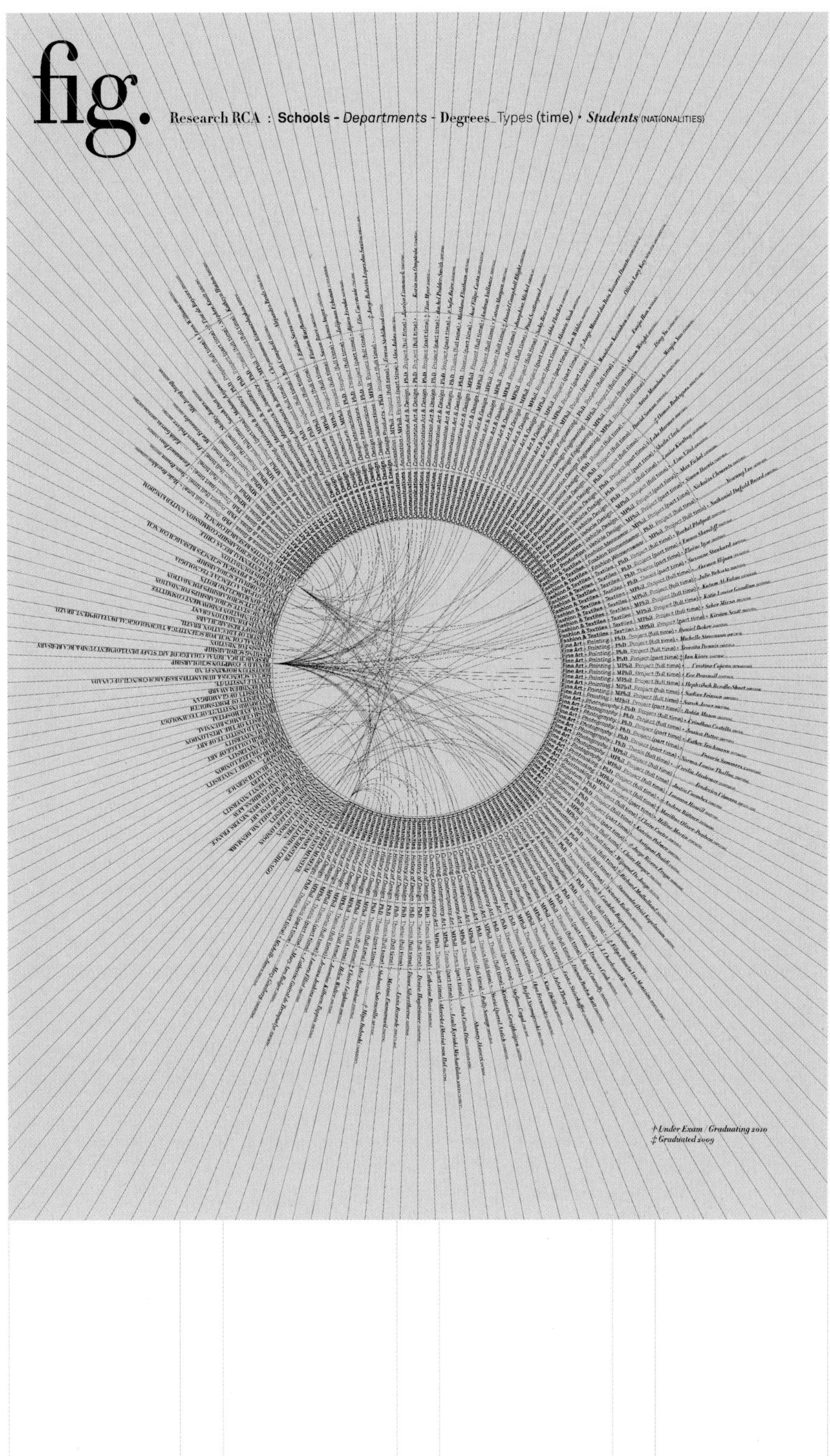

GRID SPECIFICATIONS

Page size (trimmed)	700 x 1000mm
Top margin	23mm
Bottom margin	64mm
Left margin	24mm
Right margin	24mm
Number of columns	192 radials
Number of rows	192 radials
Gutter width	N/A
Extras	N/A

RESEARCH RCA

Design: Peter Crnokrak at ±

The intention behind this design was to create a visual representation of the complex varietal make-up of internal and external college dynamics at Research RCA, and the resulting influence upon research output. To this end, the designers created an information visualization that illustrates the distribution of all students across departments. Each student was recorded according to various factors such as school, degree type, and their relationships to collaborators. The use of typography-only data capitalizes on the inherent form differences between typefaces, providing clear visual differentiation between the aforementioned categories. The end result is a complex snapshot of the Research RCA student body and the relations they hold with national and international art and design agencies and institutions.

1. Prémio Fernando Távora
Apresentação / 20 Novembro
Salão Nobre da Faculdade de Ciências, UP / 21:30

2. Obra Pedagógica
Ciclo de conferências e vídeo + projecção de desenhos e fotografias de viagens lectivas 1980—1993
Salão Nobre e átrio da Faculdade de Ciências (Praça dos Leões), 21:30

Ciclo de Conferências
4ª feiras • 21:30

23 Nov: "A Viagem"
Alexandre Alves Costa, Joaquim Vieira

30 Nov: "Viajar / Coleccionar"
Eduardo Souto Moura

07 Dez: "Fernando Távora - Eu sou a Arquitectura Portuguesa"
Manuel Mendes

Ciclo de Vídeo
Reposição das "Aulas de Teoria Geral da Organização do Espaço, Fernando Távora, FAUP, 92/93" introduzidas por arquitectos e historiadores que com ele partilharam a docência
Domingos • 21:30

20 Nov: "A Aula"
Álvaro Siza Vieira

27 Nov
António Lousa

04 Dez
Manuel Graça Dias

11 Dez
Rui Lobo
(a confirmar)

15 Jan
Nuno Tasso de Sousa

08 Jan
João Mendes Ribeiro

22 Jan
Rui Tavares

29 Jan
Carlos Machado

05 Fev
Paulo Varela Gomes
(a confirmar)

3. Reunião de Obra - Exposição
Palácio do Freixo, Porto (1996–03)
Local Museus dos Transportes, Alfândega do Porto /15 Dezembro

4. Obra Aberta
Visitas guiadas a obras de arquitectura de Fernando Távora,
5 de Fev — 6 Maio (Sábados)

Mercado Municipal de Santa Maria da Feira
11 Fevereiro

Casa da Covilhã, Guimarães
25 de Fevereiro

Casa de Férias no Pinhal de Ofir
11 de Março

Pousada de St' Marinha, Guimarães / 25 de Março

Centro Histórico de Guimarães
8 de Abril

Quinta da Conceição e Quinta de Santiago, Leça da Palmeira
6 de Maio

Casa dos 24, Porto
22 de Abril

5. A Festa
I Love Távora
Quinta da Conceição, Leça da Palmeira
06 de Maio, 22 horas

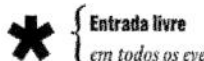

Comissariado:
Luís Tavares Pereira
Teresa Novais
Filipa Guerreiro

Beatriz Madureira (Ciclo de vídeo)
José Gigante (Festa)

Produção:
Ana Maio
Carlos Alberto Faustino

Comemorações do dia Mundial da Arquitectura

Ordem dos Arquitectos
Secção Regional do Norte
OASRN

I love Távora

20 Nov—06 Maio
2005/06

©

OASRN
Secção Regional Norte da Ordem dos Arquitectos
www.oasrn.org

Rua de D. Hugo, 5–7
4050-305 Porto – Portugal
F 222 074 250 · F 222 074 259
cultura@oasrn.org

Banif · often · TUPAI · Miele · weber

GRID SPECIFICATIONS

Page size (trimmed)	1,200 x 1,700mm
Top margin	28mm
Bottom margin	28mm
Outside margin	28mm
Inside margin	28mm
Number of columns	6
Gutter width	16mm
Extras	Baseline grid, 48pt

I LOVE TÁVORA

Design: Lizá Ramalho, Artur Rebelo, and Liliana Pinto at R2 design

This poster promotes a series of events that were tributes to modernist Portuguese architect Fernando Távora. Designers Lizá Ramalho and Artur Rebelo wanted the poster to evoke the ideological and philosophical principles that characterize Távora's work. The text is laid out using a six-column grid, but most of the poster is filled with a typographic composition suggestive of an urban plan, within which a heart can be seen.

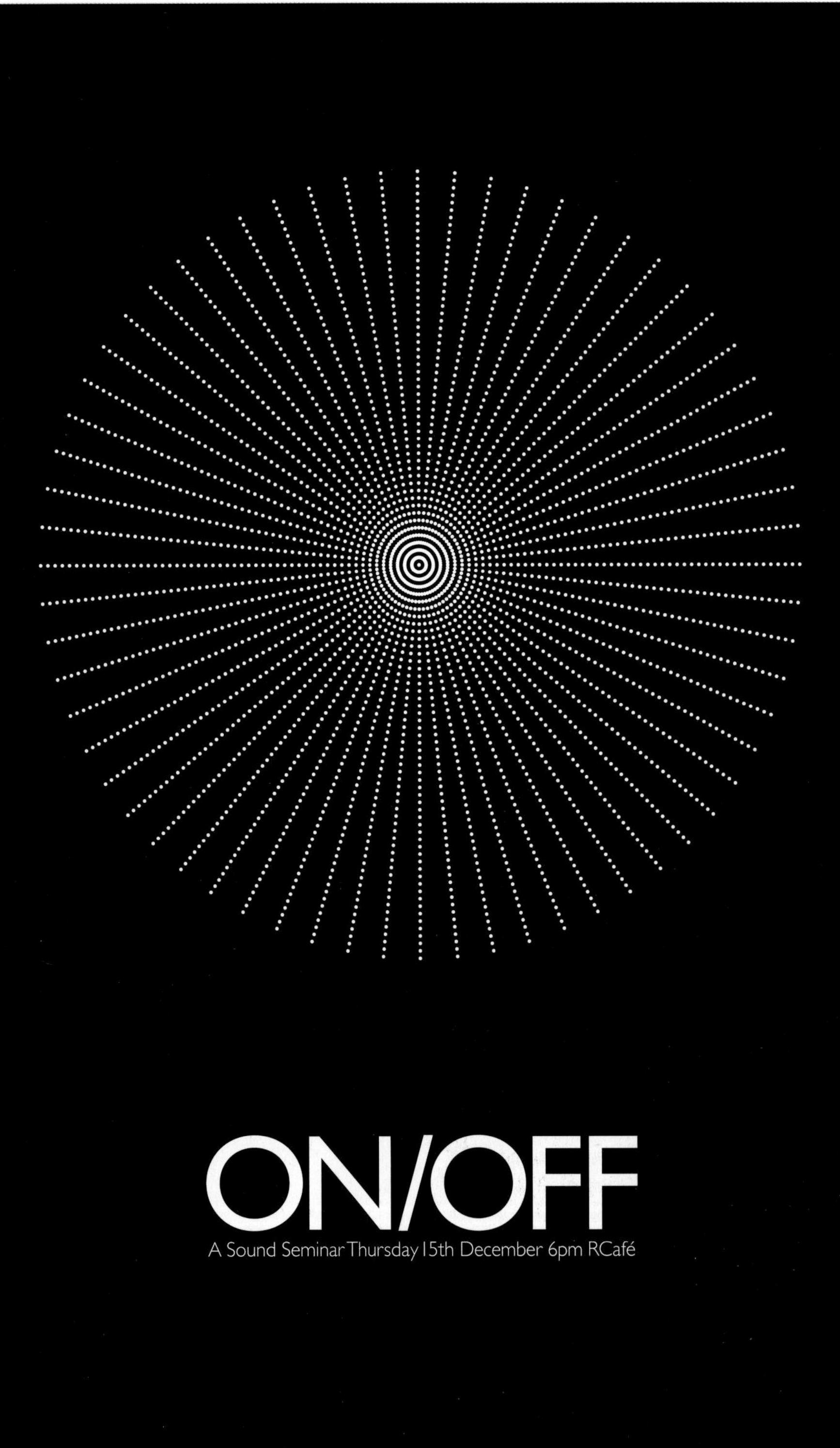
ON/OFF
A Sound Seminar Thursday 15th December 6pm RCafé

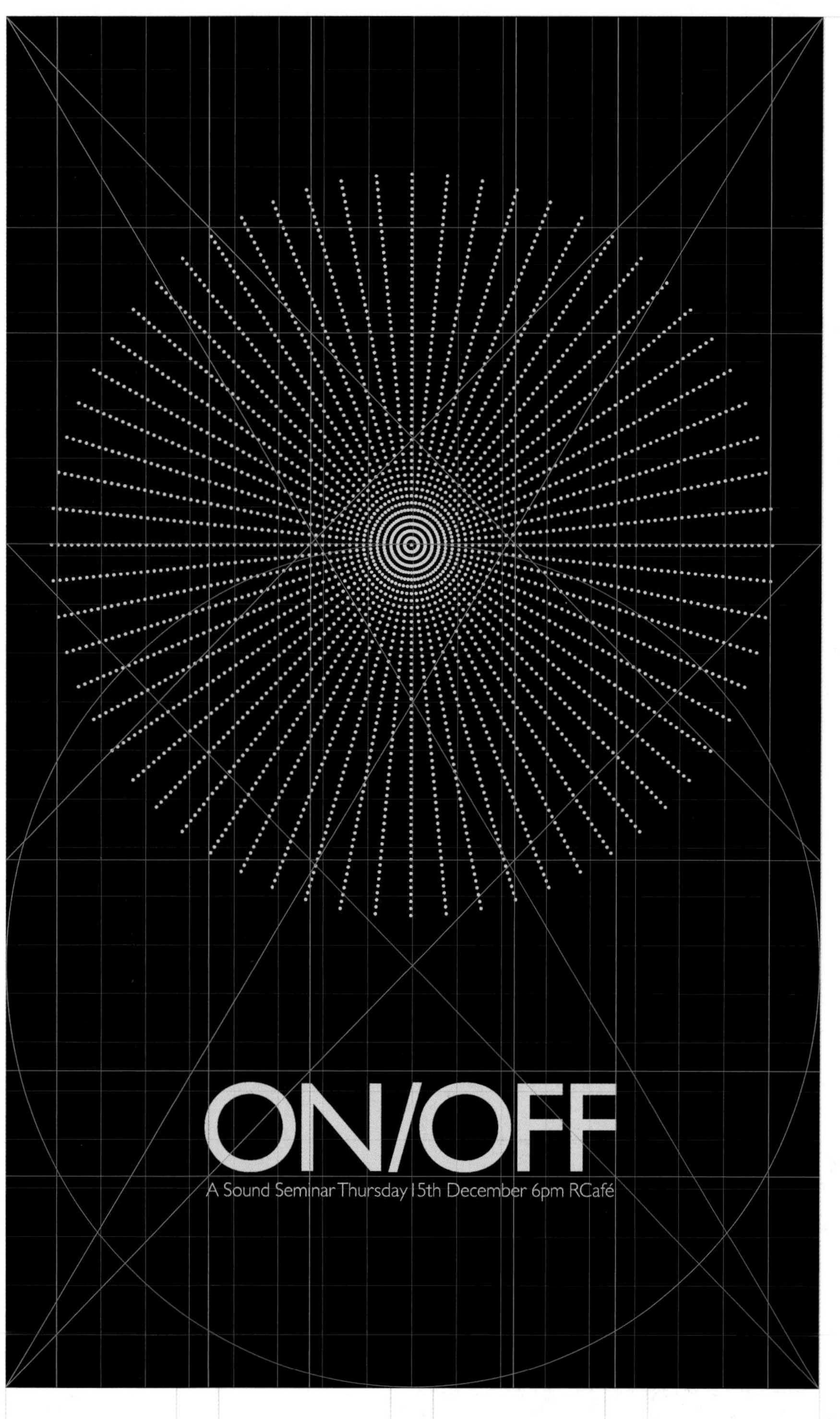

GRID SPECIFICATIONS

Page size (trimmed)	512 x 832mm
Top margin	32mm
Bottom margin	32mm
Outside margin	32mm
Inside margin	32mm
Number of columns	16
Gutter width	N/A
Extras	Baseline grid, 3.2mm; 28 fields

ON/OFF

Design: Richard Sarson

This poster advertised a series of seminars on sound that were held at the Royal College of Art, London, where Richard Sarson was a student. Inspired by Josef Müller-Brockmann and Jan Tschichold, Sarson used abstract shapes to explore visual representations of rhythm and sound, and looked to geometry to develop his grid by taking the golden section as his starting point.

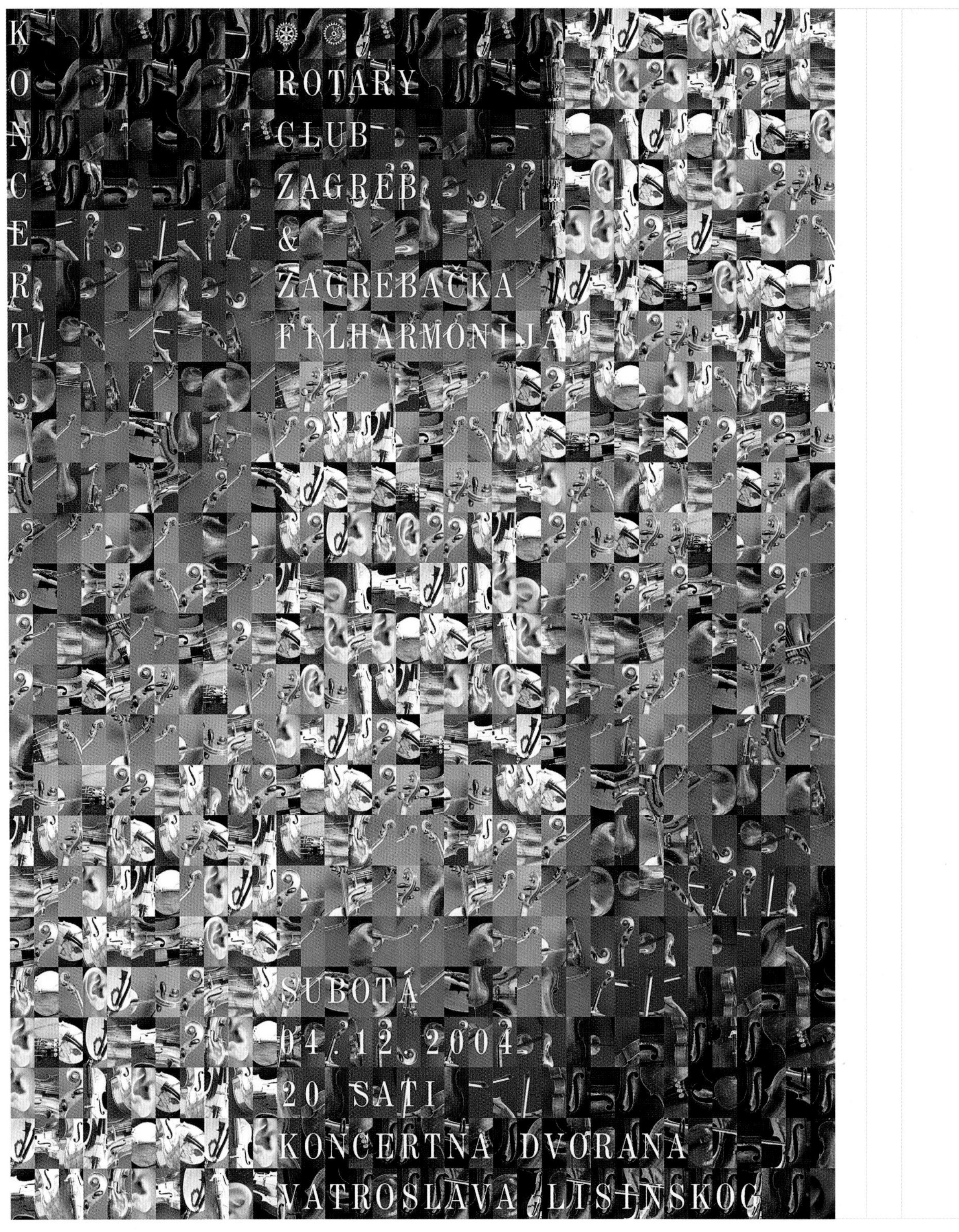
K
O
N
C
E
R
T
ROTARY
CLUB
ZAGREB
&
ZAGREBAČKA
FILHARMONIJA
SUBOTA
04. 12. 2004
20 SATI
KONCERTNA DVORANA
VATROSLAVA LISINSKOG

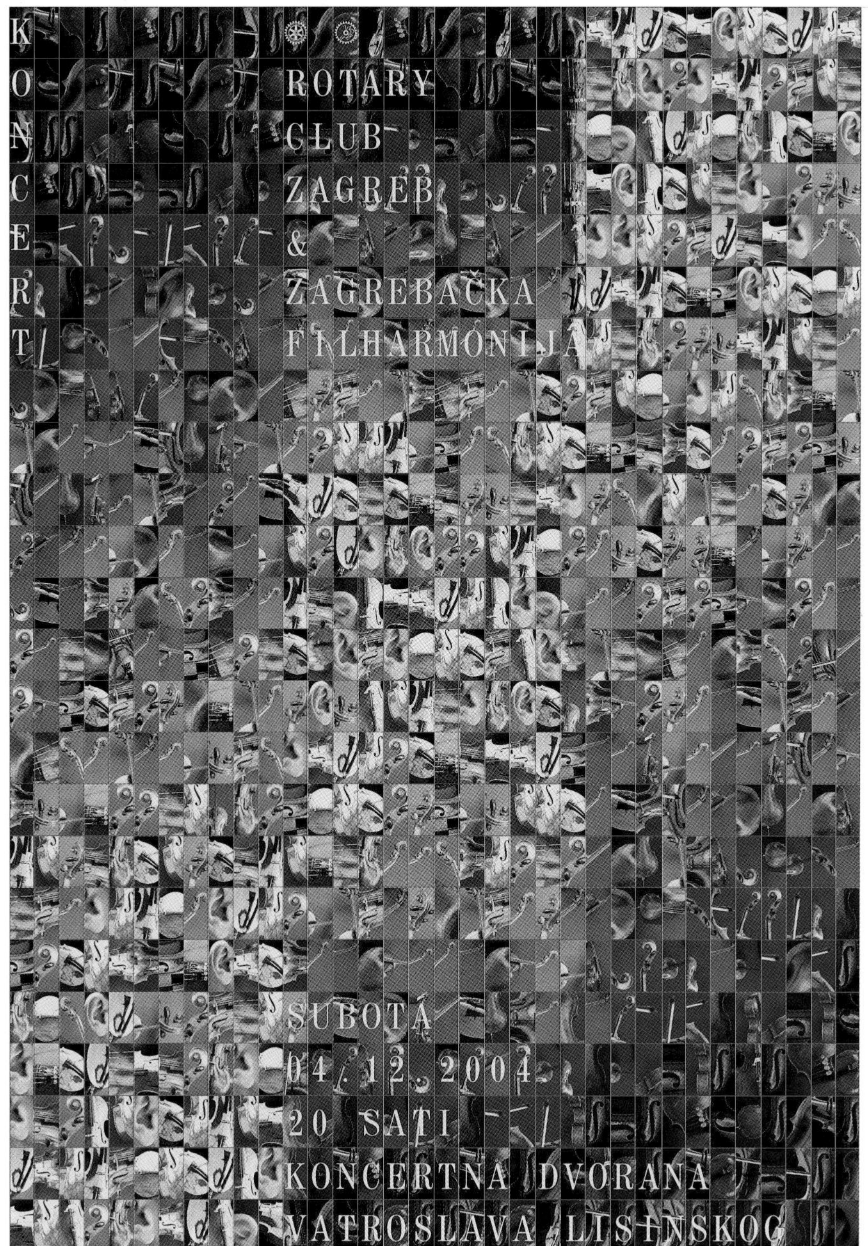

GRID SPECIFICATIONS	
Page size (trimmed)	700 x 1,000mm
Top margin	To bleed
Bottom margin	To bleed
Outside margin	To bleed
Inside margin	To bleed
Number of columns	34
Gutter width	N/A
Extras	Grid developed from base unit—portrait rectangle

ROTARY CLUB PHILHARMONIC CONCERT

Design: Boris Ljubicic at Studio International

Designer Boris Ljubicic's creative inspiration for this concert poster was the three-tonal scale of the music. The poster is divided into a grid of narrow columns and fields, each filled with an image to form a mosaic of photographs—a visual representation of the rich orchestral music to be played at the concert. Ljubicic describes the process of importing these images into the grid as similar to composing virtual music.

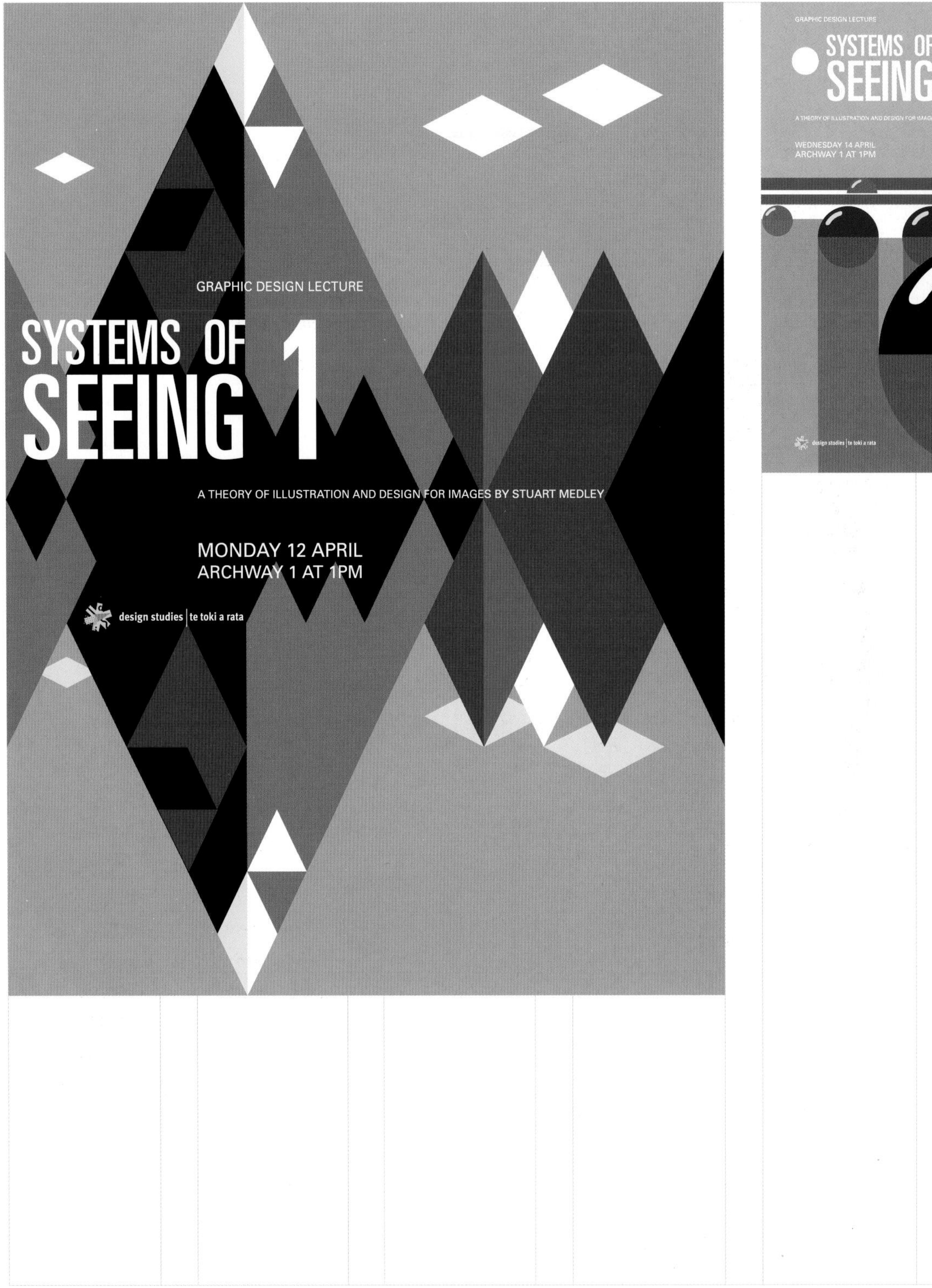
GRAPHIC DESIGN LECTURE
SYSTEMS OF SEEING 1
A THEORY OF ILLUSTRATION AND DESIGN FOR IMAGES BY STUART MEDLEY
MONDAY 12 APRIL
ARCHWAY 1 AT 1PM
design studies | te toki a rata
GRAPHIC DESIGN LECTURE
SYSTEMS OF SEEING 2
A THEORY OF ILLUSTRATION AND DESIGN FOR IMAGES BY STUART MEDLEY
WEDNESDAY 14 APRIL
ARCHWAY 1 AT 1PM

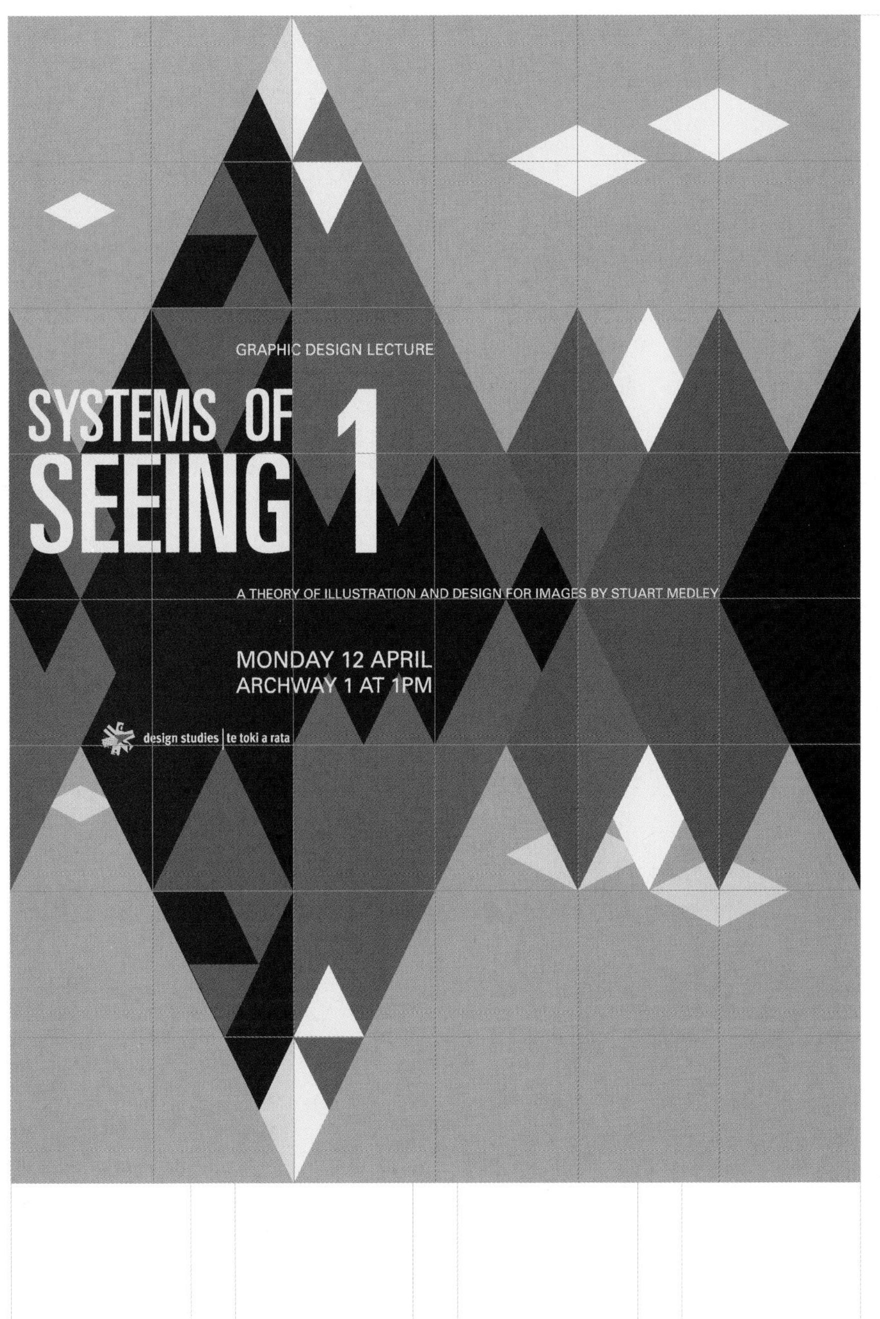

GRID SPECIFICATIONS

Page size (trimmed)	450 x 600mm
Top margin	None
Bottom margin	None
Outside margin	None
Inside margin	None
Number of columns	6
Number of rows	8
Gutter width	N/A
Extras	Grid is for visual elements only.

SYSTEMS OF SEEING

Design: Stuart Medley at Lightship Visual

Stuart Medley designed these posters to promote a series of lectures he was invited to present at the University of Otago, New Zealand. Keenly interested in theories that evaluate and quantify graphic design illustration and imagery, he refers to these as 'systems of seeing'. The grids in these posters were used to align only the image elements, and type was aligned optically without the use of margins or a baseline grid. These designs are unusual in that the imagery is gridded, rather than the type, thus presenting an interesting reversal of the accepted approach to graphic design. In keeping with the location of the lectures on New Zealand's South Island, the designer created systematic drawings of two local landmarks: Mitre Peak and the Moeraki Boulders.

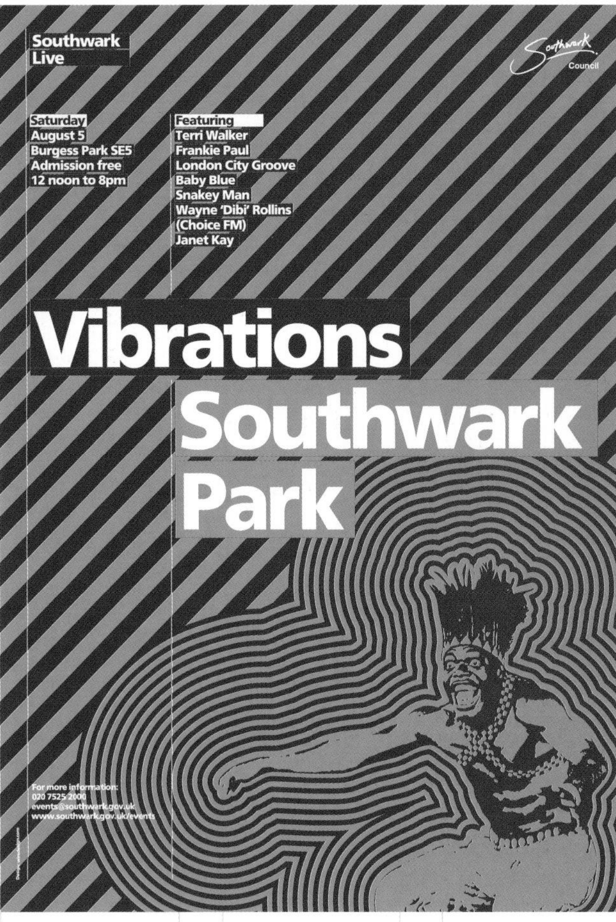

SOUTHWARK LIVE

Design: Tim Sawford at Wire

Southwark Live is one of London's largest events programs. Wire's brief was to create a functional and flexible visual identity to convey the vibrancy and diversity of the activities on offer. Designer Tim Sawford used abstract forms, inspired by the flags often seen at local events, within a multicolumn and multifield system. Colored text boxes help to make informational hierarchy clear even against the more complex photographic images.

Southwark
Council
I Love
Peckham
2006
August 7 to 13
Peckham Town
Centre
Live music, street
performance,
dance, markets,
food and art
August 10
Star Academy
Southwark
Live
For more information:
020 7525 2000
events@southwark.gov.uk
www.southwark.gov.uk/events

GRID SPECIFICATIONS

Page size (trimmed)	297 x 420mm
Top margin	10mm
Bottom margin	13.5mm
Outside margin	12mm
Inside margin	8.5mm
Number of columns	16
Gutter width	4mm
Extras	Baseline grid, 0.5mm

MyHome SIEBEN EXPERIMENTE FÜR EIN NEUES WOHNEN

SEVEN EXPERIMENTS FOR CONTEMPORARY LIVING

Interventions by: / Interventionen von:

Jurgen Bey, Ronan & Erwan Bouroullec,
Fernando & Humberto Campana,
Hella Jongerius, Greg Lynn,
Jürgen Mayer H., Jerszy Seymour

AN EXHIBITION AT THE / EINE AUSSTELLUNG IM

VITRA DESIGN MUSEUM

14. JUNI–
16. SEPTEMBER
2007

Opening hours		Öffnungszeiten	
Monday–Sunday	10 am–6 pm	Montag–Sonntag	10–18 Uhr
Wednesday	10 am–8 pm	Mittwoch	10–20 Uhr
Guided tours		Führungen	
Saturday and Sunday	11 am	Samstag und Sonntag	11 Uhr

Vitra Design Museum
Charles-Eames-Strasse 1 / D-79576 Weil am Rhein
info-weil@design-museum.de / www.design-museum.de
phone +49 (0)7621 / 702 3200
fax +49 (0)7621 / 702 3590

Vitra Design Museum

GRID SPECIFICATIONS

Page size (trimmed)	895 x 1,280mm
Top margin	85mm
Bottom margin	100mm
Outside margin	100mm
Inside margin	100mm
Number of columns	4
Gutter width	N/A
Extras	N/A

MY HOME

Design: Ludovic Balland

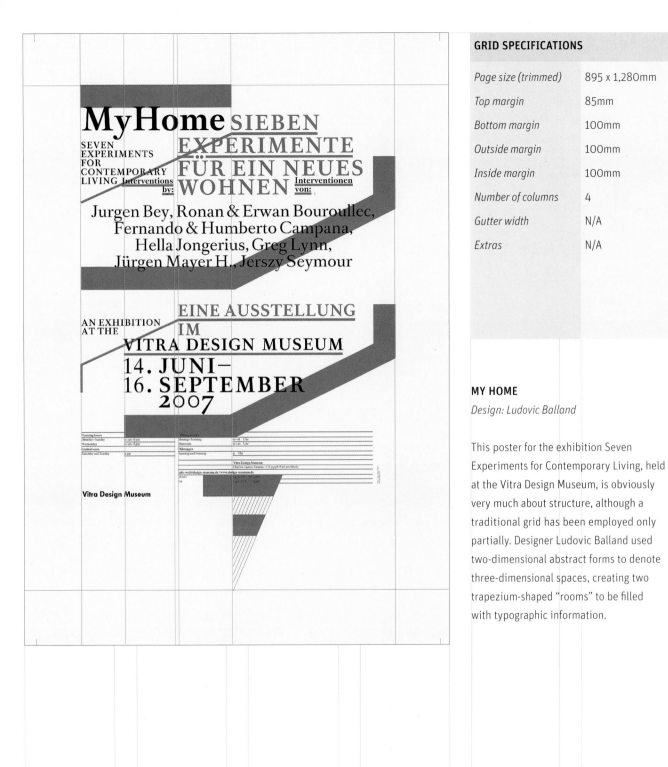

This poster for the exhibition Seven Experiments for Contemporary Living, held at the Vitra Design Museum, is obviously very much about structure, although a traditional grid has been employed only partially. Designer Ludovic Balland used two-dimensional abstract forms to denote three-dimensional spaces, creating two trapezium-shaped "rooms" to be filled with typographic information.

Index

AA Print Studio **133**
AArchitecture **133**
Abbeydale **183**
Adams, George **197**
aesthetics **10, 179**
Airside **191**
AJ: The Architects' Journal **169**
alignment **113, 203, 217**
alorenz **185**
Ambos, Grégory **133**
American Modernism: Graphic Design 1920 to 1960 **73**
Americans **73**
Amsterdam **18, 145**
APFEL (A Practice for Everyday Life) **169**
architectonics **43**
Architectural Association School of Architecture **133**
architecture **15, 58, 117, 169, 193**
art books **145**
Art Institute of California **203**
Arts and Crafts Movement **13**
ASCII **175**
Ashby Design **33**
Ashby, Neal **33**
Asymmetric Typography **15**
asymmetry **11, 15**
audio installations **179**

Balland, Ludovic **221**
banknotes **171**
bar codes **185**
BaseDESIGN **43, 193**
baseline grids **11, 18, 217**
Bastos, Nuno **55**
Bather, Zoë **27, 153, 157, 159, 183**
Bauhaus **14–15**
Bayer, Herbert **14–15**
BB/Saunders **107**
Beall, Lester **73**
Berlin **185**
Bill, Max **16**
biographies **33**
body text **10**
book covers **63**
Braques, Georges **13**
brochures **21–39, 183**
Brodovitch, Alexey **73**
business cards **117**

calendars **125**
calligraphy **11**
Capital **18**
captions **10, 63, 73, 85, 101, 129, 163**
Carrot **27**
cartography **153**
catalogs **21–39**
CDs **5, 175, 179, 187**
Chartered Society of Designers **141**
Chartier, Richard **179**
CHK Design **171**
ciphers **69**
clips **39**
color coding **43, 101**
column width **10**
comic books **63**
commentaries **187**
commercial artists **11**
compositors **13**
computers **18–19**
constructivism **14**
contact information **33**
content **11**
context **93**
conventions **11**
cookery books **89**
copy **33**
300% Cotton: More T-Shirt Graphics **79**
200% Cotton: New T-Shirt Graphics **79**
Creative Review **139**
Crnokrak, Peter **205, 207, 209**
Crouwel, Wim **18, 46**
cubism **13**
Cult-Ure **69**
Cultuur TV **39**
Curtis, Matt **163**

dadaism **14**
Daly, Wayne **133**
± Design **205, 207, 209**
Design This Day: 8 Decades of Influential Design **92–93**
Design Typography **27, 63, 73, 141**
The Designer **141**
Designs for Small Spaces **101**
Device **69, 77, 175**
diagonals **79, 113**
diagrams **27**
diaries **107**
die-cutting **205**
dimensionality **14, 16, 31, 221**
dislocation **58**
DNA Films **191**
Doesburg, Theo van **15**
Donohue, Patrick **33**
Dorfsman, Lou **73**
Douglas, Sarah **169**
Dumphy, Hannah **171**
Dunraven Secondary School **157**
Dutch **15, 18, 51**
DVDs **179**

L'École Property **27**
engravings **13**
EPs **185**
essays **187**
Esterson, Simon **141**
Europe **73, 159**
Everyone Ever in the World **205**
6=0 exhibition catalog **55**
exhibitions **41–59**
expressionism **14**

FAD Graphic Guideline **193**
fashion **79**
Fawcett-Tang, Roger **101**
Fehler **187**
Fibonacci sequence **12**
fields **11, 46, 79, 85, 93, 107, 117, 129, 139, 183, 193, 203, 215, 218**
file names **5**
Filter **35**
Fl@33 **79, 85**
flags **218**
Fleckhaus, Willy **141**
fliers **189–221**
folds **31, 191, 197**
folios **85, 147, 153, 157, 169**
font design **73, 77, 89, 141, 163**
form **11, 13, 43**
formalists **15**
Freddie Stevenson: A Body on the Line **175**
French language **16**
Frutiger, Adrian **203**
function **10, 13**
futurism **14**

Gale, Nathan **139**
geography **43**
geometry **12**, **185**, **213**
German language **16**, **185**
Germany **15**, **73**
Gerrit Rietveld Academy **145**
Gerstner, Karl **18**
golden section **12**, **97**, **213**
Gómez, Jason **92**
Grafik **129**
Graham, Ben **92**
Graphis **63**
graphs **35**
GRAy **145**
Grid Systems in Graphic Design **16**
GRID-IT notepads **19**
Groot, Arjan **51**
Gropius, Walter **15**
Gry, Lane **145**
Guardian **19**
Gutenberg Bible **19**

hanging heights **113**
hard binding **35**
Harriman Steel **31**, **151**, **199**
Harriman-Dickinson, Julian **31**, **199**
Heiman, Eric **97**
Heinisch, Damien **119**
Hidalgo, Reggie **203**
hierarchy **10**, **218**
Hochuli, Jost **73**
Holt, Mark **19**
Homeosteticos **55**
Horror Vacui: Urban Implosions in the Netherlands **51**
Hughes, Rian **69**, **77**, **175**

I Love Távora **211**
identities **79**, **105–25**, **157**, **183**, **218**
Ikon Gallery **125**
illustrated books **61–103**
illustrations **33**
images **23**, **27**, **31**, **33**, **39**, **46**, **73**, **77**, **79**, **85**, **97**, **129**, **139**, **145**, **151**, **153**, **169**, **175**, **191**, **217**
indents **129**, **133**
InDesign **5**, **147**
Industrial Revolution **12–13**
Industrial Romantic **77**
interactivity **147**
Internet **69**
Italian language **16**
Italians **12**

Jacquillat, Agathe **79**, **85**
Jagdish, Madhavi **97**
Jake Tilson Studio **89**
Joinedupdesignforschools **183**
Jorge Jorge Design **113**
journals **35**, **107**
justified setting **11-12**

Kalmre, Risto **145**
Keith Talent Gallery **171**
King, Laurence **63**
Kitty Cuts **185**
Küsters, Christian **171**

landscape images **77**
leading **141**
leaflets **21–39**
legibility **141**
Lightship Visual **201**, **217**
limited editions **92**, **179**
The Line of Forgetting **23**
LINE Series 3 **179**
linguistics **11**
Lisbon Architecture Triennial **51**, **58**
Ljubicic, Boris **215**
logos **183**
Lohse, Richard Paul **16**
London **27**, **213**, **218**
longitude **153**
loop binding **27**
loose leaves **27**
Lorenz, Angela **185**
Lost Souls Lookbook **31**
Lund + Slatto **117**

McNally, Clare **145**
Macs **175**
Madrid **43**
Maestro Design & Advertising **39**
magazines **127–71**
mailers **199**
Mamaril, Bryan **92**
manuals **145**
manuscripts **11**
MAP **153**
maps **27**, **107**, **153**
margins **12**, **63**, **217**
mass production **13**
mastheads **153**
mathematics **18**
measurement **5**, **12**
Medley, Stuart **201**, **217**
minimalism **15–16**, **113**, **179**
Miser & Now **171**
Mission Design **117**, **119**
Mitre Peak **217**
modernism **15–16**, **211**
modular systems **43**
Moeraki Boulders **217**
Monographics series **63**
Morris, William **13**
Mosaic Print **33**
movie stills **63**
Muir, Hamish **19**
Müller, Julia **51**
Müller-Brockmann, Josef **16**, **213**
multiculturalism **183**
multiple columns **11**
Murphy, Dom **125**
Museum of Modern Art **43**
My Home **221**

navigation **15**, **46**, **92**, **125**, **133**, **153**, **159**, **203**
Nazis **15**
needlework **79**
Netherlands **18**, **51**
The New Typography **15**
New York **43**
New Zealand **201**, **217**
newsletters **127–71**
newspapers **127–71**
Next Level **151**
Norwegians **117**
novels **145**

Octavo **18–19**
Old School, New School, TrueType School **201**
8vo: On the Outside **19**
On-Site: New Architecture in Spain **43**
On/Off **213**
op art **51**
Otago University **201**, **217**
overprinting **199**

packaging **173–87**
365 Pages **107**

painting **15**
panels **51**
paper stock **58**, **93**, **97**
pattern making **85**
Patterns: New Surface Design **85**
perception **10**
personalization **33**
perspective **43**
philosophy **11**, **211**
photographs **13**, **33**, **77**, **89**, **119**, **151**, **215**, **218**
physiology **10**
Picasso, Pablo **13**
Pinto, Liliana **58**, **211**
plans **27**
Plastique **163**
Porto **55**
portrait images **77**
Portugal, Pedro **57**
Portuguese **211**
postcards **31**
posters **31**, **46**, **171**, **183**, **189–221**
printers **13**, **199**
prints **63**
proportion **11–12**, **16**, **77**
psychology **10**

quadrants **33**
QuarkXPress **5**

R2 Design **55**, **58**, **211**
RA Magazine **159**
Ramalho, Lizá **55**, **58**, **211**
Rand, Paul **73**
ratios **16**, **117**
Rebelo, Artur **55**, **58**, **211**
Reed, Amber **97**
registration **199**
Research RCA **209**
Rossoni, Maggie **203**
Rotary Club Philharmonic Concert **215**
Royal College of Art (RCA) **213**
Ruder, Emil **16**, **201**
running feet **85**, **147**, **169**

Saetren, K.M. **117**
sans serif **97**
Sarson, Richard **213**
Sawford, Tim **218**
scale **43**, **77**, **85**, **117**, **139**
Schuitema, Paul **15**
Scotland **51**, **153**
screen format **39**
scribes **11**
sculpture **15**
SEA **46**, **129**
serif **97**
Serralves Museum of Contemporary Arts **55**
Seven Experiments for Contemporary Living **221**
signage **183**
sketchbooks **107**
Sorrell Foundation **157**, **183**
Southwark Live **218**
space **11**, **14**, **16**, **18**, **46**, **51**, **58**, **63**, **101**, **151**, **153**, **221**
Spanish **193**
Spencer, Herbert **63**
spiral binding **33**
spreads **63**
standfirsts **129**, **153**
stationery **113**, **117**, **183**
Stavro, Astrid **19**
Stedelijk Museum **18**
Steel, Nick **151**
stencils **58**
Stevenson, Freddie **175**
de Stijl **14–15**
structure **23**, **31**, **46**, **57–58**, **69**, **129**, **133**, **141**, **145**, **169**, **175**, **183**, **199**, **201**, **221**
Struktur **101**
Studio8 Design **157**, **159**, **163**, **183**
Studio International **215**
Sunshine **191**
suprematism **14**
surrealism **14**
Sutnar, Ladislav **73**
Swiss typography **16**, **92**, **203**
symbols **69**
symmetry **11–12**
Systems of Seeing **217**

tabs **101**
tactility **93**, **179**
TAKI **125**
A Tale of 12 Kitchens **89**
tartans **51**
Távora, Fernando **211**
Teague **92–93**
templates **157**
text **27**, **31**, **46**, **63**, **73**, **79**, **97**, **101**, **129**, **133**, **139**, **141**, **145**, **163**, **207**, **211**, **218**
textiles **51**
Tilson, Jake **89**
titles **63**, **129**
Tschichold, Jan **14–16**, **213**
Turnstyle **35**, **92–93**
tutorials **5**
Typographica **63**
Typography **16**

Uneasy Nature **97**
Urban Voids **58**
utilitarianism **27**

Vignelli, Massimo **73**
visible grids **18–19**, **31**, **69**
Vitra Design Museum **221**
Vollauschek, Tomi **79**, **85**
Volume Inc **23**, **97**
Vormgevers exhibition **18**
+/Vs **187**

Watson, Steve **92**
Weatherspoon Art Museum **97**
weaving **51**
websites **125**
Weimar **15**
Weingart, Wolfgang **201**
Wien **185**
Willey, Matt **153**, **157**, **159**, **163**
Wire **218**
word counts **10**
Worker/Parasite Manifesto **207**

Yendle, Brad **27**, **63**, **73**, **141**

Zak Group **133**
Zero **157**
Zwart, Piet **15**